£19.99

CW00346548

THE RISE OF LABOUR AND THE FALL OF EMPIRE

THE MEMOIRS OF WILLIAM HARE, FIFTH EARL OF LISTOWEL

With Selected Correspondence to and from Earl Mountbatten of Burma concerning the End of British Rule in India

William Hare, fifth Earl of Listowel, in his parliamentary robes as a peer in the House of Lords. Reproduced by kind permission of the House of Lords.

THE RISE OF LABOUR AND THE FALL OF EMPIRE

THE MEMOIRS OF WILLIAM HARE, FIFTH EARL OF LISTOWEL

With Selected Correspondence to and from Earl Mountbatten of Burma concerning the End of British Rule in India

edited by
H. Kumarasingham

CAMDEN FIFTH SERIES
Volume 57

CAMBRIDGE
UNIVERSITY PRESS

FOR THE ROYAL HISTORICAL SOCIETY
University College London, Gower Street, London WC1 6BT
2019

Published by the Press Syndicate of the University of Cambridge
University Printing House, Shaftesbury Road, Cambridge CB2 8BS, United Kingdom
One Liberty Plaza, Floor 20, New York, NY 10006, USA
477 Williamstown Road, Port Melbourne, VIC 3207, Australia
C/Orense, 4, Planta 13, 28020 Madrid, Spain
Lower Ground Floor, Nautica Building, The Water Club,
Beach Road, Granger Bay, 8005 Cape Town, South Africa

First published 2019

A catalogue record for this book is available from the British Library

ISBN 9781108487610 hardback

SUBSCRIPTIONS. The serial publications of the Royal Historical Society, *Royal Historical Society Transactions* (ISSN 0080-4401) and Camden Fifth Series (ISSN 0960-1163) volumes, may be purchased together on annual subscription. The 2019 subscription price, which includes print and electronic access (but not VAT), is £205 (US $342 in the USA, Canada, and Mexico) and includes Camden Fifth Series, Volumes 56, 57 and 58 and Transactions Sixth Series, Volume 29 (published in December). The electronic only price available to institutional subscribers is £172 (US $286 in the USA, Canada, and Mexico). Japanese prices are available from Kinokuniya Company Ltd, P.O. Box 55, Chitose, Tokyo 156, Japan. EU subscribers (outside the UK) who are not registered for VAT should add VAT at their country's rate. VAT registered subscribers should provide their VAT registration number. Prices include delivery by air.

Subscription orders, which must be accompanied by payment, may be sent to a bookseller, subscription agent, or direct to the publisher: Cambridge University Press, University Printing House, Shaftesbury Road, Cambridge CB2 8BS, UK; or in the USA, Canada, and Mexico: Cambridge University Press, Journals Fulfillment Department, One Liberty Plaza, Floor 20, New York, NY 10006, USA.

SINGLE VOLUMES AND BACK VOLUMES. A list of Royal Historical Society volumes available from Cambridge University Press may be obtained from the Humanities Marketing Department at the address above.

Printed in the UK by Bell & Bain Ltd.

CONTENTS

ACKNOWLEDGEMENTS

I am deeply indebted to Francis Hare, Earl of Listowel, for giving me permission to edit his father's memoirs for publication. Francis very generously responded to my query regarding the existence of the memoirs and immediately gave me a copy and expressed sincere happiness that the work would finally be published and reach a wider audience. Professor Emma Griffin and her successor Professor Richard Toye have both been wonderful Literary Directors at the Royal Historical Society and I am so pleased they have allowed me to include this work within the Society's invaluable Camden Series. They have also generously been very understanding with my tardiness and consistently supportive both in their official role and as British historians themselves. I am very grateful to Dr Emile Chabal and Dr Donal Lowry for advising me generously on some factual queries. My deepest debt is to Lady Diana Voss who has been a great source of help and kindness in giving every assistance to me in getting her father's fascinating story published without seeking to direct or control my role as editor. I thank her most sincerely for not only getting family papers ready for me and answering queries, but also for facilitating the permission to reproduce letters between Lord Listowel and Lord Mountbatten concerning the final months of British rule in India. Lord Listowel himself made his own acknowledgments in his preface to the memoirs which follows my introduction. I was a schoolboy in New Zealand when Lord Listowel died in March 1997 and never knew him. I first came across his name working as a university student in the New Zealand National Archives in Wellington, where there were official papers describing his visit to the country in early 1949 to try and convince the sceptical Labour Prime Minister, Peter Fraser, and members of the New Zealand Civil Service that a republican India should be welcomed into the Commonwealth despite not keeping George VI as head of state like all the other members. I was intrigued by this young Fabian aristocrat and struck by his quiet courtesy and this curiosity duly increased as I looked further at the variety of missions and roles he held. It is my hope that historians and interested readers will share the opinion of the Listowel family and my own that these memoirs and the related material are of immense historical value and add a crucial and previously unpublished witness account to many of the great events and episodes in twentieth-century British history, all told with a lightness of touch and a gentle elegance that cloaked a steadfast determination to serve, and to make the world more decent and just.

H. Kumarasingham
December 2018
Edinburgh

EDITOR'S INTRODUCTION

On 24 June 1980, William Hare, known to some as Billy Hare, fifth Earl of Listowel,[1] delivered the ninth Jawaharlal Nehru Memorial Lecture. As someone who had been the last Secretary of State for India he began his talk on the British transfer of power by stating that the story had been told before 'from the angle of the narrators'.[2] The narratives of key British players (and many Indian ones too) in the drama surrounding the demission of power in India had indeed been told either by themselves or in substantial biographies. Even the famously reticent Clement Attlee had penned accounts of this critical historical event,[3] while others like Lord Mountbatten almost never ceased to produce accounts in the public sphere on their contribution to what was unquestionably the seminal moment in the late British Empire.

This is Listowel's narrative of events. His career covered not only the transfer of power in India, but a great deal more. This is the first publication of an edition of his memoirs, encompassing his ninety eventful years. Listowel was a member of an old Anglo-Irish family. William Francis Hare's great-grandfather had been an Irish MP representing Cork and in 1800, on the dissolution of the Irish Parliament was raised to the Irish peerage as Baron Ennismore, advancing to viscount in 1816 and finally becoming the first earl of Listowel in 1822. The fifth earl's grandfather became a peer of the United Kingdom in 1869 with the title Baron Hare, which enabled him and his heirs to sit in the House of Lords. Listowel was born in London on 28 September 1906. He attended Eton where he was allegedly known as the only Labour supporter there other than the headmaster's wife, Mrs Alington. The poverty he witnessed in London as a boy reputedly kindled his interest in socialism.[4] He

---

[1] He will be referred to in this introduction and in all the footnotes as Listowel.

[2] Earl of Listowel, 'The British Partner in the Transfer of Power', The Ninth Jawaharlal Nehru Memorial Lecture, 24 June 1980, p. 1.

[3] For example, Clement Attlee, *As it Happened* (London, 1954), or Francis Williams, *A Prime Minister Remembers: The War and Post-War Memoirs of the Rt. Hon. Earl Attlee*, based on his private papers and on a series of recorded conversations (London, 1961).

[4] George Ireland, 'William Francis Hare, fifth Earl of Listowel', *Oxford Dictionary of National Biography* (Oxford, 2004).

then went to Balliol College, Oxford, but his father, Richard
Granville Hare, from 1924 fourth earl of Listowel, a Conservative,
removed him believing that his son was coming under the influence
of left-wingers at the university. As he recounted later 'I regarded the
Labour Party as representing the under-dog. It was of course, a complete break with family tradition'.[5] Indeed, his father's aggravation
was prompted in particular when it had come to his attention that
his son had appeared in a debate as plain Mr Hare dropping his
courtesy title of Viscount Ennismore. From there he went to
Magdalene College, Cambridge, but the admonitions of his father
did not curtail his left-wing sympathies as he joined the university
Labour Party. He attended many party events. After Cambridge
he completed a PhD in London and spent time studying in
Germany and France. Before he was thirty he had completed two
books on critical philosophy *The Values of Life*[6] and *A Critical History
of Modern Aesthetics*.[7] In 1931, when Listowel was twenty-five, his father
died and he became the fifth earl of Listowel. His father's anger at his
left-wing views had meant he was disinherited – though, as the memoirs relate, it is possible this was not meant to be the case. Like Attlee
and others Listowel spent time working at Toynbee Hall and sincerely believed in social justice, especially for those in poverty and
facing discrimination. While his hopes for a seat in the Commons
evaporated with his elevation – renouncing his title was not a legal
option at the time – he decided to join the sparsely populated
Labour benches in the Lords. In these years, he travelled widely
for the Labour cause including going to Spain with Ellen
Wilkinson during the civil war and also doing his best to encourage
support for China and the Soviet Union. Unable to join the
Commons he was elected to the London City Council as the
Labour member for East Lewisham in 1937. On the outbreak of
war he volunteered for the army, but was rejected for active service
due to his defective eyesight and served instead at 'home' with the
Royal Army Medical Corps and later with the Intelligence Corps.
    In 1941 he was persuaded to be the Labour whip in the Lords and
took an increasingly active role in the chamber both for Labour and
for Churchill's Wartime Coalition. Hugh Dalton confided to his
diary the weakness of the few Labour peers in the upper house.

---

[5] Listowel quoted in an interview in September 1994 with Martin Pugh in his article,
' "Class Traitors": Conservative recruits to Labour, 1900–30', *English Historical Review*,
113, 450 (February 1998), 53.
    [6] Viscount Ennismore [as Listowel was then], *The Values of Life* (London, 1931).
    [7] Earl of Listowel, *A Critical History of Modern Aesthetics* (London, 1933; recently repr.
Routledge, 2016 in their Aesthetics series).

The few did not impress this influential, but difficult senior Labour insider. Various Labour front benchers in the Lords were privately described as 'a complete nitwit', 'a pansy pacifist of whose private tendencies it might be slander to speak freely', 'a small man', 'very old indeed and deafer still'. His comments on Listowel, comparatively, seem merciful whom he describes as 'always white with stage fright and rather reassured that Labour peers were tolerated after all'.[8] Later in January 1943 over a dinner with Attlee, then deputy prime minister, the Labour leader revealed to Dalton that he had tried to get Listowel appointed to the government as under-secretary for either the Colonies or India, but was unable to persuade Churchill, mainly due to divisions of office between the coalition parties. Dalton archly divulged to his diary that he is 'quite glad that he [Attlee] didn't get in this poor little wisp of a peer, for he would have been of very little use and it would have roused great jealousies elsewhere'.[9] However, Attlee eventually succeeded and Listowel gained office as under-secretary of state for India in late 1944 and deputy leader in the Lords in Churchill's wartime coalition government. Even Dalton admitted just prior to the 1945 general election that Listowel was one of the few peers fit for office in any future Labour government.[10] On Labour's victory under Attlee he entered the Cabinet as Postmaster General and the youngest of His Majesty's Cabinet ministers, being just thirty-eight. When one considers that the average age of the Attlee Cabinet in 1945 was sixty-one,[11] it is all the more extraordinary that Listowel entered Cabinet before he reached forty. Listowel was, in Kenneth Morgan's survey of the Labour government, seen as one of the 'talented figures', who helped make the House of Lords more amenable to the government's legislation despite that chamber's almost atavistic disapproval of what Labour represented.[12] His biggest role was yet to come.

Days before his appointment as under-secretary of state for India in the wartime coalition, Listowel had sent a message to D.V. Tahmankar, the London editor of the United Press of India, for publication in the *Hindustan Times* on 14 November 1944 on the occasion of Nehru's fifty-fifth birthday. Listowel had to ask Tahmankar to write an addendum to the effect that the message had indeed been

[8] Diary entry, 27 October 1942, in Hugh Dalton, *The Second World War Diary of Hugh Dalton 1940–45*, ed. Ben Pimlott (London, 1986), 508–509.

[9] Diary entry, 5 January 1943 in Dalton, *Second World War Diary*, 542–543.

[10] Diary entry, 25 April 1945 in Dalton, *Second World War Diary*, 854.

[11] R.K. Alderman and J.A. Cross, 'Rejuvenating the Cabinet: The record of post-war British prime ministers compared', *Political Studies*, 34, 4 (1986), 641.

[12] Kenneth O. Morgan, *Labour in Power 1945–51* (Oxford, 1983), 83.

sent before he had any idea he would be appointed to the India Office. He had said

> I am glad of the opportunity to send a message to Mr. Nehru on his birthday … I met Mr. Nehru when he was in London before the war, I have read his book, and I have the greatest respect for his sincerity and strength of purpose. I feel that at this moment, when I and many of his other British friends probably differ from him about immediate issues relating to the war, it is specially important to emphasise our underlying agreement about the direction in which India must travel towards political independence and high standards of life, and to repeat my own conviction that he has a leading part to play in the future of India. I look forward to the time when he will again figure in the forefront of Indian political life.[13]

As Listowel recounts in his memoirs, his new boss, the Conservative Secretary of State for India throughout the wartime coalition, Leo Amery, was not overly impressed by this. No doubt Churchill, had it been brought to his attention, would not have been overjoyed either, being more reactionary in regard to India than Amery. This was in part caused by Nehru and Congress's different views from the Cabinet regarding the war and especially India's part in it, which not only resulted in grumbling in Downing Street but in Nehru's imprisonment. This was not an impediment, however, in the eyes of Attlee, now Prime Minister, who had kept relatively quiet on the India Committee during the coalition to serve wartime goals and save a fight with Churchill. Lord Mountbatten, the last Viceroy of India, wanted a new man as India secretary and the septuagenarian Lord Pethick-Lawrence was ready to retire. Though he said he wanted Listowel 'because I already knew him and he was deeply steeped in India and I thought would be an easy person to deal with', the young earl was an 'afterthought' according to Mountbatten's biographer, Philip Ziegler. The new Viceroy was petrified that Sir Stafford Cripps, a highly determined and long-standing Labour expert on India, would go to Delhi himself with his own plenipotentiary powers and that Mountbatten would have to deal with what he thought would be the 'third version of the Cripps offer' countering any of the Viceroy's initiatives. Consequently, Mountbatten thought Cripps might be better at the India Office – and thus far away from the action. In contrast, Listowel was more 'amenable' to Mountbatten's personal ambitions perhaps because he was not privy to them beforehand and not of

[13] Listowel to Tahmankar, 28 October 1944, IOR: L/I/1/1443, India Office Library Collection, British Library, London.

the same rank or influence as Cripps.[14] Not knowing any of this
Listowel recalled that he 'accepted not without gloomy anticipation
of the many anxieties which this great responsibility would bring;
but I had long believed, since I was a university student, that India
was fit for self-government ... [and therefore] I could not shirk'.[15]
Attlee deftly, and with the pithy clarity he was famed for, was firm
in his choice. He told the youngest of his Cabinet ministers that 'it
is quite clear to me that you have greater experience than anyone
else available for this position. You will certainly need to work
hard to catch up with the work ... I do not think you need worry
about insecurity ... I am quite sure you can do the job all right'.[16]
    Attlee, of course, had his own motives, as Listowel would learn and
candidly admitted. The Prime Minister wanted to direct India policy
himself and therefore a secretary of state for India in the Lords, like
Pethick-Lawrence before him, would mean the Prime Minister
would answer and command the subject in the House that mattered.
As Listowel remarked, India animated the typically reserved Prime
Minister, since on that subject in the Cabinet Room Attlee 'quite
unlike his usual habit of quietly listening and doodling while others
talked, became the dominant personality'. He met little opposition
from the Cabinet and seemed to have with the Foreign Secretary,
Ernest Bevin, 'at heart an old fashioned imperialist' a sort of 'non-
intervention pact at Cabinet level between those two potentially formidable opponents', which enabled Attlee's (and Cripps's) recommendations on India to fly with 'little discussion and no substantial
alteration'.[17] For all the admiration for Attlee and his historic role,
Listowel believed that Sir Stafford Cripps was the essential force in
the Cabinet in terms of its India policy. In 1978 he wrote as much
to Lady Cripps saying that her late husband 'played a more important part than Attlee in the policy decisions leading up to the transfer', even though, as Cripps's biographer Peter Clarke argues, the
contrary view is more often expressed.[18] The circumstances and realities of the Indian situation demanded imaginative, high-level
responses. Attlee, in reality, with Cripps, took the key decisions concerning India in Cabinet. Listowel was often left out of the conversation and rarely was given an opportunity to influence the big
decisions. As a small indication of this, when there was discussion

[14] Philip Ziegler, *Mountbatten: The Official Biography* (London, 1985), 356.
[15] 'Whitehall Events and Personalities, 1944–1950', undated, Listowel Private Collection.
[16] Attlee to Listowel, 5 April 1947, Listowel Private Collection.
[17] Lord Listowel, 'With Attlee for Indian Independence', Fifth Attlee Lecture, 16
February 1988, pp. 7–8
[18] Peter Clarke, *The Cripps Version: The Life of Sir Stafford Cripps 1889–1952* (London, 2002),
467 and n. 35.

in May 1947 of whether a Cabinet minister should go directly to India to 'settle matters there with full powers', Listowel, as secretary of state for India, was not considered a realistic option despite being the responsible minister.[19]

As R.J. Moore argues it is very likely, for all the flurry of memoranda and attentive communication, that the appointment of the youthful Listowel as secretary of state in place of Pethick-Lawrence gave the Viceroy 'enhanced ... freedom' on the ground in India, which Mountbatten himself admitted.[20] Listowel was no pliant tool of Mountbatten, however, and, both officially and off the record, stated his reservations in writing and at times, as Moore argues, was 'alarmed at the tenor' of statements made by the Viceroy and 'demurred at Mountbatten's intimation[s]' to Indians, since there was usually a crevice between allusion and reality, especially regarding the princely states and their rights and prerogatives.[21] In one rare hint of disagreement with Attlee, Listowel explained that he believed he should have been told in advance by the Prime Minister on his appointment as secretary of state for India that Mountbatten had been given his so called plenipotentiary powers to decide things on the spot, since, as secretary of state, 'if Mountbatten had made a serious error of judgment and anything had gone wrong in India, I should have had to "carry the can" '.[22]

Chandrika Kaul has argued that Listowel was worried about the BBC and other media giving too much of an impression of British accomplishment and celebration as independence dawned in the midst of communal violence as a consequence of Partition. This would in Listowel's words, give unintentional offence as 'we should appear to be trying to emphasise awful consequences of abandonment of power'.[23] Indeed, writing over thirty years later, he confessed that '[i]t has been said that in agreeing with such alacrity to the final Partition Plan we failed to foresee the mass migrations and massacres in the Punjab to which it would lead. This is true. We did not foresee the terrible consequences of dividing the Province'. He then asked

[19] Rowan to Attlee, 14 May 1947, document 435 in *The Transfer of Power 1942–47: Constitutional Relations Between Britain and India*, Vol. X, Nicholas Mansergh, editor-in-chief (London: Her Majesty's Stationery Office (HMSO), 1981), 818.

[20] R.J. Moore, *Escape from Empire: The Attlee Government and the Indian Problem* (Oxford, 1984), 236.

[21] R.J. Moore, *Endgames of Empire: Studies of Britain's Indian Problem* (New Delhi, 1988), 195–198.

[22] Lord Listowel, 'The Whitehall dimension of the transfer of power', *Indo-British Review*, Vol. 7, Nos 3 and 4, (1978), 24.

[23] Chandrika Kaul, ' "At the Stroke of the Midnight Hour": Lord Mountbatten and the British media at Indian independence', *Round Table*, 97, 398 (October 2008), 688.

himself rhetorically whether the 'greatest human disaster in India since the turn of the century' with millions destitute and thousands upon thousands of dead could have been averted. Listowel believed it impossible to answer such a question, but did argue that the 'sheer pace and momentum of Mountbatten's policy ... gave no time for second thoughts', which enabled the agreement of both Jinnah and Nehru to the plan to divide India. More time, Listowel argues, would have seen a breakdown of that brittle settlement that acknowledged and realised the new states of Pakistan and India.[24] In an interview for the *End of Empire* documentary series in 1982, Listowel thought that in an otherwise commendable tenure as viceroy, Mountbatten 'for once ... had slipped up' by underestimating how much the Sikhs would fight, and that the Cabinet had little idea beyond Attlee and Cripps, since 'the thing is that most members of the cabinet know almost nothing about India'.[25] Perhaps mindful of the calamity of being defeated or damaged in the House of Lords, which would derail the Attlee-Mountbatten rapid timetable, Listowel rose in the chamber to introduce the Indian Independence Bill by saying that the British 'in India have displayed an understanding not exceeded by the genius of the Romans, of the political requirements of a society utterly different from their own'.[26] As the son of a peer, he had sat on the steps of the throne in the Lords, and in 1926 had listened to Lord Irwin, the future earl of Halifax, on his way to India as viceroy. Lord Halifax spoke this time in defence of the bill and thus helped Listowel. As he recounted over forty years later, Halifax's speech 'was the only occasion I can remember in over fifty years in the House of Lords when a single speech has changed the mood of the House'.[27] Then the extraordinary bill went through easily and history was made. In one of his final telegrams to the Viceroy as secretary of state for India, on the eve of independence, Listowel praised Mountbatten as the man who had 'saved India from unimaginable disaster' and that would be 'remembered in time to come as one of the greatest feats of statesmanship in history'.[28]

---

[24] Listowel, 'Whitehall dimension of the transfer of power', 28.

[25] End of Empire Interviews: Archive Log of Transcripts, Lord Listowel, May 1982, MSS. Brit. Emp. s. 527, Bodleian Library, University of Oxford.

[26] House of Lords Debate, 16 July 1947, *Hansard*, Vol. 150, cols 802–74.

[27] Andrew Roberts, *The Hold Fox: The Life of Lord Halifax* (London, 2004), 298.

[28] Not all shared this view. The Earl of Listowel to Rear-Admiral Viscount Mountbatten of Burma, 14 August 1947 in document 480 in *The Transfer of Power 1942–47: Constitutional Relations Between Britain and India*, Vol. XII, Nicholas Mansergh, editor-in chief (London: HMSO, 1983), 726–727.

Listowel seemed willing to help India and its interim government, including assistance on questions of diplomatic representation, sterling balances and a shared condemnation of the aggressive and armed restoration of Dutch colonial rule in Indonesia.[29] Listowel, of course, not only had to deal with the Indian National Congress, but also the Muslim League. He personally had to tread carefully over the highly contentious Boundary Commission under Sir Cyril Radcliffe, where Jinnah carefully read every announcement from the India Office and was ready to pounce on any purported deviation from the agreed understanding.[30] As Listowel recalled he was not just secretary of state for India, but once it became inevitable, for Pakistan too. In 1984 Listowel gave an address on Jinnah at a memorial meeting at Lincoln's Inn. Listowel recalled meeting Pakistan's founder several times in London and once as his guest in Karachi, where Jinnah was now governor general. He found a 'relaxed and genial host, a very different person from the stern unbending figure usually depicted'. In the course of the lecture, almost forty years after independence, Listowel said that 'partition seemed to most of the British an evil to be averted at almost any cost' and yet 'from a greater distance in time we can perceive that they took too shortsighted and too self-centred a political view', since Jinnah's Pakistan is a 'secure and permanent reality', despite so many thinking it 'to be impossible'. For Listowel, of all the personalities in the drama, Jinnah was 'remarkable' in his 'clarity and inflexible determination about his vision of the future'.[31]

India (and Pakistan) were not the only things on Listowel's ministerial plate. He was also secretary of state for Burma and this was his only role after Indian independence in August 1947, till Burma's own independence in January 1948. As in India, he had to try and keep the peace between the different local factions and engender a Commonwealth connection. Listowel and the civil servant Sir Gilbert Laithwaite went to Burma to try and persuade the Burmese to accept Commonwealth membership, but, as he argues in the memoirs, a combination of misunderstanding of what

---

[29] See, for example, correspondence between Listowel and Krishna Menon regarding Indonesia in July 1947, in S. Gopal (ed.), *Selected Works of Jawaharlal Nehru*, 2nd ser., Vol. 3 (New Delhi, 1985), 358–363.

[30] See, for example, Jinnah's querying the contents of a speech made by Arthur Henderson, under-secretary of state for India, regarding the terms of reference of the Boundary Commission, July 1947, in Z.H. Zaidi (ed.), *Jinnah Papers: On the Threshold of Pakistan 1 July–25 July 1947*, 1st ser., Vol. 3 (Islamabad: Government of Pakistan, 1996), 481–482.

[31] Lord Listowel, 'Jinnah', Jinnah Memorial Lecture, April 1984, Lincoln's Inn, London.

membership meant and the Cabinet's attention on India at the cost of Burma's future relations led to an inability to find a formula for the country to stay in the Commonwealth as a republic akin to the agreement that India would later get in April 1949.[32] Listowel was candid enough to tell Karen leaders in September 1947 gathered in Rangoon that he had been unable to secure the conditions that the Karens, who had 'such long, close and intimate relations' with Britain, wanted with the new Burmese state. Starkly, he warned them that no further financial assistance could be given to Karens living in what would soon be a 'foreign state' as opposed to a Commonwealth one. Listowel confessed that this and other related issues in Burma was a 'real disappointment', in effect admitting to his audience that Britain was leaving with obligations unmet and relations less close than hoped.[33] As late as 1985 a Karen in Burma would tell a visiting academic from the United Kingdom: 'Please take a message to Lord Listowel ... Tell him about our situation'.[34]

On 11 September 1947, Listowel, no longer secretary of state for India, on his way home from Burma was in New Delhi as a guest of the Mountbattens at what was now Government House during a time when India was facing a great deal of hardship and an austerity regime meal was served among the contrasting splendour of his surroundings with a 'three-course repast consisting of some cabbage-water masquerading as soup, one piece of spam and potato, a biscuit and a small portion of cheese'. The Viceroy's press secretary, Alan Campbell-Johnson, observed that the noble earl asked afterwards 'whether this dinner had been specially laid on for his benefit!',[35] perhaps a droll comment on the rationing wartime Britain still faced after the war.

Writing in 1978 he believed that 'British statesmanship in the pre-war decade was at the lowest ebb that I can remember in forty-five years of public life' and had massive consequences on India, Pakistan and Burma: 'In the context of history, the transfer of power in 1947 was no more than a mitigation of the failure of British policy to part with it earlier, and to a united India'.[36] As

---

[32] Listowel's visit to Burma 1948, IOR/M/4/2148, India Office Library Collection, British Library, London.

[33] 'Speech by the Earl of Listowel to the Karen Leaders', 8 September 1947, document 515, in Hugh Tinker (ed.), *Burma: The Struggle for Independence 1944–1948: Constitutional Relations between Britain and Burma*, Vol. II (London: HMSO, 1984), 748–750.

[34] Julian Berger, 'Indigenous Peoples in Commonwealth countries: The legacies of the past and present-day struggles for self-determination', *Round Table*, 102, 4 (2013), 336.

[35] Alan Campbell-Johnson, *Mission with Mountbatten* (London, 1985), 186.

[36] Listowel, 'The Whitehall dimension of the transfer of power', 31.

Peter Hennessy has argued, the Attlee years were full of idealism despite dealing with harsh post-war realities. In Hennessy's astute eyes there has never been in British history a more 'progressive phase to match 1945–51'.[37] The independence of India and Pakistan in 1947, the emergence of the modern Commonwealth in 1949 and the process of decolonization during this period are undoubtedly part of this, as, of course, was Listowel.

Listowel thus found himself in the remarkable situation of successfully effecting the abolition of his jobs. With Indian and Burmese independence, his offices ceased to exist and unlike Mountbatten honours did not come his way and instead he found himself demoted to become a minister of Colonial Affairs, but typically Listowel preferred substance over style and relished the new opportunities of advancing self-government to other parts of the British Empire. In Australasia Listowel was given the tough mission of convincing the Antipodean prime ministers of the virtues of not only a republican India, but of a new conception of the Commonwealth that relaxed the hitherto constitutional requirement of keeping the Crown domestically as part of the local institutional infrastructure. Listowel was told in New Zealand, the Commonwealth member with the most intransigent attitude towards the issue at the time, that 'it would be more satisfactory to exclude India at this stage' rather than diminish the monarchy and risk change.[38] Eventually Attlee was able to convince all the Commonwealth ministers of the necessity of including republican India and with this the modern Commonwealth was born in April 1949.[39] In the Colonial Office he also had the heady task of dealing with Palestine, Malaya, and the West Indian territories among others. After the 1950 election he became a junior minister in Agriculture and Fisheries, a post he himself admitted he was most unsuited for. He remained in his job until Labour was defeated in the general election of October 1951.

Listowel was seen as a 'paternalistic' minister towards the colonies by the imperial historian D.K. Fieldhouse, but these memoirs reveal a different portrait.[40] Listowel saw Attlee as 'truly the architect of our

---

[37] Peter Hennessy, *Never Again: Britain 1945–51* (London, 2006), 454.

[38] H. Kumarasingham, 'The "New Commonwealth" 1947–49: A New Zealand perspective on India Joining the Commonwealth', *Round Table*, 95, 385 (July 2006), 441–454.

[39] See H. Kumarasingham, 'A new monarchy for a new Commonwealth? Monarchy and the consequences of republican India', in Robert Aldrich and Cindy McCreery (eds), *Crowns and Colonies: European Monarchies and Overseas Empires* (Manchester, 2016), 283–308.

[40] D.K. Fieldhouse, 'The Labour governments and the empire-commonwealth, 1945–51', in Ritchie Ovendale (ed.), *The Foreign Policy of the British Labour Governments, 1945–1951* (Leicester, 1984), 107–108.

modern Commonwealth' and himself saw it being one of great orga-
nizations for world peace and friendship out of the rubble of Empire
– unlike what he had seen of the violent ending of French and Dutch
imperialism and post-colonial hostility in Asia particularly.[41] Seeing
as he did the will of non-white territories, Listowel believed the
Commonwealth was an opportunity to redress colonial inequality
and provide a body to promote progressive policies across the developing world. Indeed, for some in the Fabian Colonial Bureau, where
Listowel was a long-standing stalwart, independence was not the
goal. As Rita Hinden explained, to the consternation of Kwame
Nkrumah in 1946, 'British socialists are not so concerned with ideals
like independence and self-government, but with the idea of social
justice.'[42] In opposition, Listowel co-wrote a Fabian publication called
Challenge to the British Caribbean in 1952, which attacked the existing
colonial system in the region and closely analysed the poor economic
and political benefits for those who lived in these British territories.
Listowel and his co-authors believed that, along with social reform,
for the conditions of the British Caribbean to improve 'There is
no answer other than in Federation' and with full collective self-
government the Caribbean could 'manage its own affairs and ...
play its full part in the shaping of world events'.[43] Just months before
going to Ghana as governor general, he wrote for the Fabian
International Bureau in July 1957 a 'Fabian Tract' entitled
'Commonwealth Future' that argued among other things that 'If
we in Britain are to pay more than lip-service to the
Commonwealth, we must be prepared to forgo an element in our
prosperity for the sake of those who lag far behind. This is the real
challenge for believers in a world-wide community.'[44]

Nkrumah, a Commonwealth fellow traveller, gave Listowel his
next dramatic job – the last governor general of Ghana in
November 1957. The famous activist George Padmore, described
by British officials, as a 'West Indian Marxist' and 'High Priest of
Pan-Africanism' then advising Nkrumah, but without an official position, apparently 'reproached' Nkrumah for wanting a European to
have the role.[45] Indeed Padmore had in fact written to the leftist

[41] Listowel, 'With Attlee for Indian independence', 1–22.
[42] Partha Sarathi Gupta, *Imperialism and the British Labour Movement, 1914–1964* (London, 1975), 325–326.
[43] Earl of Listowel, Rawle Farley, Rita Hinden, Colin Hughes, *Challenge to the British Caribbean* (London, 1952), 36–37.
[44] Lord Listowel, 'Commonwealth Future', Fabian Tract 308, Fabian International Bureau (July 1957), 30.
[45] High Commissioner to Commonwealth Secretary, 18 April 1957, The National Archives of the UK (TNA), DO 35/6199.

Ceylon government of S.W.R.D. Bandaranaike in the hope that their Governor General, Sir Oliver Goonetilleke, might replace Arden-Clarke in Ghana.[46] Nothing came of this. It seems Lord Rennell was also in the running and the sitting Governor General, Sir Charles Arden-Clarke, believed that it would be Rennell who would succeed him, but again this did not happen, perhaps due to Rennell's City and Conservative connections. The idea of a Ghanaian choice was also unattractive, since it was believed that Nkrumah did not savour the idea of another African stealing any limelight from him. So, it was Listowel who was chosen. His Fabian colours and role in India no doubt commended him to the Ghanaian leader. As his obituary in *The Times* reported, Listowel, whose outlook 'had always been a left-wing one', and as an active member of the Fabian Colonial Bureau, 'had no difficulty at all in adjusting to the "wind of change" era', that began in Ghana.[47] The *Ghana Daily Graphic* was clearly impressed that the son of a Conservative peer had joined Labour and proudly reported that when he was asked, on his selection as governor general designate, about his motives for 'embracing Labour' he replied: 'I felt the Labour Party would do more to help the ordinary people of the country than the Conservatives.'[48] Nonetheless, under the Conservative government, he was made a Knight Grand Cross of the Most Excellent Order of St Michael and St George to uphold the expectations of his new vice-regal office.

Listowel's dress and acclimatization to Ghanaian conditions clearly distressed some Britons in Ghana and was thus reported to the Commonwealth Relations Office. An MP even took the trouble to bring a letter from a Mrs Marriot to the attention of the Commonwealth Secretary, Lord Home, since Listowel's ways were conceived as 'regrettable' and 'damaging' to the Commonwealth.

> The British Community here are all very upset at our Governor-General – why the British Government sent a Socialist Irishman I can't imagine. He does not seem to care two hoots for British prestige. When they arrived back from leave, Lady Listowel's first appearance as Governor-General's wife, she arrived in slacks! Everyone there to meet them in gloves, hats, stockings etc. They gave a cocktail party for all the delegates to the African Conference and both he and Lady L. came dressed in the local native dress – kente cloth. All Africans in their best 'gents' natty suitings'.

[46] Commonwealth Relations Office Telegram to High Commissioners on 'Governor-General of Ghana', 9 May 1957, TNA, DO 35/6199.
[47] *The Times*, 13 March 1997.
[48] *Ghana Daily Graphic*, 12 November 1957.

Apparently even the Africans were livid. It's most distressing: we wonder now if they will wear kente cloth to greet The Queen.[49]

Meanwhile a retired brigadier from Suffolk, clearly not appreciating that Ghana was no longer ruled by Britain and thus no concern of the Colonial Office, wrote to the Colonial Secretary, Alan Lennox-Boyd, complaining that Listowel as 'Governor' was 'not a particularly good example of British habits and customs to have before the Africans'.[50] An anonymous letter arrived at the Colonial Office of a clipping from the *Daily Mail* describing Listowel and his new wife, Stephanie Wise, going night-clubbing and not leaving the Coq d'Or till 4 a.m., 'one of the gayest night-clubs in Casablanca' and eating couscous 'a sort of curry made of mutton and chicken' and sipping champagne. Lady Listowel 'danced with Moroccans' [double underlined by the sender] and 'exchanged jokes with Berbers who danced in the cabaret'. In the corner of the clipping was handwritten the censorious injunction that 'Governors and their wives, we understand, have to he[a]d up British prestige abroad', clearly thinking the Listowels were doing the opposite.[51] The Ghanaian press, people and politicians, meanwhile, seemed very happy that Listowel had not only chosen to get married in Ghana, but that the bride's ring was made of the famous gold of the country. Nkrumah appreciated Listowel and he was given a grand send-off in 1960, but nearly outstayed his welcome, as the plane carrying him almost failed to get airborne in time to avoid the constitutional indignity of the Queen's Representative being still on the ground as the Republic of Ghana dawned.

Not long after his return from Accra, Listowel took part in the debate in the Lords where famously Lord Salisbury attacked the Conservative Colonial Secretary, Iain Macleod, in March 1961 for being 'too clever by half' by effectively abandoning the Europeans in Africa and pursuing decolonization at, what appeared to people like Salisbury, an unseemly pace. Listowel tried to insert a conciliatory approach into the debate, but would not hide his deep concern for the African communities under British rule and tried to put on to Salisbury personally a responsibility for African self-government, as a former Colonial and Commonwealth Office minister. His intervention did little, however, to abate the rancour that Salisbury's verbal assault on the Colonial Secretary caused in the Lords and elsewhere.

[49] Ronald M. Bell MP to Lord Home, 12 January 1959, with extract of letter from Mrs Marriot to Lady Kittermaster, 30 December 1958, TNA, DO 35/9289.
[50] 13 August 1958, TNA, DO 35/9289.
[51] July 1958, TNA, DO 35/9289.

The Lord Chancellor believed it the most 'bitter' assault on a minister in his 26-year parliamentary career.[52]

Linked to these views on race, Commonwealth migration was a hot topic in post-war Britain. Harold Macmillan, then minister of defence, confided to the Foreign Secretary, Sir Anthony Eden, in January 1955 that Listowel might be the person who could raise the subject of controlling the 'problem' of immigration from the British Caribbean, since Lord Kilmuir, the Lord Chancellor, thought he might be amenable to a debate in the House of Lords. Macmillan was 'surprised' to learn this, as 'He is normally the wettest thing I know' and thought he would normally have 'been in favour of mixing up blacks and whites', but perhaps if his 'opinions are sound' he could be the peer they needed from the opposition to avoid its being seen as a Conservative ploy.[53] This assertion that Listowel was at least willing to discuss this despite his 'wetness' is confirmed by his being sounded out by other Conservatives like Lord Munster, who were worried about their party's policy being labelled as the blatant colour bar discrimination that it was. Listowel replied that he would need to discuss this with the senior Labour colonial affairs spokesman James Griffiths and get more information if 'coloured' immigration to Britain was indeed a problem and needed a policy check, a reaction, as D.W. Dean argues that was 'scarcely indicating uncompromising hostility'.[54] It could also be that Listowel's natural conciliatory nature allowed this impression and perhaps as well the reality that within Labour itself under Attlee it was discussed and later in the Wilson administration it became policy to impose restrictions on certain Commonwealth migrants that correlated to colour and race. Though this was realpolitik it was not unnatural for figures like Macmillan to be 'surprised' that they were not rebuffed by Listowel since he always aligned himself with Fabian beliefs and an association with self-determination and racial equality.

Having reached the Cabinet table before the age of forty, it was as Greg Rosen argues a little surprising to some, that Harold Wilson did not invite him to join his administration on Labour's victory in 1964. Arguably, though, Listowel found a more convivial role for his talents as chairman of committees and deputy speaker in the House of Lords

[52] *The Times*, 8 March 1961.

[53] 'West Indian Immigration', note by Macmillan to Eden, 14 January 1955, PREM 11/824, in *The Conservative Government and the End of Empire 1951–1957*, Part III: Economic and Social Policies, ed. David Goldsworthy, in *British Documents on the End of the Empire*, Ser. A, Vol. 3 (London: HMSO, 1994), document 523.

[54] D.W. Dean, 'Conservative governments and the restriction of Commonwealth immigration in the 1950s: The problems of constraint', *Historical Journal*, 35, 1 (1992), 187.

the next year and held the post till 1976.[55] Andrew Roth described him colourfully as being 'the virtually unknown Fabian liberator of India, Pakistan and Burma'. Roth went on to write that he had last met Listowel at a Labour Party function in 1996 in the Lords, the year before his death, and was asked afterwards by some party members 'the name of the slight, grey and balding peer', despite being Labour's longest-serving peer in the Lords and its first, and the House's longest-serving, chairman of committees and deputy speaker. Lord Graham of Edmonton believed that for 'Billy' this period as a committee man in the Lords was a 'golden period in his life. His patience and sympathy for all benches gave the true feeling that he was working for all, and he gained additional respect which lasted until the day he died'.[56] As chairman of committees in the Lords he was able, at least, to give female peers the pleasure of approving in December 1965 their request to wear hats while speaking in the chamber.[57] Well into his eighties, Listowel was among those to defend and represent Labour interests in the upper house, despite, especially during the Thatcher years, the sparseness and advanced age of peers on the Labour benches.[58]

Listowel was an active person and heavily involved in a wide range of public activities. It says something about Listowel that he could be invited to give lectures on, and had known personally, Attlee, Mountbatten, Nehru and Jinnah. H.V. Hodson remembered Listowel as a 'loyal party member, a sound administrator, a good listener and a good chairman, a kind, gentle and gifted man, without competitive ambition, without a single enemy'.[59] He was a founder member of the Voluntary Euthanasia Society in 1935 and served as the longest-serving president of the world's first such society from 1951 to 1980 and then again from 1983 to 1995. His fellow member, the broadcaster Ludovic Kennedy, remembered that Listowel's 'commitment to the movement was part of his devotion to human rights' and his 'wisdom, political experience and charm inspired members', who totalled over 20,000 at the time of his death with over £1 million in assets in the society.[60] His connection to the society

[55] Greg Rosen, '5th Earl of Listowel (William Francis 'Billy' Listowel)', in Greg Rosen (ed.), *Dictionary of Labour Biography* (London, 2001), 360–362.

[56] *The House Magazine*, 24 March 1997.

[57] *The Times*, 21 December 1965.

[58] *The Times*, 4 May 1989.

[59] H.V. Hodson interviewed by Qutubuddin Aziz, *Encounter* (Pakistan), 1 November 1997.

[60] Ludovic Kennedy, *The Guardian*, 14 March 1997. He spoke on the subject of voluntary euthanasia at the Cambridge Union on 26 October 1981.

may have encouraged the detailed correspondence he maintained with the Legalize Cannabis Campaign in the 1980s.[61]

Listowel's description of his role in the transfer of power to India perhaps illustrates more generally his role in British history:

> the recollections and reflections of one of the supporting cast in Whitehall may add an useful footnote to the sum of knowledge about a turning point in modern history.[62]

Listowel, while not a footnote, was never the key player. Instead through his long years in public life he was able, whether in the council room in the India Office, on the tennis court at State House in Accra, on the red leather benches of the House of Lords, at the bar after some difficult foreign mission, or in a committee room at Westminster, to judge and witness great, and not so great, events and individuals in British and Commonwealth history. Beneath the cover of a mild-mannered, quiet, courteous and bespectacled Englishman was hidden a man of many parts and views.

Listowel died on 12 March 1997 almost fifty years exactly after receiving the seals of office as secretary of state for India, metaphorically since the originals were lost (as recounted below). 1997 was also the year that India and Pakistan would celebrate fifty years of independence and that in which his old party, Labour, would achieve its greatest electoral victory since his old boss Attlee won the 1945 contest. Longevity, however, is no reason in itself to reflect upon his career. A Cabinet minister, social activist, campaigner, author, thinker, Queen's Representative, public servant, Parliamentarian and especially intimate witness of, and sometime participant in, some of the most important events of British history in the twentieth century must together focus our attention on examining and learning from the experiences and perspectives of a life devoted, sincerely and modestly, to the public good.

*   *   *   *   *

Lord Listowel lived a long life and these memoirs were completed in October 1995 just after his eighty-ninth birthday. It appeared in private circulation as *Memoirs – Earl of Listowel*. The main text of the memoirs needed hardly any alteration, since it was crafted carefully and with an eye to posterity. Thus as editor I have left the text largely as I found it with the exception of necessary formatting and, most critically, the insertion of a substantial number of footnotes. So many of the individuals Listowel came across in his long life are not

---

[61] Sean Blanchard to Listowel, 19 July 1982, Listowel Private Collection.

[62] Lord Listowel, 'The Whitehall dimension of the transfer of power', *Indo-British Review*, Vol. 7, Nos 3 and 4 (1978), 22.

as well-known as they should be, or at least not nearly as recognizable as they were when he came across them. This tendency is further accentuated when there is a need, for example, to traverse a range of people from Carlists in interwar Spain to civil servants in Nkrumah's Ghana, including a stream of British characters spanning the leaderships of Ramsay Macdonald to Tony Blair. Where foot-notes are italicized these are notes Listowel himself made and not mine. It was not always possible to find the necessary biographical information on the people mentioned and thus there are some who are unacknowledged despite my best efforts. The introduction above only skims his story since, as will be seen below in the memoirs, it is all covered clearly and tenderly in the text itself with some edi-torial explanation from me in the form of footnotes.

Interestingly Listowel only emerges as an incidental figure in dia-ries of fellow Labour figures like Richard Crossman and Tony Benn, who ignore his larger role and career. For example, from the latter at a lunch in May 1966 for former postmasters general, Listowel and Benn shared stories about how difficult it was to erase the sovereign's head from postage stamps.[63] Yet, the historian and journalist, John Grigg, on receiving an article by him in June 1980, implored Listowel to 'please expand it into a book covering, among other things, the whole of your political experience ... I should love to read such a book, and have no doubt at all that many others would be equally keen to read it'.[64] Now Listowel's memoirs can finally join the ranks of Labour primary accounts from the twentieth century, but more than most of them give a wider canvas than just the United Kingdom. Within the pages of the memoirs comes an array of experiences that demonstrate intrigu-ing variety and showcase a long political vintage. Beyond British domestic politics there are first-hand accounts of the Spanish Civil War; campaigning for pre-1949 China; giving speeches to Maori people in Rotorua; catching up with Barbara Tuchman in Washington; being greeted by Alexander Bustamante in Kingston; comforting the Kabaka of Buganda; listening to pleas for a separate Karen State while in Burma; or trying to maintain the rule of law in Ghana. Westminster, of course, figures prominently as well. Listowel's long public life meant he was in the Lords when some peers still wore top hats in the chamber; he saw the last occasion when a member of the Lords facing criminal charges was tried by his peers; he was assigned to share a room at the Palace of

[63] Diary entry, 13 May 1966, in Tony Benn, *The Benn Diaries: Selected, Abridged and Introduced by Ruth Winstone* (London, 1995), 151–152.
[64] Grigg to Listowel, 26 June 1980, Listowel Private Collection.

Westminster with Lloyd-George; and most prominently he successfully piloted through the historic India Independence Bill in a
House of Lords that was far from sympathetic to its contents.
Along the way, at home and abroad, he met a fascinating range of
political people from Churchill to Aung San, but also poets, writers
and artists, which evidenced a cultured life.

Unlike some diarists Listowel kept his own feelings and personal
life hidden. Other than the chapters on his ancestors and parents
the reader will search in vain to know anything about his family
life. Little mention, for example, of his distinguished younger brothers Richard Hare, a diplomat and professor of Russian literature;
John Hare (later Viscount Blakenham, a Conservative minister and
party chairman under Harold Macmillan; Alan Hare, an intelligence
officer and later chairman of the *Financial Times*, let alone his two sisters. Listowel was married three times. Firstly, from 1933 to 1945 to
Judith de Márffy-Mantuano, a Hungarian-born journalist and activist, who met Listowel at the London School of Economics. They had
one daughter together. Secondly from 1958 to 1963 he was married
to the Canadian blues singer Stephanie Wise. This relationship also
produced a daughter. Finally, in 1963 and for the rest of his life he
was married to Pamela Read, who had been a hairdresser in
London and with whom he had two sons and a daughter. None of
these family members are to be found in the main text of his memoirs. I have kept to this conscious style of keeping his immediate family outside the text apart from where a rare comment dictates a
footnote, but these are almost all from his childhood.

As editor, I have added an appendix containing the collection of
personal correspondence between Lord Listowel and Lord
Mountbatten in 1947, when they were respectively the last
Secretary of State for India and the last Viceroy of India. This crucial
correspondence was donated by Lord Listowel to the India Office
Collection at the British Library in 1982.[65] Twenty-five of those key
letters are reproduced here for the first time in a more accessible for-
mat with annotations and references, so that scholars and readers
interested in the last days of British rule in India can see the issues,
subjects and eccentricities of this remarkable and dramatic period.

---

[65] These can be found in the British Library's India Office Records and Private Papers
section under the reference MSS Eur C357.

PREFACE

I have had the good fortune to live through an exceptionally exciting and eventful period of British history, and to have witnessed much of it from the grandstand of ministerial office, or the humbler position of a seat in the House of Lords since 1932, which makes me the longest serving member of the House.[66]

Social reform and political change had been frozen during the Second World War, and Parliament still reflected the inertia of pre-war Baldwin and Chamberlain Conservative Governments. But with the end of the war the General Election in 1945 resulted in the return of the first Labour Government with an absolute majority of seats, under a new leadership pledged to improve conditions of life for the ordinary citizen. I am one of those who consider the Attlee Government of 1945 as having the best record of achievement in this regard since the Liberal Government of 1906.

As I had served as a junior minister in the Churchill Coalition Government during the war, I was promoted by Attlee to be a senior minister in his Government, and I had the privilege of serving first at the Post Office, then at the India and Burma Office, and finally at the Colonial Office. I was therefore able to assist in the building of the Welfare State, and in the transformation of this country from the status of a world-wide British Empire to that of an equal partner in a Commonwealth of nations and a medium-sized European power.

I owe an immense debt of gratitude to all those, in many parts of the world, who, in conversations, in letters or publications, have enabled me to recall people and events from childhood to old age which would otherwise have escaped my octogenarian memory. I am particularly grateful to my nephew, Michael Blakenham, for the gift of family letters, which gave me a link with my predecessors. But I am above all grateful to my son-in-law, Tim Voss, who first put the idea of this book into my head and who pestered me, with the connivance of my family, until I had finished it. I must also thank my daughter, Diana, for her patience and editorial skill, Diana

---

[66] It should be mentioned that his fellow Anglo-Irish peer the 4th Lord Ornamore and Browne took his seat in the Lords before him in 1927 and outlived Listowel by five years, dying in 2002.

Cullen for her skill and accuracy in carrying out the task of typing my manuscript through its numerous drafts over a period of years and Tina Brown for patiently putting the finishing touches to a manuscript I found hard to stop revising.

I
ORIGINS AND ANCESTORS

The Irish Hares

The Irish Hares are an off-shoot of the much older Hare family in Norfolk. They go back to a certain Michael Hare 'of Monktown in County Dublin', who had come to Ireland from Norfolk in the 17th Century, and died without issue in 1685, leaving a large fortune in a Will dated 1684 to his nephew John Hare, 'a native of Norfolk'. There is evidence of the relationship between the Irish and the Norfolk Hares in [the] similarity between the family coat of arms, particularly in their shields, which can be traced back by the Norfolk branch of the family to the Norman family of D'Harcourt which is believed to have fought in the Crusades.

John Hare decided to settle in Ireland, where he established himself as a merchant in Cork in 1710. He married the daughter of another Cork merchant, William Bussell, and became the father of four sons and five daughters. He added to the family fortune by his export–import business in Cork, at that time the second city in Ireland. I suppose he exported Irish dairy produce in exchange for English manufactured goods. On his death his very substantial fortune was shared between his wife and his sons.

But it was re-accumulated by his third son Richard, who made himself a gentleman by buying extensive properties in different parts of Ireland. In 1789 he paid the Earl of Kerry[67] £13,000, plus an annuity of £3,000 per annum, for a total of 20,000 acres in County Kerry, and he also bought property in the city of Cork and in the Counties of Cork and Tipperary.

He added to his holding in County Kerry in 1796 by purchasing the lands of Ennismore from Sir Maurice Fitzgerald, the Knight of Kerry.[68] His Kerry land included the site of the present town of Listowel. At that time it was a small village at the foot of the ruins

[67] Francis Thomas-Fitzmaurice, 3rd earl of Kerry (1740–1818).
[68] Sir Maurice Fitzgerald, 18th hereditary 'Green' Knight of Kerry and an Anglo-Irish Whig.

of the old castle, which had been built in the 13th Century to consol-
idate the Anglo-Norman conquest of Ireland. It was the last stronghold in Kerry to surrender to the invading British in the year 1600.

It then passed to the first Lord Kerry, and remained in the Kerry
family until it was bought by Richard Hare in 1783. But I am afraid
the contemporary records show Richard Hare to have been as ambitious and unscrupulous a politician as many others of that period. I
quote the following passage from a letter from a Mr Galbraith, the
Marquis of Abercorn's Agent in Dublin, to his principal in
London, dated November 2nd, 1797.

> The result of my enquiries since I have been here is not favourable to the
> hope of an immediate sale of Augher on good terms. The only money I
> can as yet find in the market is Mr Haires (sic). This gent has a very great
> estate and is very anxious to be a Peer, and with that intent has agreed
> about two years ago for the purchase of four seats in this Parliament at
> £2,500 each. As he is anxious to set out a Viscount in the Peerage, and
> finds the Minister boggled about gratifying him, he would to secure it pur-
> chase one or two Boroughs. But his brother-in-law, whom I know, tells me
> he fixes his price from the standard of Carlow, which was sold to Mr Bury
> about two years ago for £13,000. Mr Haire has been offering for another
> Borough, but has come to no agreement for the same cause. He was a
> great merchant in Cork in the provision trade, and lately purchased Lord
> Kerry's estate, which is at present £25,000 a year, and he is a man of expense
> and has ready money enough, from which I still have hopes of him.

Richard Hare's wealth was fortunately matched by the family's
sturdy Irish patriotism. The enrolment of his second son, Richard,
as an officer in the Irish Volunteer Army was typical of the public
spirit of the Anglo-Irish families. It should not be forgotten that a
French invasion of Ireland, where they hoped to be welcomed as lib-
erators by the Catholic population, was quite on the cards in the year
1781. Lord Charlemont,[69] the Commander-in-Chief, had been
informed by the Lord Lieutenant, that an immediate invasion was
expected, and that the City of Cork was a most likely point of attack.
15,000 men had been despatched from Ulster for the defence of the
Southern Province of Munster. I am proud to say that my gallant
ancestor, Captain Richard Hare, is listed among the Munster
Volunteers in County Cork as Captain of a Company in the Cork
Artillery. His formidable battery consisted of only two pieces, four
pounders, and his military uniform is described as blue, faced scarlet,

[69]James Caulfeild, 1st earl of Charlemont (1728–1799), commander-in-chief of the
Volunteer Army, recruited in Ireland to counter possible French invasion.

with yellow buttons and gold lace. It belonged to the Premier Regiment of the Volunteers of Ireland, later styled the Royal Cork Volunteers. He was certainly a pretty easy target for any enemy soldier holding a rifle!

By the end of the year, a Volunteer Army of about 60,000 men had been raised by Charlemont. The objectives were political as well as military. They wanted to secure for Ireland the same political and constitutional liberty, under the parliamentary system of government, as was present in England since the peaceful and glorious revolution of 1688. This was set out in a series of resolutions passed by the Ulster Volunteers at a meeting in the Church at Dungannon on February 15th, 1782. The first of these resolutions declared that 'the claim of any body of men, other than the King, Lords, and Commons of Ireland, to make laws to bind this Kingdom, is unconstitutional, illegal, and a grievance'. This was the authentic voice of the Protestants of Ireland, as expressed by their political leaders: Grattan,[70] Flood,[71] and Charlemont. The comment of Lecky, as the leading historian of the period, is certainly worth recording:

> Charlemont and Grattan, in the purity of their motives, and the high quality of their patriotism, were not inferior to Hampden or Washington. To [sic] the great unpaid armed force, which the necessities of the country had evoked – self-constituted, self-governed, and for the most part self-armed – was guilty of absolutely no acts of violence. It had made the country thoroughly defensible and had possibly saved it from invasion.[72]

Richard Hare died in 1792 having made sure that the Hares would remain among the most powerful Anglo-Irish families in Munster by providing in his will that his land should pass undivided to his eldest son, William.[73] It is also interesting to note that he left a mere £10.00 to the Presbyterian Meeting House where he had worshipped throughout his life.

The First Earl of Listowel

William Hare sat as a member for the City of Cork from 1796 to 1797, and for another constituency Athy, where he was the nominee of the Duke of Leinster, from 1797 to 1800. Both William and his brother, Richard, sat in the Irish House of Commons. I have little

---

[70] Henry Grattan (1746–1820), Irish and later Westminster MP.

[71] Henry Flood (1732–1791), Irish and later Westminster MP.

[72] [Listowel's original footnotes are in italic.] [W.E.H.] *Lecky, Ireland in the 18th Century, Volume 2.*

[73] *Born in 1751.*

doubt that both were 'placemen' who took their orders strictly from the Lord Lieutenant. The Hare family had finally arrived in the social sense, having graduated from the merchant to the land-owning class and from there to membership of the Irish Parliament.

The Union soon offered William Hare MP the ennoblement which was all he required to complement his enormous wealth. In 1799 a Motion against the Union had been carried by a majority of only 5 votes. Pitt[74] realised that his only hope of consent to the abolition of the Irish Parliament was by the lavish bribery of its members. The total cost to the unfortunate Irish taxpayers has been estimated at about £1,226,000. The average price paid to the incumbents and their patrons in the Boroughs was £15,000. In William Hare's case the lion's share of £13,500 went to his patron, the Duke of Leinster, while he was left with the paltry sum of £1,200. 20 Irish Peers in the Upper House were advanced in rank, and 28 members of the Irish House of Commons, including William Hare, who now became Baron Ennismore and Listowel, were given Peerages. To compensate the Irish Parliament for its undignified self-destruction, Ireland was to be allowed 100 members of the House of Commons at Westminster, and 48 representative Irish Peers[75] in the British House of Lords. Little did Pitt foresee at that time the vital influence of the Irish, in the 19th Century House of Commons, in the struggle for Home Rule or the balance the small minority of Irish members maintained between the opposing Conservative and Liberal Parties in the lower House.

William Hare, or Lord Ennismore as he had become after duly voting for the Act of Union in 1800, soon decided to build a country house appropriate to his new status. Some years before the Union he had bought the house and lands of Convamore, near Mallow, from the O'Callaghans of Cork. The first Convamore house was built, probably in the 18th Century, by a Colonel Bailey, who married a daughter of Lord Doneraile. Lord Ennismore proceeded to demolish the old house, and to build a much larger mansion on the site, which he handed over almost immediately to his son Richard. He employed an architect called Payne, who later built Mitchelstown Castle for Lord Kingston. The house was much admired by his contemporaries:

---

[74] William Pitt the Younger (1759–1806), prime minister, 1783–1801 and 1804–1806.

[75] *They vanished from our Upper House with the new State of Eire in 1917.* [Actually there was provision for 28 not 48 Irish Representative Peers after the Acts of Union 1800 and the Irish Free State was established in 1922 when the Irish peers ceased to elect representatives though some continued to serve in the House of Lords, as the Irish Representative Peers were able to serve for life.]

For the first in beauty and magnificence is Convamore, now the property of the Honourable Richard Hare, eldest son of Lord Ennismore. This place was much and justly admired for the singular beauty of its situation, before it derived any adventitious graces from the hand of art. The addition of a superb house and grounds, highly dressed and judiciously planted, fully entitle it to the pre-eminence here bestowed. This fine mansion is not less calculated to gratify the accomplished spectator within than without. Lord Ennismore and his son are both distinguished for their skill and love of painting, and have in consequence profusely adorned the house with pictures of the best Masters.[76]

After Lord Ennismore had handed over Convamore to his son, I believe that these Old Masters were subsequently transferred by him to Kingston House in Knightsbridge, where he lived permanently, and which had at that time one of the finest private collections of Old Masters in London. These were hung, as I remember, looking like rows of postage stamps in the large drawing rooms of Kingston House. This would explain why a later description of Convamore in 1837 omits a reference to the Old Masters:

Convamore, the seat of Viscount Ennismore, eldest son of the first Earl of Listowel, is a handsome modern mansion, beautifully situated in a fine domain stretching along the banks of the Blackwater, and commanding an interesting view of the winding of that river through rich masses of woodland to the picturesque ruins of the ancient castle of Ballyhooly, situated on a rocky prominent over the Blackwater, and, with the present church and the ruins of the former, both closely adjoining, presenting a highly picturesque and romantic group.[77]

The rural nature of Convamore and its surroundings is made clear by an amusing interchange between the second Earl and the novelist Anthony Trollope,[78] who at that time was employed in the Post Office as their surveyor in the area of County Cork. Lord Listowel wanted a Post Office opened in his local village of Ballyhooly, but Trollope replied that there would be too few literates to justify the expense. The fact was the only literate people in the neighbourhood of Ballyhooly were Lord Listowel himself and the Parish Priest! Here is Trollope's reply which I think is worth putting on the record.

[76] *A Statistical Survey of County Cork (1815), by Townsend about country seats situated on the River Blackwater near Ballyhooly.*

[77] *Lewis S, A Topographical Dictionary of Ireland, Vols 1 and 2 (London 1837 and 1846).*

[78] Anthony Trollope (1815–1882), 19th-century English novelist and author of works such as the series *The Chronicles of Barsetshire* and *Phineas Finn*.

My Lord,

I have before me a representation made by your Lordship to the Postmaster General respecting the renewal of the Post Office at Ballyhooly. I beg to remind your Lordship of a conversation I had the honour of having with you on the subject. The Postmaster General cannot establish the office at Ballyhooly at the expense of the Crown as the number of letters in the locality is found impossibly insufficient to warrant him in doing so in conformity with the regulations issued by the Lords of the Treasury on this subject. The Office can, however, be put in Operation if your Lordship will give a guarantee to the Crown to repay annually the whole expense of £4.00 per annum. In the event, however, I would wish your Lordship to bear in mind that the number of letters going to Ballyhooly after the establishment of the Office would have to depend on the guarantee given by your Lordship which would be <u>unconditional</u> and that your Lordship would be annually called on to pay the full sum of £4.00 per annum until such time as you should withdraw from the arrangement by giving the Post Office three months notice of your wish to do so. If your Lordship would wish to have the office renewal at Ballyhooly on these terms, I will thank you to notify to me your willingness to execute a guarantee to this effect. My address is Mallow.

I have the honour to be, my Lord, your Lordship's most obedient servant
Anthony Trollope

There is no record of my ancestor undertaking to pay this amount to the Post Office

I have always been somewhat surprised about the first Listowel's advancement in the peerage. For he was a Whig, and Lord Liverpool's[79] administration from 1820 to 1830 was of course Tory. His promotion to an Earldom in 1822 under such an administration has always been something of a mystery. He did not appear to take any further interest in party politics after he had left Convamore for Kingston House.

There is an amusing entry in a diary of 1818 kept by Mr Justice Day of Kerry, an old friend of the Hare family, whose father had been Rector of Listowel and was himself a 'Freeman' of the City of Cork. His mother had been a daughter of the Knight of Kerry and he was guardian of the young Maurice Fitzgerald, heir to the Knight of Kerry. He had been visiting his many friends in London and walked to Kingston House, where he 'enjoyed a hour's interview with that trifler [Lord Ennismore] and then walked back to town'. The disdainful tone of his comment may have been due to the fact that Ennismore was very much a self-made man, and looked down upon by the old

[79] Robert Jenkinson, 2nd earl of Liverpool (1770–1828), prime minister, 1812–1827.

Anglo-Irish gentry of County Kerry. It was also probably a reminder that at that time the future first Listowel was no longer interested in the important political issues of the day, and really only giving serious thought to his own future and that of his family.

He had been an absentee landlord from the time he handed over Convamore to his eldest son, Richard, until his death at Kingston House in 1837. He had lived to the grand old age of 86. He married his second wife Anne Latham when he was 67, and she placed a rather touching memorial plaque in Cork Cathedral, inscribed as follows:

> Sacred to the memory of William, Earl of Listowel. Born in Cork 1751 and departed this life at his London residence July the 13th, 1837. His remains are interred in Westminster Abbey.[80] He died in humble hope of divine mercy, through the merits of his Redeemer. Anne, his widow, erects this tablet. Also to Anne, the second wife of the above.

Kingston House, which was inherited (along with the rest of his estate) by his eldest son's eldest son, William, was the last of the great private houses, standing in their own grounds within five minutes of Hyde Park Corner, to disappear between the World Wars. It followed in the footsteps of Grosvenor House, Dorchester House, Lansdowne House, and Devonshire House.

Kingston House had been built as a country house, surrounded on three sides by fields, in the year 1770 for Elizabeth Chudleigh – the notorious Duchess of Kingston, by her husband the Duke. It was not until 1851 that Princes Gate was built on the west side of Kingston House, and still later Ennismore Gardens on the fields behind it. I remember my Grandfather telling me that, as a boy, when Kingston House was still regarded as being in the suburbs, the family used to take a house in Eton Square for 'the season' every summer, and that cows were brought over from Ireland to provide the children with fresh milk, grazing on the adjacent pasture in the rear of the family mansion, now Ennismore Gardens.

The style of architecture was that of Isaac Ware,[81] the architect of Chesterfield House, built 20 years earlier, and not unfortunately of such contemporary architects as Adam and Wyatt. Its austere, finely proportioned 18th Century exterior had been spoilt by the addition of bow windows, the front verandas, and extensions such as a large conservatory and stables, added by the first Listowel, to match his grander style of life, when he bought the house during the Napoleonic Wars from the childless Earl of Stair.

---

[80] *He was buried there because the Abbey was his parish church, Kingston House being in the parish of Westminster.*

[81] Isaac Ware (1704–1766), an architectural exponent of the Palladian style and a writer.

My grandfather enjoyed telling the story of the flight from his London home of its more widely publicised earlier occupant, the Duchess of Kingston. After a sensational trial by her peers in the Upper House of Parliament in Westminster hall,[82] she was found guilty of a felony, a bigamous marriage to the Duke of Kingston, and only escaped being branded on the hand by claiming benefit of peerage, as she was still the legal wife of the Earl of Bristol. As she was no longer the widow of a Duke who had left his property to his wife, the Duke's nephews decided to start legal proceedings to invalidate his Will. They obtained a Writ forbidding her to leave the country pending the hearing of the case, and to escape the service of this Writ, the Duchess fled secretly to France. She left, as the story goes, a dinner party at Kingston House in order to speed by coach to Dover in a friend's carriage. Her story continued in Paris but that was the last I heard of it.

The most distinguished occupant after the Duchess at Kingston was the Marquis Wellesley,[83] elder brother of the Duke of Wellington, who rented it from the Second Earl of Listowel from 1837 until he died there in 1842. His brother, the 'iron' Duke, used to ride over from Apsley House to see him. The interior had fine 18th Century features, ceilings, and fireplaces, with Regency Hepplewhite and Sheraton furniture, as well as the fine collections of Old Master paintings. It was occupied by the Listowel family from 1842 until my Grandmother[84] died there in 1937.

Richard, Viscount Ennismore

Richard, the eldest son of the first Earl, served in Parliament from 1812 to 1827, when he died suddenly at Convamore of an 'apoplexy' – presumably the word used for a heart attack.

Throughout his political life, his views were typical of the Protestant die-hards. His attitude to the Irish can be judged from a speech he made in the House of Commons in May 1823 on a Government Motion 'To continue the Irish Insurrection Acts':

> Before tranquillity could be expected to prevail in Ireland, it was necessary to strike terror in the lower orders. They must be made to know that the laws are strong and they cannot break through them.

---

[82] In 1776.

[83] Richard Wellesley, 1st Marquess Wellesley (1760–1842), held many senior posts including lord lieutenant of Ireland and governor general of India.

[84] Ernestine, Countess of Listowel, née Brudenell-Bruce (1849–1936). She is actually recorded as having died in 1936, not 1937 as mentioned throughout the memoirs.

Daniel O'Connell[85] records, in a letter to his wife dated February 25th, 1825, that he appeared before the House of Commons Committee on Irish Affairs, and was asked a few questions by Lord Ennismore, at that time a member of Parliament for County Cork. This was a high-powered Committee, which included Goulburn, Peel, Spring-Rice and Sir Henry Parnell.[86] At any rate he was not an absentee landowner, like most of his predecessors, as he spent the best part of the time at Convamore after his father had handed over his Irish property and moved his own permanent residence to Kingston House.

Richard maintained the family tradition of the Protestant Ascendency[87] by objecting to measures to remove the disabilities of Roman Catholics. He decided to oppose the Second Reading of Sir Francis Burdett's[88] 'Catholic Relief Bill' in April 1825, which was carried by a narrow majority of 268 to 241 votes in the House of Commons. He returned to the charge on May 6th urging the House not to give the Bill a Third Reading until another Bill dealing with provision for the Irish Clergy had been passed. He was answered by Mr Brougham, speaking for the Government, who said that although he was entirely willing to make 'reasonable sacrifices to conciliate the noble Lord', he entreated him to consider how completely the condition he proposed would go to nullify some of the most gracious labours in which the House had ever been engaged'. Lord Ennismore consented to withdraw his proposition and the Bill was duly passed.

The Second Earl of Listowel

My great grandfather, the second Earl of Listowel, sat in Parliament as a Whig MP for Kerry from 1825 to 1830. He became Viscount Ennismore in 1827 on the death of his father at Convamore, and succeeded his Grandfather the first Earl on his death in 1837. He sat in Parliament again, as an Irish Peer he was eligible for the Lower House, and represented St. Albans from 1841 until 1846. He then retired from Party politics, and became a courtier as an intermittent Lord-in-Waiting to Queen Victoria until his death in 1856.

[85] Daniel O'Connell (1775–1847), Irish political leader and MP known as 'The Emancipator' due to his campaign for Catholic emancipation.

[86] The MPs Henry Goulburn, Sir Robert Peel, Thomas Spring-Rice and Sir Henry Parnell.

[87] A term used from the beginning of the 17th century till the early 20th century to describe a small group of Protestant Anglo-Irish figures who dominated the political, economic and social affairs of Ireland.

[88] Sir Francis Burdett, 5th baronet (1770–1844), English MP and reformer.

His early career in the House of Commons was more sensational than successful. In 1826 he fought an election in Kerry characterised by all the worst features of violence and corruption prevalent in unreformed constituencies during that period. The Kerry election of 1826 has been described as 'the most tempestuous in the history of Kerry', and has gone down to Irish history as 'Hare's Election'. There were three candidates for the two Kerry seats. Two were sitting members, Maurice Fitzgerald, Knight of Kerry, and Colonel James Crosbie. The third candidate was William Hare. Both the sitting members had supported Catholic Emancipation. Hare, on the other hand, had a fiercely Protestant family background and his father had been returned for County Cork since 1812 by the 'high Protestant interest' – an interest entirely opposed to Catholic emancipation. As the election would be decided by the votes of the 40 shilling freeholders, most of whom were Catholics, it was fortunate and timely that Hare decided to change the family allegiance. He gave a solemn undertaking that, if he were returned, he would support Catholic Emancipation in Parliament.

Fitzgerald's seat was unassailable, so the contest lay between Crosbie and Hare. Polling day was on June 4th and the voters gathered in the Court House at Tralee. On a show of hands, the Sheriff declared Crosbie and Fitzgerald to have the majority. A supporter of Hare called for a poll. The Sheriff conceded to this request but adjourned the count for several days. This made it possible for the powerful absentee landlords such as Lord Ventry to collect their tenants who could be relied on to vote for Hare. But when the police marched back to Tralee with the enfranchised tenants, a riot broke out between the rival supporters, the military opened fire, and 16 people were killed. The Sheriff adjourned the election result until July 3rd when Hare was duly returned with Fitzgerald. The election had been blatantly 'rigged' by Hare, in collusion with the Sheriff, the military, and the police. Crosbie sent a well documented complaint to Dublin Castle,[89] but his complaint was dismissed by the Lord Lieutenant out of obvious political prejudice.

That great Irishman, Daniel O'Connell, was one of my great grandfather's Kerry constituents, and he expressed his fury about the election in several letters. Gladstone[90] wrote in one of his Diaries: 'O'Connell was the missionary of an ideal – the idea was

[89] The seat of the English administration in the country headed by the lord lieutenant of Ireland.
[90] William Ewart Gladstone (1809–1898), Liberal prime minister, 1868–1874, 1880–1885, 1886 and 1892–1894.

the restoration of the public life of his country'. On 4th July 1846, O'Connell wrote the following to a member of his family:

> Colonel Crosbie must insist on his being returned, as he had the show of hands on the first day and Hare, it is, who called for a poll. That poll is plainly illegal. The Sheriff ought certainly to be hanged; but if he escapes the gallows – which god forbid! – he will be imprisoned for months in Newgate. I will not however attend an illegal poll. This election must be set aside.[91]

He wrote a less strong letter to William himself. I quote an extract from William Hare's reply dated February 1827:

> In reply to a letter which you have done me the honour of addressing to me, I beg leave to say that far from thinking that its contents were dictated by any unkind or offensive feeling, I am thankful for any suggestion that my constituents have the goodness to offer me. I look upon Catholic Emancipation as an all important step. I regard it as a measure that would strengthen the bonds of union, tranquillity, and welfare, in a country that has been too long distracted by well grounded discontent. It is therefore my intention to pursue a course I had adopted with steadiness and zeal, unabated by any trivial circumstances, and unaccompanied by injudicious and compromising conduct.'

This was pretty strong language from my great grandfather. The reference to 'injudicious or compromising conduct' might have referred to the possibility of a duel. Duelling was of course strictly illegal, but it still happened quite frequently in the early part of the 19th Century.

As if to atone for his behaviour in the 1826 election, Hare, or Ennismore as he had now become, submitted a petition to the House of Commons in the following year from the people of Listowel protesting against their religious disabilities. He said in support of his petition:

> That he had himself witnessed the many evils which resulted from the system of exclusion which was acted on towards his Roman Catholic fellow subjects. All the disunion, ill feeling, and animosity, public and private, which prevailed in Ireland, might be traced to that source, nor could he conceive how permanent tranquillity could be secured in that country, so long as such a penal code was suffered to exist. It was a matter of infinite moment to conciliate the feelings of the people of Ireland, and by that means restore peace, order and unanimity; and he was convinced nothing could affect that most desirable object but complete and unqualified emancipation.

[91] *This dramatic reappraisal of O'Connell was in spite of Gladstone's agreement in the Peel Cabinet of 1843 to the prosecution of O'Connell for treason.*

Again in 1828, Viscount Ennismore supported a resolution in the House of Commons proposed by Sir Francis Burdett and seconded by Mr Broome:

> That this House do resolve itself into a Committee to consider the State of the Laws affecting His Majesty's Roman Catholic subjects in Great Britain and Ireland with a view to a final and conciliatory adjustment.

After condemning the laws in question, he went on to argue that coercion would not work because it would not remove the causes of violence and hatred. This could only be achieved 'by conciliation'. The resolution scraped through the House with a majority of 6 votes – 272 to 266, against the Opposition of the then Tory Government. Lord Ennismore is recorded on the list of those who voted for the Third Reading of the Catholic Emancipation Bill in 1829. He unfortunately resigned his seat in the House of Commons in 1830.

He had not abandoned his Liberal Whig allegiance when he became MP for St. Albans between 1841 and 1846. He spoke and voted in May 1843 against the Second Reading of the Arms (Ireland) Bill, which had been introduced to authorise coercion against the disaffected Catholics. He was for reform, particularly the reform of the Church, which would remove the causes of violence and the need for coercion:

> No man could deplore more than he did the agitation now going on in Ireland, which prevented the introduction of capital and the amelioration of the condition of the people; yet they should recollect that to this agitation 7/8ths of the people were parties, it should be met, not by unconstitutional coercion, but by redress of the peoples' wrongs.

He ended with a strong plea for equality of treatment of the Catholic Church in Ireland:

> If the Government had the moral courage to grapple with the ecclesiastical establishment in Ireland, he was persuaded that the difficulties with regard to the Government of that Country would cease. They should govern Ireland as they govern the distant dependencies of the Crown, whether Hindu or Roman Catholic, whether in India or Canada. They should respect her Church, and her sons would respect and support the Government.

In August of the same year, 1843, he spoke in support of a Motion on the Irish Church. The Motion proposed that the tithe revenue and property of the Irish Church should also be available to support the Catholic clergy. What he wanted was for the payment of tithes, deeply resented by the Catholic peasants, should benefit the three faiths in Ireland, Catholic, Protestant, and Presbyterian. The

House was eventually 'counted out' (that is to say less than 40 members were present) at 8.00pm in the evening.

Lord Listowel as he had now become (since the death of his father in 1837) attributed the ills of Ireland to the domination of a Protestant minority over a Catholic majority. 'No, Sir, the cause of these evils is as clear as the noonday sun, and may be expressed in three words, Protestant against Catholic. The people of Ireland were oppressed solely because they maintained that religion which was once your own – a Protestant Church was forced upon a Catholic people'. In April 1845, Lord Listowel voted for the Second Reading of the Maynooth College Bill, the purpose of which was to provide a grant for the training of Catholic Priests. This was for Gladstone the momentous issue on which he resigned from Peel's Government and ceased to be a Tory. Again reverting to the reform of the Protestant Church in Ireland, Lord Listowel said in the House of Commons:

> Let me observe that such opinions lead to the one result, namely, that in a country which numbers 8,000,000 of population, and of which less than 1/8th professes the Protestant faith, the Protestant Church ought to be cut down and adapted to the wants of those who do belong to it, and not suffer to remain as she now is, an object of distrust and of disgust, of contempt, and of annoyance, to those who do not.

His enlightened attitude led to his vote in May 1846 for the total repeal of the Corn Laws – which for so long had protected the interests of British landlords, supporting a Motion 'That all restrictions on corn should be now abolished'. In the Division Lobby he was joined by other free traders including Cobden and Bright[92] and his own Leader Lord John Russell[93].

Emerging from retirement during the last years of his life he became on three occasions a Lord-in-Waiting to Queen Victoria from 1840 to 1841, from 1846 to 1852, and finally 1853 to 1856 when he died at the early age of 54.

The Third Earl of Listowel

On the Second Earl's death in 1856 he was succeeded by my Grandfather, another William, and now Third Earl of Listowel. He was born in 1833, and after three years at Eton joined a

[92] The leaders of the Anti-Corn Law League, Richard Cobden and John Bright.
[93] Lord John Russell (1792–1878), later 1st Earl Russell, Liberal prime minister, 1846–1852 and 1865–1866.

Guards Regiment, the Scots Guard, at the age of 19. He was soon to
see active service in the Crimean War, and was seriously wounded
early in that war at the battle of the Alma in September 1854. He
was invalided home, and as a Captain served as Aide-de-Camp to
the Lord Lieutenant of Ireland in 1856. He retired from the army
on succeeding his father.

He now turned his attention to politics, where his life-long ambition was to add to his Irish honours a Peerage that would give him a
seat in the House of Lords. As can be seen from a letter from Lord
John Russell, then Prime Minster, dated May 10th, 1866:

> My dear Lord,
>   Your claims to a British Peerage shall be fairly considered with those of
> some others – of your father's merits I have the strongest impression and I
> should be happy to have his son in the House of Lords. But there is at
> least one Claim which when Irish Peers are given seats in the House of
> Lords may appear equal or superior to yours.
>   I remain, yours faithfully,
>   Russell

He persevered after Lord Russell had been succeeded as Prime
Minster by Mr Gladstone. When Mr Gladstone rewarded his support
of the Liberal party with the title of Lord Hare of Convamore in the
County of Cork, his ambition was at last realised. I quote the following letter from No. 10 Downing Street, dated November 8th, 1869:

> My dear Lord,
>   I have received the permission of Her Majesty to propose to you that you
> should become a Peer of the United Kingdom.
>   It gives me much pleasure to convey an offer the proprietary of which will I
> am sure on all hands be recognised.
>   I trust that I may anticipate your acceptance.
>   I remain, my dear Lord, very faithfully yours,
>   W.G. Gladstone

In 1873 he became, like his father, a Knight of St. Patrick[94], and in
1880 a Liberal Lord-in-Waiting to Queen Victoria, again following
in his father's footsteps. He also increased the family property in
County Kerry from 25,500 acres in 1870 to 30,000 in 1883.

His tenure of office as a Lord-in-Waiting started in May 1880, and
ended abruptly in August of that year. In that month he resigned, in

[94] The Most Illustrious Order of St Patrick, a prestigious British honour linked with
Ireland.

protest against Forster's[95] 'Compensation for Disturbance (Ireland)
Bill'. Sir Edward Hamilton,[96] who was Private Secretary to Mr
Gladstone, noted in his diary at the time 'There have been further
resignations. Listowel and Zetland.' What had this Bill done to
upset the Irish landlords? The Irish Land Act of 1870 had recognised
the tenant's right to compensation for improvements when he left or
was evicted from his holding. But it made an exception in the case of
non-payment of rent. Forster's Bill sought to remove this exception,
but only 'in exceptional circumstances'. For example, if a farmer
failed to pay his rent because his crop had failed (a frequent occur-
rence during the famine years) he would not forfeit his claim to compensation if evicted by his landlord. The Bill was to apply only in the
distressed areas, and for a limited period of time. The plea of 'exceptional circumstances' was the ground on which a tenant could appeal
to a County Court Judge against a landlord's decision to evict him. It
was this revolutionary measure which was too much for the landlords
in the House of Lords! They threw it out by a majority of 282 to 51.
Lord Granville,[97] the Liberal Leader in the House of Lords, was
astonished that more than half the Liberal Peers voted against the
Bill, though it had been carried comfortably by the Liberal majority
in the House of Commons.

It gave my grandparents great prestige when the Prince, the future
Edward the VII, and Princess of Wales stayed with them at
Convamore from April 8th to April 27th, 1885, on their visit to the
south during their tour of Ireland. The Prince had been bullied by
Mr Gladstone, who was seeking popularity, into visiting the country
and his reluctance can easily be understood by the reception of the
Royal couple in the city of Cork. As reported by the Prince's equerry,
Arthur Ellis, to Queen Victoria on April 15th:

> The fact is that the lower class, the lazzaronis of Cork, which exists in over-
> powering numbers, were rabid rebels. No other word can convey their hostil-
> ity and behaviour.

However, there was a well-dressed middle class crowd to cheer the
Prince and Princess outside the Protestant Cathedral.

Unlike his father, who had spent most of his time at Convamore,
my grandfather was an absentee landlord who lived permanently at

---

[95] W.E. Forster (1818–1886), chief secretary for Ireland, 1880–1882.
[96] Sir Edward Hamilton (1847–1908), later permanent secretary to the Treasury.
[97] Granville Leveson-Gower, 2nd earl Granville (1815–1891), Liberal peer and minister.
As well as Liberal leader in the House of Lords, he also served several times in other ministerial posts including foreign secretary, colonial secretary and lord president of the
Council.

his London residence, Kingston House, and only visited his Irish home occasionally, usually during the summer months. On some of these occasions my grandmother is said to have enjoyed her visits to Gurtinard House, the family residence in the town of Listowel. My grandfather was 80 in 1913, the last year in which I spent Christmas at Convamore.

The Fourth Earl of Listowel

On his death in 1924 he was succeeded by my father, another Richard Hare, who was born in 1866. After Eton and Oxford he joined the First Life Guards in 1890 as a Second Lieutenant. He was soon to see active service in the Boer War, and on May 30th, 1900 he was taken prisoner and held in a prisoner of war camp until the end of hostilities.

I do not think I can do better than describe the battle in which he was taken prisoner in the words of Thomas Pakenham's excellent history of the Boer War:

A still more humiliating coup (inflicted by de Wet's brother, Piet) was the capture of the thirteenth battalion of the Imperial Yeomanry at Lindley on May the 31st. To British eyes, this mounted Battalion was the social and political show-piece of the new Volunteer Army; a company of Irish M.F.H.'s known as the Irish Hunt Contingent, including the Earl of Longford and Viscount Ennismore; two companies of Ulster Protestant Unionists, including the Earl of Leitrim, a whiskey Baronet (Sir John Power) and the future Lord Craigavon; and a company of English and Irish men-about-town raised by Lord Donoughmore, who had insisted on paying their own passage to South Africa.

This patriotic band was commanded by a British regular, Lieutenant Colonel Basil Spragge; and Spragge proved himself a regular ass. They were supposed to join General Colville, who was desperately short of men. When they arrived at Lindley on May the 27th, they found that Lindley had somehow slipped back under the control of the Boers. Instead of making a fighting retreat towards Kroonstadt, as he acknowledged was perfectly possible, ('I can get out but shall lose in doing so'), Spragge sent an SOS to Colville. Then he and his men sat down on some kopjes outside Lindley, and waited to be rescued. Unfortunately Colville, who had been ordered to be at Heilbron by May the 29th, and was not fully aware of Spragge's dangerous situation, decided not to delay his Brigade by returning to rescue the mounted troops. He marched on to Heilbron, leaving them to their own devices.

On June the 1st, when the rescue column – three Yeomanry Battalions led by Lord Methuen (downgraded by Roberts) – reached Lindley and stormed the

kopjes they found the hills already strewn with dead, Spragge's dead. The rest of
Spragge's Yeomanry had surrendered the previous day when de Wet brought
up field guns. The surrender of Spragge's Irish Yeomanry was the cause of a rip-
ple of mirth in nationalist circles in Ireland.

In fact, there was a gallant Last Stand made by the Irish Hunt Company.
Lord Longford, with blood streaming from wounds at the neck, face, and wrists,
ordered his men to fight to the end. 'I knew it to be madness,' said one of the
gentlemen troopers, (son of the Irish Lord Chancellor) 'and so did everyone
else, I think, but not a man refused'.

In general raw Irish Yeomen fought no worse than British regulars had
fought in similar situations. A respectable total of 80 were killed or wounded
before the White Flag went up.

Piet de Wet's bag totalled about 530 men, including Spragge, Lord Longford
(seriously wounded), Lords Ennismore, Leitrim, and Donoughmore (and the
future Lord Craigavon), all captured, and the whiskey Baronet killed. The
wounded were left at Lindley: and the other prisoners were marched away
northwards to the eastern Transvaal. Their captors evaded the net of 20,000
British troops trying to rescue them.[98]

When my father returned home he resigned his Commission in the
Army shortly after his marriage in 1904, but insisted at the age of
48 on rejoining his old Regiment, the Royal Munster Fusiliers, on
the outbreak of the First World War in 1914. As he was no longer
fit for active service in the front line, he joined the Army Police,
and became a Provost Marshal, first in the Mediterranean, and
later in Cairo. After the war he retired from the Army with the
rank of Major.

As a young man he was an enthusiast for all field sports, and spent
much of his time salmon fishing in the River Blackwater at
Convamore, and shooting woodcock in the surrounding woodlands.
While he lived in Ireland he was also master of a famous Irish pack of
hounds, the Duhallow Hunt. He usually visited friends in Scotland
for deer and grouse shooting in the autumn. It was the age of hunting
big game with the rifle rather than the camera. My father was an
excellent rifle shot, and had been in the 'Shooting Eight' at Eton.
He went abroad for long periods to shoot big game on safari in
Africa, and came home with his trophies, to be stuffed by a famous
firm in Piccadilly.[99] Our home became a menagerie of dead animals
– stuffed or affixed by their horns to the walls.

He taught me with much patience how to use a shotgun without
risk of injury to myself or other people and insisted on my cleaning

98 *Thomas Pakenham, The Boer War, pp. 436 and 437* [1979.]
99 Most likely Rowland Ward Ltd.

the gun in his gun room every evening after a day's shooting. As he grew older, and preferred to stay at home, he became a keen gardener. He made a superb garden in our Yorkshire home, and built the rock garden with his own hands. I often marvelled how he could lift and carry enormous blocks of granite, to place them at regular intervals as steps between his rock plants. He was also a keen embroiderer and did many elaborate chair seats in gros point.

He still hankered after his Irish home after it had been burnt down in 1921. The fire was probably started by Sinn Fein in retaliation for the destruction of many small Irish homes by the Black and Tans during the 'troubles' that followed in Ireland after the First World War.

The following is an extract from The Times of the 29th October 1921:

£85,000 COMPENSATION

Lord Listowel's Burnt Mansion

At Fermoy Sessions yesterday £150,000 was claimed for Lord Listowel for the destruction of his mansion, Convamore, Ballyhooly.

His solicitor submitted to the Court a typewritten document addressed to Lord Listowel from 'Headquarters, Cork, No. 2 Brigade,' saying 'On Wednesday, the 13th instant, the enemy bombed and destroyed six houses of Republicans as reprisals for IRA activities on the 10th instant. You being an aggressively anti-Irish person and your residence being in the Battalion area of enemy reprisals, I have hereby ordered that the same be destroyed as part of our counter-reprisals, – Commandant.'

The Recorder awarded £85,202, including £55,319 for the mansion, £21,234 for the furniture, and £7,430 for pictures.

This was followed by a final sentence which reads as follows:

A schoolteacher was awarded £5,000 compensation for the loss of her husband, who was taken from his home by armed and masked men and was found by the roadside shot dead.

This statement suggests the difference in value between life and property. However, in spite of the substantial compensation payment, my father decided to sell the site of the house to a developer.

So it was a sad, but at the same time fortunate, moment in his life when my grandfather died in 1924. For the first time, at the age of 58, he could afford to buy his own country house. He chose the Oxton Estate in Devon, between Exeter and the sea. The climate, mild and damp, and the rough shooting and the trout streams, must have reminded him strongly of his beloved Ireland. It was a happy retreat

for the last years of his life. The rest of the family went there for
school holidays, and we were allowed to ask our friends to stay.
My father obviously intended Oxton to replace Convamore as the
family country seat. However it had been left for life to his youngest
son, my brother Alan,[100] who was still a schoolboy, and the trustees
sold the estate almost immediately after his death. He died there in
November 1931, having developed pneumonia after coming home
drenched to the skin after a day's shooting with a neighbour, Sir
Trehawke Kekewich,[101] with whom he was staying.

A close friend of the Kekewich family, Sir Jocelyn Lucas,[102] was
also staying at that time at Peamore, their country house. Many
years later he became a Conservative member of the House of
Commons. It was at Westminster that Sir Jocelyn spoke to me
about my father's death. When the doctor informed him that his illness might be fatal, my father expressed a wish to see a lawyer in
order to change his will. But this did not happen. When I arrived
at Peamore, my father was in the final stages of pneumonia, struggling for breath and not recognising me or others around him. I
had travelled home from Paris, where I was studying at the
Sorbonne, as soon as I heard the news of his critical illness.

I was glad to think that my disinheritance was due to an accident,
and that my father bore me no ill-will. He had obviously not
expected to die in his 60's (he was 66) and had not therefore altered
a will made when he was furious (and, I am afraid, deeply hurt) when
I became a Socialist. It was a sad story that could have been avoided
had I not been so impetuous about airing my political opinions in
public.

My father's London property, including Kingston House and
Ennismore Gardens, was inherited by my brother John.[103] When
my grandmother died there in 1937, he decided to sell the house,
which has been replaced by a large block of luxury flats. My brother
kept the best of the family pictures, the family plate, and the family
jewellery, and decided to sell the remainder of the contents by auction on the premises. My mother[104] went to the auction, and bought a
few things which she gave to me as mementos of the old family residence. I like to think that many families are now enjoying a beautiful
home that was for so long the preserve of one family only, but I still

[100] Alan Hare (1919–1995), later served in the Armed Forces and Foreign Office, and
then joined the *Financial Times*.
[101] Sir Trehawke Kekewich, 1st baronet (1851–1932), English judge.
[102] Sir Jocelyn Lucas, 4th baronet (1889–1980), Conservative MP.
[103] John Hare, later 1st Viscount Blakenham (1911–1982), Conservative MP and later
Cabinet minister in the 1950s and 1960s.
[104] Freda, Countess of Listowel, née Vanden-Bempde-Johnstone (1885–1968).

deeply regret that the old 18th Century house had to go, with the beautiful croquet lawn and back garden, where the old people played a gentle game on a summer's evening: an oasis of peace amid the roar of London traffic passing between Knightsbridge and Hyde Park Corner.

II
EARLY LIFE: 1906–1924

I was born in London at Wilton Crescent on September the 28th, 1906 almost within earshot of Bow Bells,[105] the definition of a Cockney. The following notice appeared in the press the day after my birth.

There was born yesterday an heir to the Irish House of Hare in the person of the son of Viscount and Viscountess Ennismore. Lord Ennismore, who married Lord Derwent's grand-daughter only a year or so ago, is the eldest son of the Earl of Listowel. In addition to his Irish estates, Lord Listowel is the fortunate possessor of a fine, if not large, London property. It is situated near the Albert Hall, and close to Hyde Park and Kensington Gardens. It comprises Kingston House and Ennismore Gardens. There are scores, if not hundreds of houses on the estate, and probably not one yields a ground rent of less than one hundred pounds per annum, while some of the larger mansions produce hundreds a year in ground rents. It is to this property that the Earl of Listowel's grandson, born yesterday, is the ultimate heir, as well, of course, as to the Irish estates.

I have spent the best part of my life in London or its suburbs. I cannot imagine a more pleasant or civilised city, though as a child I naturally preferred the country. My parents had a large house in Bryanston Square, No. 14, now converted into flats. They bought it soon after their marriage in 1904, and in those days it was on the unfashionable side of Hyde Park. My Listowel grandmother lived at Kingston House, the family home in Knightsbridge, and her somewhat acid comment, repeated by my mother, was that 'It would be so convenient for Paddington Station.'

It had four floors, a huge basement where the servants worked, a gentle front staircase for the family, and a very steep back staircase where servants climbed to their bedrooms on the top floor. It is curious to remember that right up to the outbreak of the Second World War there were ten domestic servants: three in the kitchen, three in the house, three male servants under the butler, and a ladies maid.

[105] The bells of St Mary-le-Bow in Cheapside, City of London.

Three women looked after me and, as time passed, my three brothers and two sisters: the nanny and a day nurse and night nurse. The third floor was occupied by the day and night nursery. My nanny must have been a perfect mother substitute, as I can think of her with nothing but pleasure, and she stayed long enough to give me the continuity of affection needed in early childhood. But her underlings were more ephemeral, and I remember vividly to this day having my ears boxed quite violently for some minor misdemeanour. In those days children saw little of their mother until they were old enough to come downstairs for their meals. But I remember being brought down to the drawing room after tea in a smart dress, where my mother or father would read to me from Hans Anderson's or Grimms' fairytales until bedtime.

My parents also had a house in Yorkshire, where they went after the London season ended in July. There we spent our school holidays: I went off to a preparatory boarding school at the age of eight. This was the Dower House on the estate of my grand-father Lord Derwent[106] at Hackness, near Scarborough. He had been a widower for many years, and was overjoyed to have his daughter and her young family within walking distance from the Hall. My grandfather's elder daughter, Sybil,[107] had married Toby Long,[108] the eldest son of Viscount Long of Wraxall.[109] She lost her husband in the first World War, and her only child in the second.

As both my grandfather's children were daughters, the Hackness property went with the title to his nephew, Peter Johnstone,[110] his nearest male heir.

Hackness was a paradise for children, especially for boys. I was able to indulge in all the country pursuits of my well-to-do contemporaries. I soon became an avid collector of wild flowers which I brought home and dried, a collector of butterflies and moths, and even, I am ashamed to say, a collector of birds' eggs. Also a collector of postage stamps, pasted into a book in the winter evenings. There was trout fishing in the becks that ran along the valleys, and larger fish in the Lake adjoining the Hall. Later still there was pheasant shooting in the Christmas holidays, the occasional grouse-shoot in September, and rabbits all the year round. In all these activities I

[106] Francis Vanden-Bempde-Johnstone, 2nd Baron Derwent (1851–1929).

[107] Sibell Vanden-Bempde-Johnstone (1881–1958), later married Ralph Glyn, 1st Baron Glyn.

[108] Brigadier Walter 'Toby' Long (1879–1917).

[109] Sir Walter Long (1854–1924), later 1st Viscount Long of Wraxall, Conservative minister and secretary of state for the Colonies, 1916–1919.

[110] His name was George Harcourt Vanden-Bempde-Johnstone, 3rd Baron Derwent (1899–1949).

was helped and instructed by my father, whose life, after he retired from the army at an early age, was spent mainly on gardening and field sports.

Hackness is still among the most perfect beauty spots in Yorkshire, nestling in one of the wooded dales that run down from the southern edge of the Yorkshire moors. But it was far more beautiful then than it is now. The old woodlands had not then been cut, and the dales were still alive with butterflies and birds. The roads were not filled with traffic and the Forestry Commission had not planted its serried ranks of sombre conifers on the moorland boundaries. It is strange how one can imagine later on the beauty one missed as a child. I had the same experience after I left Eton.

My earliest memory was registered by a combination of excitement and greed. I stayed up late and was given a pink blancmange for lighting the village bonfire for the Coronation of George V in 1911. I vaguely remember being held up by someone, probably my father, to kindle the pile of wood. The villagers gave me a gold pen-knife, which I hope my grand-father paid for, as a memento of the occasion. I promptly cut my finger. My grand-father Derwent was the kindest of men, and a typical figure of the semi-feudal landlord age. He was liked and respected by his tenants, and performed his somewhat unexacting duties as a resident landlord. He was also patron of the Hackness living.

The vicar when we first went to Hackness was a cousin of my great grandfather, who was remembered with admiration because he still rode in the hunting field when he was over 80. My grandfather was a regular church-goer, and sat at the end of the family pew in Hackness church, every Sunday at Matins and Evensong. He always gabbled the lesson at a pace that made it incomprehensible. He took the collection with the other church wardens, two of his senior tenant farmers. He liked the villagers to touch their caps as he walked through the village from the Hall to the Grange where we lived, and did not altogether approve of the village schoolmaster who gave him a smile but no salute. He adored sport in all its forms, and I think the greatest pleasure in his old age was when he succeeded in winning a Box at Lords Cricket Ground for the annual Eton and Harrow cricket match.

The only time I saw my grandfather Derwent in the House of Lords was as a sponsor of his Yorkshire neighbour, Edward Wood,[111] when the latter was introduced as Lord Irwin on his

---

[111] Edward Wood (1881–1959), later 1st earl of Halifax, Conservative MP (later peer) and minister, and colonial administrator; viceroy of India, 1926–1931; and foreign secretary, 1938–1940.

appointment as Viceroy of India in 1926. As an eldest son I sat on the steps of the Throne.[112]

He was an unselfish sportsman, giving himself the outside place in a line of guns at a pheasant shoot, or walking in line with the beaters on the hillside to pick off the high birds as they sped across the valley. Nevertheless he did care for birds. Almost every evening in the summer he walked down to the lake in front of the house with his binoculars, to watch and count the ducks and pick out any rare visitors. The lake was a sanctuary and any bird that alighted on its waters was safe from the sportsman. His old valet said he knew my grandfather must be dying when he no longer turned his head when woken in the morning to see the birds on the lawn from his bedroom window.

When I was older and trouble started with my father about my politics, although he disliked my views as much as my father, he never reproached me for holding them, and tried to help without appearing to interfere. After I was banished from the family home he offered me hospitality at the Hall for as long as I liked during my vacations. I refused his kind offer because I could not face the routine of his daily life. The succession of long and too abundant meals, and, what I most dreaded, the invariable rubbers of three handed bridge – when alone he played 'double dummy' with his lady housekeeper – which would have filled every evening between dinner and bedtime.

My father had been a professional soldier, serving in the Life Guards and later in an Irish Regiment, the Munster Fusiliers. He fought in the Boer War, when he was taken prisoner, and later released by the Boers. Although during my childhood he retired from the Army, he served behind the lines in the Mediterranean during the First World War. He loved the country, where he could spend as much time as he liked shooting, fishing, or gardening, and he hated life in London. I never saw him open a book, but he spent the long winter evenings, before television invaded the home, doing his tapestry in gros point or sticking in his postage stamps. He was an ideal companion for the outdoor pursuits of boyhood.

My mother's tastes were just the reverse. She adored London, where she found everything she liked: people, music, theatres, and was thoroughly bored by life in the country. Although she was highly gregarious, and liked nothing better than the large dinner and luncheon parties that preceded the mass entertainment of our less civilised cocktail era, she had a few intimate women friends, and quite a large number of amusing and intelligent acquaintances from the

---

[112] A privilege now granted to the eldest *child* of a peer.

world of art and letters. I remember meeting at her table James Agate[113] and Desmond McCarthy,[114] the theatre and literary critics, Alan [sic] Walton,[115] the painter, whose cottage with its rose garden that [sic] so delighted her old age when she took it over after he died, and, less frequently, Churchill's Private Secretary, the witty and effervescent Eddie Marsh.[116] Eddie was an enchanting companion, and I shall never forget his piping voice as we drove down St James's Street to his flat, squeezed into the front seat of my Austin Mini, with the running commentary on the 18th century facades as we passed.

My mother did not deliberately 'lionise' like that professional social figure Lady Colefax,[117] and her guests from the art world were always the people she really liked. She had one foot in the art world, and the other in what was then called 'society'. Here, again, she preferred quality to quantity. Among her closest friends were Mrs George Keppel.[118] She must have cared a lot about my mother, because she left her a beautiful diamond brooch with sapphire wings and ruby eyes which had been given her by her friend, Edward VII. Mrs Keppel has sometimes been thought of as little better than a courtesan, but those who knew her best thought otherwise. I would like to quote a few words from Magnus's standard biography of Edward VII,[119] spoken by Lord Harding [sic] of Penshurst,[120] at one time Head of the Foreign Office:

Everybody knew of the friendship that existed between King Edward and Mrs George Keppel, which was intelligible in view of the lady's good looks, vivacity and cleverness. I would like here to pay a tribute to her wonderful discretion, and to the excellent influence she always exercised upon the King. She never utilised her knowledge to her own advantage, or to that of her friends; and I never heard her repeat an unkind word of anybody. There were one or

[113] James Agate (1877–1947), theatre critic who worked at times for the *Manchester Guardian*, *Sunday Times* and the BBC.

[114] Sir Charles Desmond McCarthy (1877–1952), literary critic who worked at times for the *New Statesman* and the *Sunday Times*.

[115] Allan Walton (1891–1948), designer and painter. The word 'that' after 'garden' is probably an undeleted error.

[116] Edward Marsh (1872–1953), later Sir Edward Marsh, civil servant and private secretary to many senior ministers in the early 20th century, most famously Churchill.

[117] Sibyl, Lady Colefax, née Halsey (1874–1950), interior decorator, and a famous society hostess.

[118] Alice Keppel, née Edmonstone (1868–1947), long-time mistress of Edward VII.

[119] Philip Magnus, *Edward VII* (London, 1964).

[120] Charles Hardinge (1858–1944), later 1st Baron Hardinge of Penshurst, senior civil servant and colonial administrator, served twice as permanent under-secretary at the Foreign Office; viceroy of India, 1910–1916.

two occasions when the King was in disagreement with the Foreign Office, and I was able, through her, to advise the King with a view to the policy of the government being accepted. She was very loyal to the King, and patriotic at the same time. It would have been difficult to find any other lady who would have filled the part of friend to King Edward with the same loyalty and discretion.

Margot Asquith,[121] in her retirement from politics after the death of her husband, also became a friend. I can speak from personal experience when I say that Margot's impact in old age on a very young man was still tremendous. She made me feel, as I am sure she made others feel, that I was the one person in whom she was deeply interested, and I have no doubt she really may have been at that particular moment. I was convinced that she would invite me immediately to her house, and that I would be expected to play bridge with her – she was an execrable player – for stakes far higher than I could afford. My relief can be imagined when my mother smiled, and told me that I was not the first to be captivated by her charm and that I was not in danger of an invitation to her house in the country.

Another woman friend was the beautiful Lady Leconfield,[122] the chatelaine of Petworth House in Sussex, who had everything in life except children. For this reason my mother asked her to stay with our large family at Hackness. It transpired that she had never stayed in such a small house (it is now a country hotel), but that she liked the children.

So my mother was invited for a weekend at Petworth, and told to bring me with her. Luckily for me, as I was the only child in this large and portentous gathering, our hostess was fond of music, and had included among her smart guests the delightful and world-famous musicians Adila Fachiri and her sister Jelly D'Aranyi.[123] Jelly took a fancy to me, I think because she was genuinely fond of children, and her warmth quite broke through the frozen shyness with which I had been overcome. I was too young to appreciate or remember either the grand company, or the finest private collection of landscapes by Turner in the country. But I still remember Jelly.

My mother's greatest woman friend was the Edwardian hostess, Mrs Arthur James.[124] She was much older than my mother, who

[121] Margot Asquith, née Tennant, (1864–1945), later countess of Oxford and Asquith, influential and literary wife of Liberal prime minister H.H. Asquith.

[122] Beatrice Wyndham, Lady Leconfield, née Rawson (1892–1956).

[123] Adila Fachiri (1886–1962) and Jelly D'Aranyi (1893–1966), Hungarian-born sisters and violinists.

[124] Mary Venetia James, née Cavendish-Bentinck (1861–1948).

told me that she might have married Sir Edward Hamilton, Mr Gladstone's Private Secretary, who was desperately in love with her, but was forbidden by her mother because he had no money. When my mother first met her, I believe with my father on a big game shooting expedition on the Nile, she was already married to the American millionaire Mr Arthur James. They had no children, and her relationship with my mother resembled that of mother and child. As children we used to stay at Coton, Mrs James' large unheated country house near Rugby, where she had enormous week-end parties which she entertained with shooting and amateur theatricals.

In my first term at Eton, where even the new boys had separate rooms, I was given a little room in an attic at the top of the house. I shall never forget my alarm and astonishment when one evening this formidable old Lady appeared at my door, breathless after climbing so many stairs. She proceeded at once to cross question me about everything I was doing, so as to report in full to my mother when she got back to London. She had a kind heart but a somewhat overbearing manner, and during our winters in London she would set off regularly once a week with my mother to a Girls Club in the East End of the city. Like some very rich people, she had a mania for small economies, such as saving on a tip to a porter or taxi driver, and travelling cheaply (at that time third class) on the railway. The latter habit resulted in an incident which I remember to this day with acute embarrassment. I had settled into a corner seat of a third class non-smoker at Euston Station. There was only one seat left in the carriage when a familiar figure, no less than Mrs Arthur James, marched in. She spotted me immediately, cowering in my corner, and in stentorian tones made the following announcement to me, and apparently to the assembled company: – 'I thought Earls travelled First.' But there was a generation gap between my mother and Mrs James, and my mother's artistic interests and social concerns were not shared by her friend Venetia.

My mother had a genuine social conscience which was shown in her work for women; though she carefully avoided the minefield of party politics. Two subjects were taboo at meal time: religion and politics. She was a pioneer of the Women's Institute Movement, which did so much to enrich the lives of village women in the countryside. Her Village Institute at Hackness was the first in Yorkshire, and she was mentioned in the official history of the Women's Institute Movement among those who were already serving on the National Executive in the 1920s. She was particularly keen about bringing the arts into village life by the encouragement of active participation. Song, mime, and dance were already part of the village tradition, but expert advice was needed for their development. My mother became Chairman of the First Music and Drama Sub-Committee of the National Federation of Women's Institutes in 1926, and, through her initiative immediately after the last war, a combined Festival of the Arts took place in London in 1946, and was attended by the Queen Mother.[125] She was always hopelessly incompetent as a public speaker, but she had so much tact and charm that she was usually able to get her way in committees.

My grandfather Listowel was over 70 when I was born. He lived to the age of 91, becoming the second oldest member of the House of Lords, being beaten by one of his colleagues by only 11 months. He had served in the Crimean War and was severely wounded at the Battle of the Alma. That appears to have been the end of his active career in the army. I rarely saw him, but when I did he would press a golden half sovereign into my hand as a holiday tip. In the winter the family sometimes spent Christmas with him at Convamore, an enormous barrack-like house near Cork on a wonderful site above the Blackwater River and looking away to the Kerry hills. In the days before air travel the journey from London to Ireland was by no means a picnic. My parents always travelled without the children. We, my brother Richard[126] and I, were in the charge of our French governess, who was far too sea-sick on the small boat that carried us from Holyhead to Rosslare to pay the slightest attention to her charges.

My only memories of Convamore are such as any small boy would have anywhere. Baked potatoes from the bottom of a bonfire in the garden, and a vast Christmas tree dressed by my grandmother, who was extremely annoyed when we dashed for the presents underneath it, instead of admiring her work in dressing it. This was not unnatural, as having a staff of at least 20 indoor servants and nothing to do in the house, she had spent hours tying little baubles to the branches of the tree. I also remember the golden pheasants which fluttered about like farm-yard fowls in the great park. There was general jubilation when my grandfather celebrated his 80th birthday by half a day's woodcock shooting at Convamore.

I saw my Listowel grandmother even less frequently. It was a daunting ceremony for a small boy when my mother took me to tea with her at Kingston House. We rang the bell at the Porter's Lodge, and, when he had opened the gate and let us in, we were met, at the front door, by a footman with gold buttons – adorned

with my grandmother's coroneted monogram, and he ushered us
upstairs to the drawing room. There was no electric light or central
heating. I found the passages dark and the rooms large and cold.
There was nothing at the back save a croquet lawn bordering a
large and gloomy shrubbery.

I had to be on my best behaviour to make polite conversation to
the old Lady. On one such occasion, the first since I had begun to
wear spectacles, my mother told me to take them off before we
went upstairs as my grandmother would have been annoyed if she
had known that her grandchild had any physical defect. The fact
that none of us ever received a Christmas or a Birthday present
from her suggests that she found children rather a nuisance. I suspect
that my father must have suffered throughout his life from lack of
maternal affection. He was fond of his father, but he never referred
to his mother, even in the family, except as 'Her Ladyship'. Her portraits show a blonde blue-eyed beauty with a peach bloom complexion, and the first child might well have been an unwelcome
interruption in the dizzy mid-Victorian round of balls, house parties,
and long days in the hunting field that followed my grand-father's
return from the Crimea. But she was full of gratitude to my grandfather for staying up every night to bring her home from the
ballroom.

Another memory is that of the old couple calling in their motorcar
at our house in Bryanston Square every spring before the annual
Chelsea Flower Show of the Royal Horticultural Society, to save
my grandfather from having to buy a second ticket. He left a fortune
of £750,000 when he died in 1924. My grandmother went on living
at Kingston House until her death in 1937.

The golden years before I went to my first boarding school were
only marred by illness. My father was doing a last spell of duty
with his regiment at the Curragh Camp in Ireland when I was struck
down by acute stomach pain. A surgeon was summoned from
Dublin. He cut me open and sewed me up again without removing
the appendix! About a year later, just after the outbreak of the First
World War, I had another but more severe attack. This time we were
in London, and a great Australian surgeon, Sir Douglas Shields,[127]
was working at a London Hospital for the Australian Forces. He
saved my life by an immediate operation. My grateful parents celebrated my convalescence with an orgy of expensive delicacies, and

---

[127] *Sir Douglas Shields, Australian surgeon, who saved my life by appendicitis operation.* [Served as a
surgeon-in-chief to the Australian Voluntary Hospital and had a private practice in
London].

drives round the London Parks in the latest motor vehicle, an electric car.

At the age of eight and a half I was packed off to my preparatory school, Lockers Park near Hemel Hempstead in Hertfordshire. In the last week of term we used to sing the following ditty in the dormitory:

This time next week where shall I be,
Out of the clutches of R.C.C.[128]
No more Latin, no more Greek,
No more swish to make me squeak.

I mention this because it is interesting to note the study of the classics, and the use of corporal punishment, at private schools which small boys entered at the age of 7 or 8. I can remember a homesick and miserable first term, but I settled down after that, and was well enough instructed after 4 years to get a place in the Upper Fourth, the second highest Form, for a new boy at Eton. It seems that I must have been above the average entry for that Form because at the end of my first term I was given a 'double' remove, that is, I skipped the Form immediately above it, and landed in a higher Form where all the other boys had been doing Greek for one term. I was allowed extra tuition in Greek to help my frantic efforts to catch up. My Tutor was Mr J H L Lambart, an erudite classicist, later Lower Master, whose splendid collection of gramophone records enhanced my taste for classical music.

At Eton the windows soon began to open for me on worlds undreamt of in the narrow family and prep school circles. It is often said that, at any rate in those days, the public schools worshipped sport and despised or even bullied anyone with intellectual pretensions. This was certainly not true of Eton, apart from certain of the Houses where Housemasters allowed it. Elsewhere there was good natured tolerance of the 'sap', a slang word for somebody with intellectual interests. But of course, the very fact that this word had a derogatory flavour, and that the prestige of a member of the cricket eleven or the Field (school football team) was much greater than that of a Sixth Former, showed that the emphasis of school life and the criterion of success, among the boys at any rate, was brawn rather than brain. I was fortunate to be in a House where no-one ever discouraged me from 'doing my own thing', but it may not have been a disadvantage that I was good enough at games to play cricket and football for my House. My

---

[128] *Mr Craig the French Master.*

Housemaster, Mr C.H.K. Marten,[129] was an enthusiastic historian who inspired others with his own enthusiasm. This included the success of his own House on the cricket field. I remember how, on the evening before my School Certificate exam, when I should have been revising, he insisted that I must join the rest of his team for a cricket practice before a House match the following day. He was a historian who loved history, and brought the past to life for his students. He published an elementary textbook on English history, which did less than justice to his flair for teaching it. He also went regularly to Windsor Castle to teach history in private lessons to the two little Princesses, Elizabeth and Margaret.

Looking back, I think like many other Housemasters, he gave too much authority to older boys, and interfered too little with the way they ran the House. I am sure this was the usual practice in my time, when it was considered inherent in the long established doctrine of training for leadership. But of course it is unwise to give older boys power over younger boys, because they cannot have an adult sense of responsibility. The practice of 'fagging' for the senior boys, some of whom were allowed to administer corporal punishment whenever they thought fit, was wide open to abuse, and most of all when there was little supervision. I was lucky to avoid a beating because the seniors in my House were exceptionally humane and responsible, but the juniors in other Houses were less lucky. I'm glad to say when I graduated to the 'Library',[130] I never had to beat another boy. I remembered being amused when told by a prefect to warm up a lavatory seat in the outside lavatory! Even in the modern Houses the lavatory would be outside the main building, where the small boys would sit summer and winter in a row of cubicles, with each door open.

One advantage of Eton was that it gave a certain scope for individuality, and at least did not seek to impose the rigid pattern of uniformity obtaining in some of our public schools. If you were interested in a subject outside the school curriculum there was almost always someone who could discuss it intelligently, whether a 'beak' (as the Masters were called), or a visitor. As it was I was allowed to spend an hour every week with a young beak who studied philosophy, and introduced me to Hume[131] and the English Empiricists. For those like myself who were keen about politics there was the

---

[129] C.H.K. Marten (1872–1948), later Sir Henry Marten, history master and later provost of Eton; tutored Princess Elizabeth in constitutional history.

[130] House prefect.

[131] David Hume (1711–1776), 18th-century Scottish enlightenment philosopher.

Political Society. It always surprised me how willing distinguished members of both Houses of Parliament were to visit us.

There were leading figures from all the Parties, including the Labour Party, and I remember being impressed by Buck de la Warr[132] and Maggie Bondfield,[133] the first Socialists I had ever met, and I think members of the 1924 Labour Government. There was no school debating society until towards the end of my time at Eton. But I have a vivid recollection of a heated debate on the future of the House of Lords. I led for those who were in favour of abolition, while Quintin Hogg, now Lord Hailsham,[134] an outstanding Scholar from College, spoke with eloquence about the virtues of the hereditary principle in providing a second chamber to act as a safeguard of our constitution.

I suppose at this time I was a radical reformer, and I already regarded the Labour Party as the standard bearer of radical social change. My views were certainly heretical, though they were shared by the Headmaster's wife, Mrs Alington.[135] I was already vaguely, but only vaguely, aware of the gulf that separated the two nations of rich and poor as Disraeli[136] described them. Within a stone's throw of my home in Bryanston Square was a typical London slum called Lisson Grove, where you could see ragged children playing in the street without shoes or socks. At home I had never been able to talk politics, because party politics and religion were the two subjects about which discussion was strictly forbidden. Eton opened a chink of window for me on the wider society to which I belonged, and what I saw I found strangely disturbing.

---

[132] Herbrand Sackville, 9th Earl De La Warr (1900–1976), peer who held office under Labour, Coalition and Conservative administrations; president of the board of education, 1938–1940.

[133] Margaret Bondfield (1873–1953), Labour MP who served as minister of labour, 1929–1931.

[134] Quintin Hogg (1907–2001), later 2nd Viscount Hailsham and Lord Hailsham of St Marylebone, Conservative politician; served as lord chancellor, 1970–1974 and 1979–1987.

[135] Hester Alington, née Lyttelton, m. Cyril Alington, headmaster of Eton, 1916–1933.

[136] Benjamin Disraeli (1804–1881), later earl of Beaconsfield, Conservative prime minister, 1868, 1874–1880; in his novel *Sybil, or the Two Nations* (1845) referred to 'Two nations; between whom there is no intercourse and no sympathy; who are as ignorant of each other's habits, thoughts, and feelings, as if they were dwellers in different zones, or inhabitants of different planets; who are formed by a different breeding, are fed by a different food, are ordered by different manners, and are not governed by the same laws.'

III
STUDENT LIFE: 1924–1932

Although I had never been unhappy and in fact enjoyed my public school, the transition from public school to university was altogether delightful. There is a psychological uplift about being treated by adults as an equal instead of an inferior, as a rational being instead of a child, which no-one can understand who has not experienced it. I felt for the first time like a mature person, who could be persuaded by argument but not ordered about like a domestic pet. As my main interests at Eton had been history and philosophy, I decided to take my degree in what was then the new school of Modern Greats. This included the trinity of history, philosophy and economics, and covered much the same ground as is covered now by PPE.[137] My tutor was Humphrey Sumner,[138] who took what was thought to be the brightest of the new intake of undergraduates. No-one could have given a stronger visual impression of dedication to the true and the beautiful than Humphrey Sumner. His glowing eyes and parchment complexion suggested a reincarnation of Savonarola. To complete the picture he wore a flowing black cloak and a broad brimmed black hat. When you went in for a tutorial he was puffing his pipe and working indefatigably on an obscure period of Russian history. I saw him once again after I left Oxford. He descended on me one afternoon at Magdalene, Cambridge, and asked to be taken around the College and the Pepys Library. I did so with trepidation as I knew he would expect the expertise of a professional guide. I lost touch with him before he became Warden of All Souls, the crown of a great academic career.

For philosophy at Oxford at this time there was a galaxy of talent. The Master himself,[139] who lectured on Plato, Morris, the late Lord Morris of Grasmere,[140] and a young Fellow called John

[137] Philosophy, Politics, and Economics.
[138] B. Humphrey Sumner (1893–1951), fellow of Balliol College and later warden of All Souls, 1945–1951.
[139] A.D. Lindsay (1879–1952), later Baron Lindsay of Birker, academic philosopher and master of Balliol College, 1924–1949.
[140] Charles Morris (1898–1990), later Baron Morris of Granmere, philosopher; later vice-chancellor of the University of Leeds.

Macmurray,[141] a leading expert on Kant with a reputation for his brilliant lectures on the Categories of Knowledge. Another Fellow of the College who left a brief but indelible impression on me was R.H. Tawney.[142] His nephew Michael Vyvyan was a history Scholar. He arrived at Balliol at the same time as I did, and he asked me to tea in his rooms to meet his Uncle, who had come to Oxford to lecture on the topically important subject of 'Coal'. Tawney had just returned from a holiday in Italy, and we were regaled in an opulent and mellifluous prose, such as I had never heard before, with an unforgettably brilliant picture of the art and architecture of the Renaissance in Italy. He was already a major prophet of socialism, but on this occasion there was not one word about politics or economics.

My undergraduate friendships were mainly formed with those who shared my enthusiasm for the Labour Club and the Union Debating Society. It was there that I first met two friends whom I was to see often in later life when they became Members of Parliament, Dingle Foot[143] and Dick Acland.[144] From them I learned that to succeed at the Union you had to burn the midnight oil. But my closest friends were those who most regularly frequented the Labour Club. The Labour Club was a flourishing University society which secured speakers from every branch of the Labour movement, MPs, Trade Unionists, and academic Economists. Its presiding geniuses were Douglas[145] and Margaret Cole,[146] who were indefatigable in their efforts to stimulate the young. They used to ask some of us to their Oxford home, where Douglas would read a paper on the socialist theory he was at that moment embracing. I remember meeting for the first time Roger Wilson,[147] who became Professor of Education at Birmingham University, Robert Henriques[148] the novelist, and Evan Durbin,[149] who was to become the closest friend of Hugh

[141] John Macmurray (1891-1976), philosopher who held academic positions in Oxford, London and Edinburgh.

[142] R.H. Tawney (1880-1962), Fabian intellectual and Professor of Economic History at the London School of Economics.

[143] Sir Dingle Foot, QC (1905-1978), Labour MP and solicitor general, 1964-1967.

[144] *Who gave his estate to the National Trust.* Sir Richard Acland, 15th baronet (1906-1990), Liberal and then Labour MP.

[145] *Douglas Cole and his wife, Margaret, members of the Labour club, Syndicatists and lecturers on economics.* G.D.H. Cole (1889-1959), Fabian and political theorist at Oxford University.

[146] Dame Margaret Cole (1893-1980), Fabian, local government politician and co-author with her husband of mystery novels among other writings.

[147] *Roger Wilson, my best friend and later professor of education at Birmingham.*

[148] *Robert Henriques (1905-1967), novelist.*

[149] *Evan Durbin, best friend of Hugh Gaitskell, died young in tragic accident.* Evan Durbin (1906-1948), economist at the London School of Economics and Labour politician and MP.

Gaitskell.[150] Roger was a devout Quaker, and his socialism was a practical expression of his religious ethics. He combined a strong social conscience with a great sense of fun. But the friend from whom I learned most about society, though I can't say I ever felt close to him, was Frank Lee,[151] who came to Balliol after a scholarship to Ruskin College. My other friends were middle class, but Frank's father worked in the Lancashire cotton mills, and his son was an authentic voice of the working class. I was slightly afraid of his emotional intensity, and shocked by his hatred of the exploiting class. But his burning sense of social justice and injustice, and his entire devotion to the cause of the underprivileged, earned my deepest respect. His sincerity and power of argument, even though unaccompanied by the faintest spark of humour, made him a successful speaker at Union debates. He asked me once to meet his parents and spend the night at their home. The Look in his father's face when I left the skin of my kipper on my plate is something I shall not forget; ever since I have found the waste of food in the homes of the well-to-do somewhat shocking. Frank lived to become the first Labour Mayor of Northampton. But both he and his lovely wife Olive died young.

The idyll of my first year at Balliol was abruptly and most unexpectedly interrupted by one of those accidents whose repercussions are felt for the rest of one's life. I was attending the annual conference of the Universities Labour Federation when a press reporter came up to me and asked me for a personal statement about my views. I was rather flattered by this request, and told him that I had decided to drop my title and preferred to be addressed as Mr Hare.[152] This was immediately reported in the press, thereby drawing the attention of my father who, for the first time, as politics had been taboo at home, became aware that his son had become a Socialist and therefore a dangerous heretic. Roger rebuked me afterwards for speaking to the press, and of course he was right. I suppose it had flattered my vanity to find that my doings were of interest to the public. Anyway the result was disastrous. The following statement appeared in the Daily Mail on April the 27th, 1925:

> Viscount Ennismore, eldest son and heir of the Earl of Listowel, has joined the famous Fabian Society, members of which are usually called Intellectual Socialists. Its still best known members are George Bernard

---

[150] Hugh Gaitskell (1906–1964), Labour MP; chancellor of the exchequer 1950–1951; and leader of the Labour Party (and opposition), 1955–1963.

[151] *Frank Lee, scholar from Ruskin, became Mayor of Northampton.*

[152] As opposed to the courtesy title Viscount Ennismore.

Shaw and Sydney [*sic*] Webb. Lord Ennismore, who is now 19 years old, is now at Oxford and is said to intend entering politics as soon as he graduates. Six of the seven Labour peers in the House of Lords are members of the Fabian Society – Lord Haldane, Earl Russell, Lord Olivier, Lord De La Warr, Lord Thomson and Lord Gorell.[153]

The Fabian Society was still a middle class organisation of 'intellectual socialists' founded in 1884 by Edward Pearse [*sic*][154] and his friends, as an offshoot of the idealistic 'Fellowship of the New Life' by a resolution defining its aim as 'the reconstitution of society in accordance with the highest moral possibilities'. It was named after the Roman General, Fabius, who 'waited most patiently when warring against Hannibal though many censured his delays'.

There was no mention of its association with socialism until it was joined shortly afterwards by Bernard Shaw[155] and Sidney Webb,[156] who described it as 'consisting of socialists, whose aim was to re-organise society by freeing land and capital from private ownership'. It remained essentially middle-class and gradualist, avoiding the dogmatism, revolutionary violence, and class war of the Marxists, and preaching its gospel by means of Fabian Tracts exploring the evils of a capitalist society and prescribing their remedy.

My father had been devoted to me when I still shared his interests and was therefore all the more hurt at my turning against all that he held dear. His attitude was typically Victorian and as he himself said if it had been a woman or money he would have understood but for me to betray my own class was unforgivable. My father believed that I had been corrupted by the company I kept, which of course included the Master himself, Sandy Lindsay, who later became a Labour candidate for the Oxford constituency. My father wrote to me an angry letter saying that, in my own interest, he was no longer prepared to pay my fees at Balliol. As his objection appeared to be directed to the College rather than the University, I asked the Master whether I could not transfer to another College. He went to see the Dean of Christ Church and when his mission failed, I was deeply touched that he came in person, mounting the steep staircase to my little room in College, to say how sorry he was about his failure. I believe he also tried other Colleges, without success.

---

[153] *Statement in Daily Mail, April 27 1925, about my politics and membership of Fabian Society, which ended my life at Balliol when my father refused to pay university fees.*

[154] Edward R. Pease (1857–1955), founding member of the Fabian Society and trustee of the London School of Economics.

[155] George Bernard Shaw (1856–1950), Irish playwright and Fabian.

[156] Sidney Webb, later Baron Passfield (1859–1947), intellectual and Labour minister, served in various ministerial posts including secretary of state for the colonies, 1929–1931.

At this stage I heard from my father that he had found out from his old school friend Lord Willingdon,[157] at that time Governor-General of Canada, that he would be willing to have me on his staff as an honorary A.D.C. My father believed that this association with people of the 'right' social standing would assist me to see the error of my ways. I protested that this would deprive me of a university education, and, although my father attached no importance to this, my plea was supported by other members of my family. It was then that some bright and kindly ally – I don't know who it was – suggested that A.B. Ramsey,[158] who had known me at Eton when he was Lower Master – he presided over the 'Essay Society' in his garden, at which I had read an essay, might be willing to take me at Magdalene College, Cambridge.

So a place was found for me at Cambridge, and I was saved from what I certainly regarded at the time as a fate worse than death. When the news that I was leaving Balliol got around, everyone treated me with great kindness. Among the older men A.L. Rowse,[159] the historian, invited me for the weekend to All Souls, proclaiming indignantly this was the first time since Shelley[160] that an undergraduate had been sent down for his opinions. This comparison was more flattering than true. Shelley was sent down by University College for his atheism, but I had been removed by my father, and neither Balliol nor Oxford was in the least to blame for this paternal intolerance. Although I had only been up at Oxford for a year, the Balliol Society, at the instigation of its Secretary Kenneth Bell, invited me to become a member.

I have already mentioned the kindness of the Master. I wonder whether he felt, in view of his own socialist opinions, some responsibility for the bad company which my father thought I had fallen into. Lady Scott, in her beautifully written biography of her father,[161] attributes my departure from Balliol to a comment in the Morning Post which alerted my father to the fact that the Master had written a book which glorified: 'the first and greatest of all the Communists, Karl Marx'. Needless to say, this book on Marx did not in the least mean that the Master agreed with him, in fact his was a devout

[157] Freeman Freeman-Thomas (1866–1941), later 1st marquess of Willingdon, Liberal politician and colonial administrator; governor general of Canada, 1926–1931, and viceroy of India, 1931–1936.

[158] *A.B. Ramsey, Master of Magdalene College, Cambridge and former Lower Master at Eton, who offered me a place at Magdalene.*

[159] A.L. Rowse (1903–1997), historian and literary academic, fellow of All Souls, Oxford.

[160] Percy Bysshe Shelley (1792–1822), poet. His expulsion from Oxford in 1811 was the result of his part in an anonymous pamphlet *The Necessity of Atheism* printed the same year.

[161] *A.D. Lindsay – A Biography* [published in 1971].

Christian interpretation of Marxism. But my father did not read the Morning Post, although he may have known something about the Master's reputation as a socialist. In point of fact Sandy Lindsay did not influence my political opinions, and I find that in a letter to my father I pointed out that I had brought my socialism with me from Eton.

It was the writings and speeches of a French socialist leader, Jean Jaurès,[162] who had graduated in philosophy before he found a political party that agreed with his views about society, that first attracted me to socialism. Sandy Lindsay may not have been a great scholar or an original philosopher but he stood out as a good man who really believed in social justice and economic equality. His main interests as a philosopher were the ethics of political theory. His life was spent in applying ethical principles to the practical problems of society, afflicted as it then was before the advent of the Welfare State by all the ills of unemployment and lifelong poverty. The advice he gave me when I paid him a last visit before leaving the College was to take economics at Cambridge. This he said would teach me to understand the social problems which would one day confront me in Parliament. I am glad to think that I was able later on to assist in providing a wider forum for his views, and a fresh opportunity for public service. When Viscount Addison,[163] my Leader in the Lords, told me that the Prime Minister, Clem Attlee,[164] wanted suggestions for Labour peers, I thought immediately of Sandy Lindsay. He did in fact accept a peerage in 1945, and spoke in the House, rather nervously I thought, on several occasions. It was a great pity he was not offered a post in the 1945 Labour Government, ideally at the Ministry of Education, where he could have combined the administrative ability he had shown as Vice Chancellor at Oxford University with his enthusiasm for education. But unfortunately he had no 'base' such as a constituency or a trade union in the Labour Party.

Another Oxford don I had the good fortune to meet was that grand old man, Professor Gilbert Murray,[165] with whom I was already familiar from his romantic translations of Euripides. He was the moving spirit behind support for the League of Nations, precursor of the United Nations Organisation, which many of us regarded at the time

---

[162] *Jean Jaures, French socialist leader and orator.* [Assassinated in 1914.]

[163] Charles Addison (1869–1951), later 1st Viscount Addison, Labour politician and minister including serving as leader of the House of Lords for the entire Attlee administration, 1945–1951, and secretary of state for dominion affairs, 1945–1947.

[164] Clement R. Attlee (1883–1967), later 1st Earl Attlee, Labour prime minister, 1945–1951, and leader of the Labour Party, 1935–1955.

[165] *Professor Gilbert Murray, professor of Greek and enthusiast for League of Nations.* Gilbert Murray (1866–1957), classical scholar and translator at Glasgow and then Oxford.

as the principal safeguard against another World War. Every year Professor Murray despatched a band of undergraduate missionaries to preach the League gospel at public meetings during university vacations. As I was primarily interested in social work, he asked me to talk about the International Labour Office. I went out to Geneva and met Mr Butler, who had succeeded Mr Albert Thomas as Director-General of the I.L.O.,[166] and I also met Dame Rachel Crowdey [sic],[167] who briefed me about the humanitarian work of the League of Nations for women and refugees. I spent some of my summer vacation addressing almost invisible audiences in schools and village halls.

There was one other event during my Oxford career which necessitated another difficult choice between my family and society. The facts of the General Strike of May 1926 are familiar to everyone. It happened during my summer term at Oxford, and my father summoned me back to London to join him by enrolling as a Special Constable. It should be remembered that the Special Constables at that time were recruited from ex-officers and university students. My sympathies of course were on the side of the coal miners. I flatly refused to become a policeman, in which capacity I might have had to assist strike breakers and to suppress demonstrations by Trade Unionists. Instead, as a compromise, I drove patients to the London Hospitals in my little car, and later acted as an office boy for some older university students who were trying to get out a news sheet to publicise the Archbishop of Canterbury's appeal for an agreed settlement. When I returned to Oxford I was greeted by another angry letter from my father for failing to do my patriotic duty. It is curious how completely the tables have been turned in the years between the general strike of 1926 and the Heath Government of 1970. In 1926 the miners were routed by the mine owners and the Government, and were driven back to work by starvation, with lower wages and a longer working week. The Heath Government was brought down by the resistance of the miners to the refusal of a wage increase.

At Magdalene, Cambridge, I started life in 'digs', and among my earliest recollections was that of the arrival of a large consignment of books from my great-uncle, a successful stockbroker and youngest brother of my grandfather Derwent, which included J.S. Mill on 'Liberty'.[168] He was the only member of my family who tried to

[166] International Labour Organization, established in 1919 and based in Geneva.
[167] Dame Rachel Crowdy (1884-1964), social reformer and nurse during First World War, head of the Social Questions and Opium Traffic Section at the League of Nations.
[168] English philosopher, John Stuart Mill; *On Liberty* was first published in 1859.

convert me by argument, and I am ashamed to say I did not acknowledge his gift.

In spite of an excellent tutor in economics at Cambridge, in the person of Sargent [sic] Florence,[169] I found Marshall's 'Principles of Economics',[170] the textbook for students of this subject, so dull and difficult and so far removed from the problems of real life in which I was interested, that I decided to switch from economics to English. I was thus able to combine work with pleasure, and my tutor I.A. Richards[171] was an outstanding figure among younger dons in the field of English literature. In the final Tripos examination I failed to get a First Class Degree, and came in with a good Second.

I had been fond of music since early childhood, a taste encouraged by my mother who was always dashing off when we were in London to the Queen's Hall as it then was, or to the Wigmore Hall for concerts and recitals. One of my greatest blessings has been a good musical memory. I carry in my head a collection of melodies from songs, arias from operas, themes from orchestral or chamber music, that never leave me with the boredom of a vacant mind. I should perhaps say fragments rather than whole compositions. The words I usually forget, but the theme often brings these back. My feeling for music is best described by Schubert in his song 'An die Musik'.[172]

Eton gave me my first opportunity of becoming a performer instead of a listener. In accordance with my paternal upbringing a piano was an instrument for girls, but luckily there was no such restriction on the male voice. I therefore started singing lessons with a professional bass in the School Chapel Choir, and soon found myself emulating the booming tones in which my teacher uttered the haunting melancholy of Schubert's 'Der Wanderer'.[173] There was plenty of robust singing in the School Musical Society, and even in our House Quartet which introduced me to Elizabethan madrigals. But no-one took the trouble to teach me to read music. I had an excellent ear fortunately, and this was good enough for Eton. But when I went up to Oxford, and Sir Hugh Allen[174] gave me an audition for the Bach Choir, he would have failed me but for my touching enthusiasm at the prospect of singing Bach. I still regard music as queen of the arts.

---

[169] *Sargant Florence; economics don and my first tutor at Cambridge.* Philip Sargant Florence.

[170] Cambridge economist, Alfred Marshall; *Principles of Economics* was first published in 1890.

[171] *I.A. Richards, taught English Literature and my tutor for the subject.*

[172] Franz Schubert composed this in 1817.

[173] Composed in 1816.

[174] Sir Hugh Allen (1869-1946), musician and academic at Oxford and the Royal College of Music.

There was nothing at Cambridge to correspond to the Bach Choir in which I sang at Oxford, but I was invited to join a small group of undergraduates familiarly known as the 'Corncrakes', who met every week at the home of Professor Cornford.[175] He was a professor of classics and his wife, Frances Cornford,[176] was a poetess who had been a friend of Rupert Brooke.[177] They were the parents of John Cornford,[178] a poet and communist who became a Cambridge legend when he was killed in the Spanish Civil War. There we sang madrigals, gossiped over coffee and cakes, and made new friends.

The lure of politics was still overwhelming, and I soon gravitated towards the University Labour Club and the Union Debating Society. Of all the guest speakers at the Labour Club I remember most vividly the lumbering massive figure of the biochemist J.B.S. Haldane.[179] He described to us how he made himself a guinea pig for his own scientific experiments, venturing sometimes to within an inch of death. He was admired throughout the University for his defiance of our antiquated divorce laws. In those days a divorce was only possible after proof of an offence. He was in love with a married lady parted from her husband, and they wanted to get married. It was therefore indispensable for one or other of them to commit a marital offence. Haldane duly committed adultery, and obtained Charlotte's divorce, and their marriage.

He was then informed by Mr Seward,[180] the Vice-Chancellor, that the Sex Viri (responsible for the morals of the University) had decided to deprive him of his Readership on grounds of 'gross immorality'. This important body consisted of three Heads of Colleges and three Professors of Laws, with the Vice-Chancellor in the chair. He decided to appeal against this absurd decision, and the Senate had the good sense to find the charge of 'gross immorality' untenable, and to reverse the verdict of the Sex Viri.

It was at another union debate that I fast met Arthur Ponsonby,[181] later my Leader when I took my seat in the House of Lords. He told me to my surprise that Ramsay MacDonald[182] in 1929 had seriously

[175] F.M. Cornford (1874–1943), classics scholar at Cambridge.

[176] Frances Cornford (1886–1960), poet.

[177] Rupert Brooke (1887–1915), poet and soldier.

[178] Died 1936.

[179] J.B.S. Haldane (1892–1964), scientist and socialist.

[180] Later Sir Albert Seward (1863–1941), master of Downing College, 1915–1936, and vice-chancellor of Cambridge, 1924–1926.

[181] Arthur Ponsonby (1871–1946), later 1st Baron Ponsonby of Shulbrede, Liberal and then Labour politician; Labour leader in the House of Lords, 1931–1935.

[182] Ramsay MacDonald (1866–1937), Labour prime minister, 1924, 1929–1939; leader of the Labour Party, 1922–1931.

considered his recommendation to give me a peerage to strengthen the Labour Party in the Lords. At the time it was contrary to the policy of the Party to create new hereditary Peerages, and the fact that I was the eldest son of a Peer must have appealed to the Prime Minister. I daresay my age deterred him. An undergraduate socialist peer might have made the small number of Labour peers in the House of Lords look a little ridiculous. Perhaps it was as well, because my father would have had a fit if I had had the further publicity of a Labour seat in the Lords!

I attended and took part regularly in debates at the Union, and finally reached the Order Paper in the Michaelmas term of 1928, as the proposer of a Motion condemning the existing social order. This was the occasion of another disaster in my private life, and is therefore a focal point among my Cambridge memories. Soon after I came to Magdalene, I told my friends I would prefer to be addressed by my family name of Hare instead of my courtesy title of Viscount Ennismore. This was understood and accepted as a private arrangement within the university. However when my name appeared on the Order Paper of the Cambridge Union advertising the debate as 'Mr W.F. Hare', the floodgates of publicity were thrown wide open again. My photo as Mr Hare was published in a number of daily newspapers, and the Daily Express carried a fairly long and friendly story about the debate mentioning the fact that 'When it was proposed a few months ago that women should be admitted to the debates of the century old Cambridge Union Society it was Viscount Ennismore who pleaded eloquently that the word Lady should be added to Gentlemen in the Rules'.[183]

But now let me go back to the Debate in the Union which led to my final family disaster. The Motion to which I was speaking was framed in suitably sweeping undergraduate terms. 'This House believing the present constitution of society to be inefficient and immoral, cannot hope for peace in industry.' The proposer Mr W.F. Hare, seconder Mr A.J. Cooke. Mr A.J. Cooke was the Secretary of the Miners Federation of Great Britain,[184] and had led the miners through the long ordeal of the lockout, the General Strike, and the final capitulation in 1926. I had to point out that he was on the left of the Labour Party to convince my audience that the motion was also supported by moderates like myself. Mr Cooke complained that I had 'disowned him' and insisted on

---

[183] *I appeared on Order paper of Cambridge Union (debating society) as Mr W F Hare, Proposer of Motion, with Mr A J. Cooke, Secretary of the Miners Federation of Great Britain, as seconder. This was last straw for my father who banished me from home.*

[184] 1924–1931.

referring to me as 'the noble lord'. I blush to think of my own per-
formance. I had just been reading the speeches of Jean Jaures, a
French socialist leader I greatly admired, and I modelled my speech
on the long flowing periods of his impassioned Gallic oratory.
Anything less appropriate to a sophisticated Cambridge audience
can hardly be imagined. In spite of this inauspicious opening, the
debate ended to my surprise with just over 200 votes for the
Motion out of a total of over 500 votes cast. A not inglorious defeat.

But the dropping of a name and a title he had borne for most of
his life was the last straw for my poor father. He made it quite clear
that in future he did not want to see me at home during the vacations. This setback did not however discourage me from persisting
with the Union. In my last year I was elected to the Standing
Committee, and this gave me an opportunity to raise again the question of the admission of women. I was sure that if I could get the
Committee on my side, a Motion could be carried on the floor of
the chamber. Selwyn Lloyd,[185] later Foreign Secretary to Anthony
Eden[186] at the time of Suez and Speaker of the House of
Commons, was President that Term, and he agreed to summon a
special meeting for the purpose of discussing the admission of
women. I put my case, but the majority including the President
were against me. I teased the late Speaker a little about this incident
one evening at a dinner at the Speaker's House – this of course was at
a time when we were both members of different Houses at
Westminster.

Another political Opponent and good friend whom I liked
immensely was Gilbert Harding,[187] who was just as amusing in private
life as he was later on as a broadcaster. It seems strange since women
have now played such a conspicuous part in the activities of the
Cambridge Union, and have even filled the office of President,
that it took so long after their admission to Parliament for the
doors of the University Debating Society to be opened to them.

What might have made matters even worse for my family than my
escapades at Balliol, was that I now fell into the clutches of someone
even more dangerous than the Master, a Christian socialist who was
the nearest approach to a socialist saint that I ever met. His name was

[185] Selwyn Lloyd (1904–1978), later Lord Selwyn-Lloyd, Conservative MP who served as
foreign secretary, 1955–1960, and chancellor of the exchequer, 1960–1962; speaker of the
House of Commons, 1971–1976.
[186] Anthony Eden (1897–1977), later 1st earl of Avon, Conservative prime minister, 1955–
1957.
[187] Gilbert Harding (1907–1960), broadcaster and journalist.

Jack Bellerby,[188] he was a Fellow of Caius College, and he lectured on economics. He was engaged in organising an immediate and peaceful transition to what he called a 'contributive society' in place of the acquisitive society in which we live. His instrument for this purpose was a new kind of Friendly Society called 'The Neighbours'. This Society was registered under The Industrial and Provident Societies Act, and the first Articles of the Rules read:

> The Society should be called Neighbours Limited, and its object should be to collect provide and administer funds for the promotion of art, science, social welfare, and fellowship.

Every member was obliged to hold at least one share of one penny, but for each share he must donate £100 to the Society. The donation of members would be invested, and the income used for the above purposes. There was one benefit, and one benefit only, which the members themselves could derive; being a safety net for those who gave away all of their property. If their income were less than the national average wage earned at that time, it would be made up to £3 per week for a single person and to £4 per week for a married couple, with 10 shillings extra for every child. It should be emphasised that though the aim of every member of the Society was to live on no more than the average wage, the only qualification was a commitment to reduce personal consumption in order to release surplus income and capital for the purposes of the Society. There was no obligation not to exceed the average wage, and I am afraid this feat of self-denial was always far beyond me. But I hovered for a time very close to the edge, and this was enough to cause intense worry to my parents.

Needless to say the founding of this Society and my connection with it did not escape the attention of the press. I was interviewed by the Daily Sketch, and the result was an article headed 'Peer's Son to Give Up Fortune' and beginning with the following sentence:

> An extraordinary Friendly Society has been formed to enable wealthy men and women to give away their money for social purposes and live on a mere pittance allowed by the Society.

It went on to say that I intended to live in a bedsitting room in London. By that time I was 22, and my fortune consisted of a modest allowance from my father to cover food clothing and tuition fees, and

[188] *Professor Jack Bellerby, Fellow of Caius College, Cambridge and lecturer on economics, who founded a Friendly Society called 'The Neighbours'. A secular saint, who among other activities published a symposium on factory farming for the Association for the Advancement of Science. He financed the publication of my booklet on 'The Values of Life'.*

a capital sum of £2,000 given me by my grandfather Derwent when I was 21. I had told Jack Bellerby that I might be willing to hand over my capital, but before accepting he thought he should discuss it with my mother. He told me, after having a cup of tea with her at our London home, that it would evidently cause distress to her and my grandfather if I parted with my money, and advised me to keep it for the time being. The reference to the bedsitting room was highly misleading in the context of the article, when it suggested this was the next step towards a life of increasing self imposed austerity. In fact as my father had now banished me from the family home, I had absolutely nowhere to go during the university vacations. So my mother had come to my rescue by taking a bedsitter for me at No. 6 Paddington Street, not too far from my home at Bryanston Square.

My darling mother had supported me during the whole of the trouble with my father. There I resided in the holidays until an accommodation with my father made it possible for me to return home. The basis of this accommodation, which took place after I left Cambridge, was that I reverted from Mr W. Hare to Viscount Ennismore. I am glad to say that the friendly relationship that this concession made possible continued until my father's death in 1931.

But to go back to Cambridge and my friend Jack Bellerby and The Neighbours Limited. I do not believe that it ever attracted many supporters, and those who joined it were worthy rather than wealthy. I am sure that Jack Bellerby did not really expect it to transform society, but rather to offer a unique opportunity for those who believed that the accumulation and inheritance of private property and the manner of its acquisition are an obstacle to the good life. This belief has inspired secular socialists and many devout people throughout history. But, whereas the utopian socialists and monastic orders organised their new societies outside the community, The Neighbours was a new society within the existing community. You could therefore be a 'Neighbour' and remain a husband, a professional man, a good citizen standing as an active participant in local or national politics, but you became a better person by using your saved or inherited income or capital for the common good. This it seems to me was the essential originality and ingenuity of Jack Bellerby's conception. He certainly deserves a niche in the history of British Socialism in the 20th century.

After I left Cambridge, Jack Bellerby and I drifted apart. His first wife, the poetess Frances Bellerby, became a chronic invalid and he seemed to spend most of his time after he retired from Cambridge looking after her. He surfaced again in 1970 when I had a letter asking for my help with a book on factory farming. I had been a junior Minister at the Ministry of Agriculture in 1951. He told me that he had had to give the welfare of farm animals higher priority than his philosophy. He was profoundly shocked by the cruelty of some of the methods of factory farming, the battery or broiler house chicken, the sweat box, the battery calf, methods that deprive these animals of the freedom of movement and enjoyment of light and air which they would have in their natural environment. He produced his book, with a foreword by Prince Philip, in the form of a symposium on Factory Farming, which he edited on behalf of the Association for the Advancement of Science. I heard from him again once or twice, suggesting ways of bringing pressure to bear on the Minister of Agriculture for the control of factory farming.

It was at Cambridge also that I discovered Bertrand Russell.[189] His essay on 'A Free Man's Worship' was exactly in tune with my own doubts about the benevolent creator in whom I had been brought up to believe, and struck an attitude of defiance in the face of adversity which suited the circumstances of my own family predicament. It was of course in form and content quite different from his later writings, and had a poetic quality calculated to appeal to the young.[190] At the same time it helped to crystallise my thoughts about the universe in a form which I found no reason to change in later life. The universe as we know it is not hostile or unfriendly but simply indifferent to human existence, which has come about by a series of accidents, and will be brought to an end when conditions on our planet render it uninhabitable by living organisms. Mysterious as the relationships may be between mind and body, the one seems to depend on the other, and we have no evidence of the existence of disembodied minds.

My mood of defiance has changed over the years to one of acceptance of the limits that nature and society impose on the freedom of each of us to choose our own path through life.

In the cosmic sense nothing and no-one matters at all, but in an arbitrary human sense everything and everyone is of supreme importance. It was this paradox that set me thinking about human values, and occasioned the small book on 'The Values of Life' I wrote soon after I left Cambridge. It was commissioned by Jack Bellerby for private publication by Education Services, which was responsible for educational productions on behalf of The Neighbours Society. This little book was translated into Sanskrit. I never knew the

---

[189] *Bertrand Russell. His essay on 'A Free Man's Worship' opened my eyes to a new philosophy of life.* Bertrand Russell (1872–1970), later 3rd Earl Russell, philosopher, writer and activist. *A Free Man's Worship* first appeared in 1903.

[190] *Russell mentions in a letter to Donnelly that he had had a letter from Joseph Conrad 'praising' the Free Man's Worship 'in about the strongest terms in which writing can be praised'.*

translator, and I have no idea how it circulated in India. I cannot now regard it as an original contribution to philosophy, but it did express a passionate affirmation of belief in the distinction between the values that are ends in themselves, beauty, goodness and truth, and those that are merely instrumental, such as material values, to the achievement of the good life. My sense of values has not changed, and I still find love at the core of it.

I was a socialist, but not a Marxist. Marx's deterministic philosophy of history bears little relation to historical facts, and seems to have become in communist countries a substitute for religious faith. My own youthful politics can only be understood in the context of the social conditions prevailing in the 20's and 30's. This was long before the Welfare State had provided a safety net from cradle to grave, at a time when the depth of poverty, the hardship of unemployment, the glaring inequalities between rich and poor, and the bitterness of the class struggle, were such as we now find hard to imagine.

Social conditions in the 30's were exposed by Lord Boyd-Orr's[191] famous study of the nation's health in his 'Food, Health and Income' published in 1936. He asserted that 'at least a third of the population were so poor they could not purchase sufficient of the more expensive foods needed for health'. The Conservative government was ignorant of or indifferent about the extent of poverty and malnutrition, and was so alarmed by Lord Boyd-Orr's report that at first they tried to stop its publication. To my father I was simply 'a traitor to my class', as he described me in one of his letters. This was a sad mistake. For it was the middle class political leadership in this country which, with the support of the Trade Union movement, later made possible a peaceful and democratic transition to the Welfare State, and averted the violence and bloodshed which has characterised the social revolutions and counter revolutions in other parts of the world.

Let me now return to the reconciliation with my father which took place soon after I left Cambridge. When my grandfather died in 1924, my father inherited a great deal of money and decided to buy a home in the country to replace Convamore, the 'family seat' in Ireland. He chose a pretty Georgian house at Oxton in Devonshire, where the mild and damp climate must have reminded him of Ireland. The situation was lovely, the house standing in a small park facing a lake and surrounded by woods and hills. My mother told me he had bought the home without consulting her,

---

[191] John Boyd Orr (1880–1971), later Baron Boyd-Orr, public health specialist and first director general of the United Nations Food and Agriculture Organisation.

and she would have preferred something nearer London. It was just too far for a weekend in the country. But she soon made it a comfortable home for the family, and invited their friends and hers to stay.

I used to spend my summer holidays at Oxton. Walking took the place of shooting, which I had given up while I was at Cambridge. When I was a boy shooting was my favourite sport, and my grandfather always reserved some pheasant shooting, at least a few cock birds, for my Christmas holidays. But I woke up one morning with a sudden horror of wounding or killing wild animals for sport, and since then I never touched a gun or a rifle. Indeed I soon afterwards joined the National Society for the Abolition of Cruel Sports. I still hope that one day the shooting and killing of animals for pleasure will go the way of bear baiting and cock fighting.

My favourite pastime now was to go for long walks through the lanes and footpaths of the Devon countryside with my nearest neighbour, Sir Robert Newman[192] (later Lord Mamhead), the [C]onservative Member of Parliament for Exeter. He subsequently refused to accept the policy of his Party, and held his seat at Exeter as an Independent by defeating the official Conservative candidate backed by the party machine. This unusual feat was entirely due to the love and loyalty of the people of Exeter, in whose service he had spent the best years of his life. He was a very devout Anglo-Catholic, and often asked clerical friends to stay at Mamhead. I was glad when he told me that the Bishop of Norwich had described me as 'a good man without God'.

I also saw my old Oxford friend Evan Durbin again at Oxton. His home was at Exmouth, and we tramped the country lanes together. Evan was a brilliant economist. He died tragically young; drowned in an attempt to rescue his children in a rough sea off the coast of Devon.

Thinking probably that I had grown more responsible since I had left Cambridge, my father told me one day at Oxton that he intended to hand over his Irish property to me. I regarded this as a mixed blessing as my father's main interest was to get rid of it by sale, to save himself the trouble of collecting the rents. Most of the Irish land had already been sold, but he was still a landlord with considerable property in the town of Listowel and elsewhere in the counties of Cork and Kerry. I did not altogether relish the prospect of becoming an Irish landlord, particularly as I would almost certainly be an absentee, but I said that I would do my best. However I was never put to the test, after an incident that occurred while I was in London.

---

[192] Sir Robert Newman, 4th baronet (1871–1945), later Baron Mamhead, Conservative and later an Independent MP.

My father had invited a lady friend from his unmarried past for the weekend, and put this friend in my bedroom at Oxton. The lady noticed on my bookshelf a book on the evolution and reproduction of animals by a highly reputable Belgian biologist, I think it was Forel.[193] Unfortunately for me it was lavishly illustrated, and among these illustrations was one of the male and female genital organs. When my father's attention was drawn to my literary tastes he decided that I was addicted to pornography, and was therefore quite unfit to manage his Irish estates. The lady's motivation was, I fear, that of a discarded mistress, as my father did not marry until middle age.

I had been stimulated by disagreement with what I read about theories of literature to undertake a serious study of aesthetics. It seemed to me that delight in poetry and the other arts should be as susceptible to rational analysis and explanation as the phenomena of nature. I found that the psychological theory of mental equilibrium advanced by I.A. Richards and the Cambridge school was vague and totally unsatisfactory, and this whetted my curiosity to such an extent that I was obliged to seek the truth about aesthetic experience for myself. I experienced something of the passionate curiosity which Bertrand Russell describes as impelling him to write about the principles of mathematics, and which had always animated the explorer in philosophy or science. There was no comfort to be found from the professional philosophers G.E. Moore, Broad, or Wittgenstein,[194] though I attended some of their lectures and seminars. They all seemed to think that aesthetic experience and beauty defied analysis. When I told Wittgenstein that I wanted to study aesthetics and possibly write about it, he replied in his blunt rude way that I should give up the whole idea and get to know something more about philosophy. I was not deterred.

As aesthetics was then a terra incognita at English universities, I had to go to Paris, where a Chair of Aesthetics had been recently founded at the Sorbonne for a Professor Basch.[195] I decided to submit the result of my enquiry as a thesis for a PhD degree at London University.

So I went off to Paris, and installed myself in a single room in a Pension on the Left Bank run by a widow who took foreign students as paying guests. She was a simple but excellent cook, and I got on

[193] François-Alphonse Forel (1841–1912). He was Swiss.
[194] Cambridge academic philosophers, G.E. Moore, C.D. Broad and Ludwig Wittgenstein.
[195] Victor Basch (c.1863–1944), Sorbonne academic and expert on aesthetics, executed in 1944.

well with my fellow lodgers, two of them Americans and one English
student, whom I met at our evening meals. My déjeuner was usually
taken at a little Duval, a Parisian version of what at that time in
London was the Lyons establishments. In the evening I went out to
classical concerts or the opera comique, where I loved to hear
Italian tenors in arias of Verdi or Puccini. My Pension was not far
from the Sorbonne, where I went every morning by autobus. I
remember reading the whole of Goethe's 'Gespräche mit
Eckermann'[196] during my bus journeys. I had been there about a
year when I was summoned home by a telegram from my mother
saying my father was seriously ill with pneumonia, contracted after
a day's shooting in the rain with a neighbour. Pneumonia of course
was a killing disease before the days of penicillin, and he was too ill
for me to speak to him before he lost consciousness and died. I saw
him once while he was unconscious, the first time that I had seen a
dying person, and it made me desperately anxious that his painful
struggle for breath should end quickly. He was buried in the family
burial ground at Oxton, and that patriarchal figure the then Bishop
of Exeter,[197] a brother of Lord Salisbury, read the burial service.

Mr Lesley [sic] Farrer, now Sir Lesley Farrer,[198] then a junior member of the firm of Farrer & Co, and later solicitor to the Queen, had
been sent from London with my father's Will. After the funeral the
family returned to the house and he divulged its contents. One of
my Aunts, Lady Margaret Loder, thought I needed a little worldly
advice before inheriting a fortune, and told me to beware of entertaining Royalty. When she was a girl she told me the Prince of
Wales (later King Edward VII) with Princess Alexandra[199] had stayed
at Convamore on a visit to southern Ireland, and my grandfather had
complained that he had found his Royal guests extremely expensive.
This advice however turned out to be unnecessary.

The ensuing moments had exactly the qualities of extreme secrecy
and total surprise for a superb example of Victorian melodrama. The
only thing lacking was the family gathering round the dining room
table. There was a very large fortune to dispose of, the eldest son
cut off without a penny, the widow with no more than the tail-end
of a London lease,[200] the whole family, even the dead man's widow

---

[196] Johann Peter Eckermann's conversations with the scholar and writer Johann
Wolfgang von Goethe, edited by Eckermann in the mid 19th century.

[197] Lord William Cecil (1863–1936), bishop of Exeter, 1916–1936.

[198] Sir W. Leslie Farrer (1900–1984).

[199] Later Queen Alexandra.

[200] *It might give a false impression if I did not add that my mother had some money of her own inherited
from her father.*

without an inkling of what the Will would reveal. What more could one want before the curtain fell on the final scene!

What my father had done in a Will that largely decided the fate of the next generation was to place the family property in trust with Lloyds Bank for two of my younger brothers, John and Alan Hare, during their lifetime with reversion on their death to the then holder of the Listowel title. This had been made possible, by an agreement between my father and grandfather while I was still a child, to break the entail on the family property, whereby the family fortune had passed for several generations, undivided, since the time of the first Richard Hare, the merchant from Cork, with the family honours passing from father to eldest son. The entail was broken by my father and grandfather to benefit the family by reducing tax on my father's death.

My father had passed over my next brother, Richard, who was only eleven months my junior. He had the fatal defect of being an intellectual who had never shown the faintest interest in sport. By far the most intelligent member of my family, he took First Class honours at Oxford, and after marrying a remarkable Russian sculptress, Dora Gordine, became one of our leading authorities on Russian culture and the first Professor of Slavonic Studies at London University. He translated the novels of Turgeniev[201] and published several books on Russian art and literature. He died alas in his fifties, and with a hardly surprising sense of estrangement from his family.

My youngest brother Alan inherited for life Oxton, our home in the country, the Irish property, and a substantial residue of capital investment. My two sisters received the usual pittance allowed for those who had the misfortune to belong to the female sex.

It was my brother John, who became Viscount Blakenham, who inherited the lion's share, Kingston House, and the rest of the London property. He went on to a distinguished political career in the Conservative Party, first in local politics on the London County Council, later in national politics rising to Cabinet Office as Minister of Agriculture, and becoming finally Deputy Leader of the House of Lords and Chairman of the Conservative Party.

Within the next few years the inevitable happened. The Oxton estate was sold except for the consecrated burial ground, and a block of modern flats was rising on the site of Kingston House, the last of the great 18th century mansions within 15 minutes walk of Hyde Park Corner. It was, of course, before the days when our architectural heritage acquired legal protection.

[201] Ivan Turgenev (1818–1883), novelist.

I confess that I was taken by surprise, as it had not occurred to me that even my small allowance might stop, and make it difficult or impossible for me to carry on with unpaid public work or research. I had been lulled into a false sense of security by my father's promise that if my expenses increased when I married he would help me by providing further funds for my wife and children. But this was the moment of truth, and I had to make an immediate decision. It was too late at my age to train for a profession, but if I wanted money my title in those days might have given me a start in business or in the city. I did not really hesitate. I had a gut feeling that my vocation was to be a scholar and a public servant, and that would be possible only with my mother's support. She disapproved as strongly as my father of my political views but nevertheless treated me with unfailing kindness and generosity. When I took my seat immediately as a Labour peer there was another minor family crisis. It was bad enough to sit as a socialist, but this disgrace was now compounded when it was realised that on taking my seat I had Affirmed instead of taking the Oath of Allegiance to His Majesty. Not even a Christian, possibly an Atheist!

I was told my grandmother Listowel had retired to her bed for a week when she heard the news.

The time had now come when I was ready to put pen to paper. At this stage it was easier to work in London than Paris, as I could find all the books I wanted in the Reading Room of the British Museum. What I had in mind was a history of aesthetic theory, picking up the historical thread where it had been dropped by the Oxford idealist Bernard Bosanquet[202] in 1892, when his 'History of Aesthetics' was published, and bringing his seminal work right up to the present day. I had been immensely impressed by the work of the German philosophers of the second half of the 19th century and the beginning of this century, particularly the schools of Einfühlung[203] and the science of art, who, influenced by the development of scientific thought, had abandoned idealism and applied the methods of science to the problems of art and beauty. It seemed to me that they already had most of the answers, and they were almost unknown in my own country, which was still under the influence of the idealism of Benedetto Croce.[204]

I was working in London under the supervision of an excellent academic philosopher, Miss Hilda Oakley [sic],[205] at King's College. But

---

[202] Bernard Bosanquet (1848–1923), philosopher and writer.
[203] Philosophical and aesthetic term coined by German philosopher Robert Vischer in the late 19th century usually translated into English as aesthetic empathy.
[204] Benedetto Croce (1886–1952), philosopher and politician.
[205] Hilda Diana Oakeley (1867–1950), philosopher and academic.

when I finished my thesis neither she nor anyone else at English Universities knew enough about my subject to be able to judge its merits, and my old friend and teacher Professor Basch had to be summoned from the Sorbonne. His report was mainly critical, so I was relieved when at the end he concluded that my thesis 'would have been accepted for a Doctorate at the University of Paris with an honourable mention'. This was a sufficient recommendation for a Doctor's Degree at London University. My attention was also caught by his remark about the value of my thesis, if it were published, to English readers 'who wanted to find a path through the labyrinth of modern aesthetic theories.' I was lucky enough to find a publisher in Allen and Unwin, and my thesis appeared as a 'History of Modern Aesthetics'.[206] Basch told me that if it had been a thesis for the Sorbonne he would have given it a double degree of merit.

There is nothing more boring than an author who trumpets the virtues of his own book, so I will only quote two press comments, one favourable, and one unfavourable. A literary periodical 'The New English Weekly' did not like my style and simply could not stomach my 'cheap clichés' . I am sure they were right, and I have tried to mend my ways in the revised edition of my book. 'The Listener' on the other hand, a BBC publication, described my history as 'certainly the first account in English of the many important theories of aesthetics which have appeared in Germany during the last 50 years. It is our ignorance of these theories which is largely responsible for the grotesquely exaggerated importance which English writers have attached to the aesthetics of Croce, and for providing a corrective in this respect, if for no other reason, Lord Listowel deserves our gratitude'. The article concluded 'His book may be recommended as now the best introduction to its subject'.

This was not however the view of the majority of professional philosophers, who simply ignored it. It was the era of logical positivism, and aesthetics was regarded like metaphysics as nonsense, a total non-subject. A notable exception was Professor Samuel Alexander, professor of Philosophy at Manchester University, whose letter of April 30, 1933 I should like to quote:

> I was greatly delighted with your book, and I hope it will be much read, and will help the study of aesthetics in this Country.

When I first knew him he had already completed his major work 'Space, Time and Deity'[207] and was writing short pamphlets on art

---

[206] Published as *A Critical History of Modern Aesthetics* in 1933 and reissued in 2016.
[207] Published in 1920.

and beauty. He was a brilliant systematic thinker, with a twinkling eye and boyish enthusiasm, and our mutual friend, the late Miss Eleanor Rathbone M.P.,[208] told me he could be seen cycling through the streets of Manchester well into his 70s.

What pleased me most about my book was that though it was not for the general reader it was read throughout the English speaking world and in Latin America. A pirated Spanish translation appeared in Buenos Aires in 1954, and the author pointed out that there had been no history of aesthetic theories in Spanish since the 19th century. I was able to revise my first edition in 1967, when the Teachers College Press of Columbia University in New York asked me to produce a volume in an educational series.[209] I succeeded in correcting many of the mistakes in the first edition, and widening its scope but, I had not the time in a busy life to bring my history up-to-date, so the title to avoid confusion was altered to 'Modern Aesthetics; an Historical Introduction'.

After a first visit to London to read my thesis I never saw Professor Victor Basch again. In France he was a moral force as well as a great savant, and in his capacity as President of the Ligue des Droits de l'Homme[210] he had often denounced the Nazis for the persecution of their political opponents and the Jews. When Hitler invaded France he was therefore a wanted man. He fled with his wife from Paris to Vichy France after the invasion, but when the Germans occupied the whole of France they were both carried off suddenly by the fascist Vichy Police and brutally murdered, although he was by that time an old man in his seventies.

Another friendship born of a mutual interest in aesthetics was with the poet and art critic Sir Herbert Read.[211] I dealt with him rather severely in my book, and I was astonished when he offered to introduce me to Professor Constable[212] of the Courtauld Institute, because he thought his students would benefit from some knowledge of the theory of art. As a result of this introduction I was invited to give a series of lectures. I met him [Read] several times with like minded people in London, and I was always struck by a strange incongruity between his poetic and indeed heroic personality – if one reads between the lines of his story about life in the trenches in the First

[208] Eleanor Rathbone (1872–1946), social reform campaigner and Independent MP.
[209] *Revised edition of my book published by Teachers' College Press, Columbia University, New York (1967): Modern Aesthetics: an historical introduction.*
[210] Originally formed in 1898 to defend Alfred Dreyfus.
[211] Sir Herbert Read (1893–1968), art critic, historian and writer.
[212] W.G. Constable (1887–1976), art historian who in addition to being director of the Courtauld Institute, 1932–1936, held positions such as Slade Professor of Fine Art at Cambridge and curator of the Boston Museum of Art.

World War, when he was awarded a D.S.O.[213] and an M.C.[214] – and his very ordinary appearance. He was a small man with a round face like a Dutch cheese, and he spoke so softly that it was sometimes difficult to hear him. I had a letter from him in 1967 written only two months before he died, and it shows that he remained faithful for 50 years to the philosophy of life jotted down in his War Diary in February 1917. The extract from his diary reads as follows:

> Art is to my mind a thing of such fundamental value that it should colour our whole outlook on life … Allied to love, it is a complete philosophy of life. Love gives us the fellowship of our species: Art unites us with something vaster – with the whole cosmic process.

Compare this confession of faith with the following extracts from his letter to me: –

> It is very kind of you to send me a copy of the revised edition of your Modern Aesthetics. I have always jealously guarded the first edition and have often referred to it.
>
> Your 'conclusion' is a definition of the subject that I can after all these years of thought on the subject wholly agree with – what you call 'the relational character of beauty'. I still hesitate to equate art and beauty, but that is merely a semantic problem. I also agree that the metaphysical implication of our aesthetic philosophy is a form of monism.

Now that my book on aesthetics had been published, I was able to devote myself to the support of the Labour Party in the House of Lords.[215]

---

[213] Distinguished Service Order.

[214] Military Cross.

[215] *My apprenticeship to parliament was through London local government. I was elected in 1937 as one of the two members for East Lewisham forming part of the Labour majority. The Municipal Reform Party had been in power for 27 years before the 1934 election (when Labour were elected) and their main objective had been to keep down the rates as 'economy had always been their watchword'. At the end of the three years after 1934, the Labour Party led by Herbert Morrison were able to go to the electorate with a record of achievement more striking than anything that had been attempted for many years past, but with a rise in the rates of 1s and 2d. Nevertheless, in 1937 the electorate again preferred Labour, when they were sent back to finish the job.*

IV
POLITICS IN THE 1930s

1934: Spain: A Democracy in the Making

My first visit in a parliamentary capacity to Republican Spain was in the autumn of 1934. I had heard on reliable authority that a rising of the miners in the Asturias had been suppressed with extreme brutality. The Spanish Foreign Legion had been brought over from Africa, and they had meted punishment on wives and families as well as on the militant miners. It was therefore suggested that Miss Ellen Wilkinson M.P.[216] and I should go to Spain on a humanitarian mission, and to point out to the Spanish authorities that much harm was being done to our relations with Spain by the atrocity stories appearing in the British press.

We travelled directly to Madrid to make our representations to the Spanish government. We were surprised, considering our political insignificance, to find that we were received with the utmost friendliness and courtesy at the highest level, and immediately invited by Senor Lerroux,[217] the Prime Minister, for an interview at his official residence. When we told him that we would like to visit the Asturias to see for ourselves the conditions prevailing in the mining villages, he made not the slightest objection, and said repeatedly that 'la porte est ouverte'.[218] We had a long talk about the political situation, and it was clear that he did not under-estimate the difficulty of sustaining the fragile and comparatively new system of parliamentary government against the growing menace of the revolutionary extremes on the left and right. He was, however, more than willing that we should go everywhere and see everything, and wrote a letter of introduction to Commander Doval,[219] the officer in charge of military operations in the Asturias, commending us and

---

[216] Ellen Wilkinson (1891–1947), Labour MP and later minister of education, 1945–1947.

[217] Alejandro Lerroux (1864–1949), founder and leader of the Radical Republican Party, and prime minister of Spain on three separate occasions between 1933–1935.

[218] The door is open.

[219] Civil guard commander Lisardo Doval Bravo, who had a reputation for being tough on the leftists and was a friend of Franco.

including the words 'I would like to ask you to help [Listowel] in any way possible, and it is in your hands that he fulfils the mission that brings him here.' At the same time Senor Gil Robles,[220] leader of the conservative right, was denouncing me as an 'undesirable' and demanding the expulsion of our party from Spain.

We travelled by train overnight from Madrid to Oviedo, and after breakfast at a cafe in the town, prepared ourselves for a meeting with Commander Doval at 11.00 am in the town hall. We had a long wait, and noticed while we waited a small crowd was gathering outside the town hall. We knew that Oviedo was under martial law, and was surprised to see what appeared to be some sort of demonstration. At last we were ushered into Doval's office, and explained exactly what we wanted. He tried to persuade us to leave the town, on the ground that he could not be responsible for our safety in view of the indignation of the people of Oviedo. When we persisted, he eventually agreed, provided that we accepted a strong police escort. As we walked down the steps from the main entrance we found that our police escort was directing us to our waiting car. We were then told that the instructions to our driver were to take us, escorted by the National Guard, not to the town, but straight to the frontier. As the purpose of our mission was in this way frustrated, our forcible expulsion from the Asturias gave a clear impression to the outside world that the military authorities were hiding the evidence of their persecution of the miners, and that they, not the civil government in Madrid, were the effective rulers of a large area of northern Spain. Something had been accomplished; if not what we had intended.

My abrupt return to London was another but lesser problem with my family. My uncle by marriage, Sir Ralph Glyn, was a Conservative MP, and he told me that he had been button-holed by the Foreign Secretary, Sir Austen Chamberlain,[221] who complained that he had heard his nephew had been interfering in the domestic affairs of a friendly country. This reproof from a cabinet minister had upset my uncle, but he was too kindly a person to be angry with me, and I think regarded the whole thing as no more than a youthful escapade. We were also censured by the National Executive of the Labour Party for acting without their authority. It was not until 1937 that the Party sent a delegation led by Attlee to support the Republic.

---

[220] José María Gil-Robles (1898–1980), right-wing conservative and political leader of the Catholic Right during this period.

[221] Sir Austen Chamberlain (1863–1937), Conservative MP and minister; foreign secretary, 1924–1929, so not at the time of this visit, but still a senior figure in the House of Commons.

This party criticism did not however prevent Lord Snell,[222] who had taken over from Arthur Ponsonby as Leader of the Opposition in the Lords in June 1936, from inviting me to sit on the Front Opposition Bench. The Letter is so charming and characteristic that I would like to include it:

11th June 1936

Dear Listowel,

As you know, it is one of the tasks of the Leader of the Opposition to select the personnel of the Labour Front Bench, and it is my desire to carry the members with me in any changes which I think desirable.

You have now had considerable experience in the work of the House and in political life generally, so I need not remind you that occupancy of the Front Bench imposes penalties as well as privileges. Its members have to surrender some of the freedom which the back benches afford, and they have to consider much more closely whether what they do and say may help or compromise the position of the Party. These obligations are so trying at times that men like Arnold, Buxton, Ponsonby (and now Sanderson) do not care to assume them, preferring the greater freedom of the back benches.

I would not personally press anyone to change back bench freedom for Front Bench reticence and circumspection, but I should like you to consider whether or not you cared to do so. If you thought that you could stand the yoke (and I have not found it too difficult) it would be a pleasure to me to tell the members of the Party that I proposed to ask you to join those who sit on the Front Bench.

Will you please let me have a private line on the matter during the next few days.

Yours sincerely,
Snell

Needless to say, I was delighted by my promotion to the Front Bench.

1937: China: A Victim of Aggression

In 1934 and 1936 Republican Spain had been the first victim of aggression in Europe. In 1937 China became the victim of aggression in Asia, when it was invaded by Japan. I was almost immediately involved when invited in the autumn to join a group from the left wing of the Party which decided to organise support for China. The main object of this group was to mobilise public opinion and

[222] Henry Snell, later Baron Snell (1865–1944), Labour politician and Labour leader in the House of Lords, 1935–1940.

sympathy for the cause of China, and to provide humanitarian aid for the national resistance to the Japanese.

On September 30, 1937, the first meeting of the China Campaign Committee took place at the Whitfield Tabernacle, at the invitation of its pastor, the Reverend Belden. There were messages of support from Lord Cecil of Chelwood,[223] Mrs Pat Koo,[224] the daughter of the distinguished Chinese diplomat, Dr Wellington Koo,[225] Madame Chiang Kai-Shek[226] and Professor Harold Laski.[227]

The Chairman of our Committee was Mr Victor Gollancz,[228] the Vice-Chairman was Miss Margery Fry,[229] and I was asked to be its President. Margery Fry, Quaker sister of the art critic Roger Fry,[230] was one of the most dedicated internationalists I can remember. Victor Gollancz was often absent, and she did most of the work with untiring energy and superb efficiency.

Our most outstanding parliamentary supporter was the Nobel Prize winner, Lord Cecil of Chelwood, who not only supported us in the House of Lords but addressed many public meetings in London and elsewhere on behalf of China. His Opposition to the foreign policy of the Government was so strong that he moved his place on the Conservative benches to join us on the Opposition Front Bench, where he sat somewhat uncomfortably, because he disliked our domestic policy, which at the time included several measures of nationalisation, almost as intensely as he disliked the foreign policy of his own party.

We also advocated a boycott of Japanese exports, encouraged by the example of the Southampton dockers, who had refused to unload a Japanese ship, and a boycott of exports of war materials, particularly oil, to Japan.[231] I am glad to say my words, on behalf of the

---

[223] Lord Robert Cecil, later 1st Viscount Cecil of Chelwood (1864–1958), politician and diplomat who famously advocated the cause of the League of Nations.

[224] Patricia Koo Tsien (1917–2015); her professional life was spent at the United Nations.

[225] Wellington Koo (1888–1985), represented China at the Paris Peace Conference in 1919; senior diplomat who served in variety of ministerial posts for the Republic of China.

[226] Soong Mei-ling also known as Madam Chiang Kai-Shek (1897–2003), leading political figure as First Lady of the Republic of China, wife of Generalissimo Chiang Kai-Shek and sister-in-law of Dr Sun Yat-sen.

[227] Harold Laski (1893–1950), Professor of Political Science at the London School of Economics; Labour Party official and Fabian.

[228] Victor Gollancz (1893–1967), later Sir Victor Gollancz, prominent publisher and founder of the Left Book Club.

[229] S. Margery Fry (1874–1958), social reform advocate; later secretary of the Howard League for Penal Reform and principal of Somerville College, Oxford.

[230] Roger Fry (1866–1934), painter and art critic.

[231] Their action was taken in December 1937 against the liner *Duchess of Richmond*, which contained Japanese cargo and in January 1938 Middlesbrough dockers refused to load the Japanese steamer *Haruna Maru*.

China Campaign Committee, congratulating the Southampton dockers on their 'splendid example of political courage and determination' were noted in the press on December 12, 1937. The article went on to my attack on the Government which 'had not protested against the violation of the solemn international treaties to which Japan had adhered and which she had broken by invading China. The Government has not even prohibited armament firms from sending military planes and guns to the Japanese. It was time that England had the courage to stand up to fascist aggression.'

We raised funds at public meetings by press appeals and even by an art exhibition. I remember organising with Ruth Gollancz[232] an exhibition of 'Chinese Art in London', which included the finest pieces from the two best private collections in the country, those of Sir Percival David[233] and Mr Eumorphopolos,[234] shown at the Royal Institute of British Architects. Both collections were bequeathed to the nation, and are now divided between the Victoria and Albert and the British Museum. Perhaps the day will come when the world can admire both collections in a single London Museum.

Most of our funds were spent on medical supplies for the International Peace Hospitals in different parts of China. I was pleasantly surprised to read in Arthur Clegg's excellent booklet on Aid to China[235] that one of these hospitals still exists in Hopei Province. In recognition of the Committee's work the Chinese Ambassador in London told me that General Chiang Kai-Shek[236] would like to give an Honour, I think it was the Order of the Chrysanthemum. I consulted the Foreign Office, and was told that Ministers of the Crown (by that time I was a Junior Minister) could not accept Honours from foreign Governments. So I declined the flattering offer without, I hope, causing offence.

I will conclude this account of our work for China with a quotation from the Introduction to Arthur Clegg's book by the distinguished scientist and sinologist, Dr Joseph Needham.[237]

The China Campaign Committee was a great feature of life in the England of those days in the 30s, and I believe it really did much towards

[232] Ruth Gollancz, née Lowy (1892–1973), painter and wife of Victor Gollancz.
[233] Sir Percival David, 2nd baronet (1892–1964), financier and collector of Chinese art.
[234] George Eumorphopolos (1863–1939), financier and collector of Eastern art.
[235] Arthur Clegg (1914–1994), national organiser of the China Campaign Committee, 1937–1949.
[236] Chiang Kai-Shek (1887–1975), political and military leader of the Republic of China; left the mainland for Taiwan after 1949.
[237] Joseph Needham (1900–1995), biochemist, sinologist and writer.

making China that great ally in the Second World War, which it afterwards became.

So perhaps we did some good for our own country as well as for China.

1938: Spain: A Struggling Democracy

I believe that my 1938 visit to Spain is best described using extracts from my diary.

January 30th

The opportunity for which I have long waited had arrived. I was invited a few days ago to attend the opening of the Cortes on February 1st in Barcelona; it had not met since the seat of Government had been moved to Catalonia, and its last session had closed in Valencia in October of 1937. I accepted immediately, both with a view of doing my bit for the Spanish Republican Government and in order to get into direct contact with the relief problem in Catalonia. It was hoped we might be an all-party group, but the Conservatives as usual were only half-hearted. So I set out this morning from Victoria in the following company: Dick Acland (Liberal M.P.), Mrs Barbara Ayrton-Gould,[238] (Vice-Chairman of the Labour Party), and F. Montague M.P.,[239] the official delegates of the Labour Party, and Rev. Woods M.P.,[240] the representative of the Co-operative Movement.

In Paris we met the other Parliamentary Delegates to the Spanish Parliament; they included men of all parties from the three Scandinavian countries and France, and were joined later by old Emil [sic] Vandervelde[241] from Belgium. It was good to be in the company of representative people from some of the most progressive countries in western Europe.

January 31st

We travelled overnight to Perpignan, and were met there by two buses under orders to carry us to Barcelona; we should have arrived

---

[238] Barbara Ayrton-Gould (1886–1950), suffragist and later Labour MP.

[239] Frederick Montague, later Baron Amwell (1876–1966), Labour MP and peer.

[240] Rev. George Woods (1886–1951), Labour Co-operative MP.

[241] Emile Vandervelde (1866–1938), Belgian Labour politician; held several ministries in the interwar years.

by midday, but the inevitable Spanish dallying over and before the midday meal (we must have eaten Figueros out of provisions for a week) delayed us until shortly after dusk. The drive was exceedingly beautiful; in the morning through the Pyrenees, and skirting the Mediterranean during the last lap. The sun brought old women out to bask in their doorways, and cats and dogs curled up in its warmth, while the scenery varied from the rocky grandeur of snow-capped mountains to the bright spring verdure of the coastal plain, where almond orchards were already gleaming like scattered patches of pink mist. I understand now why people prefer the south of France to England in the winter months.

We reached Barcelona just after dark, and observed the precautions against air-attack; the street lights were all dimmed with a coating of blue paint, but there seemed to be no shade over the dazzling head-lamps of cars – which obviously guided the enemy planes to the main thoroughfares.

I was directed to the Ritz Hotel with a room and bath to myself; hot water was provided for our benefit, and the food was excellent.

En route I spoke to a bi-lingual Norwegian girl, Miss Gripp, who organised the Scandinavian delegates; she seemed to be quite fearless, judging from her stories about Bilbao during the bombing. The nearer to the Front, the happier she felt, she said. She was married at eighteen to an Italian and is now happily divorced. In Norway divorce by mutual consent is obtainable after one year, unilateral divorce after two years' respite; the proceedings are strictly private throughout. Their commonsense has evidently not been warped by their Lutheran beliefs.

On arrival we found our fellow-guests somewhat shaken by a severe daylight raid delivered the very day before our arrival; 300 killed and 700 wounded, the heaviest daytime casualties since the war began. By way of giving us happy dreams we were taken after dinner to inspect the damage done by a bomb up the street – about 200 yards from the hotel. A six-story building had been sliced open like a slab of cheese, the bomb exploding on the ground floor and destroying the six floors above as well as the wall facing the street. Its force was perpendicular rather than lateral, and pictures and mirrors were visible, unbroken, on the walls of rooms without floors or ceilings at the top of the house. They were still clearing away the debris and expecting to find more buried corpses. One lay covered with some sacking on the pavement. The damage was done by not more than eight planes, but one can arrive by multiplication at what a larger number could have achieved in killed and wounded. There was no military target, so this was an early example of the bombing of open cities.

February 1st

We were told to be ready at 7.30 am, as the President of the Chamber, Martinez Barrio,[242] wanted to see us at eight. We actually started in a car from the hotel at eight, not bad for Spanish punctuality, and were given some tickets for the opening of the Cortes in the building that houses the Catalonian Parliament. Then, to our amazement, instead of being driven back to our hotels for breakfast, we found ourselves speeding away from Barcelona – whither we knew not – into the mountains of the hinterland. It was a wonderful drive, and I can only compare the scenery to what one sees from above the Gulf of Cotor on the road from Ragusa to Cetinje. Higher and higher we climbed, skirting deep ravines through which plunged mountain torrents, until at last we reached a summit two thousand feet above sea-level, and spread out behind us lay the plain we had crossed, while inland the serried ranks of foothills culminated on the distant horizon in the snow-covered ridges of the Sierras. We had reached our destination, the famous and austerely beautiful monastery of Montserrat; and there, on the plain wooden benches of a long refectory, hung with marvellous tapestries from the Royal Palace at Madrid, assembled the majority of members comprising the Cortes of Republican Spain. Here, in the shadow of the Holy Grail they were re-dedicating themselves to the salvation of their country and the freedom of their countrymen. The speeches were impressive because they gave a sense of absolute unity in a common purpose.

After the Government had had their turn – Negrin,[243] Prime Minister and ex-professor of physiology at Madrid University; Alvarez del Vayo,[244] the socialist Foreign Minister; Prieto[245] (who entered Teruel in a tank before the heights of Santa Barbara had fallen) emphatic, bald, and immensely fat; Jiralt [sic],[246] bespectacled and mouse-like – representatives of the different political Parties rose from their seats. I could only understand completely when translated the speech of Dolores Ibarrure [sic],[247] the wife of a Bilbao miner. She had six children before she entered politics in 1930 or 1931, and her

[242] Diego Martinez Barrio (1883–1962), president of the Cortes, 1936–1939.
[243] Juan Negrín (1892–1956), Socialist Workers Party politician; last prime minister of Spain, 1937–1939, before the Franco regime took over.
[244] Julio Álvarez del Vayo (1891–1975), academic, journalist and Socialist Workers Party politician; foreign minister twice during the Second Spanish Republic.
[245] Indalecio Prieto (1883–1962), Socialist Workers Party politician; served in various roles during the Second Spanish Republic.
[246] José Giral (1879–1962), republican left politician; prime minister, 1936.
[247] Dolores Ibárruri known as 'La Pasionaria' (1895–1989), prominent Communist Party politician.

remarkable eloquence lent courage to thousands of luke-warm Republicans at the beginning of the Civil War. Known as 'La Passionaria' [*sic*], she spoke first for the Communist Party. She had a fine presence, a lovely voice, and perfect enunciation, but unfortunately her speech affirming loyalty to the Government of the Communist Party was read and not spoken. In all the qualities of the orator save spontaneity she infinitely surpassed the others. She was followed by a member of the Republic Union Party[248] – the Party of Barrio and Lerroux, the extreme right of the present Cortes – who spoke in exactly the same vein. Then a small and wiry Basque rose to his feet, a Catholic from the north of Spain, and his words of loyalty to the Government were echoed by the leader of the Catalan Esquerra who followed him. The picture of a people united in self-defence against a common enemy would not have been complete without an intervention from the Left Republicans – the Party of Azana,[249] President of the Republic – and from a spokesman of the Socialist Party. Possibly for the first time in the history of Spain I was witnessing the spectacle of unanimity between people who had seldom before been able to agree, a complete sinking of personal, political, historical, and religious differences in order to resist as one man the military rebels and foreign invaders. The key-note of the proceedings was the unity of all parties, creeds, and nationalities in the common cause of national defence, and of course the purpose that united them was not social revolution or class revolt but simply the determination to defend the independence of Republican soil, and to preserve their liberal and democratic institutions from overthrow by a military dictator.

The secret of this strange meeting of the Cortes in the refectory of a monastery was so well kept that the deputy for Montserrat had gone to Barcelona, and was not back in time for the Assembly! Secrecy was obviously desirable to prevent Franco[250] from using the meeting place as a target for his Italian planes from Majorca.

The adjournment was followed by the longest lunch I have ever attended, a typical Spanish orgy lasting from two till five in the afternoon. The foreign deputies were invited by the Prime Minister to attend this Government function, and I had the good fortune to sit next to the Minister for Economic Affairs. He told me that the main reason for the strength of the Franco Peseta[251] as compared

---

[248] More commonly known as the Republican Union.

[249] Manuel Azaña (1880–1940), president of the Republic, 1936–1939.

[250] Francisco Franco (1892–1975), nationalist general and later military dictator and head of state, 1939–1975.

[251] The then currency of Spain.

with the Government Peseta was not the poverty of the Government, but the fact that well-to-do Spaniards had gone abroad and sold their pesetas for anything they could get in foreign currency. He also said that, since Teruel,[252] the credit of the Government had slightly improved; instead of paying for their imports beforehand, they were able to pay on delivery. The absolute necessity for them is to have foreign currency, and they are very strict about forbidding the export of even the smallest quantity of home produce without payment in the local currency. I gathered that the foodstuffs most sorely lacking were milk – they are cut off from the main dairy-farming area of Spain in Galicia, sugar, and meat. – Relief organisations abroad should therefore concentrate on condensed milk, sugar, and tinned meat. He added that the total volume of relief that had come from abroad had made no appreciable difference to the food situation. What could demonstrate more forcibly the inadequacy of voluntary effort when faced with calamity on so vast a scale, and the necessity for Government action, independent or concerted, to stave off starvation and epidemics? An American woman, who acts for the Co-ordination Committee in Paris and has spent one million dollars from the United States in relief work, told me that the diet of the refugees consisted of chick-peas, beans, a little rice and wine, and the plight of the natives, who get a minute fraction of poor bread as well, is little better. She says the food shortage is diminishing as they are using their own farms to produce what they need at home. The shortage of clothes and blankets for the refugees is still acute. The country is mainly wine-producing and too dry to grow corn; but the peasants are starting to cultivate potatoes.

Let me return to the afternoon orgy at Montserrat. The Prime Minister proposed the health of the foreign parliamentarians and old Emil Vandervelde answered for us all. His eloquence soared above the conflict of the moment to the great historical themes it exemplified – la lutte pour la paix, pour la liberté, pour la patrie humaine.[253] In passing he mentioned the Belgian adherence to non-intervention as the reason for his resignation from the Cabinet, a statement greeted with thunderous applause. The old boy is now on his way to the Madrid Front! The venerable, white-haired Valladarez [sic],[254] the Liberal Prime Minister at the time of the last Election resulting in the victory of the Popular Front, was also

---

[252] A bloody civil war battle in 1937–1938.

[253] Roughly translated as 'the struggle for peace, liberty, and the human race'.

[254] Manuel Portela Valladares (1867–1952), Liberal Party politician and prime minister, 1935–1936.

at the luncheon; and he described how, as soon as the results were known, the Conservative leaders and chiefs of the General Staff came to him and offered to establish his dictatorship. He is an aristocrat, a Marquis, I think; and the only nobleman whom I have heard of on the Government side. And so back to Barcelona for the night.

The morning before we came over a hundred children had been killed by one bomb – they were refugees huddled in the crypt of a church in which they were sheltered; the bomb came in through the roof but didn't explode till it reached the crypt, and the only children that escaped were those who, instead of taking cover, had stayed in their beds. A bad moral, but the value of a basement refuge depends of course on the amount of building above it. At about 7.45 that evening, having emerged from a lovely hot bath, I had just shaved one side of my face when the lights suddenly went out; knowing that this was the usual precursor of an air-raid, I groped my way to an electric torch and joined my fellow guests downstairs, clad as I was only in pyjamas and a dressing-gown, and adorned with one half of a promising beard. The darkness and preoccupation of the moment were not unwelcome. After thirty-five minutes the lights went on again, and it transpired that the enemy planes had not visited us at all but had unloaded their bombs upon another town further down the coast.

Wednesday, February 2nd

A day without highlights passed in Barcelona. In the afternoon we visited one elementary school and two homes for children who were refugees or orphaned by the war. The school was most interesting; it amazed one that they could be spending so much on education while engaged in a life and death struggle. The children seemed to have everything except sufficient food; the standard of equipment was first-rate, and even included the teaching of pottery and printing and illustrating magazines and programmes of their own work. Two 'model' homes – one which was housed in the residence of a former managing director of the Catalonian Railways who had left his country mansion to a monastic order – were less interesting than others serving the same purpose, because the atmosphere of plenty was so obviously exceptional.

Our little guide, formerly a prosperous dentist in Oviedo, told me quite by accident that bull-fighting had been stopped in Republican Spain. Why do they not make the most of this humanitarian spirit in their propaganda? I am sure that 99% of English people were as

ignorant as I was of this bold attack on a brutal but very ancient
Spanish custom.

Thursday, February 3rd

Started in the morning, not more than half an hour late, on our drive
to Valencia. The scenery was admirable, and the weather perfect. So
far every day has been warm, sunny, and cloudless – just what
England ought to be like in May but seldom is. The Catalonian
coastal region is thickly set with vines and olives, but here and
there a whole orchard of almond trees was in blossom, and an occasional solitary cherry in a cottage garden. In the neighbourhood of
Tortosa the spur that runs down from Teruel reaches the sea, and
one winds along the mountain side with deep gorges below and pre-
cipitous heights above. Then the coastal plain resumes, and passing
from the province of Castellon to that of Valencia one finds oneself
among the orange groves that stretch right down to Alicante and
Malaga. They are a lovely sight at this time of the year, the golden
oranges thickly clustered round the branches and gleaming brightly
against the dark green leaves. On the road to Tarragona one is
reminded of the Roman colonies on the Levant coast of Spain by
a magnificent triumphal arch in honey-coloured stone, a feast of colour when viewed in the sunlight against the deep blue of the sky. At
Benicarlo we stopped off for another Spanish lunch, and did not get
under way again till five o'clock. As we approached Castellon just
after sundown a range of cobalt hills was outlined sharply against
the pale lemon of the western horizon. It was dark when our cars
deposited us at the Hotel Victoria in Valencia. During the last lap
we stopped at a hospital of the International Brigade to chat with
the convalescents and slightly wounded and to give them the
cigarettes for which they pined. I chatted with Asturians who had
been driven out after the civil war, with German emigrés, with
Americans and cockneys; they were for the most part genuine ideal-
ists, though there were some adventurers too. For instance, a long-
haired Irishman from Limerick boasted that he knew the best pubs
in every town from Malaga to Madrid, and didn't care a damn
about politics. We were asked to address a gathering of wounded
men who assembled in the main hall after supper. It was extraordi-
narily difficult to say anything: their courage and suffering and sacri-
fice spoke more eloquently than our poor words, and choked us with
shame at our own miserable non-intervention. There was a young
Canadian nurse – the only one in Spain, who had tremendous difficulty in getting permission to work out here; what spirit had moved

her to risk her life for the cause of these unhappy strangers in a land
so far from home?

Friday, February 4th

Before we started in the morning for Teruel the sirens sounded their
warning against an air-raid. The townsfolk ran into the houses from
the open streets and squares but there was no sign of panic or stam-
pede. It wasn't long before the all-clear followed, as the raiders had
gone to Sagunto – Roman Saguntum sacked by Hannibal[255] – ten
miles up the coast.

As we climbed from the coastal plain, with its sub-tropical vegeta-
tion, up towards the high plateau of Central Spain, the sturdy stone
pines multiplied in place of the olives and vineyards. We were soon
surrounded in all directions by a barren expanse of heath and
stone. Nestling in small fertile patches were the villages we passed
on the road, where peasants could be seen through their open cottage doors, feeding their chickens and suckling their young. We
stopped at last at a railway embankment, and though we were several
miles behind the lines our three cars were strung out so as not to present a tempting target from the air. Our little guide led us along the
railway line into the pitch darkness of a tunnel, and after we had
groped our way for about a hundred yards we were told to scale
the stationary coach standing beside us. We were then ushered into
a compartment equipped as an office, and introduced to General
Sarrabia [sic],[256] Commander-in-Chief of the Teruel forces, for this
was General Headquarters on the Teruel Front. The General was
an officer of the regular Spanish Army who had opted for the
Republic, and won one of their few victories at Teruel. He explained
that he could not guarantee our safety if we pressed on to Teruel, but
provided us immediately with a staff officer as guide when we inti-
mated our desire to visit the Front.

When we set out again in our cars we left a large interval between
each vehicle, so as not to attract enemy planes. We were in the leading car, and our officer guide halted us a few kilometres short of the
town to speak to a driver whose lorry had broken down coming from
the opposite direction. He enquired about the enemy artillery, and
was told they were shelling the approaches to the town. This had a
magical effect on our chauffeur, who fairly 'stepped on it' until we
were safely through the danger zone.

---

[255] 219 BC; sparked the Second Punic War.
[256] Juan Hernández Saravia (1880–1962), republican general.

We found ourselves at last in the streets of what had once been a beautiful 18th century town, and had now become a derelict ruin in whose streets the shells and debris of houses alone remained. To be strictly accurate we saw three inhabitants, a woman and two small children, sitting at the black mouth of a hole leading downwards into the earth – an air-raid shelter – where she and her little ones could take refuge at the first sign of enemy aircraft. After dark they went back to the remains of their home. The landmarks of the historic victory of Teruel were pointed out to us; the bull-ring on the outskirts of the town, the first objective, the Bank of Spain in which for ten days the enemy had held out, until their stronghold was finally blown up by the dynamite of the Asturian miners; and the seminary in which the Bishop of Teruel and the last of the Franco Garrison, after their water supply as well as their food had been cut off, surrendered to the Republican Militia. The appropriate chorus that accompanied us as we marched round this scene of destruction and desolation was the rat-tat-tat of machine guns, the crackle of rifles, and the occasional louder bang of trench mortars that reached us from the Front Line just beyond the city. At places the enemy were no more than 1000 yards from the outskirts, and we had to be careful not to expose ourselves to fire from their lines. The destruction wrought by explosives was not quite as complete as I remember at Ypres when I saw it in 1918, just after the First World War. The battle had not lasted as long, and the artillery bombardment was certainly not as heavy.

A lovely Moorish tower in brick, ornamented with geometrical designs in faience, supposedly unique among the Moorish relics of Spain, was almost untouched. The carved rood screen behind the Altar of the Cathedral, an absolutely superb piece of Baroque craftsmanship, was also intact; and not a single book had been removed from among the volumes of philosophy, theology, and Latin poetry in the Bishop's Library. These treasures were being cared for by the Ministry of Culture, and were to be removed as soon as possible for safe keeping to the vaults of Valencia or Barcelona.

I talked for some time with a Scotch International Brigadier named Fraser, who had been out for over a year without receiving a scratch. This period included three months without relief in the Front Line before Madrid. He told the old, old story of Franco's overwhelming superiority in the air and in heavy artillery. During the battle for Teruel the Government planes had been outnumbered by three to one. The enemy method of attack was to shell the Front Line so heavily that they expected to blow it right away. This rattled the Spanish Militia, though the International Brigade was getting used to it.

The lack of planes and guns was the reason for their bitterness against the British and French policy of non-intervention, which prevented the Spanish Government from counteracting the equipment provided by Italy and Germany for Franco. It was to prove the deciding factor in the Spanish Civil War, which was the first victory for the dictatorships over the democracies in western Europe. Russia had sent some tanks and a few planes but no soldiers, and these not until October 1936, long after the armed intervention of the Fascist powers. Military supplies from the Soviet Union simply couldn't compare with what had reached Franco from Hitler[257] and Mussolini.[258] A dour Scot volunteer, Dunbar, whom I spoke to en route, had been twice wounded 'but they haven't killed me yet'. Curious the types one meets in this cosmopolitan army; intellectuals, working men, adventurers and 'professional' soldiers – men who really enjoy a scrap, and go wherever a bit of fighting can be found.

We started back from Teruel just before dusk. We were still in the leading car, and, when a short distance from the gate we had left by, we observed the smoke of a shell bursting in the road about 200 yards in front of us. We were under fire from Franco's artillery! The little procession of cars was halted, and told to wait for a few minutes until the gathering darkness could hide us from the view of the enemy batteries. We then proceeded without any contretemps on our way, and passed strings of mules bringing supplies for the defenders of the city under cover of darkness.

At the second line we stopped to have a word with some men in the Lincoln and Washington battalions; they were bivouacking for the night on an open moor, spread out widely on account of hostile air-attack, and clustering in groups round little fires that warmed their limbs and heated their cans of hot soup. The icy wind that swept the high sierra after nightfall cut like a knife, and yet these men were not grumbling about another of their many nights spent in the open. We talked to an officer in an anti-tank battery, and one of my companions waxed enthusiastic about his guns. Personally, I could feel no spark of enthusiasm for these weapons of destruction, which appeared to me an infinitely deplorable necessity. Of course the amazing courage of men who risk their lives every day for months, living in hell without a murmur against their lot, and the camaraderie that shares the last crust and the last thimbleful of water, also belong to any true picture of war.

---

[257] Adolf Hitler (1889–1945), chancellor, then Führer (dictator) of Germany, 1933–1945.
[258] Benito Mussolini (1883–1945), prime minister and duce (dictator) of Italy, 1922–1943.

Saturday, February 5th

My driver appeared this morning at the hotel in Valencia three quarters of an hour late, excessive even for Spain, and I had to abandon
the idea of driving through to the Frontier in the day. The further
one gets from the Front, the more inefficient organisation becomes.
We had just passed through Sagunto when some bombers arrived
from Majorca. I stopped and watched the raid from the road; one
could see against the blue sky the white puffs of bursting shells, but
the planes themselves were too high to be visible.

　We didn't reach Barcelona until about four. My driver had two
oranges and a dry roll for lunch and offered me an orange; it was
difficult to refuse without hurting his feelings, so I said I generally
lunched later – it was then at least three o'clock! Our little guide
had been a prosperous doctor [or dentist, if same man as mentioned
earlier] in Oviedo and he told me that he used to visit the military
prison after the miners had been crushed by the foreign legionnaires
in 1934. The brute Doval was still in charge of the troops in the town,
and he used to torture the prisoners – giving them, for instance, salt
fish to eat and nothing to drink. The little man added that 'he
invented things' – what, I did not care to ask. His own escape
from the rebels, after living for weeks in a dark underground cellar,
was an amazing tale of adventure.

Sunday, February 6th

It was lucky I had an extra morning in Barcelona as I was able to
attend a conference of foreign relief workers. They were representatives
of England, the Scandinavian countries, Switzerland, the U.S.A.,
France and even Chile, Argentina, and Egypt. Curiously enough the
Swiss seemed to have done more work than anyone save the French.
They had their own lorries for distributing milk and other foodstuffs
among allotted colonies of refugee children. But their magnificent
efforts appeared as a drop in the ocean when compared with the magnitude of the food shortage; the problem is so enormous that voluntary
organisations, unassisted by Government money or support, cannot
possibly solve it. The food situation will deteriorate rather than improve
as the war goes on. This strictly humanitarian conference, presided
over by a representative of the rather more than half pro-Franco
General Relief Fund, passed a resolution protesting against the bombardment of open towns. An admirable band of warm-hearted human-
itarians, many of them sustained by belief in the Christian quality of
their work, ministering so far as their own limited powers would

allow, to the sufferings of a war-stricken population. They kindled hope and kindness and enthusiasm among all who met them. It is good to know there are such loveable and dedicated people in the world.

In the afternoon my driver took me straight through to La Jonquera on the Pyrenean Frontier, which we reached by the light of a marvellous moon. We chatted awhile before parting – or rather he talked and I listened. He had been with a tank for a whole year on the Aragon front near Belchite, it was hell of course, especially when he had a whole battery of anti-tank guns firing at him and 'he thought he was dead'. But now he had something – pulling a dirty slip of folded paper from his wallet – that General Miaja[259] himself was proud to have; it was a certificate of valour, corresponding to a military decoration. How lucky, poor fellow, that those few words on a slip of paper were balm for all the misery of that year at the Front. He was sharing the glory of Miaja, and what else could matter.

It was a real pleasure to taste butter once more in the French Station restaurant at Perpignan and to drink coffee with milk. But lying snugly in a luxurious sleeper and roaring through the night towards the comfort and safety of a great material civilisation, one felt a little like a deserter who slinks off home while his comrades are still in the damp dug-outs of the front line.

I was kept in touch with the tragic decline of the Republic by their charming Ambassador in London, Senor Azcarate,[260] who invited me several times to his house in Belgrave Square. We also set up a National Joint Committee for Spanish Relief of which I was Vice Chairman, which sent medical and food supplies to Spain, and helped the increasing flood of Spanish refugees. The Chairman was the Duchess of Athol[sic],[261] the 'red' Duchess of her critics, while the indefatigable secretary was Miss Eleanor Rathbone M.P. We were able to send a medical unit to Spain with the financial support of the Trade Union Congress. We also arranged for hospitality and ultimate repatriation for about 4000 Basque children.

The bombing of Barcelona, an open city, continued after we had returned, as is testified by a telegram I received at the House of Lords from Del Vayo, the Foreign Minister, on March 28th, 1938: –

I am sure that the whole of Great Britain will have shuddered with horror on reading the news of the most recent bombardment of Barcelona. But I can

---

[259] José Miaja (1878–1958), army officer and minister during the Second Republic.
[260] Pablo de Azcárate (1890–1971), Spanish diplomat; ambassador to London till 1939, when Britain recognised the Franco government.
[261] Katharine Stewart-Murray, Duchess of Atholl (1874–1960), Scottish Unionist MP; her support of Republican Spain earned the nickname the 'Red Duchess'.

assure you after having visited the entire city in which 2000 people have been killed and an equal number wounded that the worst predictions of the coming aerial warfare have been converted here into the most abominable reality.

The Spanish people turn towards Great Britain and ask you to raise your voice against the extermination of this civilian population of Barcelona and against the policy which prevents the Spanish Government from acquiring the means necessary to defend itself against this murder of more than 1000 women and children in a single day.

Signed: Alvarez del Vayo

The air attacks on Barcelona and, before that, the total destruction of Guernica, were indeed a rehearsal for the far more horrifying bombing of open towns in the World War that soon followed, and the policy of non-intervention exposed to Hitler and Mussolini the fatal weakness of the democracies. Had the legitimate Spanish Republican Government with their assistance won the Spanish Civil War, the Allies might not have had to fight the Second World War. The European Union of today is an acknowledgement of the fact that defence is indivisible.

1939: The Soviet Union: Alliance as Last Hope for World Peace

When the danger of World War was becoming more and more acute with every concession to Hitler, I became convinced that the only way to stop him was by a defensive alliance with the Soviet Union, as the one thing he really feared was a war on two fronts. I was criticised at this time for my association with communists and 'fellow travellers', as near communists were then called, but I was very glad to work with anyone and any organisation that wanted a closer relationship with the Soviet Union. One of my best friends was Mrs Isobel [sic] Brown,[262] a member of the Communist Party, with no more than an elementary education but an extraordinary gift for tear-jerking platform oratory that brought in a great deal of money for the victims of aggression.

For this reason in 1937 I served as Chairman of two conferences, one in London and the other in Birmingham, called the Congress for Peace and Friendship with the U.S.S.R.

[262] Isabel Brown (1894–1984), founding member and lifelong supporter of the Communist Party of Great Britain.

My speech in Birmingham, was reported in the Birmingham Post on November 29, and set out our alternative policy of collective security:

> The first aim of the Congress was to stress the necessity for this country to co-operate as closely as possible with the Soviet Union in defence of peace. They believed very strongly that the best chance of peace in Europe lay in co-operation between this country and the Soviet Union and France, and all those democracies anxious to preserve their own liberties and to maintain peace throughout the continent. It was obvious that by standing together and obtaining collective security they stood a good chance of avoiding another war, which might otherwise be started by some great Power which felt that it could fall upon a defenceless and isolated victim. It was clear from the part that Russia had played in the League of Nations in developments in Europe and the Far East, that Russia stood for those principles of collective security to which we were pledged and which alone offered a real hope of lasting peace.

The following year. I wrote a letter to the Manchester Guardian saying that 'the one and only way of preserving the balance in favour of the peace-loving and democratic nations, who are now the trustees of European civilisation, is to be as neighbourly with Russia as we are with France'.

It seemed to me that every concession would increase the Fascists' demands, and lead inevitably in the long run to war. The alternative advocated by the Labour Party was to make a reality of collective security by international action in support of the Covenant of the League of Nations. This of course would depend on a credible threat of the use of sanctions, in the first place, economic; and in the last resort, military. I had no idea at the time of the extent of our failure to modernise our armed forces, although I did my best to persuade my party to support re-armament. Their annual opposition to the Army estimates seemed to me the height of folly, and I think my only speech at a Party meeting was against this disastrous practice. I was relieved to find that Hugh Dalton[263] agreed with me, and that as shadow Foreign Secretary was doing his best to convert the Party. It did not help us that our most powerful supporter in the House of Commons was Winston Churchill.[264]

[263] Hugh Dalton (1887–1962), later Baron Dalton, Labour MP; minister of Economic Warfare, 1940–1942 and chancellor of the exchequer, 1945–1947.

[264] Winston S. Churchill (1874–1965), later Sir Winston Churchill, Conservative and Liberal MP; later Conservative leader; prime minister, 1940–1945 and 1951–1955. Churchill was on the backbenches at this time.

However, Chamberlain[265] and Halifax were desperately afraid of the spread of communism. Indeed, Halifax praised Göring[266] for his anti-communism when he visited Germany as a fellow sportsman. Litvinov,[267] the Soviet Foreign Minister, had offered a tripartite alliance in the spring of 1939. But this offer was turned down. It was only in the early summer that a Foreign Office official, Sir William Strang,[268] was sent to Moscow to negotiate the terms of a common front against further Nazi aggression. This was a half-hearted effort that never looked likely to succeed. Instead of sending the team of negotiators in a naval vessel through the Baltic, they travelled on a slow merchantman. Having no authority to decide, they were constantly referring back to the Foreign Office. Negotiations dragged on through the summer months until Stalin[269] lost patience, and Hitler sent Ribbentrop[270] to do an unscrupulous deal which gave him much more than we could or would offer. Halifax's worst mistake was to give the last opportunity for an alliance with the Soviet Union so little chance of success. I asked my Leader in the House of Lords, Lord Snell, to make this clear in a debate in the House: –

> We struggled hard against appeasement because it encouraged the dictators to ask for more. But since the Government abandoned this policy in March, it has failed to replace it by the system of collective security we have advocated all along. Our idea of collective security in Europe always included the Soviet Union as one of the senior partners, and the failure to build up an effective European alliance against further aggression is due to the disastrous bungling of the attempted agreement with Russia.[271]

Mr Roberts, in his admirable biography,[272] points out that Halifax wanted to avoid giving the impression that we were anxious for a deal. But the Soviet Union, like us, was animated by the strongest form of self-interest, self-preservation, and our own anxiety for a deal would not have made the slightest difference. After weeks had

[265] Neville Chamberlain (1869–1940), Conservative MP and leader; prime minister, 1937–1940.
[266] Halifax visited the Nazi president of the Reichstag, Hermann Göring, for a hunt in November 1937.
[267] Maxim Litvinov (1876–1951), Soviet minister of foreign affairs, 1930–1939.
[268] Sir William Strang (1893–1978), later 1st Baron Strang; diplomat and later permanent under-secretary at the Foreign Office, 1949–1953.
[269] Joseph Stalin (1878–1953), dictator and general secretary of the Communist Party of the Soviet Union, 1922–1952.
[270] Joachim von Ribbentrop (1893–1946), German ambassador to London, 1936–1938, and Nazi foreign minister, 1938–1945.
[271] Extract from letter to Lord Snell dated 22 July 1939.
[272] Andrew Roberts, Holy Fox: The Life of Lord Halifax (London: 1991).

passed without any progress the Russians began to doubt our sincerity. Halifax ought at least to have gone himself, or sent a Cabinet Minister with plenipotentiary powers, instead of a bunch of civil servants without the political weight or authority to conclude the all-important defensive alliance. The opportunity for such an alliance, which would have faced Hitler with – a war on both fronts, East and West, the threat he most feared, was lost by the anti-communist prejudice of Halifax and Chamberlain.

V
ARMY LIFE

When I decided to join the Army I thought I should first seek guidance as to how membership of the armed forces could be squared with my parliamentary duties. So I wrote to the Lord Chancellor, Lord Simon,[273] better remembered as Foreign Secretary in the 1930's, to ask his advice. Lord Simon stated that: '[t]he same point arose, of course, in the last war and I remember the discussions about it when I was serving'; and summarised his views as follows:

> The first point is I think, that a member of either House who joins the armed forces, must in the main be his own judge as to what is proper and appropriate. No-one can restrain a member for doing his full duty as a member of the legislature, and he is under no reproach for doing so. Of course if he offers to take active military service and is accepted this must be some restraint upon his political activities, but how much is I think, for him to say.

This reply had the clarity and good sense of a great lawyer who was also a fine parliamentarian. I fear Simon has been underestimated as a person, whatever view you may take about his politics, at least that was my experience. He was extremely kind to me when I first joined the Coalition Government as a junior minister, inviting me to a simple tête-à-tête dinner at the Lord Chancellor's flat in the House of Lords with his Irish wife, who looked after us without the assistance of any servants. This letter gave me exactly the encouragement I needed to be a serving soldier without deserting the little band of Labour supporters in the House of Lords.

After offering myself as a recruit, I went to see a doctor who would report on my fitness for military service. His verdict was that my defective eyesight made me unfit for active service, so that I could only be in the army as a non-combatant. So I plumped for the Royal Army Medical Corps [RAMC], which offered me a useful humanitarian role, and possibly also exposure to the risks of active service if sent out with a Field Ambulance.

---

[273] 1st Viscount Simon, formerly Sir John Simon (1873–1954), Liberal and later National Liberal MP and peer; served in many high offices; foreign secretary, 1931–1935, and lord chancellor, 1940–1945.

I joined the army as a private soldier in the RAMC, and was immediately posted to their training depot near Aldershot. I'm afraid I didn't carry a Field-Marshal's baton in my knapsack. But little did I suppose I would be the only private soldier in the Army whose subsequent incarnations would include that of Cabinet Minister and Governor-General. I had not realised that all the officers in the RAMC were doctors, so that the training of the recruits was entirely in the hands of the NCOs (Non Commissioned Officers), a very efficient but extremely tough lot of men who had risen from the ranks. I don't think I had seen an officer, and certainly had not spoken to one, until a benevolent Major gave me a lift in his car as I was walking wearily back from the railway station to the Camp. All the volunteers were allocated to 'C' Company, the other Companies being made up of conscripts, and our Company was expected to be the smartest and keenest in the Battalion. We were mainly middle class, which was not exactly a recommendation to our Company Sergeant. I really blotted my copy book with him on my first Sunday, when, being an agnostic, I refused to go on Church Parade. He hadn't of course the faintest idea about what I meant, but obviously thought I wanted to shirk the Parade. He therefore sent me with other minor delinquents to scrub the floor of the dining hall. I was obviously suspect from the moment I was given leave to travel up to London for meetings of the House. I attended when asked by my Leader for support, and there was soon friendly comment in the press about wartime democracy in the Upper House, when I appeared in my private's uniform among the elderly Field Marshals.

The daily routine was morning parade, with a great deal of shouting if buttons were not gleaming and boots shining. Then a good deal of square bashing, and long route marches around the neighbouring countryside. An unforgettable lesson I learned from my time in the RAMC Camp was the real meaning of comradeship. The extraordinary kindness and helpfulness to each other of a crowd of mainly ordinary working men, torn from their homes and struggling to cope with army discipline for the first time, was an experience of human nature at its best I had never had before.

One morning at parade our sergeant announced that anyone who could speak German should report to the Company office. There I was told that German speakers were wanted at the War Office for a language test. This seemed to offer a possible escape route, but I did not feel too sanguine as I had spoken little German since I left Eton, where we learned to read Goethe and other classics, which were splendid literature but really quite useless for the purposes of ordinary conversation. However, the intelligence officer who put me through my paces when I came up to London was I am afraid impressed by Eton, Cambridge, and the Lords, and rather shocked by my humble status. Anyway, I was most grateful to him for his recommendation that I should be accepted for training by the Intelligence Corps.

This resulted in instant release from the RAMC, and a posting in civilian clothing to a course at the Intelligence Corps training college at Matlock in Derbyshire. They had taken over the Hydro there, a comfortable tourist hotel at this picturesque holiday resort. The surrounding countryside was really delightful, and I enjoyed many pleasant walks up the steep hillsides and through the woods that are typical of Derbyshire, in the company of young men with a similar background and education. It was somewhat like going back to school again, with a military rather than academic choice of subjects studied in class.

I managed to survive the course, and emerged as a Second Lieutenant in the Intelligence Corps. As the Corps consisted entirely of officers, I had no further drudgery in the ranks. It was a pleasant change to eat in the Officer's Mess, and have a batman to look after me.

My first posting was to London District, located at that time in a block of modern flats off Curzon Street, a very convenient spot for me as I would be able to continue to combine my military duties with attendance at the House. I had a flat with one bedroom and sitting room in Pimlico at Dolphin Square, and it was an easy journey by bus to Victoria and then on to Piccadilly. My first job in the Map Room I found extremely dull, but things brightened up when I was moved to a large office upstairs, where I found myself in the company of a GSOIII[274] – Captain Webster, a classics Don at Oxford, a GSOII[275] – Major Villiers, who had been seconded from the Brigade of Guards, and as my fellow dogsbody, second Lieutenant Freddie Ayer,[276] another Don from Oxford. From that moment, Freddie, the founder of logical positivism, became a life-long friend whose infectious cheerfulness and wonderful sense of humour made his company an unfailing delight. He was quite the reverse of the stuffy and reclusive philosopher, having friends, male and female, old and young, and in all walks of life. As a young man he had stood as a Labour candidate for the Westminster Borough Council in Soho, but though his sympathies were always with the Left, I do not think he ventured again into active politics. But let me now go back to life at London District.

[274] General staff officer, Grade III.
[275] General staff officer, Grade II.
[276] A.J. Ayer, also known as Freddie Ayer (1910–1989), later Sir Alfred Jules Ayer, philosopher and Oxford academic.

Our main function was to interrogate German prisoners of war, but as there were very few German prisoners at that early stage in the war, we were never fully employed. Those we captured were some pilots and crews of planes brought down over the United Kingdom, and a few sailors from a naval vessel intercepted on the high seas. I was occasionally sent to the 'cage', as it was called, in Kensington Palace Gardens,[277] where they were held. According to the Rules of War, prisoners of war, whether taken either by the Germans or the Allies, were under no obligation to answer any questions other than giving on request their name, rank, and number. So I was much astonished to find how anxious they were to talk about their homes, their work as civilians, indeed the whole of their lives before they were caught by the Wehrmacht. I never heard whether any of the background information we provided had been of military value.

Major Villiers was reluctant to use a member of the Lords for some of the morally dubious intelligence work going on in London. I told him I hoped that he would not feel any such scruples, and at last he gave me what he considered quite an important assignment. He said that a good deal of secret information was reaching the enemy from London, and it was suspected that this was due to careless talk by British officers in public places while they were back on home leave. One of the most popular places where officers spent a cheerful evening was at the Café Royal in Regent Street.[278] My assignment was to sit in civilian clothes at a table one evening, strategically placed to listen to my neighbours in uniform, so as to be able to report back on any indiscretions I might hear. I carried out my instructions to the letter, but I could only report the next morning that the noise in the supper room was so deafening that I could not overhear anything. After the complete failure of my first attempt at espionage, and the boredom of my under-employment at London District, I was quite relieved to hear from my Leader in the Lords, Lord Addison, that his Chief Whip had resigned, and I was his only supporter with the necessary experience for the Front Bench. As this would be a whole time job I would have to leave the army. Lord Addison applied to the Adjutant General for my release, and as no-one appeared anxious to keep me in my present occupation, I reverted immediately to 'civvy street' and the Opposition Front Bench in the Lords, succeeding Lord

---

[277] The London office of the Combined Services Detailed Interrogation Centre, known colloquially as the London Cage, run by MI19 of the War Office to interrogate enemy prisoners of war; allegations of torture surround its existence.
[278] 68 Regent St., once a famous meeting place and restaurant, now a hotel.

Strabolgi[279] as Chief Opposition Whip. I had already had some valuable experience of the Whip's office, as I had been an Assistant Whip in 1938.

[279] Joseph Kenworthy, 10th Baron Strabolgi (1886–1953), Labour MP and peer. Listowel succeeded Strabolgi as chief opposition whip in the Lords in 1942.

VI
PARLIAMENTARY MISSION TO
AUSTRALIA AND NEW ZEALAND: 1944

In the spring of 1944 I was asked to join an all party Parliamentary Delegation organised by the Empire Parliamentary Association to visit our opposite numbers in Australia and New Zealand. The object of the exercise was to strengthen Empire ties at the Parliamentary level. The delegation was to consist of British and Canadian Parliamentarians, who would be the guests of the Australian and New Zealand Parliaments. The British Delegation was led by a senior Conservative member of the House of Commons, Colonel Wickham,[280] and, as I was the only representative from the Lords, I was asked to act as the Deputy Leader. This arrangement also helped to keep the balance between the parties.

We were meeting our Canadian colleagues in New York. We left Glasgow on April 5th, but did not arrive until April 13th, as the zig-zagging northerly course took us seven and a half days. Our ship was a converted luxury liner, armed against submarine and air attacks.

New York and Washington

We were greeted on arrival by the Australian Trade Commissioner, who deposited us at the Gotham Hotel. We were told that our Australian meat-boat had been held up for repairs, so we were likely to stay in New York for two or three weeks. We were warned by our Secretary, Sir Howard d'Egville,[281] to keep off the Presidential election, as many Republicans felt about Roosevelt as the Duke of Northumberland felt about Lloyd George after his Limehouse speech.[282]

[280] Edward Thomas Wickham (1890–1957), Conservative MP.
[281] Sir Howard d'Egville (1879–1965), hon. secretary of the British-American Parliamentary Group and later secretary general of the Commonwealth Parliamentary Association.
[282] David Lloyd George, later Earl Lloyd-George of Dwyfor (1863–1945), Liberal chancellor of the exchequer, 1908–1915 and prime minister, 1916–1922. Lloyd George delivered a speech in Limehouse, in the east end of London, on 30 July 1909, in which he castigated

We found that he had also informed Congress of our arrival, and that Senator Connolly [*sic*],[283] Chairman of the prestigious Foreign Relations Committee of the Senate, had summoned a meeting of Senators and Congressmen to greet us in Washington. Wickham, Summers,[284] Butcher,[285] Summerskill[286] (our sole lady member), and myself were packed off to represent the delegation at the capital.

The following morning we went off to the British Embassy to meet Halifax.[287] The only interesting news was that Cordell Hull[288] had already drafted official proposals for a post-war peace-keeping organisation (later the U.N.). Halifax had advised that these proposals should be disclosed to the Senate before we were informed, so that the State Department could say that no foreign power had been consulted. I did not have the feeling that Halifax was the right man for Washington. He had obviously been dumped by Churchill to get him out of the Foreign Office. It was no good telling the Americans that India was none of their business, which he said was his stock answer. He was not such a good 'mixer' as Lothian,[289] his predecessor, and Americans like good 'mixers'. But Sir Gerald Campbell,[290] the Minister at the Embassy, told me he was more popular than when he first arrived, because he had lost a son in the war.[291]

We went on to a very satisfactory meeting with the Congressmen and Senators invited by Senator Connolly. They were all equally friendly, but I was astonished how little some of them knew about

rich dukes like Northumberland and Westminster for their reluctance to improve the conditions of their numerous working-class tenants. He had Northumberland in mind when he increased the vigour of his rhetoric a few months later on 9 October in Newcastle where he famously quipped that 'a fully equipped duke costs as much to keep as two dreadnoughts and they are just as great a terror – and they last longer.'

[283] Senator Thomas Connally (1877–1963), US Democratic senator and chairman of the Senate Foreign Relations Committee, 1941–1947 and 1949–1953.

[284] Gerald Spencer Summers (1902–1976), later Sir Gerald Spencer Summers, Conservative MP.

[285] Herbert Butcher (1901–1966), later Sir Herbert Butcher, 1st baronet, National Liberal MP.

[286] Edith Summerskill (1901–1980), later Baroness Summerskill, Labour MP who served as a minister in the Attlee administration.

[287] *Some people did not like his reputation as a Master of a pack of fox hounds, others his lack of small talk and refusal to travel around the country meeting people (whereas his predecessor, Lord Lothian, had been very popular for this very reason).* Lord Halifax was ambassador to Washington, 1940–1946.

[288] Cordell Hull (1871–1955), US secretary of state, 1933–1944.

[289] Philip Kerr, 11th marquess of Lothian (1882–1940), diplomat and official; ambassador to Washington, 1939–40, died in office.

[290] Sir Gerald Campbell (1879–1964), diplomat who had served as consul general in New York and from 1941 was minister in the British embassy in Washington.

[291] Halifax's son Major Peter Wood died in active service in North Africa in 1942. His youngest son Richard Wood lost the use of both his legs the same year also during battle in the Western Desert.

this country. Had the British Parliament got two Chambers? Was the Lords still more powerful than the Commons? However, there was probably just as much ignorance at home about their parliamentary system.

We were all invited onto the floor of the Senate on the following morning, where we walked about and chatted while a debate was actually in progress. We were chaperoned by the Republican Senator Burton[292] of Ohio who explained the informality of the pro-ceedings. Most of the speeches were intended for publication in the local press, but there was genuine debate about important subjects like post-war co-operation or foreign policy.

At lunch, misgivings about us were fired point-blank. What about India? What about Palestine? Luckily I had been forewarned about their pre-occupations. After lunch our Congressman host took us round the House Office Building. He showed us the two spacious offices, where his two secretaries were hard at work. I doubt whether any legislature in the world had better facilities or a larger budget. The following evening we were asked to a dinner party given by Walter Nash[293] at the New Zealand Legation. An excellent party, including Mr Fraser[294] (the Prime Minister of New Zealand) and his wife, en route for the Prime Ministers' conference in London. I had a long talk with Fraser after dinner. He was rather long-winded and less clever than Nash. He favoured more frequent meetings of Dominion and U.K. Prime Ministers in different capitals, and peri-odic meetings between Dominion and U.K. Foreign Secretaries. Following the example of Australia, he wanted a permanent Imperial Secretariat with headquarters in London. Remarkably prophetic![295]

Taking a little time off in the National Gallery, I ran into a party from the Embassy including the Archbishop of York (Temple)[296] among the Italian Primitives. We saw him later at a lunch given by the English Speaking Union, a huge affair with several hundred guests. He spoke with moving simplicity about the spirit of the Russian people and the devastation of Europe. There was a roar of applause when he finished, and the following day the press ran riot with 'Right Honourables' and 'His Graces' – one paper even

[292] Senator Harold Hitz Burton (1888–1964).

[293] Walter Nash (1882–1968), later Sir Walter Nash, New Zealand Labour MP; New Zealand resident minister in Washington, 1942–1944, while remaining deputy prime minister and finance minister; prime minister, 1957–1960.

[294] Peter Fraser (1884–1950), New Zealand Labour prime minister, 1940–1949.

[295] Eventually established in 1965 as the Commonwealth Secretariat situated at Marlborough House.

[296] William Temple (1881–1944), archbishop of York, 1929–1942.

describing him as 'Primate of all-England'. Poor old Canterbury![297] The Americans were really touched by his humanity.

I pulled off one sensational press story whilst I was in Washington, maddening for my colleagues as it filled the columns of the morning press the very day after they had delivered important speeches.

When I went to bed my first night at the Waterman Park Hotel, I put my shoes outside my bedroom door, as I would at a London hotel, expecting that they would be picked up and cleaned in the morning. As they had not turned up at 10.00 am, I phoned the housekeeper to find out what had happened. She told me, quite rightly, that I left them in the passage at my own risk, that shoes were rationed, and that I would be lucky to recover them. But I had not brought a second pair of walking shoes, and with no coupons it would be impossible to buy a pair. Without them I would be immobilised in the hotel for the day, and faced the prospect of going back to New York by train in a pair of antique carpet slippers. In desperation I phoned d'Egville. He did not seem at all pleased to hear about my sartorial crisis. His only somewhat curt advice was to phone the Embassy. I hesitated. I was a British subject in distress, but was lack of footwear sufficiently distressing to enlist the sympathy of the Embassy? At that moment there, was a knock on the door. I opened it. There stood a young man with the missing shoes. They had been found in another passage. I suspect the housekeeper had threatened the boys on my floor with the sack unless the shoes were returned immediately. I told Tom Wickham the story. He told the Press. The next morning it appeared on the front page of the morning papers as startling evidence of the hardships of wartime Britain, where even a Lord comes over with shoes so shabby and down at heel that the hotel staff thought he had left them out intending that they should be thrown away! Anyway, this was the news-story that put the British Parliamentary Delegation on the map in Washington.

Having paid our respects to Congress in Washington, we returned to New York. I remember particularly a delightful luncheon party at Lady Gosford's pent-house in Park Avenue. Mildred Gosford[298] was a very old friend of my mother. She used to come to London quite often, having married an Irish Peer. But she and her husband had separated, and she now lived in New York, where her father, Mr Carter, a wealthy banker, had smoothed the path for a smart

---

[297] Temple would, nonetheless, eventually be enthroned at Canterbury Cathedral in 1942 and thus reach the highest ecclesiastical post in the Church of England. York is second only in rank to the archbishopric of Canterbury.

[298] *Lady Gosford was a bridge playing friend of my mother married to a penniless Irish peer, not an unusual alliance in those days.* Mildred Acheson, née Carter, Countess of Gosford (1888–1965).

social life. She had immense charm, wit, and beauty, and enjoyed a life of hospitable and cultured ease. It was a small party, and the star guests were the playwright Granville-Barker[299] and his wife. He was a great raconteur, and told a splendid story about Churchill and Clemenceau.[300] Churchill, who was proud of the fact that he had just been elected as an Elder Brother of Trinity House,[301] wanted to tell Clemenceau of his recent distinction. So he said in his bad French 'Je suis devenu le frère ainé du Trinité'. To which Clemenceau replied 'Quelle responsabilité'.[302]

Lady Gosford immediately capped this story with another. Clemenceau met an English political figure at a party, and asked him what he meant by saying that he was about to celebrate his golden wedding. He replied: 'You see this lady beside me – she and I have been living together for 50 years'. 'Oh' said Clemenceau, 'Of course, and now you are going to marry'.

I soon realised that the word 'politician' was slightly derogatory, and that admiration and respect went to the well established and highly successful business community. I was therefore very pleased to be asked to lunch at Morgan's in Wall Street, where I had an introduction from Stafford Cripps[303] to one of the partners, Tom Lamont. I waited in his private office, which was covered with framed letters from Lloyd George to Pierrepont [sic] Morgan[304] thanking him for lending Britain money in the first world war. It was a most interesting lunch, with Whitney, Luffingwell, and other members of the Board. There was a sudden hush in the conversation when I said I was a 'Labour' whip in the Lords. But it picked up again immediately, and nowhere did I learn more about America than from my charming, courteous, and highly intelligent hosts.

I had a special affinity for the Lamont family, whom I met later at their home, as their son Corlius[305] was a fellow socialist and had written a book on the subject. I heard a lot about the Stock Exchange,

[299] Harley Granville-Barker (1877–1946), actor, critic and director.

[300] Georges Clémenceau (1841–1929), prime minister of France, 1917–1920.

[301] A private corporation and charity under a Royal Charter from Henry VIII charged with safeguarding seafarers and shipping. Elder Brethren of Trinity House form much of the Court of Trinity House and are often drawn from Royalty and Naval Officers. Churchill had been First Lord of the Admiralty twice.

[302] 'I have become the elder brother of the Trinity', to which Clémenceau replied, 'What a responsibility!'

[303] Sir Stafford Cripps (1889–1952), Labour MP and later chancellor of the exchequer, 1947–1950. Cripps led a mission to India in 1942 and was part of the 1946 Cabinet mission there to respectively gain Indian co-operation in fighting the Second World War and to form a credible plan for British withdrawal from the subcontinent.

[304] John Pierpont Morgan Jr (1867–1943), US ,Wall Street financier and banker.

[305] *Corlius Lamont died in 1995, after a life spent in advocating socialism.*

and I was struck by the use of Federal taxation to check speculation by varying the amount of the tax according to the length of time an investment had been held.

I met Norman Thomas,[306] the socialist candidate for the presidency, with Roger Baldwin,[307] the champion of human rights. Thomas lectured me as if at a public meeting, and was not afraid of unpopularity by advocating a negotiated peace. It was also good to see an old personal friend, the historian Barbara Tuchman.[308] I had met her first in London during the Spanish Civil War, when she came over to Europe to support the Republican cause. She was an excellent speaker, and already engaged in writing history. She won the Pulitzer Prize soon after her return with her book on the first world war: 'The Guns of August'. She had the remarkable gift of popularizing without distorting history.

On April 28th we finally sailed for Australia on the Sydney Star, a cargo boat of 15,000 tons with passenger accommodation. Our party consisted of us, three Canadian parliamentarians (Conservative, Liberal and CCF[309]), and four Dutchmen going out to do war work. We were loaded with a cargo of explosives, so we hoped to avoid trouble with submarines. We were packed like sardines, three in a cabin, an extra bunk being fitted above the others. I shared with Tom Wickham and Spencer Summers. It grew steadily hotter as we went south, but an electric fan kept the cabin cool enough to sleep at night, though the portholes were blacked out.

The Pacific lived up to its name, calm and sunny, some porpoises and flying fish to watch from the decks, and, a few days out of Panama, our first albatross. There is no more beautiful bird to watch, as it glides over the waves without even moving its wings, and skims so close to the surface that it seems almost a miracle that it does not crash into the water. They followed us all day, and came onto the deck for scraps. They seemed never to feel fatigue, and it is this apparent lack of effort that lends such supreme grace to their movements. I won the sweepstake on the time of crossing the equator, and stood the whole crew bottles of beer for lunch. The Southern Cross was disappointing, like a crucifix, with four

---

[306] Norman Thomas (1884–1968), Socialist Party of America candidate for the US presidency six times from 1928.

[307] Roger Baldwin (1884–1981), one of the founders, later executive director, of the American Civil Liberties Union.

[308] Barbara Tuchman (1912–1989), American historian and writer; won the Pulitzer Prize for her 1962 book *The Guns of August*.

[309] Canadian political party Co-operative Commonwealth Federation.

sham diamonds. But some magnificent sunsets. Coleridge[310] was wrong about green being peculiar to English sunsets. But, of course, a long sea journey is dull, and I read all my books, some of them twice, and was reduced to bridge and deck games. The guns were not manned, thanks to our radar, then a novelty, which detected an empty case of oranges floating half a mile away. We only ran into one gale, in the Tasman sea off the coast of New Zealand, when the spray was driving right over the decks, and we all stayed below.

The whole journey from New York took 29 days, a week to Panama and 22 days from Panama to Sydney. What a lot people miss in these days of air travel.

Australia

We berthed in Sydney Harbour on June 4th. On June 7th we dined at the Australia Hotel with Sir Thomas Gordon[311] to meet some business magnates. They seemed pleased that Britain had brought the whole wool clip for the duration and one year afterwards at 15 % above the pre-war price. We went on to Canberra and visited a station of 7000 acres, which gave us a fair idea of the staple wool industry. The capital had been planned for a population of 50,000, and was only inhabited by about 12,000. There was no trade or industry, and it had the Federal Parliament but only part of the Federal Administration. Several government departments had their headquarters in Sydney or Melbourne, and some ministers had homes elsewhere. The tug-of-war between the States and the Federal Government had left the capital without the grandeur or prosperity of a capital city, though in a wonderful setting of mountain scenery in the heart of the continent.

At the state dinner in the Parliament Buildings, I had the good luck to sit next to Mr Chiffley [sic],[312] the Commonwealth Treasurer at that time and, of course, a future Prime Minister. He was a railway trade unionist of genuine working-class origin, with a first rate brain and no interests to distract him from his job. Our High Commissioner, Sir Ronald Cross,[313] told me he rarely attended

[310] Samuel Taylor Coleridge (1772–1834), poet and writer.
[311] Sir Thomas Stewart Gordon (1882–1949), Australian businessman, chairman of the Allied Consultative Shipping Council from 1942.
[312] *I found Mr Chiffley, at that time Commonwealth Treasurer, the most congenial of the Australian Ministers.* Ben Chifley (1885–1951), Australian Labor MP, treasurer, 1941–1949 and prime minister, 1945–1949.
[313] Sir Ronald Cross, 1st baronet (1896–1968), Conservative MP who later became British high commissioner to Canberra, 1941–1945 and governor of Tasmania, 1951–1958.

social functions. He was the Minister in charge of post-war reconstruction, and seemed to think a lot could be done to improve the
social services, such as housing, if only agreement was ultimately
forthcoming from the State Governments.

The highlight of the evening was a fine speech without notes from
the grand old man of Australian politics, 'Billie' [sic] Hughes,[314] then
over 80. I was a little surprised that Menzies[315] and Faddon[316] were
heckled by their political opponents, in spite of their long and dignified record as elder statesmen. Fifty senators and members of the
House of Representatives had come to Canberra expressly for the
occasion.

On June 14th we left Sydney by air for Melbourne. Crossing the
Australian Alps we missed Kosciusko, the highest peak, on account
of thick cloud, but had a splendid view of snow-covered mountains
as we passed over them. We were taken from the airport to the
Menzies Hotel, and we lunched at Parliament House with members
of the Victoria Legislature. There was a 'hung' Parliament, with a
coalition between the UAP[317] and Country Parties, and the Labour
Party [sic] was in Opposition. I replied to Premier Dunston [sic][318]
with a short speech on Britain in wartime. He wanted legislation
to give more powers to the Commonwealth Government, and,
after the war, massive immigration and industrial expansion. There
was a Lord Mayor's reception in the afternoon. The impression
was one of intensive patriotism exuding 'Britishness' from every
quarter.

In the next few days I visited several arms and aircraft factories. On
June 16th I met Sir Isaac Isaacs,[319] the first Australian
Governor-General of Australia, having been before that Chief
Justice. He was 89 and still deeply concerned about the Jewish prob-
lem and the need for a common home for the Jews, although he was
not a Zionist. He was essentially more of a scholar than a politician.

[314] William 'Billy' Hughes (1862–1952), prime minister of Australia, 1915–1923; subsequently served in several ministerial posts; died while still a member of the House of
Representatives in 1952 aged 90.
[315] Robert Menzies (1894–1978), later Sir Robert Menzies, Liberal prime minister of
Australia, 1939–1941 and 1949–1966.
[316] Arthur Fadden (1894–1973), later Sir Arthur Fadden, Country Party prime minister
1941 and treasurer, 1940–1941 and 1949–1958.
[317] United Australia Party.
[318] Albert Dunstan (1882–1950), later Sir Albert Dunstan, Country Party premier of
Victoria, 1935–1943 and 1943–1945.
[319] Sir Isaac Isaacs (1855–1948), Australian politician and judge, governor general of
Australia, 1931–1936. Not only first Australian-born person to hold the post of governor
general, Isaacs was also the first appointment as the sovereign's representative in a dominion who was not personally known to the monarch.

At dinner I met a number of British and Australian military leaders, including Admiral Sir Guy Royal [*sic*],[320] Commander-in-Chief of the Australian Naval Forces in the South West Pacific under General MacArthur.[321] I was glad to get an impression of McArthur from a close colleague, as I was expecting to meet him later at Brisbane. He told me that McArthur had two distinct personalities: theatrical and tough before press and public, while in private he was a quiet, clear headed, staff officer with an amazing grasp of strategy. As he did not get on well with Admiral Nimitz,[322] he was planning his offensive against Japan without him. McArthur's view was that the allied strategy should be more 'island hopping' to eliminate Japanese aerodromes and bases between New Guinea and Japan. Japanese pockets in South East Asia could then be left to starve or die of malaria. November 1942 had in fact been the turning-point of the war in the Pacific, the Japanese having given up the offensive after their defeats in the Coral Sea and Midway, but they would fight on until the invasion of Japan itself. Australians have never forgotten that, earlier in 1942, Japanese submarines got among their coastal shipping, and sank 7 ships with iron ore between Whyalla and Newcastle.

Lieutenant General Northcote, Chief of Staff to General Blamey,[323] said that the number of Australian Army and Air Force personnel in the South Pacific was slightly larger than that of the Americans – 500,000 to 450,000 – and that most of the land fighting had been done by the Australians. They all seemed to like Prime Minister Curtin,[324] and he was even liked by McArthur. On July 9th we lunched with Prime Minister Curtin at the Canberra Hotel. He had a rather disconcerting cast in his left eye, which made you uncertain about whether he was looking at you. He said he wanted unassisted migrants from Europe after the war, but did not agree with the trade unions about excluding migrant labour. He would accept any nationality other than German. He was in favour of reciprocal arrangements for admission to full benefit of social services, including pensions, though this would mean a

[320] Admiral Sir Guy Royle (1885–1954), first naval member of the Australian Commonwealth Naval Board (chief of the Royal Australian Navy), 1941–1945.

[321] General Douglas McArthur (1880–1964), US general and supreme Allied commander of the South-West Pacific Area from 1942.

[322] Admiral Chester Nimitz (1885–1966), US admiral and commander-in-chief of the United States Pacific Fleet from 1941.

[323] General Sir Thomas Blamey (1884–1951), later Field Marshal, Australian officer and commander; held many positions during the War; commander of the Allied land forces tasked with defending Australia and responsible to MacArthur.

[324] John Curtin (1885–1945), Labor prime minister of Australia, 1941–1945.

financial loss to Australia and gain to Britain. It was clear now that Britain would no longer be able to protect Australia and New Zealand without the support of the United States.[325] But Britain should still speak for the Empire, and carry more weight on matters of foreign policy and defence with the support of the Dominions. He would like Australia associated with the shaping of imperial policy in Europe as well as in the Pacific, which would depend on the fullest possible exchange of information and consultation on important issues. He was disappointed that his ideas about an Empire Council and a permanent Imperial Secretariat had been defeated in London by the representatives of Canada and South Africa. But he had arranged for a continuation after the war of collaboration between the Defence Departments in Whitehall and those at Canberra. In discussing post-war relations he emphasised the importance of exchanges of visits at all levels. For Empire ties were based on understanding and goodwill between the people of the mother country and the Dominions. He certainly had the breadth of vision to speak for Australia as a whole, and to grasp its importance not just to the Empire but for the entire outside world.

I spent my first evening at Brisbane with Cooper,[326] the Premier, and other members of the Executive Committee of the Queensland Branch of the Australian Labor Party. They were very proud of their record of 26 years of Labor rule, the longest of any Parliament in the Commonwealth. They said their system of compulsory arbitration in disputes between employers and employees, applied by the State and Federal Courts, had prevented stoppages during the war. Queensland was also the only State with unemployment insurance.

I also had a long talk with O'Leary,[327] the Director of Native Affairs for the Queensland Government, who considered that Queensland had done more for the Aborigines than any other State.[328] The best organised Aboriginal community was in the Islands of the Torres Straits, where they had a large measure of

---

[325] This led to the establishment of the Australia, New Zealand United States Security Treaty of 1951 (ANZUS).

[326] Frank Cooper (1872–1949), Labor premier of Queensland, 1942–1946.

[327] Cornelius O'Leary (1897–1971), director of Native Affairs in Queensland, 1942–1963.

[328] Questionable opinion to say the least. Queensland was a conspicuous laggard in terms of Aboriginal rights. It was the last state in Australia to recognize and provide voting rights for Aboriginal people and Torres Strait Islanders in 1965. Several other legislative and cultural forms of discrimination against Aboriginal and Torres Strait Island people persisted well into the late 20th century. Queensland refused to recognise Aboriginal land rights and this was famously challenged in the court case Mabo v. Queensland. The Queensland government view was rejected by the Australian High Court in judicial decisions in 1988 and 1992.

autonomy. Since the war they provided a garrison to guard the Islands, the only aboriginal contingent in the Australian Army. These men are not pure Aborigines, as they contain a mixture of Javanese and Polynesian strains. Before the war they lived by pearl fishing. On the Queensland mainland, apart from a pocket on the Western side of the Cape York Peninsula, there were no tribal Aborigines left: the able bodied males having been recruited by the farmers for labour gangs to cut sugar cane and help them at busy times of the year. In Queensland I had my first experience of the tragedy of the Aboriginal inhabitants of Australia.

I was delighted to find some first rate contemporary art in galleries in Melbourne and Sydney. The most striking figure among contemporary painters was William Dobell,[329] whom I met in the Sydney Art Gallery. He told me he had studied at the Slade,[330] under Tonks,[331] and that the Old Masters who had most influenced him were Goya and Rembrandt.[332] But he was typically Australian in his portrayal of character, which he pushed to the point of caricature. He was not far from Will Dyson[333] or Lowe.[334] Another young artist painting tavern scenes with a Dutch gusto was Russell Drysdale.[335] Perhaps the most popular school of painting, to which Roberts[336] and Streeton[337] belonged, was a school of landscape artists, depicting vast expanses of sparse pasture, dotted by the ubiquitous gum trees, where the sheep farmer grazed his thousands of sheep on a sheep station in the outback. Streeton above all, gave you a marvellous sense of great distances, the blue haze of the intense summer heat, and the brilliant tones of a land continually drenched in sunlight.

But only today has any artist tried to portray the great Australian desert, far more typical of the continent than pastoral countryside, because it covers more than half the whole area. The first Australian to reveal the real Australia to outsiders was an Aboriginal artist, Albert Namatjira.[338] I flew over thousands of miles of the Australian desert, and at Alice Springs I saw for the

[329] William Dobell, (1899–1970), later Sir William Dobell, Australian artist.
[330] Slade School of Fine Art, London.
[331] Henry Tonks (1862–1937), Slade Professor of Fine Art, 1918–1930.
[332] Francisco Goya (1746–1828) and Rembrandt van Rijn (1606–69).
[333] William Dyson (1880–1938), Australian painter and cartoonist.
[334] Possibly this is referring to the great political cartoonist David Low (born in New Zealand), whose work was prominent in the British press during these years.
[335] George Russell Drysdale (1912–1981), later Sir George Russell Drysdale, Australian artist.
[336] Probably referring to the Australian artist Tom Roberts.
[337] Arthur Streeton (1867–1943), later Sir Arthur Streeton, Australian artist.
[338] Albert Namatjira (1902–1959), indigenous Australian artist.

first time the desert at close quarters. The colouring is magnificent, tropical in its strident tones and absence of chiaroscuro. In the foreground the flaming orange-red of the sun-drenched desert, stretching away towards the horizon until suddenly interrupted by a huge mass of naked rock, violet in the distance, and silhouetted against the bluest of blue skies. This is not a white man's country, it is far too hot and barren, and it is not surprising that it has been discovered for art by one of the Aboriginals who lived and hunted there since the old stone age. For Albert Namatjira and his colleagues this is their homeland, where he and his ancestors have lived in tribal harmony since the 'dreamtime', before man and nature became divided.

New Zealand

During our stay in New Zealand we drove by car 2,200 miles in about a fortnight, starting from Auckland and covering both Islands before we returned to our starting point. At every town where we stayed there was a civic reception, and every evening we split up to address private gatherings of our respective Parties. Party feeling in New Zealand ran so strong it was impossible for us to meet Labour and National supporters together. In Wellington we lunched with the Empire Parliamentary Association, and met a number of Ministers and members of both Houses. None of the politicians seemed to be of the calibre of Fraser and Nash, and I did not feel that Holland,[339] the genial farmer who led the Opposition, had the mettle of a potential Prime Minister.

We dined with Fraser and his Cabinet at the Waterloo Hotel in Wellington on our return journey. The Prime Minister had just returned from a conference of Prime Ministers in London. He had been disappointed by the lack of support for the idea of improving the machinery of imperial co-operation after the war, but was pleased by the new practice of monthly meetings between the United Kingdom Prime Minister and the Dominion High Commissioners in London. He was worried about the future damage from flying bombs, which he had encountered during his time in London. He thought the war in Europe might be over in six months, but that the war in the Pacific might last for two years after that (without the atomic bomb and surrender of Japan it might have been so). He was immensely cheered by the land, sea, and air

[339] Sidney Holland (1893–1961), later Sir Sidney Holland, New Zealand National Party leader and later prime minister of New Zealand, 1949–1957.

reinforcements promised by the United Kingdom for the war against Japan.

It was not until we reached Rotorua that I realised the high artistic level of the Maori civilisation. You have to see the carved pillars and woven panels of a Maori meeting house, and the grace and rhythm of poi and haka dancers, to realise what a natural aptitude the Maoris have for art. I had a foretaste of this when I listened to the delightfully witty speech of the Maori Bishop Bennett[340] at a Labour meeting at Nelson. I had the good fortune to be asked by our leader, Tom Wickham, to make a speech of thanks on behalf of the delegates for the ceremonial welcome given us by the Arawa Confederation when we met them on July 27th. I was asked by the Arawa to give them a copy of my speech for their tribal records, and the New Zealand Government did me the honour of printing and publishing it with a Maori translation and an introduction by Mr Parry,[341] the Minister of Internal Affairs. As my meeting with the Maoris at Rotorua was the most memorable event in my visit to New Zealand, I would like to place on record the actual words in which I expressed the admiration and gratitude I felt and shall always feel for their gallantry and artistic genius.

Let me first say how much we appreciate the wonderful reception you have given us at Rotorua and the delightful entertainment you have provided for our benefit, a welcome that typifies the traditional spirit of Maori hospitality.

We come to you as messengers from the far-off Mother Country, from the people of Britain, and from the two Houses of the most ancient Parliament in the Empire. The message we bring you is a message of heartfelt thanks for your magnificent contribution to the war effort of the Allies, both in the fields and factories of New Zealand and on the battle fronts wherever you have engaged the enemy. Without a moment's doubt or hesitation, in spite of the momentous choice before you, you decided to send your young men to fight beside us in far distant Europe. It was only two days after our declaration of war on Germany that your four representatives in the New Zealand Parliament asked the Government to allow the Maoris to volunteer for military service. Your response to this call to the colours was so immediate that by the spring of 1940 a Maori Battalion was ready to sail, fully trained and fully equipped, from Wellington. Every man who left his home to serve overseas went out of his own free will. You accepted unanimously and without constraint, what from the days of the Greeks and Romans to the present time, has always been regarded as the highest obligation of citizenship. There

[340] Frederick Bennett (1871–1950), bishop of Aotearoa (head of the Maori Anglican Church), 1928–1950.
[341] William Parry (1878–1952). New Zealand Labour minister of internal affairs, 1935–1949.

were no laggards among the Maori race. No other people engaged in this worldwide conflict have been able to mobilise its men and women for an all-out military and industrial war effort without resort to compulsion in one form or another.

The minimum age for service overseas was fixed in New Zealand at 21. But young Maoris had a convenient habit of skipping inconvenient birthdays, and the Maori Battalion was the youngest Battalion in the New Zealand Brigade. We have not forgotten how, after France had fallen in the summer of 1940, at the blackest and most critical moment in the war, your Battalion was manning our defences in the south of England, waiting in readiness to protect our homes from the German invaders. Nor have we forgotten how the Maoris emerged from their baptism of fire. Their fame as fighters in this war was first to reach the ears of the general public during the campaign in Greece. It was there that they held the Pass of Petras on Mount Olympus for a whole day against a vastly superior force, allowing the main body of British and New Zealand troops to withdraw in safety towards the sea. Without any pause for rest after the fatigue of the day and night fighting in the retreat from Greece, your men were again thrown into the front line in defence of Crete. It was in Crete that one of those bayonet charges, which make the Maori so redoubtable a foe in hand to hand fighting, cleared German air-borne troops from a vital aerodrome in the heart of the Island. After the loss of our last foothold on the continent of Europe, the Maoris were in the forefront of the long North African campaign. Their grim ferocity at the battle of Alamein attracted Field Marshal Rommel's[342] attention, and he gave them the nickname of 'the Scalp Hunters'.

After Alamein, the Maoris swept forward with the victorious Eighth Army through Libya, Cyrenaica, and Tripolitania, until at last they were halted on the borders of Tunisia by the formidable fortifications of the Mareth Line. It was in the turning movement for which the New Zealand Division is now famous, which outflanked Rommel and obliged him to withdraw from the strongest defensive position in Tunisia, that some of the outstanding exploits of Maori gallantry are recorded. By capturing and holding with his platoon an important mountain feature, in spite of the repeated counter-attacks of a crack German Grenadier Regiment, Lieutenant Moana Ngarimu[343] won the most coveted distinction in the British Empire, the medal that bears on its face the simple inscription 'For Valour'.[344] It is not forgotten how, wounded severely in the shoulder and the leg, bleeding profusely and in great pain, he told his company commander he would prefer to stay with his men, and how he died twelve hours later with his face to the enemy. Less than a month

---

[342] Field Marshal Erwin Rommel (1891–1944), German commander in North Africa.

[343] Second Lieutenant Moana-Nui-a-Kiwa Ngarimu (1918–1943).

[344] Motto of the Victoria Cross, highest award for gallantry in Britain and, formerly, in the Commonwealth.

afterwards, by storming another key point in the Tunisian Highlands, Lieutenant Wikiriwhi[345] and Lance Sergeant Manahi,[346] of the Arawa, won the D.S.O.[347] and the D.C.M.[348] respectively. The Maori Battalion, mourning its dead and wounded heroes, but never lacking successors to fill the gaps in its ranks, still marched forward in the vanguard of the Mediterranean campaign, and even now is battering at the gates of Florence. I hope that this wartime comradeship between Maori and Pakeha[349] may lead to an even greater mutual understanding, appreciation, and esteem when the war is over. Both peoples have their own part to play, and their own contribution to make, to stability and progress in the post war world. You Maoris have a different history, a different culture, a different language and different traditional customs from the Pakeha. You will be contributing your share to this partnership, not by allowing these vital differences to be ironed out by European influences, but by jealously preserving the best that is in your own traditions and supplementing them with whatever you can gain from the methods and habits of the West. In the application of science to life, whether it be in matters of animal husbandry and the cultivation. of crops on the farm, or in saving the lives and safe guarding the health of mothers and infants, of growing children and adults, there is a great deal you can usefully pick up from the scientific discoveries and the skilled technicians we have brought with us from Europe.

But do not forget that our system of mass production in factories has killed the artistic instincts of craftsmen, and that an all-enveloping and standardised ugliness is the price we have paid for our lace curtains and plush carpets and luxury hotels. It would be a tragic loss if your wonderful artistic talents were submerged by the advancing tide of cheap industrial products.

Your language is an instrument that lends itself naturally to the music of poetry and the spoken word. The rhythmic sense and grace of movement which animate your poi and haka dances are as beautiful and as inevitable as a bird in flight, and your mastery of intricate pattern and balanced design has left an indelible imprint on woven flax, carved wood, and polished greenstone. I beg you to cherish this precious talent you have inherited from your ancestors, to preserve it from the vulgarity of European and American commercialism, and to remember, above all, that no-one can take it from you but yourselves.

It is only by this inherent power of imagination and aptitude for art that you can enrich the New Zealand of tomorrow. Pakeha society is built on a foundation of extreme individualism, which encourages each man to pursue

[345] Later Captain Matarehua Wikiriwhi (1918–1988).
[346] Lance Sergeant Haane Manahi (1913–1986).
[347] Distinguished Service Order.
[348] Distinguished Conduct Medal.
[349] Maori term for New Zealanders of European heritage.

his own advantage with little regard for others, and spreads the social qualities like thin veneer on the surface of a harsh and universal struggle. This has led to many grave evils and injustices, which are still far from being remedied. But you are accustomed by tradition to habits of friendly co-operation. You are brought up to share your possessions, you learn to live for each other and not for yourselves alone. This keen sense of social solidarity, and a courtesy, neighbourliness, and hospitable kindness to go with it, derive from the ancient traditions you have inherited from your forefathers. Thence also proceed those martial qualities which have always distinguished the young Maori. Judging from past history over many hundreds of years, there is real danger that a society which idolises comfort may in the course of time grow decadent and soft. Men may neglect to prepare themselves in days of peace for the hardships and perils of the battlefield. There can be no better antidote than the qualities you have inherited from the brave men who challenged the Pacific in their canoes six hundred years ago. The marvellous powers of endurance, the high courage, and the spirit of chivalry you have shown in the course of the war would be just as valuable to New Zealand, to the British Empire, and to the world, in the years of peace that lie ahead.

I beg you therefore to honour the traditions that have been handed down to you, to supplement them by whatever they may require to adapt your way of life to a competitive and individualistic society, and to form from this blending process a modern code of behaviour that will be as valuable to your children as your fathers' was to you.

The 19th century was a time of rapid change, of great hardship, and profound tribulation for the Maori people. For many years your very existence trembled in the balance. But the long and bitter conflict has ended in reconciliation and friendship and mutual respect between the Maori and the Pakeha. I believe you are emerging from the valley of shadows into the sunlight of a new and brighter era in Maori history. Your spirit has revived, your numbers are increasing, and you have been shown your entire fitness, in peace and war alike, to enjoy the rights and to discharge the duties of free and equal citizens in a modern democracy. You deserve the very best the future can give, and I do wish you from the bottom of my heart, the utmost success in the difficult but not impossible task of marrying your ancient and splendid traditions to the inescapable demands of a dominating white civilisation. Kia Ora.

Return Journey

The Leader of the House of Lords, Lord Cranborne[350] had informed our High Commissioner in Australia that, owing to the death of Lord

[350] Robert Gascoyne-Cecil, Viscount Cranborne, known as 'Bobbety' (1893–1972), later 5th marquess of Salisbury, Conservative peer and minister who was leader of the House of

Snell, the Labour Party Deputy Leader in the Lords, I had been asked by Churchill to take his place in the Coalition Government. It was therefore desirable that I should return home as soon as possible. I left Auckland on July 31st on a special naval Boeing Clipper, provided by Admiral King,[351] with few passengers and a bunk for the night which was the last thing in comfort. My title seemed to bother the Americans; in one document I was described as a 'British Pier'.

My first stop was at Suva in the Fiji Islands. I dined at a hotel as the guest of the Chief Secretary of the Colony, who told me that the Indian half of the population was entirely indifferent to the war. He indicated that he had noticed a considerable improvement in the impetus of the Colonial Office when Lord Cranborne succeeded Lord Moyne,[352] and he was busy preparing post-war plans for the Colonial Office regarding the development of social services, such as education and housing, and the expansion of the brick and copra industries. The plane on which I was travelling refuelled the next day at the Anglo-American Condominium of Canton Island, where I enjoyed the spectacle of a great white coral reef. The next day, August 2nd, I became conscious again of wartime conditions when I arrived at Honolulu. The population was mainly Japanese, which caused problems of security, and there was a 10.00 pm curfew every night. I stayed at the Moana Hotel, in a room overlooking an unforgettably green sea changing gradually to blue as it receded into the distance. Through my travels, there had been a sudden change of climate, from winter to summer and I bathed the following morning on a deserted Waikiki beach. The war had banished the usual hordes of American tourists, and I had the beach and the ocean to myself. The sea was smooth as a millpond, and the swimming magnificent. Never could conditions have been more perfect for the ideal holiday, and it was sad to be leaving that evening by Pan-American for San Francisco.

From Honolulu, I caught a morning plane, a venerable Douglas, to Washington on August 5th, where people were sweltering in an afternoon temperature of 95 degrees F. The British Embassy was in a tizz, because Lord Beaverbrook[353] could not be moved from the bar of the Mayflower, where he was negotiating an important

Lords, 1942–1945 and 1951–1957, and also served as colonial and dominion secretary during the War.

[351] Admiral Ernest King (1878–1956), US admiral and commander-in-chief of the United States Fleet and chief of Naval Operations.

[352] Walter Guinness, 1st Baron Moyne (1880–1944), Conservative MP and peer, colonial secretary and leader of the House of Lords, 1941–1942. Assassinated in 1944.

[353] Max Aitken, 1st Baron Beaverbrook (1879–1964), 'press baron' and wartime minister; lord privy seal, 1943–1945.

agreement. I do not know whether he was wanted on the telephone by the Cabinet, or they thought he should move to the Statler Hotel which was air-conditioned. Before I left I had a last glimpse of the Mellon Collection. The next day I caught the night Clipper from Baltimore to Newfoundland. I finally reached Ireland at Foynes Airport in the Shannon Estuary, and caught a passenger plane to Bristol. August 8th was a Bank Holiday, and I travelled from Bristol to London by British Rail. There were 15 in my compartment, mostly parents returning from a visit to their evacuee children. No complaints in spite of heat and fatigue. I was home at last, after a most fascinating experience.

VII
DEPUTY LEADER, HOUSE OF LORDS, COALITION GOVERNMENT: 1944

I arrived home from Australia at the start of the summer recess. I was told that the Prime Minister could not see me until the House sat again in the autumn but that the only qualification that Churchill insisted on for his junior Ministers was that they had served at some time during the war in the Armed Forces. I was fortunately able to satisfy this requirement by my short period of service in the R.A.M.C and the Intelligence Corps.

I finally met with Churchill on 1 November 1944, when I arrived at 10 Downing Street, I had to wait for an agonizing 15 minutes in the waiting room. The decor was heavily utilitarian and topical with four pictures by war artists, a stuffed platypus from the Australian Government,[354] and a bronze bust of Churchill himself. I was summoned by a Secretary to the Cabinet Room, and found the Prime Minister sitting alone in the middle of the long Cabinet table reading some papers. He seemed to expect me to start the conversation, so I congratulated him on how well he was standing up to his long journeys. He said he did not mind travel, and intended to go out to Australia as soon as the war with Germany was over.[355] He then told me that he would like me to go to the India Office as Under-Secretary; Lord Munster,[356] the present junior Minister at the India Office, would move to the Home Office, a very busy Department. My freedom from departmental business would give me plenty of time to assist Lord Salisbury[357] as Deputy Leader in debates in the House of Lords.[358]

---

[354] Sent at Churchill's request by the Australian Minister of External Affairs, H.V. Evatt in 1943. It was named 'Splash'.

[355] This never happened.

[356] Geoffrey FitzClarence, 5th earl of Munster (1906–1975), Conservative peer, parliamentary secretary for India and Burma, 1943–1944.

[357] Bobbety Gascoyne-Cecil was still Viscount Cranborne at this time and only became marquess of Salisbury in 1947.

[358] *My post as Deputy to the Leader of the House of Lords signified the partnership between the Labour and Conservative parties in the Lords. As a junior minister at the India office I would have few departmental duties and would be free to assist Lord Salisbury in debates in the Lords.*

I started to thank him but he pulled me up quickly with 'There is no need to kiss anybody's hand.'[359] A rhetorical note crept into his voice when he wanted to emphasise the need to keep the Coalition alive until the end of the German war, and the educational value to the Labour Party of its experience in the wartime Coalition. 'The Country would benefit in time to come', he said, 'because the Labour Party, essential to our party system of Government, will have learnt an invaluable lesson from its wartime partnership'.

I could not have been more fortunate to find a Secretary of State as my boss who was no ordinary run-of-the mill politician. Leo Amery[360] had long experience as a Cabinet Minister, after a brilliant academic career culminating in a fellowship at All Souls College at Oxford. As a firm believer in the value of the Commonwealth, he had an unrivalled knowledge of its leaders and their policies. The first question he asked me was whether there had been any political content in a message of greetings I had sent to Nehru,[361] when in prison, on his birthday. If my answer had been 'yes', I have little doubt that my life as an Under-Secretary would have ended there and then.[362] He then asked me to lunch with him at his home in Eaton Square where he told me that the average life of an Under-Secretary at the India Office was about 12 months, and expressed the hope, in which I heartily concurred, that I might be lucky enough to survive for a slightly longer period.

Leo's main contribution to my education was by allowing me to attend the meetings of the India Committee of the Cabinet, as an observer not as a full member, although I was allowed to ask questions. This Committee had been set up by Churchill in 1942, under pressure from Cripps after his return from Russia,[363] but I did not come upon the scene myself until January 1945. The India and Burma Committee, as it was officially known, was the powerhouse of Indian policy. Its members were chosen for their knowledge of India or their departmental responsibility for its affairs, and they had time for consideration and long discussion of matters of policy which was not possible at meetings of the whole Cabinet.

---

[359] A ceremony describing prime ministers and secretaries of state formally receiving the seals of office from the Sovereign. This honour is not extended to junior ministers.

[360] Leo Amery (1873–1955), Conservative MP, secretary of state for India and Burma, 1940–1945.

[361] Jawaharlal Nehru (1889–1964), leading Indian National Congress politician who was jailed at different periods for 'civil disobedience'; later first prime minister of India, 1947–1964.

[362] *Leo Amery was careful to show that any expression for my sympathy with Indian nationalists would not be acceptable.*

[363] Cripps served as ambassador to Moscow, 1940–1942.

Simon, Anderson,[364] Grigg,[365] Butler,[366] Amery, Cripps, with Attlee in the chair as Deputy Prime Minister, were all figures that had played a part in the history of India. They were a galaxy of talent such as seldom if ever before, since the time of the East-India Company, had sat around a table to decide the future of the sub-continent. I also obtained a liberal education in world politics, as my boss was one of the Ministers who received the Foreign Office Telegrams, reports to that Department from British diplomatic missions all over the world. Luckily for me, he always underlined the important telegrams with a red pencil, which lightened an otherwise extremely time-consuming task.

My duties in the Lords involved me in a lot of public speaking on subjects I knew very little about. As there are many fewer Ministers in the Lords than in the Commons, even the junior Ministers have often to speak for several Government Departments. I found myself the spokesman for the Ministry of Health and the Board of Trade as well as speaking on matters concerning the India Office. This was no mean task, as the Ministry of Health in those days included housing and local government among its responsibilities, and the planning of a post-war housing drive was a matter of burning public interest. Indeed, the rapid building of flats and houses at low rents, which had been halted by the war, and rendered even more urgent by the air raid damage to our great cities, was at that time the most pressing of our domestic problems. Lord Woolton,[367] at that time Minister of Reconstruction, put the case for the Government's housing proposals, and I on several occasions replied to his critics on the Opposition benches, having been an observer at the Cabinet Committee on Post-war Reconstruction. I also deputised quite often for my Leader, Lord Salisbury, when he was away on Government business. Some useful social legislation was passed in spite of Parliament's primary concern with the war effort, and I was proud to play a small part in the raising of the school leaving age, the introduction of family allowances, and the start of the mainly post-war housing drive.

[364] Sir John Anderson, later 1st Viscount Waverly (1882–1958), senior civil servant, politician and colonial administrator; governor of Bengal, 1932–1937 and chancellor of exchequer, 1943–1945.

[365] Sir James Grigg (1890–1964), civil servant and minister; finance member of the viceroy's Executive Council in India in the 1930s; returned to Britain in 1939 to be permanent under-secretary of war and then a Cabinet minister as secretary of state for war, 1942–1945.

[366] R.A. 'Rab' Butler, later Lord Butler of Saffron Walden (1902–1982), Conservative MP; president of the Board of Education, 1941–1944; chancellor of the exchequer, 1951–1955; and home secretary, 1957–1962.

[367] Frederick Marquis, Baron Woolton (1883–1964), later earl of Woolton, Conservative peer; minister of food, 1940–1943; minister of reconstruction, 1943–1944; and chairman of the Conservative Party, 1946–1955.

A curious situation arose towards the end of my time as Deputy Leader. Lord Salisbury was chosen as one of the ministerial team to represent the U.K. at the drafting of the Charter of the United Nations at San Francisco. In anticipation of a fairly long absence from the House, he wanted to prepare me to take over while he was away. He had prepared for me an amusing and penetrating character sketch of each of his senior ministerial colleagues. Would that I had kept it! This was accompanied by much sound advice about the management of the House. But my temporary elevation was not to be. When this proposed arrangement for dealing with business during his absence reached the ears of Churchill, it was instantly vetoed. After all, Lord Woolton was a member of the War Cabinet, and a staunch Conservative in an almost completely Conservative Chamber, which made him obviously the best man for the job. There can be little doubt that Churchill was right. So I remained Deputy Leader, while Lord Woolton became Acting Leader of the House. This little episode illustrates the truth of the old saying that there is no love lost at the top in politics.[368]

Early in 1945, after the end of the war with Germany, the Coalition Government broke up, and Churchill formed a Conservative caretaker Government, to tide the country over until the first post-war General Election. I tidied up my own office at the India Office, and bumped into my successor, Lord Scarbrough,[369] who had had some useful experience as Governor of Bombay, on the way out of the building. There was no need for a formal handover, so I just wished him good luck.

When the Coalition broke up, it was typical of Churchill's magnanimous personality to present each of his retiring Ministers from the various shades of the political spectrum with a bronze plaque: inscribed on one side with the words 'Salute to the Great Coalition' framed in a laurel wreath, and on the other, in my case, 'Listowel from Winston Churchill'. The word 'Great' is not I think an exaggeration, when one considers what the Government did for us and for the rest of the free world.

When I look back on the wartime Coalition Government, I suppose it was one of the most gifted, remarkable, and successful Governments in our history. It was indeed a ministry of all the talents. The struggle for our national survival had united the parties,

---

[368] *Lord Salisbury's dislike of Lord Woolton may have contributed to the controversy over the Acting Leadership whilst he was away.*

[369] Sir Roger Lumley (1896–1969), later 11th earl of Scarbrough, Conservative MP then peer, colonial administrator; governor of Bombay, 1937–1943; and under-secretary of state for India and Burma, 1945, in Churchill's Caretaker Administration.

and brought the best men from every walk of life into the Government service. The outstanding personalities in all three political parties – Conservative, Liberal, and Labour – were in the Cabinet, which also included two of the most successful figures in the business world, Lord Woolton and Lord Leathers[370] who respectively had fed the Nation and organised the shipping which carried the food and other wartime necessities. The unity between the parties and the classes reflected the determination of public opinion in our mature democracy to present a united front to the forces of aggression that threatened our national survival.

I would like to include at this point a charming letter I received from Lord Salisbury after the general election in 1945, in reply to a letter I had written to thank him for his kindness to me as Deputy Leader in the Coalition.

Personal

My dear Billy (may I?),

How very nice of you to write me such a charming letter. It has given me immense pleasure. I have always been extremely conscious of my deficiencies as Leader of the House, so, though I am well aware that I do not deserve the kind things you say about me, it was none the less delightful to read them.

May I, in return, say how much I have enjoyed working with you. I feel sure that you have a big future in the House of Lords. Everyone likes you, which is half the battle, and if it is not impertinent for me to say so, your speeches as Deputy Leader have been quite admirable.

It will certainly be a large job for me to lead the Opposition. But you can be quite sure that, so far as I am concerned, there will be no fractious Opposition to the Government, and my impression is that that will be the view of the vast majority of their Lordships. Whether you have got the cure for all our ills I am not so certain; but at any rate the country has decided that they wish you to try your policy out, and if, for instance, you can find a solution to the housing problem, I should imagine that everyone, whatever their party, will breathe a sigh of relief.

At any rate I hope and believe that their Lordships' criticisms – if they do criticise – will always be constructive, and we shall avoid any small wrangling.

Yours ever,

Bobbety[371]

---

[370] Frederick Leathers, 1st Baron Leathers (1883–1965), later Viscount Leathers, British industrialist who served as minister of war transport, 1941–1945.

[371] *I had a charming letter from Bobbety Salisbury's son thanking me for arranging for his father's bust to be placed in the Lords in recognition of his 45 years of service.*

VIII
POSTMASTER GENERAL: 1945

I think we were all astonished by the result of the election in the autumn of 1945.[371] Never before had the Labour Party won a clear majority of seats in the House of Commons. Churchill had gone to the electorate as the victorious war leader, far superior to a mere Party Leader, to whom the people of Britain owed more than to anyone else in the competing political parties. But the war had held up the progress of social reform and economic advance, and the men coming home from the front were looking for a new deal. This had been forecast in the vision of the future adumbrated by Sir William Beveridge[372] in his famous Report on post-war society.

Those who like myself had been Labour Ministers in the wartime Coalition were not unnaturally expecting to be offered a post in the new Government. I had heard that the new Minister of Agriculture, Tom Williams,[373] who had served as a junior Minister in this Department during the war, wanted me as his spokesman in the Lords. This was the most important of the junior appointments in the Upper House, because the majority of Peers were landlords and many farmed their own land. So I was pleasantly surprised when the new Prime Minister, Mr Attlee, offered me the much more interesting and responsible appointment of Postmaster-General. As he had at one time held this office himself,[374] I felt sure that he would not have chosen me if he had not thought I would be up to the job, and this was very reassuring. At the same

---

[371] The result was declared on 26 July 1945 with Labour winning a landslide, gaining 393 of 640 seats.

[372] Sir William Beveridge (1879–1963), later Baron Beveridge, academic and briefly Liberal MP. Author of the 1942 report 'Social Insurance and Allied Services' (better known as the Beveridge Report), which among other things argued the need to abolish the 'five giants' of want, squalor, ignorance, idleness, and disease and has influenced the policies of all British post-war governments, but particularly those of the Labour government of 1945.

[373] *Tom Williams was a delightful person and I would have been delighted to serve under him if Attlee had not thought otherwise.* Tom Williams (1888–1967), later Lord Williams of Barnburgh, Labour MP and minister; minister of agriculture and fisheries, 1945–1951.

[374] Attlee served briefly in 1931 as postmaster general in Ramsay MacDonald's minority Labour administration.

time, with no previous experience of industry or business, I was not a little alarmed, as the youngest of His Majesty's Ministers of Cabinet rank,[375] by the prospect of becoming the largest employer of labour in the country and the head of what was in fact a huge business concern. The office of Postmaster-General had a long and respectable ancestry. It can be traced to 1510, when Henry VIII appointed Brian Tuke[376] to be his Master of the Post, in charge of all the King's Messengers. But the modern Postmaster-General had a great deal more to do than his Tudor predecessor. He was responsible for the Postal Service, which employed over 100,000 postmen to deliver 30,000,000 letters or parcels every day, not to mention the members of the staff of branch Post Offices and Sorting Offices in all the Regions of the Post Office throughout the United Kingdom. He also ran the inland and overseas telegraph and telephone services, and was the banker to whom half the population entrusted its savings. The duties of the Postmaster-General were further increased during my term of office by the transfer of responsibility for the British Broadcasting Corporation, after the winding up of the wartime Ministry of Information. For the efficiency or inefficiency of all three services I, and my excellent Assistant Postmaster-General in the House of Commons, Mr Burke,[377] were responsible to Parliament. We were sometimes referred to as that dangerous couple, Burke & Hare (the notorious murderers).[378]

But I need not have worried. I was in fact no more than a glorified public relations officer, I suppose rather like the Chairman of the Board of Imperial Chemical Industries, or of any other great company in the private sector. The services provided by the Post Office were of course administered by the Director-General, or the professional heads of each of the separate organisations in the field of communications for which I was responsible. I well remember the dapper and elegant Sir Thomas Gardiner,[379] in his Savile Row suit, the Director-General of the Post Office, at its headquarters at St. Martins-le-Grand, coming every morning for several days to my office while he explained to me the ramifications of the Post Office and the many different duties that I was expected to perform. I sat at my huge desk and listened attentively, feeling as I did when as a University student I was imbibing a tutorial from my learned tutor.

---

[375] He was 38.

[376] Sir Brian Tuke (d.1545), court official who served Henry VIII and Cardinal Wolsey.

[377] Wilfrid Burke (1889–1968), Labour MP, assistant postmaster general, 1945–1947.

[378] Spate of infamous murders that occurred in Edinburgh committed by William Burke and William Hare in 1828.

[379] Sir Thomas Gardiner (1883–1964), director general of the Post Office, 1936–1945.

On my first morning I was slightly daunted by the attendant with his top hat and red coat, who greeted me and showed me to my new office. But I soon found that the Post Office was a very friendly place and that there was no need to be tied to my desk in London. It was far more exciting to visit the telephone exchanges and Post Offices in other parts of the country, meeting some at any rate, of those who worked there. Northern Ireland was one of the Regions into which the Post Office was divided, and it was pleasant to go there while a British Minister was still welcome everywhere in the province.

I was fortunate enough to arrive at the Post Office in 1945, when officials were already considering the issue of Victory stamps. Everyone was entirely confident that Parliament and the public generally would welcome such an issue. So I had to set about finding the best artist I could to design the new stamps. Of course I had to point out to any artist wishing to submit a sketch for consideration by the Post Office the limits within which he would have to work. The major factor was the Monarch's head, which would appear in the centre of the stamp. In those days it had not been removed to the top corner.[380] One advantage at any rate, for the design of British stamps, at that time alone in the world, was that it did not have to include the name of the country issuing the stamp. In recognition of the introduction of the penny postage by Sir Rowland Hill[381] in 1840, an invention which brought the post for the first time within reach of the ordinary wage earner, other countries who had since profited from our example had agreed to allow us to leave out the name of our country. My instructions to the designers were the first step of a process that lasted for about a year.

As soon as the artists were ready with their sketches, these were submitted to a number of important bodies for advice about their artistic merits and acceptability to the public. These expert bodies included the Post Office Advisory Council, the Council for Art and Industry, and the Royal Fine Arts Commission. In this way the designs of inferior artistic quality or lesser public appeal were weeded out, leaving the best of the artists sketches for submission to the King. It was at this stage that I received a summons to Buckingham Palace.

The common opinion that the Royal approval of the new postage stamp is a mere formality, like the approval of Acts of Parliament, is entirely erroneous. His Majesty showed a keen and expert interest in

---

[380] *The design of new stamps, such as the issue of victory stamps, was limited by the placing of the monarch's head in the centre. Placing it in the corner has really made modern designs possible.*

[381] Sir Rowland Hill (1795–1879), postal reformer and official.

the various designs, and had himself to choose the sketch that was ultimately used for a new issue. The Monarch can always suggest a minor alteration, and I believe the King liked to consult the Queen about the rendering of his own head. I need hardly say that this does not affect the constitutional position, whereby the Post Master General has the entire responsibility for whatever is finally decided, and must be prepared to accept either the brickbats or the applause of the press. Having received His Majesty's decision, the path was then clear for the printing of the many millions of new stamps as were likely to be required. There must be a sufficient number to meet the first day rush of enthusiastic collectors worldwide, and to cover ordinary public demand for a reasonable period of time. As a footnote to my experience of producing a postage stamp I should perhaps add that I was extremely nervous about the correct protocol for my first meeting with the King.

I should obviously bow when entering the room, but how should I leave it? I thought that it would be rather rude to turn my back on His Majesty, and so I started to shuffle uncomfortably towards the door, wondering how soon I would collide with a piece of furniture. But His Majesty, with perfect tact, solved my predicament by turning right round and looking out of the window.

The only direct contact I can remember with the BBC, was during the fuel crisis in the winter of 1947, when I was asked by the Cabinet to find out whether the Corporation could save a certain amount of electricity. This was rather a delicate matter, and could only be framed as a request, as otherwise it would look like an attempt by the Government to interfere with the sacred independence of the BBC. Sir William Haley[382] responded immediately with fine public spirit by making some domestic cuts in BBC programmes and hours of broadcasting, which saved a very large amount of precious coal. During my term of office I found myself faced with the difficult responsibility of re-appointing the Chairman and Board of Governors of the Corporation. I was much relieved to find that the Cabinet regarded this task as so important that it was taken entirely out of my hands.

Soon after my arrival at St. Martins-le-Grand I received a charming and encouraging letter from my immediate predecessor, Captain Crookshank M.P.,[383] whose universal popularity was a very useful asset. I should like to quote this letter dated August the 8th, 1945.

[382] Sir William Haley (1901–1987), newspaper editor and official; director general of the BBC, 1944–1952.

[383] Harry Crookshank (1893–1961), later Viscount Crookshank, Conservative MP and minister; postmaster general, 1943–1945 and leader of the House of Commons, 1951–1955.

My dear Listowel,
       I was profoundly touched by your kind letter of yesterday and thank you for it. I can only wish you as happy a period of office at St. Martins-le-Grand as I have had myself. Of course if I can be of any (unofficial) help to you, I am at your service 'pro bono G.P.O. [General Post Office]'.

    In spite of the election and all the rest of it, I can't some how feel any different to all those members of your Party with whom one worked amicably for so long until three months ago – that I imagine is the secret of British political life!

Yours sincerely,
Harry Crookshank

It was not surprising that with his genial personality Churchill appointed him as Leader of the House of Commons in his post-war administration.[384]

One of my first duties after my appointment was to attend the launching of the 'Monarch', the largest cable ship in the world, which had just been completed in a shipyard on the east coast. It had been built and equipped to lay and repair submarine cables, in the vast cable network which connected us by telephone and telegraph to the American continent and overseas countries of the Commonwealth. There was a comfortable cabin reserved on board for the owner of the ship – the Postmaster-General. I was told by my officials that a minor repair was required for the cable between London and Copenhagen, and that the Danish Post Office would be delighted if I was to join the ship for the visit. When I asked the Prime Minister for his permission, he immediately grasped the opportunity this offered to inform the Danish public about the work of the Labour Government. So I delivered a lecture in Copenhagen about the recent improvements in our social services, including the introduction of the National Health Service. I had no other chance of 'showing the flag' elsewhere on this magnificent ship during my period of office.

I soon learned several things about the Post Office that one could only learn from the inside. I had not realised that persons as well as things can be sent through the post by express messenger, so that I could also post myself if I wished to do so. As a Post Office messenger has to accompany the goods, this is a convenient method of travel for unaccompanied children or blind persons. This facility has not always been used as it was intended. In the campaign for Women's

---

[384] *The tolerance and mutual respect between the parties in the last sentence of Captain Crookshank's letter has certainly diminished since the war, but still exists and makes democracy work.*

Suffrage, two leading Suffragettes posted themselves to 10 Downing Street. On this occasion the Post Office was thwarted in achieving successful delivery, when the Prime Minister's Butler refused to accept these dangerous postal packets.

Sometimes the official heart gets the better of the official head. Many letters reach the Post Office at Christmas addressed to Santa Claus in some especially cold corner of the globe. If the letter includes the writer's name and address, the correct course is of course to 'return to sender'. But when a letter came from an obviously poor home, the hat went round among postmen or sorters, so that a doll or a teddy bear can arrive on Christmas morning with love from Santa Claus.

I spent many hours in my office when I first came to St. Martins-le-Grand on the saddest of my official duties, the signing of letters of condolence to the next of kin of every employee of the Post Office who had lost his or her life in the war, at home or abroad. 70,000 men and women from the Post Office joined the services on the outbreak of war or soon afterwards. Of these 3,800 gave their lives as soldiers, sailors or airmen, while 415 died at their posts as civilians. General Eisenhower[385] paid them a fine tribute in a letter to my predecessor, Captain Crookshank.

I quote:

> The building of the necessary forces for the operations had involved the construction of a network of communications radiating from points of vital importance in the United Kingdom. The greater part of the work has been undertaken by Engineers and Staff of the General Post Office. It is my great pleasure, on behalf of the Expeditionary Force, to pass on my sincere appreciation for their contribution of the long hours they have worked and the co-operation they have given toward our success.
>
> Signed: Dwight Eisenhower

This of course was in reference to the Normandy landings.

One of the most important functions of the Postmaster-General had always been the issue of postage stamps. This was a matter of concern not only to the philatelist but to stamp dealers all over the world, and also to the Government, which earns substantial revenue from the sale of postage stamps. It is hard to decide how often to make a new issue, and this difficult and important decision rested with the Postmaster-General. Before the last war it was customary for a new permanent issue to appear at the beginning of every

---

[385] General Dwight 'Ike' Eisenhower (1890–1969), supreme commander of the Allied Expeditionary Force, 1943–1945, and later Republican President of the United States of America, 1953–1961.

reign with the head of the new Monarch engraved on each denomination. These permanent issues, starting from the famous Victorian 'Penny Black',[386] have been supplemented, since the Empire Exhibition at Wembley in 1923, by a number of special issues to commemorate events of outstanding significance in our national life. Since the last war, there has been a larger number of special issues that at any time since the introduction of the postage stamp, and they have continued to multiply, so that the original purpose of special issues has been to a large extent diluted by the interests of the Treasury.[387] We are now more like some foreign countries who have always regarded stamps as no more than a revenue-producing commodity, and are constantly putting new designs into circulation.

Too often the fate of Ministers, just as they have got the hang of how a new Department works, has been to find themselves transferred to another Department they know absolutely nothing about. This is exactly what happened to me. I must admit that when Mr Attlee asked me, in the spring of 1947, to leave the Post Office for the India Office, I parted with a pang of regret from a great public service and complex business undertaking, which after a year and a half of intensive study I felt I had just about begun to understand. I was sorry to say goodbye to the senior officials who had given so much time and effort to the education of a pupil now about to leave them. I would also miss my regular talks with the Leaders, Mr Geddes[388] and Mr Edwards,[389] of the two great Trade Unions, the Union of Post Office Workers and the Post Office Engineering Union, whose co-operation and support had made it possible to avoid any industrial strike. To these, and many others at all levels of the Post Office, I shall always be grateful for their kindness.

I still enjoy a pleasant reminder of my happy days at the Post Office whenever a new issue of postage stamps comes along, and my postman brings me a First Day Cover with an example of each new postage stamp in mint condition. As neither I, nor any member of my family collects stamps, I have kept these examples of each new issue long enough to give them better value, when I have sold them to give the proceeds to charity. But I suppose it was natural for the Prime Minister, looking for a successor in the House of Lords to

[386] Issued in 1840.

[387] *There has been a very large increase in the number of 'special issues' of postage stamps since my day and the Treasury has defeated the Post Office.*

[388] Charles Geddes (1897–1983), later Lord Geddes of Epsom, trade unionist, general secretary of the Union of Post Office Workers, 1944–1956.

[389] John Edwards (1904–1959), trade unionist and Labour MP, general secretary of the Post Office Engineering Union, 1938–1947.

Lord Pethick-Lawrence,[390] to choose me, with my experience of India as a Minister in the wartime Coalition to fill this gap in his Cabinet.[391] I remembered the advice of a very old friend, Sir Gilbert Laithwaite,[392] in the Civil Service: 'In politics you should never ask for anything and never refuse.'

---

[390] Frederick Pethick-Lawrence (1871–1961), later Baron Pethick-Lawrence, Labour MP and peer, secretary of State for India, 1945–1947.

[391] *I only found out later from Mountbatten that I was his choice.*

[392] Sir Gilbert Laithwaite (1894–1986), civil servant and diplomat; private secretary to the viceroy, 1936–1943; deputy under-secretary of state for Burma, 1945–1947 and for India, 1947; and permanent under-Secretary for Commonwealth Relations, 1955–1959.

IX
SECRETARY OF STATE FOR INDIA UNTIL
INDEPENDENCE: 1947

As a Junior Minister at the India Office, I joined as an observer the India and Burma Committee of the Cabinet under Attlee's chairmanship in autumn 1944. The agenda of our meetings was a mirror image of the conflict between Wavell,[393] who had succeeded Linlithgow[394] as Viceroy the previous year, and Churchill. He had been sent to India by Churchill as a professional soldier who would keep India quiet until the end of the war, without meddling in politics. It was intended as a strictly law and order job.[395] It must have been a rude shock to the Prime Minister when he soon found out that this professional soldier, not only understood politics, but took a strong view about the immediate necessity for constitutional advance, without waiting for further progress until after the war.

Wavell had set out his opinions in a long letter to the Prime Minster, which I found on my desk when I arrived at the India Office, and I quote the concluding sentences:

> Above all, there is the question of credibility. We have lost the trust and confidence of Indians by promising so much and doing so little, and we have now to convince them of our sincerity. But the real essential is a change of spirit, a change that will convince the average, educated Indian that the British Government is sincere in its intentions, and is friendly towards India … if we want India as a Dominion after the war, we must begin by treating her more like a Dominion now … if certain measures which I would suggest were taken now … I believe it would be possible to effect a considerable improvement.

These modest measures of reform were the main subject of discussion by the India Committee until the Churchill Wartime Coalition

[393] Field Marshal Archibald Wavell (1883–1950), 1st Viscount Wavell, later Earl Wavell, army officer and colonial administrator; viceroy of India, 1943–1946.

[394] Victor Hope, 2nd marquess of Linlithgow (1887–1952), Conservative peer and colonial administrator; viceroy of India, 1936–1943.

[395] *Another reason for sending Wavell to India was because Churchill wanted to replace him by Montgomery.*

Government broke up in May 1945. It might have been expected that a Committee of the calibre of Simon, Anderson, Grigg, Butler, Amery, Cripps and Attlee; men of immense political experience and first-hand knowledge of India, would welcome an immediate policy to increase Indian participation in their own system of government. However, owing to Churchill's unyielding opposition to Indian self-government, the unfortunate Viceroy found no support except from Amery, the well-intentioned but helpless Secretary of State, and on some occasions from Cripps.

Attlee must have been torn between his personal opinions, and his duty, as the Prime Minister's representative on the Committee, to oppose even the smallest step forward while the war continued. He was well aware that Churchill's attitude had not altered since his antagonism to the 1935 India Act, and neatly described it, and the reaction of his Cabinet, in the following words: 'The Cabinet has always deferred to the Prime Minister's passionate feelings about India'. So nothing serious was done by Churchill's Coalition Government to prepare India for the great leap forward that took place so soon after the war. Attlee was unable to come out in his true colours until after the General Election in July 1945. He made sure that Indian independence was again included in the Labour Party's Election Manifesto.

When the India Committee of the Cabinet was reconstituted by Attlee after the Labour Election victory in 1945 it consisted of Stafford Cripps, Ellen Wilkinson, A.V. Alexander,[396] A. Henderson,[397] Lord Stansgate,[398] Lord Pethick-Lawrence, the Secretary of State for India, and myself, with Attlee again in the Chair. This was scarcely a team that could compare in knowledge or intellectual calibre with Churchill's, but the presence of Cripps and Attlee gave it an indispensable link with India and its leaders.

At our first meeting on 17th August, 1947,[399] Cripps and Attlee declared bravely that we must quickly work out a policy to realise the long term undertaking in the Cripps' war time offer. It will be remembered that the essence of what had been offered to India in 1942,[400] when the war was going against us, was a completely

[396] A.V. Alexander (1885–1965), later 1st Earl Alexander of Hillsborough, Labour MP and minister; first lord of the Admiralty, 1940–1945, and minister of defence, 1946–1950; member of the 1946 Cabinet Mission to India and later Labour leader in the House of Lords, 1955–1964.
[397] Arthur Henderson (1893–1968), later Lord Rowley, Labour MP and minister; last under-secretary of state for India and Burma, 1945–1948.
[398] William Wedgwood Benn (1877–1960), later 1st Viscount Stansgate, Labour MP, peer and minister; secretary of state for India, 1929–1931.
[399] 1945.
[400] The so called 'Cripps Offer'.

independent Indian Union as soon as hostilities were over, which would later decide whether or not to stay in the British Commonwealth. Thus it was plain to us from the start that our job was to replace British by Indian rule within the lifetime of the Labour Government. Little did we expect that our assignment would be complete within two years.

The Committee was guided by two strong personalities, Attlee and Cripps: the latter playing the major role. For Cripps was the only member with recent first hand experience of India, which he combined with personal acquaintance or even friendship with all the Indian leaders. He dominated the deliberations of the India Committee by his formidable fund of knowledge, his resourceful and inventive mind, his dialectical skill, and his strong political will. This impression was not confined to those who shared his politics. Wavell was often an observer at our meetings. He noticed with grudging admiration in his Journal, when recording his unfavourable impression of the India Committee, that 'Cripps is of course the directing brain'.

I soon learned about the abject and humiliating thraldom in which the Viceroy was held. He was fettered hand and foot by the Churchill Government, and could do nothing without the express authority of the India Committee or the Cabinet. He even had to ask permission when he wanted to meet Indian political leaders as recounted by Wavell to Mountbatten[401] in Simla in 1944. Wavell had asked permission from the Secretary of State to meet with Gandhi[402] when the latter was released from prison on account of illness. He had been mortified when this request was turned down, and he said Churchill was furious about Gandhi's release. He simply could not see how he could go on governing India with such restrictions imposed upon him. Mountbatten then asked him why he had not simply arranged to see Gandhi on his way between prison and hospital for an informal talk: Wavell replied that this would have been against his orders. He had a soldier's conception of obedience to his superiors.

I had met Wavell from time to time in London, when he had returned for discussions with Churchill and the Secretary of State. On social occasions he could be an embarrassment. He lacked the

---

[401] Admiral Lord Louis Mountbatten (1900–1979), later Earl Mountbatten of Burma, naval officer and colonial administrator; supreme Allied commander, South-East Asia Command, 1943–1946; last viceroy of India, 1947; first governor general of India, 1947–1948; chief of the Defence Staff, 1959–1965.

[402] 'Mahatma' Mohandas Gandhi (1869–1948), Indian freedom fighter and Indian National Congress leader; assassinated 1948.

small change of polite conversation, and at meals sitting between two ladies there could be long silences. This innate reserve deprived him of the diplomatic qualities needed for many useful and important personal relationships in public life especially in India. But appearing before a Committee of Ministers, he became a different person. If he was not as quick as some in oral argument, he had immense fluency and complete mastery of his subject.

The recommendations of the India Committee had of course to be endorsed by the Cabinet, and it was in the Cabinet Room that Attlee took the lead. He, not Cripps, put the case for the Committee, and it was inevitably agreed by the whole Cabinet. The only colleague whose Opposition he may have feared, because at heart he deplored the dissolution of the British Empire, was that of the Foreign Secretary, Ernest Bevin.[403] But there seemed to be a tacit agreement between the two men that, if Attlee gave Bevin a free hand over foreign policy, Bevin would give Attlee a free hand over India. So it was that the recommendations of the India Committee sailed through the Cabinet with little discussion and no substantial alterations. The absence of argument was not due to indifference, but a general agreement between Ministers about the direction of policy, which had indeed been laid down in our Election Manifesto in 1945.

Our first year and a half, from 1945 to 1946, was a record of abortive attempts to bring the Hindus and Muslims together. But the differences between Nehru and Jinnah,[404] who were heavily at odds over the claim to a separate State of Pakistan, could not be reconciled by the Cabinet Mission to India in 1946 or by the London Conference of Indian Leaders that followed it.

Wavell, after his failure to bring the parties together at the Simla Conference,[405] now realised we were drifting towards sporadic and dangerous violence and ultimate disaster, and that we must have a long term plan for the future of India. He offered us two alternatives, either to enforce British rule for at least 15 years, or to abdicate by a phased withdrawal. The former would entail the reinforcement of the Indian Army by 4–5 Divisions of British troops. This alternative was quickly dismissed as unacceptable to public opinion in the aftermath of the world war.

[403] Ernest Bevin (1881–1951), trade unionist, Labour MP and minister; minister of labour, 1940–1945 and foreign secretary, 1945–1951.

[404] Mohammad Ali Jinnah (1876–1948), Indian and Pakistani politician and head of the Muslim League; first governor general of Pakistan, 1947–1948.

[405] A meeting convened by Wavell of main Indian political leaders in June 1945 to agree a plan for Indian self-government and unity, held in Simla, the summer capital of the Raj. The plan was hamstrung by disagreements over Muslim representation, among other things.

The second alternative was a phased withdrawal of our armed forces, civil servants, and those British civilians who wished to leave, by stages from British India, starting from the four Congress Provinces in the South, while holding temporarily the Muslim majority Provinces in the North. The total withdrawal was to be completed by March 31st, 1948. It should be noted that Wavell was the first person to suggest a fixed date for the termination of British rule. Apart from Pethick-Lawrence, who to the end was loyal to the Viceroy, the India Committee was unanimous in its rejection of the defeatism of a proposal which was based on complete pessimism about the chances of finding agreement between the two communities. At home the country would have been divided by the outrage of the Conservatives amid Churchillian cries of 'scuttle'. It now became clear that, as neither of the alternative policies offered by Wavell were acceptable, we must look for a new Viceroy to bring us out of India with the widest possible measure of agreement between the Communities.

I have no direct evidence of the origin of the choice of Mountbatten to succeed Wavell, as neither Attlee nor Cripps discussed it with me. But he had already been talked about by Ministers in 1942 and 1943, when consideration was being given to a successor to Linlithgow. Churchill had in mind to give one of two top posts to Mountbatten at this time, either that of Viceroy of India or that of Supreme Commander in South-East Asia. He decided in accordance with the wishes of the Americans and Chiefs of Staff to send him to South East Asia. This, fortunately, was exactly what Mountbatten himself greatly preferred. But I suspect that Cripps was already considering a successor for Wavell in 1946, when he was in New Delhi with the Cabinet Mission, as he hated the Viceroy's defeatism. Sir Prenderil [*sic*] Moon[406] states that Mountbatten's name was mentioned in the presence of Major Short, the Mission's advisor on the Sikhs. In his view at least Cripps already had Mountbatten in mind as the man he wanted to replace Wavell. In his autobiography Attlee claims that Mountbatten's name came to him as an 'inspiration'. But his memory of events was not always reliable, and it is hard to imagine that Mountbatten's name never came up in talks with Cripps.

Mountbatten considered that Attlee may have been influenced by Mountbatten's actions as Supreme Allied Commander South East Asia[407] after the Japanese surrender: –

---

[406] Sir Penderel Moon (1905–1987), colonial and Indian administrator, and writer. Among works he wrote after leaving India in 1961 were *Divide and Quit* (1961) and editing *Wavell: The Viceroy's Journal* (London, 1973).

[407] *Mountbatten's Headquarters in South East Asia were in Ceylon.*

Here I had a case of 125 million native populations in the liberated area with whom I had to deal. Practically all my staff and certainly all the Civil Affairs Officers who had been recruited for military administration wished to re-impose Colonial rule in Burma, Malaya, Singapore, North Borneo, etc. The Governments in Paris and the Hague wished to do this by force of arms without incidentally having any Military means of doing it. At every turn I was faced with the fact that I was a voice crying in the wilderness, feeling convinced that the time had come when not only had the British but the French and the Dutch and any other Colonial powers to make friends with their Colonial populations and try and persuade them to remain voluntarily in an overall form of Commonwealth, British, French or Dutch ...

When I was recalled for the Potsdam Conference and Winston lost the election I went to see Attlee, my new boss, and I told him exactly what I was doing and what my policy was and confessed to him that I kept it as secret as possible from Whitehall because I knew that Winston would fire me immediately if he knew what I was doing. So Attlee said that he entirely agreed with my policy and gave me his word that he would back me up to the hilt if I continued doing what I had set out to do.[408]

Mountbatten also believed that Attlee may have approved of his handling of Nehru's visit[409] to Singapore and Malaya: –

Practically, the whole of my staff were against Nehru's visit to South East Asia. On my return from one of my routine visits to different parts of my vast command I enquired what preparations had been made for Nehru's visit to Singapore. I had then discovered to my horror that the local Military Authorities in Singapore were about to issue an order that all Indian Troops were to be confined to Barracks while Nehru was in the area, that they were in no circumstances to provide any form of transport for him or his people and that his visit should be played down in every way possible.

I immediately got hold of my best Indian Brigadier, Muchu Chaudhury,[410] and put him in charge of Nehru's visit personally with full authority from me. I lent Nehru one of my own cars for his personal use. I had him met by a senior officer of my staff who brought him to see me in Government House in Singapore and I then drove with him in an open car, very much against the advice of my staff, through the streets of

[408] *Letter from Mountbatten to me dated 3 October 1978.*
[409] In March 1946.
[410] J.N. 'Muchu' Chaudhuri (1908–1983), later General J.N. Chaudhuri; senior Indian Officer in the British Indian and Indian Armies and diplomat; later military governor of Hyderabad, 1948, and chief of the Army Staff, 1962–1966.

Singapore to the Indian Red Cross where we were to see Edwina[411] who was working with them. That evening he dined with us and we made lifelong friends'.

There followed a crucial meeting between Cripps, Attlee, and Mountbatten, when Mountbatten laid down the conditions on which he would accept the Viceroyalty. The most fundamental condition was the request for plenipotentiary powers. After Wavell's difficulties, Mountbatten was convinced of his need for such powers, indeed, Mountbatten stated that Churchill's refusal to allow Wavell to meet Gandhi was 'uppermost in my mind when I demanded plenipotentiary powers from Attlee'.[412]

Mountbatten gave a graphic account of the reception of such a request:

'Mr Attlee consulted Sir Stafford Cripps, and even after 22 years I can remember his next words 'You are asking for plenipotentiary powers over His Majesty's Government. No-one has been given such powers in this century'. There was silence for quite a while, and then he went on 'Surely you cannot mean this.' Escape at last, I thought, as I firmly replied that I did mean just that, and would understand, if, as a result, the appointment was withdrawn. Cripps then nodded his head, and Attlee replied 'All right, you've got the powers and the job.' It was interesting, I thought, that Cripps was the first to indicate agreement, and that Attlee took his cue from him.[413]

There was indeed no precedent for any Viceroy to have this power, though Mountbatten was not the first to ask for it. Lord Morley[414] refers in his recollections to the occasion when this request was put to him, as Secretary of State for India, by the then Viceroy, Lord Minto,[415] and curtly refused. 'This notion of the free hand', he wrote, 'is really against the letter and spirit of the law and constitution.'

Whatever the merits of the constitutional argument, Attlee was surely right to agree. No-one but Mountbatten would have had a

[411] Edwina Mountbatten (1901–1960), later Countess Mountbatten of Burma; during the Second World War worked for Red Cross, also superintendent-in-chief of St John's Ambulance, 1942; last vicereine of India, 1947.

[412] *Letter from Mountbatten to me dated 3 October 1978.*

[413] *Mountbatten's Nehru Memorial Lecture.* Lord Mountbatten, 'Reflections on the Transfer of Power and Jawaharlal Nehru', 2nd Nehru Memorial Lecture, Cambridge, 14 November 1968. The last sentence of the above quotation does not appear in the speech.

[414] John Morley (1838–1923), later Viscount Morley of Blackburn, Liberal MP, peer and minister, and writer; secretary of state for India, 1905–1910, and, briefly, in 1911.

[415] Gilbert Elliot-Murray-Kynynmound, 4th earl of Minto (1845–1914), colonial administrator; viceroy of India, 1905–1910.

chance of success in the mission he was undertaking to bring about Indian independence had he been obliged to refer back to Whitehall before every decision. It was one of those rare conjunctions in history between the right man and the right moment. If Attlee had consulted the Cabinet, there would also have been the risk of a disastrous 'leak'. One can imagine what they, particularly Bevin, would have thought of Mountbatten's 'plenipotentiary powers'.

The other condition not accepted without considerable argument was the fixing of a terminal date for British rule in India. He had to overcome Attlee's reluctance to be pinned down to a precise date, but his refusal to compromise resulted in agreement that the Raj would end not later than 20th June, 1948.

I did not know until 1978, when I had a letter from Mountbatten, that at this meeting he had also asked for my appointment as Secretary of State for India:

Dear Billy,

What you may not have known is that I coupled with the grant of plenipotentiary powers the request that Pethick-Lawrence should be removed from the Secretary of State for India on the grounds that he was a quarter of a century older than me and of a different generation. I asked for somebody to be appointed of my generation and preferably younger than me and I had the temerity to suggest your name personally for although I did not know you well you were exactly the sort of person I felt I could work with. This proved to be absolutely the case and I should like to take this opportunity of thanking you personally for the wonderful support you gave me all the way through.

Yours ever,
Dickie[416]

It was understandable that Mountbatten preferred a young man who would do what he was told, without too much argument, to a much older man who already had strong views of his own about India.

When Mountbatten left for India at the end of February he carried with him a directive from Attlee to secure agreement for a united India, comprising British India and the Princely States, and broadly in line with the scheme of the Cabinet Mission which had visited India the previous summer. But if the two major parties, the Congress Party and the Muslim League, were still not agreed to participate in the Government of a United India, he was to advise the Cabinet how and to whom to hand over by June 1948.

[416] *Letter from Mountbatten to me dated 3 October 1978.*

I was appointed Secretary of State for India in April, and my appointment evoked the following letter from Mountbatten: –

The Viceroy's House,
New Delhi
22nd April 1947

My Dear Listowel,

I feel I must write in extension of my telegram to reiterate my congratulations on your courageous assumption of so heavy and responsible a task, and to assure you of my loyalty and cooperation.

There are momentous times ahead, but I am heartened by the thought that we shall be in partnership for them, and that I shall have your guidance and support in my handling of affairs on the spot.

Yours sincerely,
Mountbatten

Mountbatten set out on his task in characteristic fashion. For the first week in New Delhi he spent his time making friends with Jinnah and renewing friendship with Nehru, the leaders of the League and Congress respectively, and their families, without even breathing a word about politics. He then put his plan for a united India to the two party leaders. He reported to us with deep regret that Jinnah was adamant about the establishment of Pakistan as a separate nation, and would accept nothing less. They could only agree to disagree. He was therefore in the process of drawing up his own plan for the division of India. Such a plan, we of course realised, was the only safeguard against an even greater evil than partition. For if the British left India within a year, without any agreement between Muslims and Hindus to set up a separate Government for the predominantly Hindu and Muslim areas, the two communities would fight for mastery, and the sub-continent would break up, like the Mogul Empire of the 17th century, into a welter of warring fragments. This was the situation as I found it when I arrived at the India Office at the end of April 1947. We were still waiting for the promised partition plan.

We did not have long to wait before it reached us in London, brought by Lord Ismay,[417] personal adviser to Mountbatten, to explain its contents. It was considered by the India Committee at three long meetings in the first week of May, and approved with only minor alterations on May 8th. Attlee was asked to report to the Cabinet on May 13th. In the meantime we heard, to our dismay,

[417] General Hastings 'Pug' Ismay (1887–1965), later Baron Ismay, army officer, official and minister; chief of staff to Viceroy Mountbatten; secretary of state for Commonwealth Relations, 1951–1952; and first secretary general of NATO, 1952–1957.

that Mountbatten had changed his mind about the plan. In his own words 'he had a hunch' that he should show it to Nehru, in spite of the contrary advice of his staff. Nehru, he said, was aghast when he had studied it. But our feelings in Whitehall can well be imagined. We were being asked to reverse a decision that had just been taken at Cabinet level.

I took the view that the Viceroy must be allowed to change his mind, but that he would be unlikely to convert the Cabinet unless he came home to put his case in person. I consulted Lord Ismay, as I knew Attlee would consult him, but he disagreed, probably wishing to protect his master from an unwelcome recall to London. It would also put him in the shade. I always turned to Cripps for advice in an emergency, and this seemed just such an occasion. I found, to my relief, that he, Cripps, agreed with me, and said he would tell Attlee he was in favour of Mountbatten's recall to London. The Viceroy's account of this episode is slightly different; he has said that the alternative to his return was to send a Cabinet Minister to New Delhi. This may have been suggested privately by Attlee, but I was unaware of it. If the suggestion was made I am delighted Mountbatten turned it down.

So it was that Attlee, instead of reporting to the Cabinet about the partition plan on May 18th, simply informed his colleagues that Mountbatten had been asked to return for talks with the India Committee. On the following day Mountbatten appeared before the Committee to explain the reasons for his change of mind, and to submit a revised plan which he said met Nehru's agonising doubts about its predecessor. We were told that Nehru's main objection to the original plan was that it would allow the Provinces to choose independence, either alone or in groups. He thought the Princely States would follow suit, and that this would result in the 'balkanisation' of India.

The revised plan closed this loophole by confining the Provinces to a straight choice between India and Pakistan, and in this form it was acceptable to both Congress and the League. Mountbatten went on to inform us that both new nations now wanted to stay in the Commonwealth, while reserving the right to secede, but only if their independence could be expedited to a much earlier date than we had anticipated. We were particularly surprised and delighted by the change in the attitude of the Congress leaders, who had so recently declared for an 'Independent Sovereign Republic'.[418] Mountbatten pointed out that Jinnah had always wanted Pakistan to become a Dominion in the Commonwealth, with the same status

---

[418] A resolution passed in the Indian Constituent Assembly on 22 January 1947.

as the old Dominions. Congress realised that this would place them at a serious disadvantage, and had therefore asked for a similar constitutional status provided only that the transfer could be effected much earlier than June 1948.

We could hardly do less than agree without a murmur to a scheme that had the blessing of both the Viceroy and the two religious communities. We also agreed to do our utmost to bring forward that date of independence to the autumn of the current year, in spite of the Parliamentary problems that such a timetable would confront us. We had at last achieved a goal that had eluded us for so long, and Wavell for even longer, an agreement between the two main religious communities, the Hindus and the Muslims, about the future of India after British rule. The leaders of both communities had had the wisdom to accept a compromise. For Jinnah the partition plan gave him a 'moth-eaten' Pakistan, because it obliged him to share Bengal and the Punjab with Nehru. The Congress leader disliked it equally because he had lost his dream of a united India.

Our agreement to bring forward the date of independence to the autumn of 1947 meant that we must have the consent of parliament before the summer recess at the end of July. There were two equally important conditions for the success of our effort to get the Bill through both Houses before the recess. The first was the time it would take to draft the Bill to transfer power to the two new Dominions, and the second being the support of the Conservative Opposition in both the House of Lords and House of Commons. Mr Rowlatt,[419] the senior Parliamentary draftsman, assured the Indian Committee that he could prepare a Bill within 6 weeks of receiving our instructions. We finalised our instructions on May 22nd and Attlee told the Cabinet on June 26th that a draft Bill was ready. I do not suppose any Bill of this constitutional importance in our whole Parliamentary history has ever been drafted so quickly. In the first draft, the Bill was entitled 'The India (Dominion Status) Bill'. But Cripps immediately pointed out that Indian opinion would think that we were giving something less than complete independence, and that this key word should appear on the face of the Bill. So the title was changed to 'India (Independence) Bill' by the Cabinet on June 26th.

The support of the opposition parties was essential to a quick passage of the Bill through Parliament. Attlee knew that he would have no trouble with the Leader of the Liberal Party,[420] but had the good

[419] John Rowlatt (1898–1956), later Sir John Rowlatt, parliamentary draftsman; later first parliamentary draftsman to the Treasury, 1953–1956.
[420] Clement Davies (1884–1962), Liberal MP and leader of the Liberal Party, 1945–1956.

sense not to tackle the Leader of the Conservative Party, Winston Churchill, himself. Instead he asked Mountbatten, whose war record was much admired by Churchill, strongly as he disapproved of his political ideas, to undertake this delicate task. Not the least of Mountbatten's services to India, was his success in persuading Churchill, the lifelong opponent of Indian self-government, to support the Bill. His assent made freedom the gift not just of the Labour Party, but of the whole nation. His conversion was due to the acceptance by both new countries of Dominion Status, and the agreement of both leaders to stay in the Commonwealth after independence. We were fortunate that Churchill was a statesman as well as a Party Leader, and too big a man to turn such an issue to party advantage. He alone could have made the Conservative Party face the embarrassing volte-face after its attack on the Government in February for leaving India.

Before the terms of the Bill could be settled, we had to decide about the future of the Princely States, which at that time occupied about one-third of the geographical area of India. As the paramount power, the India Committee took the view that we had no right under our Treaties with the States to transfer unilaterally our duties and obligations to anyone else. But it was obvious that after British troops and the British administration had been withdrawn from India we could no longer fulfil our obligations to protect the Princely States. The paramountcy of the protecting power would therefore lapse with British rule, and they would become completely autonomous. The choice before them would therefore be either to join one of the two Dominions, or to sustain their precarious independence without the buttress of British power. So the Bill provided that paramountcy would terminate on the date of the transfer of power. It was one of Mountbatten's outstanding feats of diplomacy, which he owed not a little to his royal blood and cousinship,[421] that he persuaded the vast majority of the small autocracies to accede to one or other of the two new Dominions. It was not his fault that Kashmir and Hyderabad stood out, leaving a legacy of bitter conflict to India and Pakistan.[422]

To return now to the progress of the Bill through Parliament. The final stages of its preparation were a race against time. The deadline was July the 10th, which meant that it had to be taken through both

---

[421] Mountbatten was the second cousin of George VI, Emperor of India.

[422] *It should be remembered that Nehru's home was in Kashmir and Hyderabad was the largest and best armed of the India States.* Hyderabad was incorporated into the Indian Union by military intervention in September 1948, while Kashmir, which lies between India and Pakistan, remains a hotly contested area and issue for both states.

Houses in a fortnight. Mountbatten had expressed a keen wish to discuss the text of the Bill with the Indian Leaders. The request was without precedent, as no United Kingdom Bill had ever before been submitted for scrutiny and comment by politicians in other countries. The idea was strongly supported by Cripps, but Attlee, with characteristic caution, was afraid that the Opposition might scent a breach of parliamentary privilege, and wanted us to wait until he had seen and spoken to them. He reported that the Opposition Leaders had no objection, provided that they saw the Bill first.

We did not receive the Congress and the Muslim League comments on the Bill and Mountbatten's comments on their comments until shortly before the India Committee met at 9.30 pm on July 3rd. That evening the Committee sat until midnight adding the amendments asked for by our critics, and it was just possible to get a copy of the amended Bill to the Clerk at the Table of the House of Commons by 1.00 am, the latest possible time if the Bill was to reach the House that day. It was printed during the course of the night, and formally presented to the House by the Prime Minister at 11.00 am on July 4th.

With the blessing of all three political parties, it was certain that the Bill would have a smooth passage through Parliament. The built-in Government majority assured its acceptance by the Commons, but I had some anxious moments in the Lords. A single successful amendment would have sent the Bill back to the Commons, breaching our agreement with the Indian leaders and delaying the Bill and with it Indian Independence, until after the long summer recess.

There was some uneasiness about our treatment of the Princely States, which were thought by some Peers to have been given less than a fair deal. This view was expressed by Lord Salisbury, a former Leader of the Lords, and Lord Templewood,[423] who, as Secretary of State for India, had been responsible for the 1935 Government of India Act. Several amendments had been tabled. I was greatly relieved when, sensing the feeling of the House, after a speech supporting it by Lord Halifax, none of these amendments were even moved.[424] This made it possible for the Royal Assent to be given to the Bill by a Royal Commission sitting in the House of Lords on

[423] 1st Viscount Templewood, formerly Sir Samuel Hoare (1880–1959), Conservative MP, minister, and diplomat; secretary of state for India, 1931–1935; foreign secretary, 1935 and lord privy seal, 1939–1940.

[424] *The speech of Lord Halifax, an ex-Viceroy, was the only occasion I can remember in 63 years when a single speech has changed the opinion of the House.*

Friday July 18th, only two days ahead of our deadline. To mark the significance of this historic moment in our parliamentary history, there was a 'five-man' Commission of Privy Councillors on the wool-sack, such as is normally reserved for the Royal Assent to the Dissolution of Parliament before a General Election. The Royal Commissioners, seated on either side of the Lord Chancellor,[425] were Lord Lytton[426] (former Governor of Bengal), Lord Llewelyn [sic][427] (a Cabinet Minister), Lord Stansgate (former Secretary of State for India), and myself.[428]

The Punjab tragedy[429] was an inevitable consequence of the division of British India, and it could only have been avoided if the unity of India had been preserved. By the time Mountbatten went out it was already too late. The divisive process became increasingly difficult to reverse from the moment when the Muslim League became committed to Pakistan in 1940. As Mountbatten relates: –

> I never had a chance of convincing Jinnah that he was wrong in insisting on complete partition because he was so pathological on the subject that one could not move him. On the other hand I understand that he only gradually became so obstinate and at one time might have been moved if the right arguments had been put to him in a way that he would have considered them seriously. Personally I could visualise having the chance of converting him to a unified India if I had been able to get there before his mind had been made up in this obstinate manner. He was the key to partition as Gandhi realised when he made his famous suggestion to me that I should reform the Cabinet making Jinnah the Prime Minister.[430]

There can be no doubt that the British alone had the power to transfer their sovereignty to a united India. Gandhi had asked for dominion status at the Round Table Conference in 1931, and he was the voice of the majority. Before 1940 the transition could have undoubtedly been made without providing separate homelands

---

[425] William Jowitt (1885–1957), 1st Viscount Jowitt, later Earl Jowitt, Labour MP, Labour peer and minister; lord chancellor, 1945–1951.

[426] Victor Bulwer-Lytton, 2nd earl of Lytton (1876–1947), Liberal peer and colonial administrator; governor of Bombay, 1922–1927.

[427] John Llewellin (1893–1957), later Baron Llewellin, Conservative MP and peer; minister in the wartime coalition; first governor general of the Federation of Rhodesia and Nyasaland, 1953–1957.

[428] The five peers dressed in their robes of scarlet and ermine for the occasion, witnessed by Attlee at the bar of the House, as the Royal Assent was given for this historic Act that enabled the ending of British rule over India.

[429] This refers to the bloody division of the critical state of Punjab, as a result of the Radcliffe Boundary Commission demarcating the borders between India and Pakistan, and the chaos of the migration of whole communities forced to leave their homes.

[430] *Letter from Mountbatten to me dated 3 October 1978.*

for the two religious communities. But British statesmanship in the decade of appeasement was at the lowest ebb that I can remember. It is not surprising that the vision was lacking and that the last opportunity was thrown away. The 1935 India Act might have been that opportunity, if we had insisted on its implementation instead of allowing the Princes to exercise their veto. Instead of granting the self-government which had been promised since 1917, or insisting on federation, we clung to power under the cloak of respectability lent by protection for the minorities until we were forced to part with it by our own reduced circumstances after five years of war. The transfer of power in 1947 was no more than a mitigation of the failure of British policy to part with power earlier to an united India.[431]

I stayed with the Mountbattens for a few days in New Delhi after independence, during the dreadful massacres in the Punjab. Lady Mountbatten dashed off, quite regardless of personal risk, to look round the hospitals where the sick and wounded were being treated. She must have seemed very different from the dignified but somewhat aloof Vicereines to whom India was accustomed. Her immense energy and exceptional ability as a public speaker won her a unique place in the affections of the ordinary people. One of the first things she did after moving into the Viceroy's House was to see for herself the living conditions of the multitude of servants whose homes were in the Viceregal compound, and to urge immediate improvement of their wretched quarters. She would go long distances in the heat of the Indian summer to visit a hospital in some remote part of the country.

I was determined to meet Mahatma Gandhi before I left India. This was not altogether easy to arrange as he was staying, as he often did, in the home of a sweeper. I naturally suggested that I should see him there, but he replied that he would prefer to come to meet me. I was really astonished that he had such a wide and up to date knowledge of politics, not merely the politics of India, but the political situation in the UK. This rare combination of the politician and the saint was surely something unique, and without it a smooth and rapid transfer of power would have been difficult, if not impossible.[432]

It was the combination of Gandhi and Nehru that made possible the transfer as early as August 1947. The agreement of Congress was of course indispensable. But Congress itself depended on the support

---

[431] *Due to our policy of giving independence to our colonies, we were the only colonial power in South East Asia to leave on good terms with the incoming governments, as compared with the French in Indo-China and the Dutch in Indonesia and Timor. This set the pattern for independence for our other colonies such as Ceylon/Sri Lanka.*

[432] *Ghandi [sic] retired from politics with a broken heart after the decision to divide India.*

of the Indian masses. It was Gandhi, not Nehru, who touched the hearts of the peoples of India. His belief in god as the source of truth which laid down the moral law which forbids untouchability, the caste system and the inequality of women, and which insisted that non-violence was the only way in which these evils could be removed; this was the teaching which went over the heads of the Congress leaders and made the Indian masses his devout disciples.

My most vivid recollection of Mountbatten in his new role of Governor-General was to find him directing as Chairman the work of the Indian Cabinet Committee dealing with the war in the Punjab. It was certainly a novel role for a constitutional Governor-General, and must have shocked some of his colleagues in the old Dominions. Another typically Mountbatten touch to show that he was sharing the food shortage with the rest of India, was to serve spam for lunch at Viceroy's House. I had only tasted this insipid meat substitute once before, during the war when meat was rationed on a weekly basis. In the evenings we were deluged with war films. I did not get the impression Mountbatten had much time or taste for reading.

The curtain that rose over the two new Dominions of India and Pakistan, fell simultaneously on the 89 years of the Indian Empire. On August 15th the India Office ceased to exist, and the last of a long line of Secretaries of State for India became extinct.

My only remaining duty was to hand over my Seals of Office to the King. His Majesty, who had just started his autumn holiday with his family at Balmoral, was good enough to say that he would like to thank me personally for what the India Office had done to bring about the transition from Empire to Dominion. For the journey from London, a Viking of the King's Flight was placed at my disposal. I arrived at the castle half an hour late for tea. The Royal Family had waited, with characteristic courtesy, for my arrival, and when we sat down at a small table on the terrace I noticed with relief that I seemed to be the only guest. The little Princesses, Elizabeth and Margaret, waited on us, handing around the scones and cakes.

After tea the King said he would like a word with me in his study. He was obviously extremely pleased that a member of his own family had played the leading role in the achievement of Indian independence, and thanked me for the help I had been able to give him from Whitehall. Having in mind, I suppose, the shower of honours Mountbatten had recommended for his staff, and the Earldom he had conferred on his cousin, he asked me whether my services had been recognised. This was a somewhat embarrassing question, as Attlee had not in fact at that time offered me anything. I forget what exactly I said, but I think my answer was that I had only been in office for a short time, and had not expected recognition of my brief tenure of the Cabinet post. When the King told me he meant to keep the Seals of the Secretary of State in his library at Windsor, I had to confess that my Department had failed to find them, and thought that they must have been lost in the distant past.

I was glad to find that Lady Delia Peel,[433] an old friend of my mother, was the Lady-in-Waiting at the time, as she was able to tell me about the etiquette of the Royal Family, and it made my weekend very much easier. I was not even surprised by the piper who marched round the table at dinner in the evening.

The attainment of Dominion Status in August 1947 was of course no more than a device to give self-government at the earliest possible moment, and did not pre-judge the decision India would ultimately take in the Constituent Assembly following independence as to whether it would remain a member of the Commonwealth. When it transpired that India did want to stay in the Commonwealth, but as a Republic instead of a Monarchy, the dangerously divisive problem again arose as whether these decisions could be mutually compatible. It was certainly clear that the Crown link could not be severed without the agreement of the existing Commonwealth countries, and Attlee was determined to do his utmost to obtain their consent, and at all costs to avoid a breakup of the Commonwealth. Burma had already left the Commonwealth after declaring itself a Republic.[434]

In March 1949 he therefore despatched his emissaries to prepare the ground for the coming Prime Ministers Conference in London, which would be a turning-point in the history of the Commonwealth.

These emissaries were chosen from the Ministers and Officials who had had considerable experience of Indian and Commonwealth affairs. They were Sir Norman Brook,[435] then Secretary to the Cabinet, who went to Canada, Mr Gordon Walker[436] who went to Pakistan and Sri Lanka,[437] Sir Percival [sic] Liesching,[438] Head of the Commonwealth Relations Office who went to South Africa,

[433] Lady Delia Peel, née Spencer (1889–1981), Woman of the Bedchamber to Queen Elizabeth from 1938.
[434] In January 1948.
[435] Sir Norman Brook (1902–1967), later Baron Normanbrook, civil servant; secretary to the Cabinet, 1947–1962.
[436] Patrick Gordon Walker (1907–1980), later Lord Gordon-Walker, Labour MP and minister; under-secretary of state for Commonwealth Relations, 1947–1950; secretary of state for Commonwealth Relations, 1950–1951; and, briefly, foreign secretary, 1964–1965.
[437] Then named Ceylon.
[438] Sir Percivale Liesching (1895–1973), civil servant; permanent under-secretary of state for Commonwealth Relations, 1949–1955.

while I was sent to Australia and New Zealand. The purpose of our mission was to persuade the Prime Ministers of the other Commonwealth countries that the flexibility of the bonds uniting the Commonwealth would allow them to be stretched so as to accommodate, for the first time, a Republic. This meant that the advantages of keeping India within the Commonwealth outweighed the disadvantages of losing the common link with the Crown. This, broadly, was the argument we were briefed to put to the old Commonwealth countries.

There were affirmative responses from Canada, Pakistan, Sri Lanka and South Africa, and I found that my old friend Prime Minister Chiffley, when I met him in Canberra, was keenly aware of the importance to Australia of the closest possible relationship with his Asian neighbour. But I had a very different experience in New Zealand. There I found Prime Minister Fraser to be dead against any weakening of the position of the Crown, for which he said the people of New Zealand had such a strong affection. I had two long sessions with him on successive days, but I could not shake what he regarded as the traditional loyalty of the people of New Zealand to the Crown. Far from being a dour Scot, he was so voluble that I found it quite difficult to get a word in when I wanted to meet his arguments.

So I returned to London with a confession of failure. Attlee, however, told me not to be too despondent, as he was sure Mr Fraser would come round when he found that he and the other Prime Ministers were against him. Attlee's forecast was right, and at the Commonwealth Prime Ministers Conference in June 1950[439] it was decided unanimously to find a place in the Commonwealth for the new Republic of India. I had a note from Attlee thanking me for my contribution, in visiting the Southern Dominions, to the success of the Commonwealth Conference.

The King would acquire the additional title of 'Head of the Commonwealth' – first suggested in the Cabinet by Cripps – as well as those already appertaining to the British Sovereign, although losing the 'I' in his signature of George, 'R & I' ('Rex et Imperator').[440] This momentous decision made it possible within the next 30 years to transform the old Commonwealth of British origin into the new Commonwealth of today, with a majority of

[439] Actually it was at the conference of Commonwealth prime ministers in April 1949 at which India's status as a republic within the Commonwealth and the King's position as head of the Commonwealth were enshrined in the 'London Declaration', at the conclusion of the conference.
[440] Due to ceasing to be Emperor of India.

Republics among the predominantly African and Asian membership. Thus the decolonisation of the British Empire, starting from India and Pakistan, led to more rather than less goodwill between the United Kingdom and its former dependencies, who now enjoyed not only their freedom from colonial status but, as well, a new world-wide partnership between free and equal nations.

India: 37 years after independence

I paid my last visit to India in 1978, when I was invited by the UK branch of the Commonwealth Parliamentary Association [CPA] to lead a delegation of members of both houses to visit their branches throughout India. Our party consisted of six members of the House of Commons and myself. They asked me to be their leader and Mr Hugh Rossi MP[441] to act as deputy leader. They also included Dame Janet Fookes,[442] as member of the Speaker's Panel of Chairm[e]n and Deputy Speaker in the House of Commons and Mr Ian [sic] Lawrence,[443] now a QC and member of numerous committees in the House of Commons.

Starting from New Delhi where we were welcomed by Mr Hegde,[444] Speaker of the Lok Sabha and president of the branch. The CPA had no less than six branches in India, which gave us a chance to pay a fleeting visit to six states as well as New Delhi. We paid our respects to the President of India[445] at the Lutyens Palace of the Viceroys, now the Rashtrapati Bhavan. The interior was still draped in mauve, the dreadful colour chosen by Lady Willingdon when her husband was Viceroy. We met the Prime Minister, and several of his Cabinet colleagues, and the Speaker arranged a dinner for us to meet Mrs Indira Ghandi [sic][446] and other Opposition leaders. It was amusing to note that one sign over a large store in Main Street read 'By Appointment to Queen Mary'. India has accepted the Raj as an episode in its history, much as Russia had accepted the Tsars. We attended meetings of the two chambers, including 'Question

[441] Hugh Rossi (b.1927), later Sir Hugh Rossi, Conservative MP and minister.

[442] Janet Fookes (b.1936), later Baroness Fookes, Conservative MP and later deputy speaker of the House of Commons, 1992–1997.

[443] Ivan Lawrence QC (b.1936), later Sir Ivan Lawrence QC, Conservative MP and criminal barrister.

[444] K.S. Hegde (1909–1990), Indian judge and Janata Party MP; speaker of the Lok Sabha, 1977–1980.

[445] N.S. Reddy (1913–1996), president of India, 1977–1982.

[446] Indira Gandhi (1917–1984), Congress Party leader and prime minister of India, 1966–1977 and 1980–1984; assassinated 1984.

Time' in the Lower House, where the badinage made us feel quite at home. As I am not writing a 'Traveller's Guide to India', I shall only mention my outstanding impression of six states we visited on our way south from Delhi. I shall not forget the Taj Mahal, the Red Fort, the palaces of four Maharajahs with their splendid water gardens or the famous rock cut temples with their splendid examples of Hindu sculpture. In Bombay, we were taken across the Bay to the Elephanta Caves to see some more splendid Hindu sculpture. I cannot end without a word of thanks to Shri Rikhi, Secretary to the Lok Sabha in New Delhi, who was our guide and friend throughout our travels.

My Indian visit in 1978 was an experience for which I can never be sufficiently grateful to my Indian hosts and can only repay with a love for their country and people that will last all my days.

X
SECRETARY OF STATE FOR BURMA
UNTIL INDEPENDENCE: 1947–1948

The Japanese had given Burma 'independence' in August 1943 and appointed Ba Maw[447] as Head of State, U Nu[448] as Foreign Secretary, and General Aung San[449] as Minister of Defence; after releasing them from jail where they had been put after the Japanese invasion in 1942. However, the Burmese resented the Japanese as much as the British and Aung San was biding his time before turning his Burmese National Army [BNA] against the Japanese.

In March 1945, Mountbatten, without any political authority, stated that it was the British Government's aim to help Burma attain complete self-government. His object was to encourage the BNA in its rising against the Japanese, and to avoid a colonial war by securing the support of Aung San for the British. On the same day, Mountbatten received a telegram from London discounting the value of the Burmese nationalist movement. London was relying upon the advice of the former Governor of Burma, Sir Reginald Dorman-Smith.[450] Dorman-Smith, a former Conservative Cabinet Minister for Agriculture, had left Burma for Simla when the Japanese invaded in 1942, and had therefore been out of touch with recent political developments in Burma. He had taken with him some pre-war Burmese politicians, whose advice he relied on in spite of their total loss of influence and support in post-war Burma and who hoped to replace Aung San and his Anti-Fascist

---

[447] Ba Maw (1893–1977), Burmese political leader who served as chief minister of Burma under British colonial rule, 1937–1939, and, under the Japanese, was head of state, 1943–1945.

[448] U Nu (1907–1995), sometimes called Thakin Nu, Burmese political leader who served as the first prime minister of independent Burma, 1948–1956, and later in 1957–1958 and 1960–1962.

[449] Aung San (1915–1947), Burmese political leader, president of the Anti-Fascist People's Freedom League, 1945–1947 and chief minister of Burma, 1946–1947; assassinated July 1947.

[450] Sir Reginald Dorman-Smith (1899–1977), Conservative MP; governor of Burma, 1941–1946. Between 1942–1945 he was in exile, mainly in Simla, due to the Japanese occupation.

People's Freedom League [AFPFL] supporters when civil government had been restored by the British.

Mountbatten, whose main objectives were to enlist the resistance movement and to avoid a subsequent colonial war, was soon at odds with Dorman-Smith. He suggested that General Aung San should be told that he would be asked to serve on the Governor's Executive Council when Civil Government had been restored. Dorman-Smith refused even to consider this proposal. His Opposition was even more determined against the treatment of the BNA as an ally, and the suggestion to embody it in the loyal Burmese Army. But Mountbatten, of course, had his way while military government continued. Rangoon was retaken on May 2nd 1945 and he arranged for Aung San to meet Field Marshal Slim[451] to co-ordinate the campaign against the Japanese. In Field Marshal Slim's view: 'I have always felt that, with proper treatment, Aung San would have proved a Burmese Smuts.'[452] In June there was a victory parade in Rangoon. 'I am sure', wrote Mountbatten, 'that having Aung San and his army take part in the Review, will have done more to prevent strife and civil war and establish friendship, than anything else I could have done.'

Another step forward towards friendship with the national movement was made by the replacement by Mountbatten of Major-General Pearce[453] who, shortly after Rangoon was taken, had advocated trying Aung San as a traitor, by a new Chief Civil Affairs Officer, Major-General Rance,[454] who shared the view that it was essential to work with the young Burmese political activists.

As an observer at the meetings of the India and Burma Committee of the Cabinet, in which capacity I was appointed by Leo Amery – Secretary of State for India during the Coalition Government – I had watched the development of our Burma Policy as it proceeded pari passu with our Indian Policy. The basic principle enunciated

---

[451] Field Marshal Sir William Slim, later 1st Viscount Slim (1891–1970), army officer and official; GOC of the Fourteenth Army, 1943–1945 (sometimes referred to as the 'Forgotten Army'), made up of numerous troops from across the Empire-Commonwealth, mainly concentrated on task of retaking Burma; chief of the Imperial General Staff, 1948–1952 and governor general of Australia, 1953–1960.

[452] Reference to the South African Afrikaner Field Marshal Jan Smuts who, despite not being British, was later, after the Boer War, a strong ally of Britain and its Empire.

[453] Major-General (later Sir) Charles F.B. Pearce (1892–1964), officer and colonial administrator; served in various roles in colonial Burma including finance secretary and secretary to the governor.

[454] Major-General Sir Hubert Rance (1898–1974), officer and colonial administrator, director of civil affairs in Burma in 1945, after the Japanese withdrawal; later last governor of Burma, 1946–1948, and governor of Trinidad and Tobago, 1950–1955.

again by the Committee in December 1944, was 'to establish self-government in Burma within the Empire.' Sir Reginald Dorman-Smith advocated a seven year reconstruction period of direct rule, following the period of military rule, and even then British trustee-ship, instead of independence, for the whole area of Burma not inhabited by Burmese.

The Coalition Government finally declared its Burma policy in a White Paper on May 17th, 1945 which was in summary that: first, the period of direct rule should be three (and not seven) years; second, when parliamentary government had been restored, a new constitution for Dominion status within the Commonwealth would be drawn up; and third, the hill areas, comprising about half the total area of Burma, would be excluded unless the inhabitants decided to join Burma. This was in contrast to the nationalists' demands for an immediate transfer of power to a provisional government in readiness for a republic comprising the whole of Burma.

After the end of the war with Japan, Dorman-Smith threatened to resign if Mountbatten failed to hand over to him. Against his better judgment – he said this was the only bad mistake in his life – Mountbatten bowed out in October 1945. Dorman-Smith's attitude to nationalist movements was illustrated by his response to Wavell's request that he receive Nehru in Burma. According to Wavell, the response was to the effect 'By all means send Nehru to Rangoon and I will put him straight into jail.'

The new Labour Government continued the White Paper policy as confirmed by wire from Pethick-Lawrence, the Secretary of State, to Dorman-Smith on September 21st: 'You should proceed on assumption that HMG's policy is that of the late Government's White Paper'.

In January 1946, Mountbatten told Dorman-Smith, on the advice of Wavell, that no Indian troops could be used in Burma and that he was not able to guarantee the use of the few British and Commonwealth Regiments in South East Asia Command. There was therefore no way of stopping a rebellion. Dorman-Smith did not report to London that he could not carry out the White Paper policy without provoking an armed uprising.

Indeed, there soon followed a crisis that could have sparked off an armed rising in Burma. In March 1946 Dorman-Smith asked Pethick-Lawrence for permission to arrest Aung San on a charge of murder arising out of the war against Japan. Mountbatten was of course consulted, and disagreed with the Governor because insuf-ficient evidence had been collected to warrant an arrest. He was in fact furious about this, because he knew what the arrest of Aung San would mean. He told Rance, then a member of his staff:

'That I will not for one moment contemplate allowing so gross a piece of disloyalty to my express wish, nor such an arrant act of treachery to the Burman Defence Army, who rose on our behalf long before the Fourteenth Army or Fifteen Corps could give their rebellion army support, as to arrest Aung San and throw him into jail while we decide to try him or not.' We wisely accepted Mountbatten's judgment and refused the Governor's request.

Then chance took a hand as it does so often in politics. In March 1946 Pethick-Lawrence happened to be abroad. Attlee took over the Burma Office. 'As soon as I began to read Pethick's papers I realised we would have to change our line', recorded the Prime Minister, 'the new policy could be described as following Mountbatten instead of Dorman-Smith'.[455] Mountbatten urged Attlee to dismiss the Governor before he involved us in a major war with Burma. This advice was probably crucial in the Government's decision to replace Dorman-Smith when he fell ill and returned to London in August 1946. The replacement was Major-General Rance, who confirmed that the White Paper policy was unworkable and that Aung San must be involved in policy. Accordingly, the India and Burma Committee's directive to Rance was to include a representative team from the Anti-Fascist People's Freedom League, Aung San's party, and to involve Aung San, despite the unresolved murder charge. Rance took over at the end of August.[456] His arrival was followed almost immediately by a police strike in Rangoon, which spread to Government employees until it was almost a general strike. Rance immediately met Aung San, who agreed to join the Governor's Executive Council, with a number of his own colleagues also members of the AFPFL. A new Executive Council, for the first time representative of the nationalist movement, was thus set up by the end of September.

The Nationalist majority in the new Executive Council made it plain that they would accept nothing less than independence. On November 13th we had a letter from Rance ending with these words: 'there is a new spirit of nationalism abroad, tempered and restrained, but quite unyielding. His Majesty's Government must either make terms with it quickly, or prepare without delay to hold the country by military force.' Almost exactly what we had heard from Wavell about the situation in India. So we decided to invite a delegation from his Executive Council to London for discussions. The invitation was accepted, and the London meeting between

---

[455] *Attlee still Chairman of India and Burma Cabinet Committee followed Mountbatten's advice when it conflicted with Dorman-Smith's, the Governor's.*

[456] *Note the turning point of a peaceful transition for Burma with the appointment of Rance as governor.*

British Ministers and the Burmese Delegates took place between January 13th and January 27th, 1947. We all realised that if we failed to reach agreement at the end of our talks, there would be serious anti-British violence, possibly civil war, in Burma. This was positively the last chance for a peaceful solution of the Burmese problem.

The first meeting at No. 10 Downing Street was on January 13th, when a statement of principle was made by the Prime Minister and Aung San and handed to the Press. The subsequent meetings were held in private. The British team, led by the Prime Minister, included Lord Pethick-Lawrence, A.V. Alexander, Sir Stafford Cripps, Christopher Mayhew,[457] Arthur Bottomley,[458] and myself. Attlee in his opening speech said that we wanted Burma to be free and to choose her own form of constitution when she reached independence: 'it is for the people of Burma to decide their own future. We have no desire to retain any unwilling peoples within the Commonwealth and Empire. Our intention is to hasten forward the time when Burma shall realise her independence either within or without the British Commonwealth.' Aung San replied that 'whatever internal differences there may be in our country, we are one on the right of our country to full and unfettered sovereignty – the day of independence for our nation should be made possible within a year from now'.

The outcome of the conference was complete agreement between Attlee and Aung San about the road to, and timing of, independence. The forthcoming General Election would be for a Constituent Assembly to frame the constitution for the new country, though there would also be direct negotiations between Aung San and the frontier peoples to work out a scheme to bring them into a united Burma. He made it clear that he wished the frontier peoples to have a free choice between separate independence and union with ministerial Burma. I should perhaps explain that under British rule, Burma had been divided between the mainly Burmese area in the south, for which Ministers here were responsible, and the frontier areas in northern Burma under the direct rule of the Governor. Finally, the Governor's Executive Council would become an Interim Government, without prejudice to his existing powers, which would last until independence. In the meantime the interim government would be treated as a self-governing Dominion Government.

---

[457] Christopher Mayhew (1915–1997), later Lord Mayhew, Labour (and later Liberal) MP and junior minister; under-secretary of state for foreign affairs, 1946–1950.

[458] Arthur Bottomley, later Lord Bottomley (1907–1997), Labour MP and minister; under-secretary of state for Dominion Affairs, 1946–1947 and last secretary of state for Commonwealth Relations, 1964–1966.

But the meeting was not to end without one of the most unpleasant examples of political chicanery I can remember. On Sunday January 26th at 10.30pm, just as we thought that there was nothing left to do but the dotting of a few i's before a short ceremony of appending signatures to the final document, Thakin Ba Sein[459] and U Saw[460] staged a walk out. We were discussing the date for publishing the agreement. Just at this moment Thakin Ba Sein said he wished to speak. He told us he could not regard the agreement as satisfactory to Burma. One difficulty was that his country would not be independent within a year. Then U Saw said that he agreed with Ba Sein, and neither of them could be parties to the agreement. They walked out of the meeting at No. 10.

My friend Tin Tut[461] was quick to point out to us after they left the meeting that their real motive was to get back to Rangoon before Aung San, so that they could denounce him as a tool of the British for the concessions he had made, before he could return to Burma in time to reply to their accusations. It should be remembered that U Saw, as a former Prime Minister of Burma, had considerable prestige, and led the important opposition Party which was hoping to overthrow Aung San. What astonished us, and even enraged the calm Attlee, was that neither U Saw nor Ba Sein had expressed any dissent when the matter to which they so strongly now objected in the agreement had been discussed at length at earlier meetings. Then Aung San, speaking for all the other members of the Burmese Delegation, said he would like to proceed without the two dissentients. The agreement was signed in Downing Street with only two dissentions on January 27th. From that moment a peaceful transition to independence was assured.

On his return to Burma, Aung San lost no time in approaching the leaders of the frontier areas about their willingness to unite with the Burmese in an independent Burma.[462] He was relieved to find that they were most anxious to co-operate, in order to bring their independence forward to the earliest possible date. This was confirmed by their representatives at a conference of the hill peoples at Pang Long[463] in the middle of February, when they decided, provided

---

[459] Thakin Ba Sein, Burmese Socialist politician.

[460] U Saw (1900–1948), Burmese politician, prime minister of British Burma, 1940–1942; implicated in the assassination of Aung San and consequently executed in 1948.

[461] Tin Tut (1895–1948), Burmese civil servant and AFPFL politician; first minister of foreign affairs in Burma, 1948; assassinated the same year.

[462] *Only a Burmese leader could have united the frontier areas and British Burma.*

[463] More usually known as Panglong. This conference in February 1947 and the agreement that followed saw key ethnic groups accept a united Burma in return for significant autonomy in the regions.

that their autonomy was preserved, to unite with the Burmese in a Federal State, and in the meantime to join the Interim Government and to send their representatives to the Constituent Assembly. The presence of a British Minister, Arthur Bottomley, contributed to the success of the Pang Long Conference, as he was able both to convince the Northerners that we were genuine about wanting their independence, and that we were also seeking their willingness to unite with their Burmese neighbours in the south to achieve it. At last the long separation between the Frontier Areas and Ministerial Burma would be ended, and the country could move forward towards a free and united Burma.

The Constituent Assembly to determine the democratic constitution of the new Burma would meet in June, and in discussing the procedure with Rance, Aung San mentioned that he intended to propose a resolution as follows: 'that Burma should be a Sovereign Independent Republic.' It was immediately apparent to Rance that the severance of allegiance to the Crown would put Burma outside the Commonwealth. Aung San agreed to this interpretation of his proposal, but replied that to keep the Crown link would break up his Party and let in the Communists.[464] This was the cruel dilemma that faced Burma, because it was the first of our dependencies to become independent after the war, before any provision had been made for Republics to remain in the Commonwealth. Rance anticipated the change in the relationship with the British Crown that made it possible later on for India, and all subsequent British dependencies that became Republics after their independence, to remain in the Commonwealth. What he said in a telegram to me dated June 9th, 1947 was this:

> The conclusion I reach therefore is the time seems right for a new conception of association within the Commonwealth, not necessarily owing allegiance to the Crown, especially for those countries which have no ties of blood, culture, or religion.

His foresight came unfortunately too late to save Burma for the Commonwealth, or to burden it with the subsequent misfortunes of that unhappy country.

U Nu visited us in London in June as a member of a Goodwill Mission, and confirmed that quite apart from the objections against recognising the British Monarch as Head of State, the communists would say that the AFPFL 'had sold Burma to the British' on the

---

[464] *Aung San had no personal objections to the Crown but realised that even titular British sovereignty would break his party and let in the Communists.*

basis that dominion status was not true independence. When this matter came up at the India and Burma Committee, Cripps echoed Rance's sentiments in suggesting the consideration of a modified form of Commonwealth association, as India would undoubtedly raise the question in due course and in the meantime, provision should be included in the prospective Treaty with Burma allowing her to return to the Commonwealth within a year of independence. The conclusion of the Cabinet Committee was however to refuse any concession to Burma.

I have sometimes wondered why Attlee did not accept Cripps' suggestion, which would have enabled Burma to return to the Commonwealth as a Republic with the agreement of the old Dominions. I suppose he probably thought that Burma was not worth the long and difficult process of consultation with the other Commonwealth countries, or that even if this procedure had been adopted, as it would be later in the case of India, they would not have been in favour of changing the constitutional framework of the Commonwealth for the sake of Burma.

I found U Nu a delightful personality, with much more intellectual ballast than the run-of-the-mill politician. The arrangements made for his reception here had to be changed as soon as we knew what he really wanted. The Foreign Office had booked him for a popular show in London and a suite at a comfortable London hotel. Instead, he insisted on a separate bedroom for himself and his wife, and a visit to the Shakespeare season at Stratford-on-Avon instead of the London theatre. He explained to me that he was himself a playwright, and a devotee of Shakespeare and Bernard Shaw. The plays of Shaw had persuaded him, while still a University student in Rangoon, not to write in blank verse. One of his plays had been translated, and he gave me a copy asking for my honest opinion. This was distinctly embarrassing, as the play was typically Shavian, and I prefer action to argument in the theatre. However he was much too good natured to take my comments amiss.

U Nu invited me during this visit to stay at his home in Burma, but I told him that, much as I would like to do so, and to visit his country as soon as possible, I doubted whether I would have time for a private visit as well. U Nu, after a somewhat rackety youth had become a 'born again' Buddhist, a total abstainer, and a celibate who practised daily prayer and meditation. I am sure he would have been happier as the Abbott [sic] of a Buddhist Monastery than he was subsequently as Prime Minister of Burma. For us the main difficulty of his devoutness was that he was constantly threatening to retire. We could only get him to stay in politics by accepting a time limit. Aung San himself had pleaded with him to join the Constituent Assembly, but he would only agree on condition that he could retire altogether from politics in six months time. His admiration for our culture and way of life made him an invaluable friend at the highest political level in Burma. Little did I think when he left London that I should next meet him as Prime Minister of his country.

Normally I did not go to my office on Saturdays, but on the afternoon of Saturday July 19th I had a telephone call from the Duty Officer to say that an urgent telegram awaited me from the Governor. It was to be the worst Saturday afternoon I can remember in all my life. The message from Rance read: 'An attack has been made on the Executive Council at about 10.30 this morning by three Burmans armed with Sten guns, five Counsellors have been killed, and Aung San himself wounded.' This message was shortly corrected to include Aung San among the victims, though not until I had already sent him a telegram of personal sympathy. One of the Counsellors who survived described what happened.

The Executive Council normally met at Government House, but the agenda did not concern the reserve powers of the Governor on that occasion, so it had met at the Secretariat. This was the case on the morning of Saturday July 19th. At about 10.30am three men armed with Sten guns and in army uniform burst into the Council Chamber, having shot the guard outside the door. They opened fire point blank at the assembled counsellors. Aung San stood up as they entered, and received the first volley in the chest. They then fired to his right and left, killing six counsellors, and mortally wounding two others. Only three of those present survived. The assassins had also intended to kill U Nu after the attack on the Secretariat, but luckily he was out when they got to his house. There was an immediate danger of a rising organised by U Saw's supporters and the Communist Party, who spread the rumour that the British were responsible for the murders. The Rangoon Press was already accusing us of complicity in the crime. Calm was restored by Rance's presence of mind in asking U Nu, who was the President of the Constituent Assembly, to form a new Council of Ministers, which was sworn in the following day. He immediately issued a statement denying the complicity of the British Government or the Governor in the murder plot.

But it soon emerged from the enquiry set on foot by Rance that acts of negligence and even corruption in the Burma army had contributed significantly to the disaster. In June and July there had been two mysterious thefts of arms and equipment from the Army Ordnance Depot. In each case a bogus police party with forged documents had perpetrated the thefts. It transpired later that two British officers had been in the pay of U Saw.[465] One had forged the police documents, the other had sold the arms to U Saw. The officer in charge of the Ordnance Depot had revealed in a statement to the Military Police, and reported straight away to the Chief of Staff of the G.O.C., that U Saw in his cups had admitted to him that he was responsible for the arms thefts. Having read the statements of the officer in charge of the Ordnance Depot, this senior officer locked it up in his safe and forgot about it, instead of informing the Burma Police. He did not remember this vital statement until after the assassination. Rance notes in his memoirs that after he had read the incriminating statement he said aloud 'Good heavens, if we had known of this earlier, the assassination could probably have been prevented.' He informed U Nu immediately, emphasising secrecy, and U Nu's reaction also was that the murderers could have been foiled. What is really remarkable is that neither he nor any of his ministerial colleagues exposed the role of British officers in the assassination of their colleagues. As Kynev Nien, a senior Burmese civil servant, reported to Maung Maung,[466] a Burmese politician: 'As Nu had said and [the British] had agreed "what had happened had happened, the point is to get Independence quickly without fail and not to provoke the British Authorities into … revoking promises".'

Of course they had an undertaking from Rance that the culprits would be apprehended and brought to justice. If the true story had 'leaked' at this moment, and it had reached the press, Europeans would have been as much at risk all over Burma as they were in India during the Mutiny.[467] However this inaction by the British authorities did lead some Burmese to wonder whether the British officers were acting under orders.

I have dwelt at some length on the events of July the 19th, 1947 because they represented a turning point, in the history of Burma. Would the internal strife that marred the early years of Burmese independence have been avoided if Aung San had not been killed at the early age of 32? Could this country with its enormous natural resources, have gradually developed under wise leadership, like another United States of America, bringing peace and plenty to a union of peoples speaking many different languages and professing many different religious faiths? This is how Rance, who knew

---

[465] *It was successfully hidden from the press and the public that British officers in the Ordnance Depot had been bribed to hand over the weapons used in the murder. How many people still know the truth? A judicial enquiry then would have meant disaster.*

[466] Maung Maung (1925–1994), Burmese politician and writer.

[467] In 1857.

SECRETARY OF STATE FOR BURMA UNTIL INDEPENDENCE 149

Burma and its leaders better than any other Englishman, put the question himself, and answered it:

> The question will always be asked – if Aung San and his associates had not been assassinated on that fateful day in July 1947, would Burma's troubles in 1949 and succeeding years have arisen? In my view, as long as Aung San held the confidence of the Burmans and the Hill Peoples (possibly less the Karens) I don't believe they would. Aung San was a much stronger character than his successor, U Nu, and with the assistance of Mahn Ba Khaing,[468] a popular Karen leader, the Karen troubles of 1949 may not have escalated to the heights they eventually did.

I, with my much more limited knowledge, would entirely agree with Rance.

Aung San had the qualities of a soldier-statesman, like Washington,[469] and as the founder of independence had become the focus of a nationwide patriotism. He loved his army, and kept a battalion with him as his body guard. This would certainly have prevented a military dictatorship. I only knew him slightly myself, but I had observed at the Attlee/Aung San meetings in Downing Street that he spoke with blunt directness and quiet determination, using few words, in a way we associate more perhaps with soldiers than politicians. Let me quote Rance again:

> I met Major-General Aung San for the first time in June 1945 and I was immediately impressed by his personality, which showed itself by his transparent honesty, his sincerity, his simplicity in dress, and his directness in thought and speech.

It was not surprising that Field Marshal Slim liked him: 'the greatest impression he made an me was one of honesty. He was not free with glib assurances and he hesitated to commit himself, but I had the idea that if he agreed to do something he would keep his word'. His daughter, Aung San Suu Kyi[470] has written a touching short biography of the father she was too young to remember – she was still a baby when he died – in which she describes what he meant to the peoples of Burma:

---

[468] Mahn Ba Khaing (1903–1947), Burmese and Karen politician; minister of industry, among those assassinated in July 1947 with Aung San.

[469] George Washington (1732–1799), leading commander of the American forces who later served as the first president of the United States of America, 1789–1797.

[470] *The spirit of Aung San lives on in his daughter, Aung San Sui Kyi.* Aung San Suu Kyi (b.1945), Burmese politician; released from house arrest in 2010; minister of foreign affairs and state counsellor of Myanmar since 2016; author of *Aung San of Burma: A Biographical Portrait by his Daughter* (1984).

Aung San's appeal was not so much to extremists as to the great majority of ordinary citizens who wished to pursue their own lives in peace and prosperity under a leader they could trust and respect. In him they saw that leader, a man who put the interests of the country before his own needs, who remained poor and unassuming at the height of his power, who accepted the responsibilities of leadership without hankering after the privileges, and who retained at the core of his being a deep simplicity.

Would that he could have lived to see her awarded the Nobel Peace Prize in 1991, when she was under house arrest in Burma. The Nobel Committee described her 'non-violent struggle for democracy and human rights' as 'one of the most extraordinary examples of civil courage in Asia in recent decades.'

Alas, it was a saintly man who abhorred violence and detested politics, not a strong man who had learned that force was necessary to uphold freedom, who inherited the leadership after the tragedy of the July massacre. As Rance noted: 'The only thing I would every say against Nu is that he utterly lacked a capacity for ruthlessness in the months leading up to, and following, independence. If he had been of a more ruthless mould, I think Burma might have escaped a great deal of its post war insurgent difficulties.'[471] Indeed, U Nu often told the story of the cobra that got away because he, U Nu, spent so long deciding whether or not he had the right to take its life. This respect for life is typical of Buddhism.

Our next step, now that it had become clear that Burma would leave the Commonwealth, was to negotiate a Treaty to regulate relations between Britain and Burma after it had become a foreign country. Attlee had intended to send out Cripps in September to handle negotiations on our side, and to discuss arrangements for the transfer of power, but a serious balance of payments crisis, including a possible run on the pound, obliged the Chancellor to stay at home, and I was asked to take his place. The proposal was made by Attlee to U Nu on August 15th, and welcomed by the latter.

On the flying boat between Calcutta and Rangoon I met Randolph Churchill,[472] not altogether surprisingly in the bar on the lower deck of the plane. My heart sank, remembering that his father,[473] Lord Randolph Churchill,[474] had annexed Burma. I was

---

[471] *U Nu of Burma by Butwell published by Stanford University Press (1963), quoted on page 90.*

[472] Randolph Churchill (1911–1968), Conservative MP, journalist and son of Winston Churchill.

[473] Grandfather.

[474] Lord Randolph Churchill (1849–1895), Conservative MP and minister; secretary of state for India, 1885–1886, under whom Burma was annexed to British India in late 1885; father of Winston Churchill.

therefore much relieved when he told me he was en route for Singapore, not even stopping overnight in Rangoon. I arrived in Rangoon on September 1st, accompanied by Sir Gilbert Laithwaite as head of the Burma Office and my Private Secretary, Ronald Harris.[475] We were met at the airport by the Governor, who disregarded protocol, U Nu, and some Cabinet colleagues: and I drove off immediately to Government House.

It surprised me to hear that I was the first Secretary of State to visit Burma, and was therefore the first holder of my Office with first hand knowledge however slight of the country. My welcome was assured by my press statement stating our policy:

> His Majesty's Government will introduce the necessary legislation (i.e. the Independence Bill) at the beginning of the autumn session in October, and they will do everything in their power to hasten the passage into law and to complete the necessary Parliamentary processes by the end of the present year.

The following morning I paid courtesy calls on the Prime Minister and on Mrs Aung San,[476] the General's widow, a remarkably lovely and intelligent lady who had been formerly a trained hospital nurse. I was given a civic reception at the Town Hall, and presented with an address in a beautiful silver casket.[477] I had lunch with U Nu and his party colleagues and also with the business community at the Rotary Club. The most memorable of my experiences was a visit to the greatest Pagoda in Burma, the Schwedagon.[478] A short account of my stay in Rangoon was subsequently published by the Government of Burma, and there is a paragraph about my visit to the Pagoda:

> One Sunday morning on September the 7th, Lord Listowel and Sir Gilbert Laithwaite visited the Schwedagon. Lord Listowel and party offered flowers and symbolic umbrellas to the Pagoda. Lord Listowel also laid gold leaf on the superstructure of the Pagoda and tolled the second largest bell in Burma. In fact he is the first Earl who has ever climbed barefoot the Upper Platform of the Pagoda to offer gold leaf. In those good old days the 'Footwear Prohibited' notice was most annoying to our European friends but times have changed. His Lordship found it easier to walk the Burmese way. This was in itself a significant thing which endeared him to the Burmans.

[475] Ronald Harris (1913–1995), later Sir Ronald Harris, civil servant at the India Office, 1944–1947.
[476] Khin Kyi (1912–1988). She later served as Burma's Ambassador to India, 1960–1967.
[477] *I passed this casket to the Burma Office for its archives when I returned to London.*
[478] More usually spelled as Shwedagon.

There is another rather charming passage at the end of this record of my visit to the Schwedagon.

> Lord Listowel lingered for more than two hours on the Pagoda platform. Then he retraced his footsteps at the request of the gentleman who offered him the philosopher's stone. He said goodbye to the flower girl at the Western entrance. He shook hands with her. She looked rather plump. Perhaps towards the end of this year when His Majesty the King announces in Parliament the transfer of power and subsequently the grant of independence she will be a proud mother. The baby will be a free Burman. This is very auspicious.

Most of my time, however, was spent at Government House, meeting people from all walks of life and all parts of Burma. My task was to find a modus vivendi between the Burmese and the Karens, and to agree the terms for a Treaty that would regulate our relations with Burma after independence. I had hoped that if I was successful with the Karens it would avert the civil war that would otherwise be almost inevitable, and unfortunately happened later. I was asked by U Nu to explain to the Karen leaders what he was prepared to offer them, and to do my best to persuade them to accept. They could have a separate Karen State in the Karen majority area, the independence of the Karenni Karens would be respected, and there would be safeguards for the Karen minority in Lower Burma. I met their leaders separately, and told the Karennis they could no longer expect subsidies or protection from His Majesty's Government after independence. Finally, I addressed a farewell speech to their ten representatives, expressing my sadness that they could neither agree among themselves about what they wanted, nor accept the generous offer of the Burma Government. I thanked them for their help in the war against Japan, and wished them well for the future. My effort as a mediator had been a total failure. Rance asked me to publish my speech to the Karens when I got home, but it remains I imagine in the archives of the Burma Office. I was glad to find later that in a letter I brought home from U Nu to Stafford Cripps, the former attached no blame to me for my failure. I quote from his letter:

> Lord Listowel will tell you that the great efforts he made to secure a settlement of the Karen question failed in the end. The failure was certainly not due to any fault on the part of the Mission, which contacted all sections of Karen opinion and did its best for the Karens.

The Treaty under negotiation would come into effect from the moment Burma became a foreign country and would include all important matters of mutual concern, such as contractual obligations, nationality, finance, defence, and trade. For the Burmese the most important provision of the Treaty was contained in Article 1:

> The Government of the United Kingdom recognises the Republic of the Union of Burma as a fully independent Sovereign State.

It was certainly our intention that the Treaty should give Burma the best possible start in life as a new member of the community of nations, and it was therefore drafted to go as far as we could to meet the urgent need for armed security and financial support. I only wish we could have gone much further to compensate Burma for the total devastation caused by the Japanese invasion and our failure to prevent it.

The financial settlement of the Treaty wiped off £15,000,000 of Burma debt, and allowed the balance to be repaid over a period of ten years. A distinct advantage for Burma was the continuation of Commonwealth preferential treatment for her trade, pending the agreement to the drafting of a Commercial Treaty. But more important still was the assistance offered by a Defence Mission led by a junior Minister, John Freeman,[479] to build up her armed forces under the supervision of British advisors from our own army, navy, and air force. We also offered military training in the United Kingdom for Burmese personnel. All British troops would be withdrawn as soon as possible after the transfer of power. In return, Burma would not receive a Service Mission from any foreign country. The Treaty was signed in London by Attlee and Thakin Nu [U Nu] on October 17th, amid the Victorian splendour of the conference room at Lancaster House.

It only remained to draft the Burma Independence Bill, and to get it through Parliament before the Christmas recess. The one difficulty we had in drafting it was to fix the date for independence. We were naturally anxious to meet the wishes of the Burma Government, and they had informed us that the 'auspicious' date would be January 6th, 1948. So, in accordance with their express wish, this date went into the Bill. Our dismay can be imagined when on November 4th, the day before the Second Reading of the Bill in the House of Commons, we received a telegram from Rangoon asking us to change the date to January 4th, because 'the large body of opinion

---

[479] John Freeman (1915–2014), Labour MP and junior minister at the War Office, 1947; later high commissioner to India, 1965–1968.

here regard that as most auspicious'.[480] I told Attlee immediately about this request for a last minute change; and he seemed unruffled, promising that 'the adjustment would be carried into his speech' on the Second Reading the following day and made in Committee. He did this rather neatly I thought, with due allowance for Burmese sensitivity, and the astrological scepticism of the House of Commons. An unopposed amendment to advance the date was duly moved at the Committee stage of the Bill.

The debate that followed Attlee's speech showed that the Conservative Party though opposing the Bill, was by no means united in its opposition. The official line was indicated by Churchill, who denounced the Government for breaking up the Commonwealth and described Aung San as a 'traitor rebel leader'. Other Conservative speakers followed in the same vein, but R.A. Butler, who had been the Conservative's spokesman on the India Independence Bill, was conspicuous by his absence from the House. I suspect that his absence was in fact a deliberate manoeuvre to avoid a painful conflict between Party loyalty and intellectual integrity. He probably knew more about Burma than any of his Party colleagues, having been a junior Minister at the India Office at the time of the 1935 India Act,[481] with the added advantage of a family connection through his Uncle Harcourt Butler,[482] who at one time had been Governor of Burma. Four Conservative backbenchers supported the Bill, and three actually voted against their Party and on the side of the Government. It was a signal to Burma that even a Conservative administration would not necessarily be unfriendly or reverse the present attitude of the Government. This impression must have been reinforced by the expressions of goodwill towards Burma emanating from all sides of the House, whether or not the speaker was in favour of the Bill. Arthur Henderson made an excellent winding up speech in reply to his critics in the House of Commons, and the Bill was given a Second Reading by 288 votes to 114.

The Bill reached the House of Lords for its Second Reading on November the 25th. I opened with a much longer speech than I had intended, which must have been intensely boring for most of my audience, for whom Burma was a far off country about which

---

[480] *U Nu however stated in his autobiography that he was sceptical of astrology, and denied that it had played any part in his political decisions. He asserted that he was offered two dates for independence and he chose the earlier date.*

[481] Butler was under-secretary of state for India, 1932–1937.

[482] Sir Harcourt Butler (1869–1938), colonial civil servant and administrator; served in India; governor of Burma, 1923–1927.

they knew very little. But I was obliged to outline the provisions of the prospective Treaty covering defence, finance, and commercial relations, as well as the historical background of our policy for treating Burma as a dependency that had reached maturity, the stage for independence. Lord Munster, who had been a junior Minister at the India and Burma Office during the war, replied for the Opposition, but the best case against the Bill was made by the final Opposition spokesman, my old friend and Leader, Lord Salisbury. In the finest speech in either House he deplored the abandonment of our responsibility for Burma, I quote: 'Sixty years of British trusteeship', he said 'recklessly cast away', and he then extolled the peace and prosperity brought by the long period of British rule.

I was supported by my predecessor, Lord Pethick-Lawrence, and in an eloquent speech from Lord Samuel,[483] Leader of the Liberal Party. But the temper of the House was bound to be against the Government, and I was relieved that, on the wise advice of Lord Salisbury to respect the decision of the House of Commons, the Bill received its Second Reading without a vote. It passed into law without amendment on December 4th, as we had hoped, before the Christmas recess, and in good time for the hoisting of the flag of Burma in place of the Union Jack on January the 4th, 1948.

I had friendly letters from both Cripps and Attlee when I retired from the Burma Office:

11 Downing Street
20.12.47

My dear Listowel,

... I should like to say how much I have admired your conduct of India and Burma affairs during this most difficult year. Much of the credit for the smoothness and quickness of action is I know due to you personally.

Thank you for it.

Best of luck,
Stafford Cripps

---

[483] 1st Viscount Samuel (1870–1963), formerly Sir Herbert Samuel, Liberal MP and peer, minister and colonial administrator; leader of the Liberal Party, 1931–1935; home secretary, 1931–1932, and Liberal leader in the House of Lords, 1944–1955.

10 Downing Street

3.1.48

My dear Billy,

Thank you so much for your generous letter. We are all greatly indebted to you for the good work which you did at the India and Burma Office. You took [it] on at a most difficult time. I greatly admire the way in which you tackled the problems before you and the clarity with which you presented your views.

Although your new post is outside the Cabinet, I think that you will find plenty of interesting and responsible work to do.

With all good wishes,

Yours ever,

Clem

This was the longest letter I ever had from Clem Attlee; he hated prolixity.

Attlee has been described by Roy Hattersley[484] as 'the greatest of all British peace-time prime ministers'. I entirely agree. The independence of India was the greatest of his achievements, and he had prepared for it over a long period of time. During the war-time Coalition he had been Deputy Prime Minister and Chairman of the Cabinet's sub-committee on India. He continued as Chairman after the 1945 General Election. By having the Secretary of State in the Lords – first Lord Pethick-Lawrence, followed by me – he made sure that he would be the party spokesman on India, and was later able to pilot the India Bill through the House of Commons. When asked towards the end of his life which of his many political achievements he valued most, he is believed to have said 'India, I suppose'. A typical understatement.

[484] Roy Hattersley, (b.1932), later Lord Hattersley, Labour MP and writer.

XI
MINISTER OF STATE FOR THE
COLONIES: 1948-1950

My appointment to the Colonial Office, as the very first Minister of State, was a far better reward for me than the honours that had been showered on the Viceroy and many others after Indian independence. I was thankful to Attlee, not only for giving me another post in his Government, though outside the Cabinet, but particularly because it gave me a chance of doing something constructive about my concern for the inhabitants of the many dependencies whose lands we had taken in 'the scramble for Colonies' – the words are those of Lord Derby,[485] Colonial Secretary in 1884.

I had spoken frequently for the Labour Opposition in the past in the House of Lords on the Colonies, and I never lacked an expert brief from the Fabian Colonial Bureau.[486] The Fabian Society had taken a special interest in the Colonies thanks to the knowledge and enthusiasm of two of its members, Rita Hinden and Marjorie Nicholson.[487] They not only provided expert advice to members of both Houses of Parliament, but befriended many young colonials, mainly students, while visiting London for the first time. Many of the young men and women they assisted, such as Tom Mboya[488] from Kenya, Lee Kuan Yew[489] from Singapore and Kwame Nkrumah[490] from Ghana, were to become leaders of the National movements in their own countries. The Fabian Colonial Bureau,

[485] Edward Stanley, 15th earl of Derby (1826–1893), Conservative peer and minister; secretary of state for the colonies, 1858–1959 and 1882–1885; remarked 'there is something absurd in the scramble for colonies' in a letter to the Foreign Secretary, Lord Granville, in December 1884.

[486] *My maiden speech in 1932 had been on the colonies.*

[487] *I owe an immense debt to Marjorie Nicholson and Rita Hinden, particularly the latter, for their invaluable 'briefs' on colonial problems for my speeches in the House of Lords.* Successively Secretaries of the Fabian Colonial Bureau and anti-colonialism campaigners and writers.

[488] Tom Mboya (1930–1969), Kenyan activist and trade unionist; minister in Kenya's post-independence government; minister of justice, 1963–1969; assassinated 1969.

[489] Lee Kuan Yew (1923–2015), secretary general of People's Action Party, 1954–1992; prime minister of Singapore, 1959–1990.

[490] Kwame Nkrumah (1909–1972), Ghanaian and Pan-African activist; first prime minister of Ghana, 1957–1960; first president of Ghana, 1960–1966.

which was founded in 1940, did a useful service in making these young people aware that they had many friends in this country who supported their demand for more rapid progress towards independence.

My parliamentary interest in the Colonies had already been noted by the Colonial Office, which asked me to serve in a personal capacity on an Advisory Committee on Social Welfare and Economic Development in the Colonies. I had also become a trustee of a hostel for African students living in London, members of the West African Student Union or WASU.

So I had a limited but useful background of experience, which at any rate demonstrated a keen and abiding interest in the Colonies and their inhabitants, at the time that I took up my new job at the Colonial Office in 1948.

We now had three Ministers at the Colonial Office, the Secretary of State, Mr Creech-Jones [sic],[491] the Minister of State, myself, and an Under-Secretary, Mr Rees-Williams,[492] who sat in the House of Commons. His career in that Chamber was cut short by a peerage, and he chose for the title a Welsh place name, that of 'Ogmore'. This choice of name caused some merriment among our colleagues when, after an eloquent defence of corporal punishment in Hong Kong, a witty member of our own Party rose to suggest that 'Flogmore' would have been a more appropriate title for the new Peer.

We three Ministers made a broadly geographical division of our Ministerial responsibilities. The most important area from the standpoint of parliamentary and public interest was undoubtedly the African continent. This went to the Secretary of State, together with his overall supervisory function which meant inevitably that he had to remain in touch with the Cabinet in Whitehall and therefore was unable to travel. The detailed work on economic development and constitutional advance for the African territories went to the Under-Secretary as a member of the House of Commons, and I was put in charge of our lesser known possessions in South-East Asia and the West Indies.

Our then system of administration of the Colonies was to have one lot of officials, the professional members of the Colonial Service, working in the field, and quite another lot, the civil servants in the Colonial Office, issuing instructions to them as directed by the Secretary of State from their offices in Whitehall. This dichotomy

[491] Arthur Creech Jones (1891–1964), Labour MP, minister and trade unionist; secretary of state for the colonies, 1946–1950.

[492] David Rees-Williams (1903–1976), later 1st Baron Ogmore; Labour MP, peer and minister; under-secretary of state for the colonies, 1947–1950.

was mitigated by the somewhat infrequent meetings in London between Ministers and senior civil servants at home and Colonial Governors and Chief Secretaries from the Colonies. In practice, it gave the Governor of each Colony a pretty free hand. The current system of a single Foreign Service under the Foreign Secretary, with diplomats brought home for a few years at the Office after each period of service in a foreign country, has always seemed to me a far better system.

I should like to start with a brief account of our Colonial Policy when we formed the new Government in 1945. Our policy of de-colonisation was important not only in its effect of radical constitutional change in the Colonies, but because it was continued by our successors, prolonging in this field the bi-partisan policies pursued by the Political Parties during the war. It was dictated by our belief in the inherent right of colonial peoples to independence. Our objective was explained by the Secretary of State in the first White Paper he published in 1945, defining our Colonial Policy as 'Guidance of the Colonial Territories to self-government within the Commonwealth'. This was echoed twelve years later in a famous speech by Mr MacMillan [sic][493] about the 'winds of change' which were blowing over the British Empire.[494]

While we shared the broad aims of Colonial policy with the Conservative Party, we differed very sharply about the tempo and the manner in which these aims were to be realised. We hoped to quicken the tempo, and to bring about a genuine partnership between rulers and ruled as they worked together for a common goal. We were determined to stop the traditional subordination of labour to capital in the economic field, as well as to lay foundations of democratic self-government in the field of politics.

The former task often involved greater difficulties and more drastic changes than the latter. It meant that the land, the minerals, and other natural resources of a Colony should not be allowed to become the monopoly of any one company or group of people inside or outside the Colony. Natural resources should be developed for the benefit of the whole community, and wealth should not be taken abroad by absentees, or unfairly divided between the owners of capital and the men and women they employed to produce it. Our policy for controlled economic development – promoting the growth of

[493] Harold Macmillan (1894–1986), later 1st earl of Stockton, Conservative MP and minister; prime minister, 1957–1963.

[494] Refers, especially, to a speech Macmillan made in Cape Town to the South African parliament on 3 February 1960, in which he said a wind of change was blowing through Africa and that decolonization in the continent was a reality.

indigenous agriculture and related industries required for a balanced economy – was in stark contrast to the economic imperialism – imposing one crop economies – of the 19th century. In those days, economic development went forward with little regard for the welfare of the local inhabitants.

The usual practice of 19th century British companies was to go concession hunting in promising areas, imposing often ridiculous bargains on ignorant native societies, in search of the cheap and profitable production of food stuffs, raw materials, and valuable minerals, wanted by the expanding industries of Europe and America. The ruthless individualism of capitalist enterprise had a shattering impact on tribal societies, and the introduction of firearms ensured that what could not be secured by agreement could always be taken by force. During this time wealth was drained from Colonial Territories, and most of the profits of trade and production were enjoyed by alien shareholders, middle-men, and managers of European companies.[495]

In our view the only firm foundation for self-government was a healthy and well-educated people, enjoying a reasonable standard of life, and not prevented by ignorance and poverty from understanding and supporting the development of local and national political institutions. Having such a background, constitutional advance could steadily progress to extension of the suffrage, democratic representation on Legislatures and Legislative Councils, and sharing executive authority with the official members of Governors' Executive Councils.

It was against this background of economic exploitation and political stagnation, only mitigated by a limited amount of western technology and investment, that our plan for the future of our Colonies had to be measured. We believed that the State should play an important part in assisting economic development in the Colonies. This was an entirely new conception of the function of the home Government. Colonial Governments had hitherto been mainly concerned with security: protection of its territory from without, and preserving law and order within: and raising sufficient revenues to obviate grants from the home Government. We now wanted Colonial Governments to regard social welfare and economic growth as among their direct and most important responsibilities. Education and health which in the 19th century were left mainly to missionaries and philanthropists, economic planning and control, which had been left hitherto to private business interests, should become essential

---

[495] *We wanted colonial governments to promote social welfare and economic growth, instead of leaving the fate of their inhabitants to the vagaries of private enterprise.*

instruments for Colonial Governments to improve the standard of living and general welfare of those for whom they were responsible.

The extent to which both our political and economic programmes for individual Colonies were carried out depended primarily on the Colonial Governors. My experience has been that they were almost always men of outstanding character and ability who had reached their position in the Colonial Service after many years in different parts of the globe, starting as District Officers and graduating by hard work and devotion to the people they served, often in dreadful climatic conditions. This country has been fortunate to find a body of public servants who chose to spend their lives so far from home, and exposed to the risks and hardships of an often unfriendly and dangerous environment.

We were assisted in our aim to prepare the Colonies for self-government, by the fact that the vast majority (96%) of those employed by Colonial Governments were of local origin. We now proposed to train locally born people to qualify for service in every grade of the technical and administrative services and not purely the lower grades. Commonwealth Development and Welfare grants were now being spent on scholarships required for the higher branches of the Colonial Service.

The expatriate element of 4% was recruited and trained in the United Kingdom, returning at regular intervals for refresher courses and to compare notes with colleagues from other parts of the globe. There was a very large increase of numbers in 1946, as recruitment had stopped during the war. Sir Ralph Furse[496] was our most valuable recruitment adviser as he had an unerring eye for the right man to serve in the Colonies. But we made it clear that, in spite of the prospect of working themselves out of a job on the transfer of power, the security of appointments in the Colonial Service was no less than that of candidates for the Home Civil Service. Our conscience about neglect of the Colonies had been deeply stirred by the report of the Royal Commission on the West Indies (the Moyne Commission) in 1939.[497] This evidence of neglect made it possible for us to ask the British taxpayer to contribute to Colonial Welfare at a moment when our own country was in grave peril, in the first year of the Second World War.

[496] Sir Ralph Furse (1887–1973), civil servant; director of recruitment, colonial service, 1931–1948.
[497] *For the first time a home government recognised responsibility for its colonies in the 1945 Colonial Development and Welfare Act. The neglect revealed by the Moyne Commission's Report on the West Indies in 1939 was a real eye opener and shocked public opinion.* The Commission toured the British Caribbean in 1938–1939. Its report was not published till 1945 and outlined in detail the poor conditions and welfare provisions in the region.

We decided, in order to secure a minimum standard of welfare in each territory, and to promote maximum development of local resources in land and minerals, together with the transport infrastructure on which this would depend, to seek from Colonial Governments the preparation of Ten Year Plans to cover the whole field in each particular territory. The success of these Plans would of course depend on the money that could be put into them, and local funds would obviously not suffice. It was an Act of Parliament, the Colonial Development and Welfare Act of 1945, which really started the ball rolling. Under this Act the assistance available from the United Kingdom funds was raised to a total of £120,000,000 over a period of ten years. This made it possible to plan long term schemes of public works, social services, and agricultural improvement, and to consider wider schemes for regional development of health and communication services. The impetus given to colonial development after the war can be judged by comparing this figure with the figure of £5,000,000 per annum allocated by the original Colonial Development and Welfare Act of 1940.

These Ten Year Plans were eventually prepared for most of the Colonies. They were drawn up in the territory and had generally been worked out by the local Government in consultation with representatives of the local population. A large proportion of the money that went into each Ten Year Programme was provided out of local revenues and loans. We tried to preserve an element of balance between local funds and external aid, so as to prevent even a suggestion of political pressure from the United Kingdom.

Another step forward was taken by the passage of the Overseas Resources Act in 1947. This Act set up two Development Corporations, a Colonial Development Corporation, to operate in the Colonies, and an Overseas Food Corporation, to function anywhere in the world. The objectives of the Corporations were to bring about a 'speedier and more widespread development of our territories overseas for the benefit of the Colonial peoples, whose low standard of living can only be raised by greater use of their natural resources', and also to benefit 'the inhabitants of this country and other countries which are still suffering from the acute shortage of agricultural produce brought about by the ravages and devastation of the war.'

After the unfortunate appointment of Mr John Strachey[498] to operate the Overseas Food Corporation, resulting in the total failure and considerable wastage of public money on his scheme for growing groundnuts in East Africa, the Colonial Office wisely decided to

[498] John Strachey (1901–1963), Labour MP and minister; minister of food, 1946–1950.

put a man with business experience in charge of the Colonial Development Corporation which owed much of its success to the appointment of an astute businessman Mr Garro Jones,[499] later Lord Trefgarne, to head it, and make a sound choice of schemes with a good chance of ultimate commercial viability.

For the Corporation was obliged by Statute to 'break even' in the long run. The money allocated to the Corporation could be spent by Colonial Governments on essential infrastructure, on social services, or on public utilities, according to the requirements of any particular scheme. In carrying out its operations it could act either on its own or in association with a Colonial Government or in partnership with private enterprise. By the end of 1956 it was operating 66 projects, mainly for agriculture and forestry, but including mines and factories. It was intended to operate in an area of marginal profitability, situated between the highly profitable undertakings of private enterprise, and the unremunerative public works provided by Colonial Governments, but partly owing to some initial mistakes, it became later on mainly concerned with advancing loans to successful private companies and territorial Governments.

I will now pass on to particular Colonial Territories with which I had to deal as a Minister, sometimes from Whitehall, sometimes in Parliament, sometimes in a Colonial territory when I was inspecting my areas of responsibility.

Palestine

On April 7th, 1948, I moved the Second Reading of the Palestine Bill in the House of Lords. The object of the Bill was to enable us to terminate our administration of the Mandate on May 15th, and to withdraw all our troops by August 1st. We were asking the League of Nations for a special Session 'to consider the question of a future Government of Palestine'. We were thus refusing to stay on to enforce the truce between the two communities although we knew that it was most unlikely that any other country would be willing to take over from us. Lord Salisbury, for the Conservative Opposition, concurred in our proposal. The political background of the Bill was our determination not to allow our own troops to continue to be involved in policing the stormy relations between Jews and Arabs. Ernest Bevin had no soft spot for the Arabs, and none for the Jews. I have already explained that Attlee had given him a free hand in

---

[499] George Garro-Jones (1894–1960), later 1st Baron Trefgarne, Labour MP and peer; founding chairman of the Colonial Development Corporation, 1947–1950.

foreign policy, and his main concern was to save British lives even if it meant leaving Palestine to its undeclared war. In my view, this hardly reflected the attitude of a Trustee, which had accepted this responsibility from the Trusteeship Council of the League of Nations. We could not even plead that circumstances had changed for the better since our acceptance. However, we were now able to redeem the pledge which we gave in the Balfour Declaration,[500] and to recognise the new State of Israel,[501] albeit surrounded by Arab countries.

The Malayan Federation

I was delighted to be advised by Sir Thomas Lloyd, the Permanent Under-Secretary at the Colonial Office,[502] that I would be more useful to the Colonies by visiting them than by speaking for them in the House of Lords. Accordingly, in the winter of 1948, I was pleased to be asked to visit the Malayan Federation.

My first stop on my journey was Malaya where I attended the opening meeting of the Federal Legislative Council in Kuala Lumpur. The Council represented all the main ethnic communities in the Federation: the Malays, the Chinese, and the Indians; and was appointed by the British High Commission for Malaya,[503] pending the return to normal conditions after the war which would permit an electoral roll and direct elections. The setting up of a Federal Legislature was the first step towards eventual self-government as agreed by the British with the Sultans of the Malay States.

I delivered a message of goodwill from the Secretary of State, and made the acquaintance of many interesting figures in all the communities. None more informative and personally charming than Dato Onn,[504] the Prime Minister of Johore, and Leader of the majority Party, United Malays National Organisation. Many years later I heard from someone who had been present on that occasion that I was still remembered in the Federation for my black top hat and tail-coat, an outfit I had borrowed from my youngest brother who had acquired it to attend the Eton and Harrow Cricket Match at Lords. It was the very first time that such an outfit had been seen

---

[500] Made in November 1917 by the foreign secretary, Arthur Balfour, to aid the establishment of a 'national home for the Jewish people' in Palestine.

[501] That came into existence in May 1948.

[502] Sir Thomas Lloyd (1896–1968), permanent under-secretary of state for the colonies, 1947–1956.

[503] The de facto British official in charge of the territory from 1948.

[504] Dato Onn Jaafar (1895–1962), Malay political leader; chief minister of the state of Johore, 1947–1950; first leader of the United Malays National Organisation.

in Malaya. It appeared that everything else I had said in my numerous speeches had by that time been forgotten.

I had been armed just before I left London by a long letter from Malcolm MacDonald,[505] who had been Commissioner-General in South East Asia with oversight of the whole British area, written from Ottawa, where he had just arrived as High Commissioner, introducing me to all the leading personalities I would be likely to meet. He had been extremely popular in South East Asia, having the rarest quality in British officials out there, namely 'the common touch'. It was not forgotten that he had slept with the Dyaks and other tribes in their Long Houses (communal dormitories) in Borneo and Sarawak.[506]

I made a most interesting tour of the Federation: watching the rubber tappers at work in the rubber plantations, calling formally on several of the Sultans in their Istanas, and visiting the old Settlements in Penang and Malacca. The East coast of Malaya, with its magnificent beaches, then unspoilt by hotels or other tourist attractions, was particularly inviting. Sir Edward Gent,[507] the High Commissioner to Malaya, and Sir Ralph Hone,[508] with his special knowledge of the whole of the British South East Asia, also explained the intricacies of the political situation.

The Communist rising started in June 1949, the month after my visit had ended. What really astonished and alarmed me was that none of the senior British officials whom I met had the faintest suspicion of any danger from the Communists. Their preparations for an armed rising must have been going on for months, but no inkling of it had reached the British authorities. Their intelligence service must have been totally ineffective to have picked up nothing from the many Malays and Chinese who knew exactly what was going on. Absence of contact between British Colonial Service officials and the local population was unfortunately not uncommon.

[505] *Malcolm MacDonald was a really delightful and civilised man who might have enjoyed an academic life more than politics.* Malcolm MacDonald (1901–1981), Labour and National Labour MP, minister, diplomat and colonial administrator; secretary of state for the colonies, 1935 and 1938–1940; commissioner general for the United Kingdom in South East Asia, 1948–1955, and governor of Kenya, 1963.

[506] *The absence of contact between British Colonial officials and the local population has never been better illustrated than by the total surprise at the communist rising in Malaya in 1949. The gap between officials and ordinary people was sadly common.*

[507] Sir Edward Gent (1895–1948), colonial service; governor of the Malayan Union, 1946–1948, and high commissioner of the Federation of Malaya, 1948.

[508] Sir Ralph Hone (1896–1992), civil and colonial service; deputy commissioner general for the United Kingdom in South East Asia, 1948–1949 and governor of North Borneo, 1949–1954.

The first-hand experience I gathered from this visit was extremely useful when I found myself replying in November to a Motion of Lord Mancroft[509] in the Lords, 'calling attention to the situation in Malaya'. I explained that the violence in Malaya was a legacy of the war against Japan. The resistance movement against the Japanese was organised by the Malayan Communist Party, and this was led by Chinese Communists. In the interval between the withdrawal of the Japanese from Malaya and the establishment of the British military administration in August 1945, the Malayan Communist Party had assumed control of the country, and hoped to set up an independent Malayan Communist Republic. Terrorist violence did not begin until June 1948, when the Communist Party decided that the patient penetration of the trade unions and propaganda in the villages had failed completely to smooth the constitutional path to power. They had exchanged one foreign master for another, and neither could be removed except by force. The Communist doctrine was that all Bourgeois Governments be removed by force: this was despite the British promise (considered to be bourgeois propaganda) to withdraw in any event. It should also be remembered that when British rule was re-established in Malaya we discriminated seriously against the Chinese. Malays were the only Asians admitted to the senior ranks of the Civil Service. Malay schools were paid for from public funds, but the Chinese had to pay for the education of their own children. The best soil for rice crops was owned by Malays, and made inalienable. Our discrimination resulted from the fear of the Communist Party.

After a couple of nights at Government House in Singapore, well situated outside the city, where Gimson,[510] the ageing Governor, was about to retire, I flew on to Kuching, for a short visit to Sarawak and North Borneo. I had had some correspondence with Rajah Brooke,[511] who for many years had treated Sarawak as the family property, and had been bought out after the war by the British Government. He retreated to Singapore during the Japanese occupation of Sarawak, and conceded the territory to us in 1946. But he still considered that he should be consulted about his former domain. We now had a British Governor, Charles Arden-Clarke[512] who was already

---

[509] Stormont Mancroft, 2nd Baron Mancroft (1914–1987), Conservative peer and junior minister.

[510] Sir Franklin Gimson (1890–1976), colonial service; governor of Singapore, 1946–1952.

[511] Charles Vyner Brooke (1874–1963). Rajah of Sarawak, 1917–1946; the last of the Brooke family to be the ruling 'White Rajah' of Sarawak.

[512] Sir Charles Arden-Clarke (1898–1962), colonial service; governor of Sarawak, 1946–1949; governor of the Gold Coast, 1949–1957; and governor general of Ghana, 1957.

trying to associate representatives of the ethnic communities with his administration. Trade and commerce were in the hands of the urban Chinese, who were the dominating element owing to their wealth, though of course few in number compared with the indigenous Dyaks; but the Governor held a fair balance between town and country.

I had also accepted an invitation from the Sultan of neighbouring Brunei, on the advice of the Colonial Office, as the oil fields of Brunei were the largest in the British Empire and could be damaged by political instability.

The Sultan of Brunei was one of the richest men in the world thanks to his royalties from the sale of oil, and there was obviously some risk from an absolute monarch reputed to have a somewhat unstable character. His instability I found to be due to addiction to alcohol, and though he was well disposed towards the British, and wanted to visit the United Kingdom, he did not appear to take his political responsibilities very seriously. So it was with considerable relief that I passed on to my next port of call. It started from Jesselton,[513] the capital of British North Borneo, which had been bought from the Chartered Company of British Borneo for £1,400,000 in 1946. There I was warmly greeted by the burly figure of the Governor, Peter Twining (later Lord Twining),[514] who took me under his wing during my visit. He was a man with an infectious humour and prodigious enthusiasm for the economic development of the area.

The West Indies

I had been instructed by Attlee to report to him personally, not to my Secretary of State, on my visit to South East Asia, and a report was duly drafted and delivered to the Prime Minister. He evidently thought that ministerial visits to the Colonies were a good thing, because in the autumn of 1949 he approved of a similar visit to the Caribbean, again suggested by the Colonial Office.

Attlee told me that he was particularly anxious that I should not miss the Leeward Islands, as he had appointed as Governor there, Oliver Baldwin,[515] son of the late Prime Minister. Oliver Baldwin had become an undistinguished Labour member of the House of

---

[513] Today called Kota Kinabalu.

[514] Sir Edward 'Peter' Twining (1899–1967), later Lord Twining, colonial service; governor of North Borneo, 1946–1949, and governor of Tanganyika, 1949–1958.

[515] Oliver Baldwin (1899–1958), later 2nd Earl Baldwin of Bewdley, Labour MP and colonial administrator; governor of the Leeward Islands, 1948–1950, recalled in 1950.

Commons, but Attlee insisted that 'something must be done for him' as son of the late Prime Minister and now he wanted to know how he was getting on. I said of course that I would make a point of seeing him when I reached Antigua.

Curiously enough, I had known Oliver much longer than Attlee. As a young man I sometimes went to Hyde Park on Sundays to listen to the orators at Hyde Park Corner. One evening I saw Oliver, whom I had first met at Eton, addressing a small crowd from a soap box. My home in Bryanston Square was quite close, and when he finished I asked him back for dinner. We talked politics afterwards, but his brand of socialism was not mine, and we did not meet again until I stayed with him at Government House in Antigua. He was an excellent host, but when I went around the Island I found to my dismay that he was not on speaking terms with most of the planters despite having become in the meantime Earl Baldwin of Bewdley. I was not surprised, as he was not the sort of person to keep quiet about politics, even in a position of representing the Crown that demanded political neutrality. On my return I duly reported my experience to Attlee, and I think Oliver was recalled very soon afterwards.

I had a pretty extensive programme including visits to the small islands of the Windwards and Leewards, Barbados of course, and the larger islands of Trinidad and Jamaica. After covering the mainland territories of British Guyana and British Honduras, I was due to finish at the British Virgin Islands, hitherto unvisited by any British Minister.

The pattern of these visits was always the same. Usually there was a dinner party at Government House on the night of my arrival, to introduce me to the Chief Justices, the Prime Minister, and other notabilities in the Colony. Then, according to the length of the visit, I would make a complete tour of the Colony by car or plane, being met and shown around by members of the local authorities, and by farmers and businessmen responsible for local agriculture or industrial undertakings. There were frequent short speeches of welcome to which I replied. It was always a fascinating experience, superbly organised by the Governor, and I cannot imagine how anyone could get to know more about the life of a Colony in so short a time.

I can remember a few highlights of my tour of the West Indies.

Barbados

In Barbados, I presided at a meeting of all the Colonial Governors in the West Indies. This was useful, not so much as a formal gathering, but because it enabled Governors, who seldom met because their territories were separated by such enormous distances, to compare notes in a relaxed atmosphere. I believe this was the first meeting of its kind, and I do not know whether it has been repeated.

British Guyana [*sic*]

The colony I remember best is British Guyana, which seemed at that time to be a land of great promise, if only the Indian minority and the African majority were able to get on better together. Both had able leaders in Mr Jagan[516] and Mr Burnham[517] but there was a good deal of fear on both sides and this was not diminished by the rapidly growing Indian population. A good start was being made however by sending the children of both communities to the same schools. The Governor, Sir Charles Woolley,[518] accompanied me on a fascinating tour by air of the whole Colony.

We landed on airstrips in jungle clearings, and met a number of the indigenous Amerindians in their villages. In one village school I picked up an English textbook, and read the following sentence: 'The Scottish nobleman strode out from his castle into the snow'. As the village children in the heart of British Guyana had never heard of Scots or noblemen, or set eyes on a castle, or, of course a fall of snow, I suggested that a textbook based on local life in the tropics might be rather more suitable. Few Amerindians had the opportunity of a higher education, but their capacity was shown by the co-pilot of our plane, who belonged to the Arawak tribe of Amerindians.

I was greatly impressed by the magnificent sight of the Kaieteur Falls, which is one of the grandest waterfalls in the world, in the same class as the Victoria Falls on the Zambesi. Perhaps by now it has been harnessed to provide hydro-electric power for the local industries, such as mining and forestry in the interior and sugar and rice along the fertile coastal belt.

At New Amsterdam, I saw a ship with a cargo of cattle which had just come down the trail from the Rupunini River. Having seen them a few days earlier in good shape on the savannahs of the interior, I

[516] Cheddi Jagan (1918–1997), chief minister of British Guiana, 1953 and 1961–1964; president of Guyana, 1992–1997.
[517] Forbes Burnham (1923–1985), prime minister of Guyana, 1966–1980, and president of Guyana, 1980–1985.
[518] Sir Charles Woolley (1893–1981), colonial service; governor of British Guiana, 1947–1953.

was shocked by their emaciated condition. It was a relief to hear that the cattle owning companies were planning to send the meat by air to the coast. In the sugar plantations, some planters were starting to move the workers from their old barrack lines into modern housing. I hope that these barrack lines are now a memory of the past.

Jamaica

In Jamaica I was royally entertained at his house in Kingston by the Governor, Sir John Huggins[519] and his charming wife Molly. I was invited to a meeting of the House of Assembly, where I sat next to the Speaker and gave a short address. I had been greeted on the pier on my arrival by Sir Alexander Bustamente [sic],[520] the leader of the majority Labour Party. He was a colourful personality, a powerful orator, who was recorded as riding through a village on a Palm Sunday on a donkey, to show his attachment to the bible. His opposite number, Mr Manley,[521] was a brilliant and distinguished lawyer, who had also been Prime Minister of the country. During my three days at Government House I was taken for an extensive tour of the Island, including the still popular seaside resort at Montego Bay. It was interesting to find a Co-operative Land Settlement – a new type of land tenure – and young light industries, such as a textile factory, saving expensive imports. Jamaica suffered seriously from violent fluctuations in commodity prices, and I assured the sugar producers that we would do our best in the United Kingdom to secure long-term contracts and a reasonable price level for sugar.

British Honduras

My most vivid recollection of British Honduras is the quantity and ferocity of the insect population, and the delightful and entertaining personality of the Governor, Sir Ronald Garvey.[522] I spent a very pleasant week with him on roads often degenerating into rough tracks that linked the villages of the picturesque and mountainous countryside. Traces of the ancient Mayan civilisation, which of

---

[519] Sir John Huggins (1891–1971), colonial service; governor of Jamaica, 1943–1951.

[520] Sir Alexander Bustamante (1884–1977), chief minister of Jamaica, 1953–1955 and prime minister of Jamaica, 1962–1967.

[521] Norman Manley (1893–1969), chief minister of Jamaica, 1955–1962.

[522] Sir Ronald Garvey (1903–1991), colonial service; governor of British Honduras, 1949–1952.

course had been destroyed by the Spaniards, remained sometimes in pretty good condition in ruined shrines and powerful sculpted stone figures, and many place names were reminders of the centuries of Spanish occupation.

It was the only West Indian Colony whose existence was challenged by a foreign neighbour. The presence of British troops was essential to prevent an invasion from Guatemala. The locals were not at all afraid. According to my host, a common saying in the villages was, 'Let's swot those Gwats'. We offered to submit the legal claim of Guatemala to the International Court of Justice, but this offer was always refused. Apart from an abundance of citrus fruit, there was little scope for agriculture, and less for industry in this poor Colony.

I had a kind letter of regret from Ronald Garvey on my departure in 1950 from the Colonial Office which also showed his robust commonsense. Princess Alice, Countess of Athlone,[523] was visiting the new University of the West Indies in Jamaica, of which she was Chancellor, and it had been suggested by the Colonial Office that she might spend a few days in British Honduras. He said in his letter:

> I have never been more reluctant to make a decision than when I decided that the Princess Alice visit should be cancelled. The trouble was that one 'boo' or one bottle thrown from a street corner would have set the world press agog – and that would have done more damage than the visit would have done good.

Starting on my homeward journey, I called at Trinidad, and was given a fleeting glimpse of the scenery and wildlife of the beautiful Island of Tobago. I stopped next at Grenada, provider of nutmeg for the Chicago meat industry, then at St. Lucia still unspoilt by tourism, St. Kitts and Nevis, and finally ended my Island tour at Antigua. There I found that my digestion had collapsed after the long succession of large typically English dishes at endless Gubernatorial dinners. I therefore cruelly abandoned the British Virgins, who may still be languishing for a handsome young Minister from Whitehall, and, when I was well enough to travel, I set out for home.

I paid an all too brief return visit to the West Indies in 1989, when I was sent by the Lord Chancellor to represent the House of Lords at the celebration by Barbados of the 350th Anniversary of its House of Assembly. It had been an independent member of the Commonwealth since 1966, but remained perhaps the most British of the former British Colonies in that part of the world by its long-

---

[523] Princess Alice was chancellor of the University of the West Indies (previously University College of the West Indies), 1950-1971.

standing and much admired system of Parliamentary Government, and its passionate addiction to cricket.

While my memories of my tour of the West Indies were still fresh, I took advantage of the recent Report of the Standing Closer Association Committee on the Federation of the British Caribbean Territories, which had been chaired by my old friend Sir Hubert Rance, to initiate a debate in July 1950 in the House of Lords to 'call attention to the recommendations in the Report on the future of the British West Indies'. As the idea of the Federation had been mooted as long ago as 1945 by Colonel Oliver Stanley,[524] when he was Colonial Secretary, it was entirely uncontroversial, and could now be discussed without any Party animus in the light both of this Report and of debates in the West Indian Legislatures.

The argument for a self-governing Federation was economic as well as political. At the moment we were in the anomalous position of having a British Cabinet Minister at one and the same time responsible for helping West Indian producers to get the best possible price for their primary products, namely sugar, and for securing the lowest possible price for the home consumer. The producers should obviously be allowed to negotiate the best price they could get in the world market, preferably through a regional marketing organisation. But this would not be practicable if the larger territories, Jamaica and Trinidad, continued to stand outside a Federation.

I pointed out that they were too poor to run their own show without the grants they were getting from the British Government: 'None of the West Indian Colonies, save possibly Trinidad, could possibly afford to pay for an independent administration, the wide range of social services and the cost of administering the territory and defence'. Accordingly, they needed to pool their expenditure to survive after political independence. At this point I entered a caveat:

it would be dangerous to rush straight away into political union. The main reason is the unpreparedness of public opinion. In the long run the only solid foundation for a Federal structure would be a general desire among ordinary people in the British Caribbean to live together under the same Government. Few who know the region at all well would maintain that at the present time the general desire among ordinary people for political union is felt by more than a minute fraction of the population. I had the privilege last October to visit all the Islands and the two mainland Territories, and this gave me an opportunity of talking to members of all sections of the population. I confess I returned in grave doubt whether the word

---

[524] Oliver Stanley (1896-1950), Conservative MP and minister; secretary of state for the colonies, 1942-1945.

'Federation' is in the mind, or even the vocabulary, of the ordinary estate
worker, small farmer, or townsman.

I followed this caveat with another: 'if the leading Territories
achieve their own political maturity outside a Federal framework,
it would be very difficult for all the Territories to come together'.
It will be remembered now that the ill-fated and essentially artificial
Federation, after misjudged encouragement from Whitehall, only
lasted for four years from 1958. Deserted by Jamaica after a referendum, Trinidad soon followed, and both Colonies became independent members of the Commonwealth. The enormous distances
that separated the units had prevented their inhabitants from acquiring the ties of common citizenship or even knowledge of each other.
The superiority of Jamaica and Trinidad in wealth to any of their
poorer neighbours was another obstacle. The concept of a West
Indian Federation as a new Dominion of the Commonwealth, linked
with Canada in the western hemisphere, was a concept emanating
from Whitehall, but not taking into account local circumstances in
the British Caribbean or the prevailing spirit of nationalism among
the local inhabitants.

The appointment of Hugh [*sic*] Rance as Chairman of the
Standing Closer Association Committee was followed by the
Governorship of Trinidad, which was the last official post before
his retirement. When he came home he took a little house near
Farnham in Surrey, and settled down to write his memoirs. We
met for lunch occasionally, when he came up to London with his
charming and indefatigable wife, Noël. But his health had been
undermined by life in the tropics. He had picked up amoebic dysentery in Burma, and when he came back he had recurrent heart
attacks. He was also in serious financial difficulties because, although
he had served under Mountbatten as a Major-General, and was subsequently a Colonial Governor, he found that his retirement pension
was awarded to him in the substantive rank of Major in the Army.
He also had no private means. As Attlee had assured him that he
would not suffer financially if he continued after Burma in the public
service, I decided to put his case to the Prime Minister.

I was greatly relieved to be told that Attlee had a fund, placed
apparently at the disposal of every Prime Minister by the Treasury,
to be used in the public interest entirely at his discretion. He immediately suggested that he would like to draw on this fund to supplement Rance's meagre pension. His health did not improve and I
had a letter in February, 1974 saying that he had had another stroke
in December, and that he was still seeing his devoted former Private
Secretary, Phillip Nash. He was struck down by a final stroke on

February 23rd of that year. There was a memorial service at St. James's, Piccadilly, packed by his old friends and colleagues. I had lost the best friend I had made in my travels as a Minister to many parts of the world, and the country had lost a great public servant. He had saved us from a civil war in Burma, and had always placed public service before self advancement. Perhaps the most surprising of the gifts of this professional soldier was a genius for friendship. Wherever he went, in Asia, Europe, or the West Indies, he left countless friends who had benefited from his good advice or simply enjoyed his cheerfulness and good humour. In his last letter he told me that he had spent more time talking than shopping in the local village high street![525]

My career as a Minister at the Colonial Office ended with the General Election. I was a little nervous, after the Conservative victory in 1950,[526] that the new Government would not appoint another Minister of State at the Colonial Office. In that case I would have been the first and last Minister of State at the Colonial Office to hold that appointment, and it might have been thought that this was an example of 'jobs for the boys', Attlee having had to find me another post after my retirement from the Burma Office, and there being no vacancy at that time in his administration. So I was considerably relieved when almost the last appointment by Mr MacMillan was that of Alan Lennox-Boyd[527] to the Colonial Office in my former capacity. He was subsequently promoted and became one of the most outstanding and successful Secretaries of State in that Department. It was a loss to the nation when he was killed in a road accident.

---

[525] *One of the pleasantest by-products of my colonial tours was meeting and making friends. I remember particularly Charles Arden-Clarke, who preceded me in Ghana and 'briefed' me superbly at home before I went out. Another was Hubert Rance and his delightful wife, Noel. He came home with amoebic dysentery, which he never entirely threw off. I shall always remember him with gratitude for his kindness to me in Burma.*

[526] A general election was held in February 1950, but Attlee's Labour government remained in office despite a large fall in its majority. As a result of the October 1951 general election, a Conservative administration was formed with Winston Churchill as prime minister.

[527] Alan Lennox-Boyd (1904–1983), later 1st Viscount Boyd of Merton, Conservative MP and minister; secretary of state for the colonies, 1954–1959.

XII
GOVERNOR GENERAL OF GHANA:
1957–1960

The first intimation that I might be asked to go to Ghana as Governor General came in a 6d Air Letter hand-written by Kwame Nkrumah from the Prime Minister's Office in the Castle[528] at Accra, and dated May 5th, 1957. There was something rather pleasantly informal about the use of the cheap Air Mail service for such an important communication. The letter, in green ink, read as follows:

My dear Lord Listowel,
   It is the intention of the Government of Ghana to appoint the next Governor-General from the United Kingdom. I know the part you have played in the socialist struggle in Great Britain. I also know of your services as Chairman of the Fabian Colonial Bureau[529] while I was in London during my student days. In these circumstances, I would be very pleased to know whether it would be possible for us to consider your name among those from whom we might choose a Governor-General. It would a privilege for Ghana if we were able, by appointing you, to honour the work which you did in the achievement of Indian Independence and which you have done in the cause of colonial freedom. As you will realise the matter is urgent and I should greatly appreciate an early reply.

Yours very sincerely,
Kwame Nkrumah

The qualifications for which I had been selected for the post of Governor-General were unusual, at that time I should imagine unique. It would surprise me if any of my predecessors had been chosen as an active socialist, who had contributed to the work of the Fabian Colonial Bureau – I should add not in the distinguished capacity attributed to me by Nkrumah. Indeed, I may have been the first member of the Labour Party to represent Her Majesty in this distinguished capacity. My other alleged qualification was also

[528] Christianborg Castle, the seat of government in Ghana.
[529] *I was never Chairman of the Fabian Colonial Bureau although I was a member.*

unusual. This was that I had shown myself in the House, and as a Minister, a firm supporter of what he described as 'the cause of colonial freedom', in other words the rapid progress towards the break up of the British Empire. Anyway, whatever credentials I was thought to have were certainly ideological and not personal. For I can only remember meeting Nkrumah once, on a visit to London when he had been entertained by my Labour colleagues in the House as the Leader of the Convention Peoples Party. So why on earth did it occur to him to ask me?

My name had not even been suggested to Nkrumah by the British Government, although, at an earlier stage, British ministerial assistance had been offered in the search for a suitable candidate. I was informed that a Conservative Peer, Lord Rennell of Rodd,[530] had been invited to attend the Ghana Independence celebrations in March 1957, at the suggestion of a Cabinet Minister, Mr R.A. Butler, in order that he might make the acquaintance of Ministers in the Ghana Government. It was of course perfectly natural that a Conservative Government should put forward a member of their own Party with a successful record in the City and no connection with Party politics. But it did not turn out that this was the sort of person for which Nkrumah was seeking. He did however write to Mr MacMillan to thank him warmly for his efforts.

I strongly suspect, though I have no direct evidence, that my name was suggested to him by his constitutional adviser, Geoffrey Bing.[531] I had known Geoffrey for many years as a left-wing Labour M.P., said by some to be 'a fellow traveller', though I have no evidence to support this allegation. His good qualities were often underestimated. He certainly upheld the rule of law in Ghana, and kept Nkrumah on the path of constitutional propriety. He and his wife, Teddy, loved Ghana, and because they had no children of their own, adopted and educated a Ghanaian child, who later graduated in medicine and became a doctor. Nkrumah had a lot of advisers, but he listened more to Geoffrey than the others. His influence at this time has been underrated and it was used for the good of Ghana.

My first reaction was to consult my friends in the Labour Party. For acceptance would mean giving up Party politics at a time when the Opposition in the House of Lords was still limited to a very small band of hereditary Peers, and I was their Front Bench spokesman for Commonwealth and Colonial Affairs and also their elected representative in the Labour Shadow Cabinet. Albert

---

[530] Francis Rodd, 2nd Baron Rennell of Rodd (1895–1978).

[531] *I am now certain that Bing suggested to Nkrumah my invitation.* Geoffrey Bing (1909–1977), Labour MP, and later attorney general of Ghana, 1957–1961.

Alexander, who had succeeded Addison as my leader in the Lords,[532] had no doubt that I should accept. Clem Attlee, also in the Lords by that time, took the same view. They both said that they regarded this offer as a means of giving important service to a Commonwealth country, and my experience there would be a valuable asset when I returned to politics at home. My mother was willing to pull up her roots in London, at any rate temporarily, to help me with the hospitality I would be expected to dispense. My colleagues' advice, and the prospect of more exciting and possibly more constructive work than I was doing here, convinced me that I should accept. I even had illusions from the distance of London about fostering a new African democracy.

As soon as Nkrumah had received my letter of acceptance, he put the official machinery in action. This meant submitting my name to the Queen for her approval, and informing the United Kingdom High Commissioner in Accra that he had done so. He himself was due in London for a Prime Ministers Conference in June and, as soon as he arrived, the Queen's secretary, Sir Michael Adeane[533] now Lord Adeane, rang him up to say that the Queen had approved my appointment. He also wrote to me to inform me that Nkrumah had been told of the Queen's consent, and that an official announcement to the Press would be made from the Palace on 23rd June.

I would like to put on record the way in which the Governor-General of a Commonwealth country is appointed, because it is still so often misunderstood. It was astonishing that The Times newspaper congratulated the British Government on the suitability of their choice. What The Times had evidently forgotten was that such appointments are always made on the advice of Her Majesty's Prime Minister in the Commonwealth country concerned, and not on the advice of the Prime Minister of the United Kingdom. The important question of who should advise the Crown was decided as long ago as the Imperial Conference in 1930.[534] The matter had arisen at that time from the determination of Mr Scullin,[535] the Prime Minister of Australia, to appoint for the first time in Australian history a native born Australian, Sir Isaac Isaacs, to succeed Lord Stonehaven[536] as Governor-General when he retired in

---

[532] Actually, Alexander succeeded Jowitt, not Addison, as Labour leader in the House of Lords in 1955.

[533] Sir Michael Adeane, later Lord Adeane (1910–1984), private secretary to Queen Elizabeth II, 1953–1972.

[534] It was at the Imperial Conference of 1926 that this convention was accepted.

[535] James Scullin (1876–1953), Labor prime minister of Australia, 1929–1932.

[536] John Baird (1874–1941), 1st Viscount Stonehaven, Conservative MP and minister; governor general of Australia, 1925–1930.

1930. King George V was not altogether convinced that this Australian could hold such a post without involvement in local political controversy. When Lord Passfield, then the Secretary of State for the Dominions and Colonies, was told of this impasse, he was alarmed at the prospect of the King being dragged into Australian politics, so he decided to put the question as to who should tender advice on the agenda of the next Imperial Conference. The Conference resolved that in making the appointment of Governor-General the King 'should act on the advice of His Majesty's Ministers in the Dominions concerned'. This wise decision has ever since preserved both the complete autonomy of Commonwealth countries in relation to the United Kingdom, and the principle that the Crown is above politics and must always therefore act on advice.

I met Nkrumah when he came to London in June for the Commonwealth Prime Ministers conference, and he discussed in a most friendly way the practical problem of where I should live in Ghana. Christiansborg Castle in Accra had been the home of my predecessor, Sir Charles Arden-Clarke, and of the British Governors of the Gold Coast ever since Cape Coast had ceased to be the capital. Because the rulers of the country had lived there for so long the Castle had become the symbol of authority in Ghana. Nkrumah had therefore rightly taken it over as the head-quarters of his Government as soon as he was released from prison (together with other leading members of the Conventions People's Party [CPP]) and made Prime Minister by the Governor. Nkrumah himself preferred to live in a bungalow attached to the wing of the new State House. He explained that he had found it very unpleasant to be so close to the sea as his books were sprayed with sea salt.

The non-availability of the castle meant that a new house would have to be built for the Governor-General, and that temporary accommodation would have to be found pending its completion. I hated the idea of a poor country spending a lot of money on a grand house, but I realised that the Ghana Government would insist that the prestige of the country depended on a suitable residence for the Sovereign's representative. It was eventually decided that I should live for the time being at Flagstaff House, then occupied by General Packard,[537] the Commander-in-Chief, West African Forces, while the State House was being completed by the addition of residential accommodation and offices as a permanent residence for me in

[537] Lieutenant General Sir Douglas Packard (1903–1999), army officer and administrator; military adviser to West African governments, 1956–1958.

Accra. I had strongly protested when it was suggested that I should be temporarily 'rusticated' by staying at Government Lodge at Cape Coast, which was 90 miles from the Capital, while the work on the State House was going on.

Nkrumah then generously offered to give me the Lodge at Cape Coast as a weekend house by the sea while my office and official home would be in Accra.[538] I accepted this offer, and it was confirmed by a Government statement to the Press and a radio announcement in Accra on September the 26th, 1957. The announcement read as follows:

> State House will be the Governor-General's official residence. Extensive modifications and improvements of residential quarters are being made in order to ensure that suitable accommodation and other facilities will be available to him. It is anticipated that this work will take some months to complete, and in the interval the Governor-General will use Flagstaff House in Accra as a temporary residence. He will also use Government Lodge, Cape Coast, as a country residence.

When I arrived in Ghana I immediately realised how quickly the scene changes. For Nkrumah had already re-allocated my 'country residence'. Government Lodge at Cape Coast was already occupied by a Mr Hagan,[539] the newly appointed Commissioner for the Western Region of Ghana. I did not of course complain or even mention the matter to Nkrumah, as it would have been an embarrassment to me to occupy two large houses, one of which I would have seldom used and would therefore have remained empty most of the time. My only regret was that the old Government Lodge at Cape Coast had an unusually lovely garden with a great variety of hibiscus and bougainvillaea and a superb view over the sea.

I heard from Nkrumah at the beginning of July that everything could be ready for me by the end of November. It was therefore something of a shock when on returning to London from a holiday towards the end of August, I received a strange and somewhat disturbing letter from Nkrumah written at the end of July. It called for a complete change of plan. The letter was this time in typescript, and asked me to come to Ghana 'early in October'. At this point there was a marginal entry in green ink as follows: 'But if you could possibly come in September it would be a great help to me'. Something had evidently gone wrong.

---

[538] *I suspect the offer of 'a country residence' was used as bait.*

[539] J.E. Hagan, Ghanaian politician; regional commissioner under Nkrumah.

The reasons given by Nkrumah in his letter were that the public 'was anxiously waiting for my arrival' and that the judiciary had become disorganised because the Chief Justice who was acting as Governor-General was unable to perform satisfactorily both his judicial and his administrative duties. I understood Nkrumah's reasons better when I arrived in Accra and learned of events in July. When Nkrumah had disembarked at Takoradi on July 22nd, returning from his visit to London for the Prime Ministers Conference, he found that much of his popularity had suddenly evaporated. In Accra a new party opposed to the CPP had been formed by the Ga, the leading tribe in Accra, and the price of basic foods such as yams and plantains had rocketed. There had been angry shouts and jeers from the 'Tokyo Joes', as the rowdies were called, on his drive through Accra to the Castle. Ever sensitive to the reactions of the public, my presence was needed to divert attention from the political Opposition and economic grievances that threatened to erode his popularity.

I replied that while I was most anxious to help him by coming out earlier than he had asked me to do, I was not willing to live outside Accra, and I could not therefore arrive earlier than at a time when Flagstaff House would be ready for me: I understood by the middle of October. But by the time Nkrumah received my letter at the end of August he seemed to have recovered his nerve. He had appointed his strong man Krobo Edusie [sic][540] as Minister of the Interior, and he had already decided on a number of measures to curb his opponents. I heard from him at the beginning of September to say that he had not wished to hurry the Packards or the Public Works Department, and it would be alright for me after all to come out in November, in time for the opening of the Legislative Assembly on 12th November.

I spent my last weeks in London seeking advice from those who [sic] with long experience of Ghana. I am truly grateful for the advice I received from all quarters – businessmen, politicians, officials, academics – and other people who had lived in the country. Having spent my life in party politics, I suppose it was natural that the advice most commonly offered was the need for political impartiality and detachment. This was perhaps excessively underlined in a ridiculous note I had received from an official in the Dominions Office:

I think it is essential for Lord Listowel to bear in mind that what Ghana is going to demand of him is the same feeling of well-founded confidence, imperturbability, goodwill and above all impartiality, which she is used to

[540] Krobo Edusei (1914–1984), Ashanti and Ghanaian politician; minister of the interior, 1957–1958.

finding in Governors and Governor-Generals from this country. The Ghanaians will expect him to be a figure above the level of day to day politics and Party manoeuvres. Dr Nkrumah will look to him for the kind of encouragement and advice which he so badly needs, the Opposition will hope to have the same advice and encouragement if and when they get into power, and both sides are likely to watch Lord Listowel's words and actions to see whether he is favouring the other side at their expense …

Who could quarrel with these words of pompous official wisdom emanating from an office in Whitehall, and directed clearly at my record as a party politician in the Lords. What the note certainly lacked was the slightest understanding of Nkrumah's personality, or the virtually one party system of Government that was already developing in Ghana.

But to one of my mentors I owe an incalculable debt for his patience and wisdom. This was Sir Charles Arden-Clarke, who had returned from Ghana in May after serving for three months as Governor-General, following several years as Governor of the colony. His home was not far from my mother's house in Suffolk, and he came over for long talks at weekends in the summer. I had met him first in Sarawak when he was Governor there, and I stayed at his house in Kuching on a visit to South East Asia while I was a Minister at the Colonial Office, so that I knew him already as an old friend. In Sarawak he was beloved by everyone, Malays and Dayaks alike. This capacity for friendship had made him equally popular in Ghana. He was the first British official to recognise the National Movement in Ghana to be represented by the CPP under the leadership of Nkrumah, whom he released from prison to make Prime Minister and Chairman of the Cabinet. He was I think the finest all-rounder of the many able Colonial Service Officers I had met on my travels, combining administrative talent of the highest order and sound political judgment with lightness of touch and a genius for personal relationships. I have always regretted that on his retirement he was not given a seat in the Lords, where his advice on the winding up of our Colonial Empire would have been immensely valuable. I can not help thinking that his many tiffs with Whitehall may have cost him the recognition due to one of our greatest public servants.

Another wise mentor I should certainly mention with special gratitude was Sir Robert Jackson.[541] He was an old friend of Nkrumah,

---

[541] Sir Robert Jackson (1911–1991), UN and Australian official, special commissioner of the Preparatory Commission of the Volta River Project, and chairman of independent Ghana's Commission for Development, 1957–1962.

whose advice about the Volta Project had been particularly valuable, and which he was largely responsible for bringing to a successful conclusion. He seemed to be in constant motion, so much were his views in demand throughout the Commonwealth, and it was always difficult to pin him down. His delightful wife, the author and economist Barbara Ward,[542] was an authority on Ghana as she had also lived there for some years. They were both indefatigable and highly skilled conversationalists, and I regretted that, as I did not meet them together, I never found out which was the more voluble, or which would give way first to the other. The administrative arrangements for my departure to Ghana were superbly negotiated by Sir Gilbert Laithwaite, the Permanent Under-Secretary at the Commonwealth Relations Office, who had been Private Secretary to Lord Linlithgow when he was Viceroy of India. Some people even referred to the 'Linlaithwaite' Viceroyalty.

I still dreaded finding myself without the invaluable civil servant advisers I had had during my whole ministerial career in Whitehall. I would obviously have to depend for advice on my Ghanaian Secretary, who would be looking over his shoulder at his own civil service career and his political masters. It turned out that my Ghanaian secretary, Michael Dei-Anang,[543] who was a delightful person and became a life-long friend, was required (as I had expected) to pass on information about me to Nkrumah. For the first time therefore I had to form my political judgments entirely alone, the greatest challenge I had ever experienced.

Only a few details now remained to be settled before I left London. I do not as a rule think a great deal about my own clothes, but it was important that the Governor-General of a new country, that had so recently put an end to its colonial status, should not appear in clothes that symbolised the colonial past. I was therefore relieved when the Lord Chamberlain allowed me to acquire what was known as the 'new style' Governor-General's uniform, which was in blue serge with a military peaked cap in place of the old style white uniform of a Colonial Governor with a plumed helmet. I had to put up with the fact that the new style uniform was painfully hot to wear in the tropics, not being available in anything but English winter weight, which of course had been entirely suitable for the Governor-General of Canada.

[542] Barbara Ward, later Baroness Jackson of Lodsworth (1914–1981), British economist and academic.

[543] Michael Dei-Anang (1909–1977), Ghanaian official and writer; secretary to the governor general of Ghana, 1957–1959, and principal secretary, Ghana Ministry of External Affairs, 1969–1961.

The prospect of my first experience of wearing my uncomfortable uniform as I descended onto the tarmac at Accra Airport did not appeal. For a Commonwealth Relations Official had drawn my attention to a photograph in The Times of Lord Dalhousie[544] descending, complete with his plumed helmet, from an aircraft at Salisbury Airport, where he had just gone out as Governor-General of the Central African Federation. With their usual thoroughness and attention to detail they pointed out that a gentlemen's lavatory on the Strato-cruiser would be large enough for me to change my clothes in. So I was immensely relieved when I received a letter, just before starting, from the Chief Justice, Sir Arku Korsah,[545] who was acting as Governor-General until I came out, and did so again with much success whenever I was away on leave, to tell me that Ministers and other distinguished Ghanaians who intended to meet me at the Airport would be wearing lounge suits. This was the first of many kindnesses for which I have to thank Sir Arku. In fact as I was not even wearing a hat when I arrived: I noticed the furtive disappearance of several trilbies behind the backs of their owners. Nkrumah was among those who greeted me on my arrival, and I was quickly whisked away to my new home to prepare for an evening talk with him.

The evening meal with Nkrumah on the day of my arrival revealed the two matters mainly on his mind. The first and foremost was the Queen's visit to Ghana. Could she come in August, the coldest month in the year, when she would find the climate more like her own country's? But, of course, he would welcome her whenever it suited her to leave the UK for a brief visit to Ghana. I undertook to convey his invitation in my next letter to her secretary, Lord Adeane.

The other matter of immediate concern to him was his relationship with the Paramount Chiefs. The gist of what he said was that the policy of the Government was to respect their traditional functions, provided that they did not 'interfere in politics'. But unfortunately some of the Chiefs were engaging in active politics. This was as I soon realised, something of an understatement considering their mutual hostility. He told me that he wanted me to meet them and 'to say things to them I cannot say'. He expected them to listen to me because of my constitutional position, which was one which to some degree they

---

[544] Simon Ramsay, 16th earl of Dalhousie (1914–1999), Conservative peer and colonial administrator; governor general of the Federation of Rhodesia and Nyasaland, 1957–1963.

[545] Sir K. Arku Korsah (1894–1967), chief justice of Ghana, 1957–1963; summarily dismissed in December 1963 by Nkrumah on acquitting defendants accused of plotting a coup and of attempting to assassinate Nkrumah.

also shared. I, as Governor-General, was a symbol of the nation. They, as Paramount Chiefs, were symbols of their tribe, and in both cases there was status but without authority. This status could only be successfully sustained by the strictest political neutrality. It struck me at the time as interesting that the similarity of status between the Chiefs and Governors was recognised during the time when Ghana was a British Colony. It was implicit in the mode of address between Chiefs and Colonial Governors. You began a letter to a Chief with the words 'My good Friend', and ended with the words 'Your good Friend', and the Chief to whom you had written would reciprocate.

I made a point of getting around the whole country every year, so I visited annually each of the five Regions. On every occasion I was invited to meet the Paramount Chiefs of the Region, who greatly enjoyed the traditional greeting of a ceremonial welcome known as a 'Durbar'. Quite a long time after my first talk with Nkrumah about the Chiefs, I heard from my Secretary, Michael Dei Anang, that the Cabinet had decided that in future there were to be no more Durbars for visits from the Governor-General. It was Nkrumah's habit when he had anything controversial to convey to me to tell my private secretary to pass on his view. I realised immediately that this would be an unpopular decision because it would deprive the Chiefs of a traditional demonstration of their own status among their people and of their loyalty to the Crown. But of course I replied that I would be careful for my part to observe the 'no Durbar' policy.

So on my next visit to the Regions I was amused to find that the Chiefs had discovered a way of getting around this difficulty. They did so by continuing the traditional ceremony not as an official occasion with the official title, but simply as a private welcome to a distinguished visitor. They appeared just as before in full regalia sitting under their state umbrellas, surrounded by their sword bearers, drummers, and dancers. I felt that I was doing my bit to make my visit an unofficial occasion by not wearing uniform. However, as I had invested in a grey top hat and grey suit for the races at Accra, which I had been obliged to attend in order to present a cup to the winners, this Ascot outfit, which had never been seen outside the capital, enabled me to turn up in an attire which was extremely gratifying to my hosts because befitting the dignity and courtesy that they had expected. I have mentioned my attendance at the Accra Races as one of my official duties. It was fortunate for the bookies that I was not a betting man, as the winner was always known to a select few who had been told which jockey had no large stones in his pockets.

The authority of the Chiefs was now limited to matters of customary law, including of course family relationships, and religion, though their influence on their own people was very considerable. The traditional system of African chieftaincy was one that I thought a lesson for the present day, as it had a secure foundation in the consent of the tribe. A Paramount Chief was not an autocrat as British Governors had been, but resembled much more closely a constitutional monarch, being obliged to act in accordance with the advice of the Elders of his Council, and liable to be deposed or 'de-stooled'[546] if he failed to carry out his constitutional duties. The members of his Council consulted the village Elders, and the village Elders had their ears close to the ground and knew what their people wanted. With this firm foundation in public opinion African traditional rule in Ghana had been more genuinely democratic than British colonial

But, on the other hand, it was entirely different from Parliamentary democracy in the sense that we understand it. The essence of our system is we can change our Government, and therefore change or even reverse the policy it is pursuing, without bloodshed or violence, by the simple process of persuading our fellow citizens to put their vote in the ballot box. But once a Chief, after fullest consultation with his Council, had arrived at a decision, any further argument or opposition became treasonable. That is why in Africa you can never have a 'loyal opposition'. It follows from this that when the multi-party system of Parliamentary Government has been tried out in Africa, it has almost always become one-party rule. Another interesting and useful aspect of tribal society was absence of private ownership of land. The land was owned by the tribe and allocated to farmers by the Chief, but they had reasonable security of tenure and could pass on their farms to their children.

Most important of all the Chiefs in Ghana was the Asantahene, the King of the Ashantis. They had been essentially a warrior people, and had dominated the Fantis in the South until we finally defeated them in 1900 after several Ashanti wars. At one time we had banished their King,[547] deporting him to the Seychelles, and had also tried to take away their 'Golden Stool', the traditional symbol of the Ashanti Kingdom. But when I arrived in Ghana the position of the Asantahene and his Chiefs had been restored, though they had never come to terms with the nationalist movement, which was

[546] The stool is the symbol of chiefly or royal authority such as the Ashanti Golden Stool of the Asantehene.

[547] Prempeh I was exiled to the Seychelles after a defeat at the hands of the British in 1900.

essentially a movement of the common man, emanating from Nkrumah's Government in Accra. In the 1956 General Election their representatives had formed an opposition party, the National Liberation Movement, which challenged the Convention Peoples Party. Nkrumah told me that he was in danger of being stoned in the streets if he visited their capital in Kumasi. Indeed, when Arden-Clarke last went there as Governor he was booed by the crowds and his car was stolen. Nkrumah's policy of uniting all the Regions of Ghana under the control of the central Government had deprived them of the autonomy they had hoped to retain under the federal constitution which they had wanted and we had hoped for.

I decided that one of my first duties would be to pay my respects to the Asantahene, and to do my best to build a bridge between the Ashantis and the Southerners. I was received in Kumasi with the utmost courtesy, invited to stay at the Palace, and presented with an Ashanti 'stool' – the symbol of chieftainship – and a splendid Kente cloth from the foremost weaver in the country. The Asantahene himself was something of a royal recluse simply attending to his official functions, and he had not been abroad or even visited Accra. So it occurred to me that a good and entirely non-political way of returning his hospitality would be to invite him to stay with me at Accra for the annual Race Meeting. This turned out to be a huge success, as there were a number of Ashantis at the racecourse, and there was a tremendous cheer when he was recognised. It was just the right ambience for him to meet Nkrumah and Government Ministers, as well as the social and plutocratic elite of Accra. This introduction lead to a relatively harmonious relationship developing between the Ashanti and the coastal peoples which I regard as one of my most useful achievements whilst I was in Ghana.

The system of succession in Ashanti was that, while the successor was always in the same family, the actual successor was not the son, but a nephew of the Asantahene. He was chosen, not by the Asantahene, but by the tribal elders. His charming successor a much younger man, I used to meet later in London during his annual visit for Ascot and the London Summer Season.

I had hoped on my arrival that I would see Nkrumah regularly every week to keep in touch with the affairs of the country, but this hope was soon disappointed. At first I lured him by inviting him for tea and a game of tennis. He adored lawn tennis, but was one of the worst players I have ever known. I had the greatest difficulty in losing every match, but he was desperately anxious to win. I soon discovered that if he had heard that I or my ADC had a cold he would not come near my house. I had the misfortune to contract a long bout of jaundice soon after my arrival in November 1957, and this kept Nkrumah away for several months. He had a chronic fear of infection and was constantly worrying about his health. He never travelled without a doctor, and he also consulted the traditional African herbal or 'witch' doctors. Much of his conduct, not only his valetudinarianism, is explained by fear. This is an emotion more easily understood in Africa than in an European environment where, apart from war, most of our natural stimuli of fear have been removed. Long before the first attempt on Nkrumah's life, which did not occur until after I had left Ghana, he would stay for long periods without emerging from his home in Flagstaff House.

His seclusion began after the so-called Amponsah-Apaloo conspiracy in 1958,[548] and therefore as my political concerns grew my ability to get hold of Nkrumah lessened. My political worries began when one morning early in January 1958 the Chief Justice, Mr Van Leer,[549] came into my office to explain the circumstances of a case in which a magistrate had convicted a Cabinet Minister, Mr Krobo Edusei, and the Chief of Police, Mr Madjety [sic],[550] of contempt of court. The reason for the judgment was that, in spite of a Writ of Habeas Corpus, two men had been deported, thus removing them from the jurisdiction of the Court. He, Mr Van Leer, had been invited to attend a Cabinet meeting the previous day where he explained that the verdict was correct in law, and there was no right of appeal. He had added that though the magistrate insisted that the contempt should be 'purged', he would be entirely satisfied by an apology from both Defendants. But the Government, instead of accepting this mild compromise, was determined to override the sentence of the Court. A Bill had been passed through Parliament that very morning exempting the Minister and the Police from any sentence or penalty the magistrate might impose.

When I reported this blatant interference with the course of Justice in my fortnightly letter to Lord Adeane, the Queen's Secretary, it elicited in reply a letter showing little awareness of the authoritarian trend in Ghana. The letter referred to the recent arrests of Amposah and Apaloo, both Members of Parliament under the Preventive

[548] A suspected conspiracy directed by Opposition MPs R.R. Amponsah and M.K. Apaloo to assassinate Nkrumah and carry out a coup d'état.

[549] Listowel is referring here to Justice W.B. Van Lare (1904–1969), who was a judge of the Supreme Court of Ghana, 1957–1963, and served as acting chief justice for a period between 1957 and 1958.

[550] E.R.T. Madjitey (1920–1996), Ghanaian police officer and later diplomat and opposition politician; inspector general of police, 1958–1964, and leader of the opposition, 1970–1972.

Detention Act, as well as to the contempt of court case. I quote the last paragraph:

> As you say, these events of Parliamentary and Constitutional importance are typical of the growing pains of a new country and, no doubt, when Dr Nkrumah returns from India, he will take steps to arrange for an open trial of the detained Members, and will also be able to reassure you that it is no part of a policy of his Government to interfere with the normal course of justice.

These fortnightly letters and replies were not copied to the British Government as my official relationship was with the Queen and throughout my time in Ghana I dealt exclusively with the Palace.

As Nkrumah was away, I immediately summoned his senior Minsters, Mr Botsio[551] and Mr Gbedemah,[552] to tell them exactly what I thought, and to warn them that if there had been a breach of the constitution I would have resigned. When I reported the matter to Nkrumah on his return from India, he expressed concern about my concern, but otherwise seemed to dismiss the matter as a storm in a teacup. I told him I could not agree with his view and, at a later stage, emphasised the need to maintain the independence of the judiciary by safeguards in the new Constitution.

It transpired much later, after an enquiry by a distinguished British Q.C., Mr Granville Sharpe [sic],[553] that the unfortunate Members of Parliament were entirely innocent. I think it was fear rather than any rational view of his security that started him on the road to preventive detention, and this also, because he was not a deliberately cruel man, enabled him to justify the hardship and suffering he inflicted on many of his political opponents and their families.

Soon after I arrived in Ghana I heard from the Commonwealth Office that they were considering a suitable honour for Nkrumah, and that they would like to make a recommendation to the Prime Minister. The honour that they had in mind was that of Companion of Honour. I replied that I thought that this honour would not really appeal to him, as it had only been added recently to our Honours System by Winston Churchill, and had not even the traditional dignity of the Orders of Knighthood.[554] I therefore

---

[551] Kojo Botsio (1916–2001), Ghanaian politician; minister of foreign affairs, 1958–1959, and 1963–1965.

[552] Komla Agbeli Gbedemah (1912–1998), Ghanaian politician; minister of finance, 1957–1961.

[553] Justice Gilbert Granville Sharp (1894–1968), Liberal politician and barrister; justice of appeal of the Supreme Court of Ghana, 1957–1962.

[554] The Order of the Companionship of Honour was founded in 1917. Membership confers no title. Churchill was a Companion, but did not found or instigate the Order.

suggested instead, knowing his veneration for the Queen, that a distinction involving a personal relationship with the Monarch, such as a Privy Counsellorship, would really please him immensely. It turned out that the offer of this honour, when followed by the invitation to Balmoral, were the two events which had given Nkrumah most satisfaction during my time in Ghana.[555]

Thanks to Nkrumah's respect for the Queen, I knew Nkrumah would take seriously my only weapon as a constitutional Governor-General and Commander in Chief. The threat of resignation. In this respect I was in a stronger bargaining position that the Monarch, who could never resign from the office of Sovereign and could hardly use the threat of abdication. It was most unlikely that Nkrumah would do anything that might be construed as disrespect for her representative. Indeed, I was increasingly conscious of the fact that my presence in Ghana was doing a valuable service by delaying for three years his transition from Prime Minister to Head of State and Commander of the Armed Forces. My apprehensions about the future, after my departure, were borne out by events. For Nkrumah then immediately despatched a large contingent from the Ghana army to support the African forces in the Belgian Congo actively engaged in a war with the Colonial Power, and dismissed the Chief Justice for acquitting his alleged would-be assassins.

I remember one evening, after a game of tennis, being told by Nkrumah that after reading how Lenin had started to construct an electrical power supply throughout Russia immediately after the 1917 revolution, and while that country was still ravaged by famine, he had decided that Ghana must be immediately industrialised to bring about in his country the higher living standards and all the other benefits of the industrial revolution in Europe. But of course he had ignored the fact that Russia already had a 19th century industrial background, and that some of the infrastructure and technical know-how had survived the devastation of the European war and the civil war that followed it. This mistake in priority for manufacturing industry in an agricultural country resulted in a wasteful and uneconomic use of the large cocoa reserves, and was disastrous for the whole Ghana economy. The reserves built up under the colonial administration were quickly used up, and the burden of foreign debt still carried by the Ghana Government started to accumulate. Prestige expenditure, such as sending diplomatic missions to South America and other parts of the world to countries with which

---

[555] *The Queen was undoubtedly a 'mother' figure for Nkrumah. The invitation to Balmoral was a superb example of royal tact.*

Ghana had little or no connection, added further to the growing public debt.

Although Nkrumah always declared himself to be a socialist, his idea of socialism had little to do either with social democratic principles of common ownership of capital, or with the revolutionary doctrine of Karl Marx and the Communist Party. What he had in mind was what is often called state socialism, and this consisted simply of a transfer of industry and capital investment from private to state ownership. This was in fact a straight forward expression of African nationalism, because, as there was almost no African middle-class in Ghana, it meant replacing the European or Lebanese entrepreneurs and shareholders by an indigenous bureaucracy. But there was nothing in this policy to bring about greater equality in the ownership or the distribution of wealth, and it simply entailed a transfer of capital from existing owners, mainly expatriates, to the Government of Ghana.

Professor Arthur Lewis,[556] at that time economic advisor to the Ghana Government, came to see me on 24th December, 1958 to explain why he had resigned to take up his new post as Deputy Director of the Special Fund at the United Nations. He had differed with Nkrumah he said over economic policy. The immediate reason for the Professor's resignation was an increase of 50% in the Five Year Development Plan, most of which would be spent on prestige projects in Accra. He showed me Nkrumah's letter accepting his resignation. The letter did not contest the soundness of the economic advice he had received but went on to say: 'I am a politician and must gamble with the future.' My heart sank because he had lost the one man who could have saved Ghana from the crushing burden of debt caused by his impulsive extravagance. I note that the last words in my diary for 1958 were 'end of a miserable year: country heading for bankruptcy and autocracy'. It took me only a year to see the direction in which Ghana was drifting.

Nkrumah failed to understand that economics were more important to the welfare of the people of Ghana than politics. His favourite motto was 'seek ye first the political kingdom'.[557] For example, it was a serious mistake when the central Government reduced the subsidy and the cost of anti-capsid spray, which greatly handicapped the cocoa farmers.

Nkrumah did however have the imaginative vision of the statesman to conceive bold and original policies, and the determination

---

[556] Arthur Lewis (1915–1991), later Sir Arthur Lewis, economist and educator, born on St Lucia; chief economic adviser to the Ghanaian Government, 1957–1958.

[557] 'Seek ye first the political kingdom and all things shall be added unto you.'

to carry them out against heavy odds, although unfortunately at times this was not tempered by realism. This gift of imaginative leadership gave him an important place in African history as well as that of his own country. He will be remembered as a leading figure during the period of emancipation from colonial rule in Africa, and as the father of the new nation of Ghana. He used to say that the achievement of independence for his own country would be fragmentary and incomplete so long as one square inch of African soil remained unfree. That was why he called the first Pan-African Conference, the all-African Peoples Conference in Accra in 1958, to which the leaders of all the national movements in the different colonial or ex-colonial territories in Africa were invited.

National freedom was to be only the first step towards African unity. However, Nkrumah's fellow African leaders did not at all approve of his idea of uniting the continent behind, still less under, the Ghana leader. When Nkrumah insisted that political unity with a resulting pooling of sovereignty must precede economic unity, it seemed to many that this insistence on overriding national sovereignty would be merely divisive, because at this point it became even harder to get agreement between African Governments. Nonetheless, his vision of a United States of Africa contributed to the far less ambitious remit of trade and economic cooperation given to the Organization for African Unity [OAU]. It may be said that he founded the OAU, a disappointment to him but an invaluable organ for economic cooperation between African countries.

Unfortunately, the practical effect of Nkrumah's African policy was that Ghana was obliged to play a part in Africa far-exceeding its size and financial resources. Large sums of money were dissipated on funds for freedom fighters in other African countries, and a fabulous Palace known as Job 99 was built on the site of my poor little State House as a meeting place for the Heads of African States. Nkrumah himself spent more and more time touring the world in his capacity as an African and world statesman, and it was hardly surprising that many Ghanaians began to feel that he should put Ghana first. He antagonised most of his neighbours by using his freedom fighters as agents directed against any African leader with whose policy he disagreed, and there was widespread complaint about his interference in the internal affairs of neighbouring countries.

The direct effect on me resulting from his meddling in his neighbours' affairs was that I was never allowed to visit either Togoland or the Ivory Coast, as Nkrumah detested Olympio[558] and Houphouet-

---

[558] Sylvanus Olympio (1902–1963), first president of Togo, 1960–1963.

Boigny[559] with equal intensity. Indeed, he went so far as to finance the reunion of the Sanwys, whose tribe was divided by the territorial boundary between Ghana and the Ivory Coast, and he greatly encouraged the Ghanaian Ewes to agitate for a union between Togo and Ghana.

His feeling for Africa was not in the least racist, and the Commonwealth appealed to him because it cut across racial boundaries and contained an even wider cross-section of mankind than the African continent. He regularly attended the conference of Commonwealth Prime Ministers in London, and it was he who first put forward the idea of a Commonwealth Secretariat, now at Marlborough House, London, which has been the most successful addition to the machinery of Commonwealth co-operation since the war. I was surprised when he told me after his return from a Prime Ministers conference in London, that the Prime Minister he liked best of those he met was Menzies of Australia. I thought he would have had much more in common with Nehru, because Nehru after all, was like him, a socialist and a republican, and it was in fact the example of India that encouraged Nkrumah to adopt the policy of making Ghana a Republican country within the Commonwealth. But Nehru unfortunately had also expressed strong disapproval when Nkrumah told him about his statue in Accra. Nehru had explained that he would not allow any statue of himself during his own lifetime to be put up in India, and I think also suggested that it was undesirable for Prime Ministers to have their heads on postage stamps. He had no use for a 'personality cult'.

The Greeks used to talk about the tragic flaw that doomed the tragic hero to his fate This, alas, became more and more apparent in the corrupting influence of power on Nkrumah's career as a statesman of African and world renown. Perhaps his finest hour was when as a former 'prison graduate' he led his country from colonial rule to independence in 1957.

Although Nkrumah had not told me himself, I was told by those who knew him well, Robert Jackson among others, that my term of office was intended to bridge for about three years the transition from Monarchy to a Republic within the Commonwealth. Ghana would thus become the first African country to follow in the footsteps of India, which had pioneered the difficult path of Republican independence without loss of Commonwealth membership. The example set by the Ghanaian Government was to be of special importance to British Africa, as it was followed by most of our other dependencies when they reached the final stage of sovereign Independence.

[559] Félix Houphouët-Boigny (1905–1993), first president of the Ivory Coast, 1960–1993.

This constitutional change was not sought because Nkrumah, or indeed, anyone else in the Government of Ghana, entertained a theoretical preference for a Republic, or felt less than the highest regard for the British Monarchy. In fact, the traditional institution of Chieftainship in Ghana, whereby a paramount chief always acted on the advice of his elders, and was careful not to meddle in party politics, was very similar to the British system of constitutional monarchy. But the Crown was still associated in many minds with colonial rule, and it was essential for Ghana to acquire the appearance as well as the substance of full nationhood. This was brought home to me in a vivid way in 1958, the second Christmas after my arrival in Accra. Just before Christmas, I received a card of good wishes from a Chief living in the depths of the Bush congratulating me warmly on my successful administration of the country! I was careful not to tell this story to Nkrumah, as I was afraid that the Chief might get into trouble. But it does illustrate what many simple, unsophisticated people would, no doubt, continue to believe as long as the laws of the country were made, and justice dispensed, in the Queen's name.

Nkrumah's personal attitude to the Queen was little short of idolatry. As mentioned, he wished her to come to Ghana, ideally while she was still Queen of Ghana, and therefore, Head of State. But, of course, this was not to be. When it became clear to the Palace that the Queen was expecting another baby, and that she would be unable therefore to travel to Africa in 1959, the question arose as to how the bad news should be broken to Nkrumah. It was decided to soften the blow of cancelling the visit by sending an emissary to break the news personally to Nkrumah.

Martin Charteris (now Lord Charteris of Amisfield),[560] at that time Assistant Secretary at the Palace, was sent to Accra in an aircraft of the Queen's Flight, and I asked Nkrumah to meet him at my house, where he would be staying. Nkrumah's features were always expressive, and I have never seen such a look of despair on a man's face as when he was told that a visit would not take place in November 1959, and would have to be postponed indefinitely.

Every effort was made by the Royal Family to mitigate Nkrumah's bitter disappointment. Prince Philip[561] agreed to visit Ghana in Her Majesty's place in November 1959, and I now record my recollections of that visit.

---

[560] Sir Martin Charteris (1913–1999), later Lord Charteris of Amisfield, courtier, assistant private secretary, 1953–1972 and private secretary to Queen Elizabeth II, 1972–1977.
[561] Prince Philip, duke of Edinburgh (b.1921), consort of Queen Elizabeth II.

Prince Philip arrived in Accra in the evening of 23rd November. While I was waiting with Nkrumah at the airport for his arrival I was pleasantly surprised when my companion remarked that 'on looking around I do not see enough Union Jacks'. Prince Philip's first engagement that evening was a state drive with Nkrumah in an open car through the beflagged streets of Accra. Nkrumah's comment after the drive was that he had witnessed 'the warmest demonstration that he had seen in Ghana in the course of his whole political career'. It continued like this, with crowds lining the streets wherever he went, during the whole of the 6-day visit. Nkrumah accompanied his guest almost everywhere in person, finding it a convenient way of increasing his popularity, except on a trip to Kumasi, and he thoroughly enjoyed his vicarious popularity. Prince Philip was by far the most popular visitor during my stay in Ghana, and none of the African Heads of State who came to see Nkrumah in Accra had anything like the same reception from the public.

The first evening of the visit is etched indelibly in my memory, and I can revive even the minute details from a note made at the time. I had arranged a dinner at the State House to give the Prime Minister and my own household an opportunity to meet the Prince. Early in the day I was given a message to say that the Prime Minister wanted a private dinner, that is to say, just me and my wife, Nkrumah and his wife, Prince Philip and his aide Admiral Bonham-Carter.[562] This of course would save the Prime Minister from appearing on the stage with fewer camp followers than his host. So the dinner table was re-arranged, and my household met the Prince for cocktails before the meal. Early in the evening there was an urgent telephone call from Robert Jackson to say that the Prime Minister wanted to bring Kwame II[563] to the State House for a few minutes before the dinner. I described the ensuing scene in the following note:

> Prince Philip taken away from cocktails at 20.45 to meet Kwame II. Baby appears in doting father's arms at 20.50. Obvious difficulty in keeping eyes open, but allows Prince Philip to pinch cheek. Thereupon emits tremendous howl, and is whisked away in arms of nurse. Mrs Nkrumah looks on without saying a word.

The secret of Prince Philip's success was extremely hard work combined with personal charm. He breakfasted at 8.00am and was out of the house by 9.00am. He was usually not in bed before 12.00pm after a day of continuous movement and constant conversation in the

[562] Rear Admiral (later Sir) Christopher Bonham-Carter (1907–1975), naval officer and courtier; treasurer to Prince Philip, 1959–1970.
[563] Gamal Nkrumah (b.1959), eldest son of Kwame and Fathia Nkrumah.

tropical heat. He never allowed himself to show any sign of fatigue or boredom, and took immense trouble with everyone he met at the endless ceremonies and numerous introductions which filled his working day.

I put on paper some thoughts on the value to Ghana of the Duke's visit. In the first place, it was a lesson in the importance of a common loyalty overriding the claims of party, creed, or class, to the symbol of national unity. This lesson was particularly valuable for a new nation like Ghana, deeply torn by party strife and tribal rivalry. Prince Philip was indeed the first visitor since independence who had as favourable a comment in the Opposition Press as in the Government Press. His photograph in the company of Dr. Busia,[564] the Leader of the Opposition, appeared in the only Opposition newspaper, the Ashanti Pioneer.

Secondly, it had strengthened the ties between Ghana, the United Kingdom, and the Commonwealth. I had observed that the 'Union Jack' had not appeared in public places in Accra since independence. On this occasion and during the whole of the visit it was hoisted everywhere with the other Commonwealth flags.

Respect and affection for the Crown were expressed in many public speeches, including those of the Prime Minister and the Chairman of the Accra Municipal Council. Many individual Ghanaians who saw Prince Philip or shook his hand must have realised for the first time their link through the Crown with the peoples of the United Kingdom.

Eventually the postponed visit of the Queen to Ghana was fixed for 1961, when Her Majesty could come as Head of the Commonwealth, and not as Queen of Ghana. But it was not until the postponement of the Royal visit that Nkrumah decided to advance the date of the Republic. As the severance of the link with the British Crown concerned the other Commonwealth Countries, he was careful to inform them of his intention. But he regarded his friendship with Mr MacMillan as being an almost avuncular relationship, and he liked to seek the good advice of the British Prime Minister in dealing with other Commonwealth Governments. It was, therefore, to Mr MacMillan that Nkrumah addressed a letter in July 1958 informing him that he intended to make Ghana a Republic within two years, but not before 1960.

On the day he wrote to MacMillan, I received an official letter informing me of his proposal that Ghana should become a

---

[564] Kofi A. Busia (1913–1978), Ghanaian politician and academic; opposition leader; went into exile and returned, on Nkrumah's fall, to be prime minister of Ghana, 1969–1972.

Republic as soon as the necessary changes had been made in the existing constitution. He asked me to disclose the intention of his Government to Her Majesty during my summer leave in the United Kingdom. He went on to emphasise that in view of the need for consultation with his United Kingdom and Commonwealth partners there would be no change in the Ghana Constitution in 1959. Finally, he said, would I ask Her Majesty to give him an audience to discuss his plans during his visit to the United Kingdom in August 1960. This I did, and the unexpected and welcome result was an invitation to Balmoral. The photographs of himself with the family corgis taken on the terrace of Balmoral stood henceforth on his study table.

It occurred to me that if I retired a year earlier than my three year term as Governor-General it would be possible for Ghana to have the first African Governor-General in the Commonwealth.[565] I explained my reasons in a letter to Hugh Gaitskell, the Leader of the Opposition in the House of Commons, on March 9th, 1959.

> I have told the Prime Minister I would like to hand over to a Ghanaian before the Queen's visit. I think Ghana should have an African Governor-General before it becomes a Republic, which is likely to happen next year, and it would be a distinction to have the first African Governor-General in the Commonwealth. There is a sound precedent for this in India. You will remember that Rajagopalachariar [sic][566] succeeded Mountbatten for a short time as Governor-General of India before India became a Republic. They had, of course, to ask an Englishman when I came here because of the deep division between Ashanti and Southern Ghana. This division is now healed, and an African nominee of the Prime Minister would be just as acceptable in Ashanti as anywhere else in the Country. The Asantahene has in fact been staying with me for the last few days for the Independence Celebrations, his first visit to Accra since 1953, and has been enjoying himself enormously.
>
> The Prime Minister ... has not yet made up his mind, and I should like to be guided by his wishes, but I don't want to give the impression that I am unwilling to do my job here for as long as I am wanted. I hope you think I am taking the right line, and I should be grateful for your views.

Gaitskell agreed, and was delighted by the prospect of my help in his Election Campaign in the United Kingdom if the General Election came in the autumn. After some time for reflection, Nkrumah told

[565] This distinction would go a few months later to Nnamdi Azikiwe, commonly known as 'Zik', who became governor general of Nigeria, 1960–1963.

[566] C. Rajagopalachari (1878–1972), Indian political leader and official; last governor general of India, 1948–1950.

me, that he would like me to stay. The real reason for this decision
was I am sure nothing to do with my job. He was simply afraid of
having a retired African Governor-General, as a possible focus for
political discontent, living in Ghana after he had become President
of the Republic. Events were to show that his fears were not altogether without justification. While I for my part was immensely
relieved to be able to stay for the full term of my appointment. I
felt I was doing a useful job for my adoptive country, and would
be spared immediate return to a poky little flat in Pimlico without
a salary or full-time employment.

At the end of 1959, Nkrumah again wrote to Mr MacMillan that
the most suitable date for his purpose would be June 1960, as this
would allow time for consultation with Commonwealth Prime
Ministers, after the Republican Constitution had been endorsed by
plebiscite in April, following the approval of the Ghana National
Assembly in March. The Commonwealth Prime Ministers
Conference took place in London in May 1960 and it was agreed
unanimously that Ghana, after the declaration of the Republic,
could continue to be a member of the Commonwealth. Ghana
was following India in this respect.

Nkrumah's political dexterity was shown in framing the questions
addressed to the electorate in the plebiscite: one for the Republic, the
other for the Presidency; insisting that each voter must be sure to
answer both questions. The public was not in the least concerned
about the change in the constitution, but of course the majority
wanted the leader of the nation to become its first President, and
how could you have a President without a Republic? Not surprisingly
the result of the plebiscite was to give an overwhelming majority in
favour of Nkrumah and his proposed constitution. Dr Danquah,[567]
the oldest of his political opponents, would have been easily defeated
without the additional handicap of a rigged poll. Nkrumah made
sure that every vote in the polling booth was known by the CPP.

Nkrumah also showed deftness of touch in other dealings. For
example, at one time he came to see me before his departure abroad
saying that he was leaving his two chief Ministers, Botsio and
Gbedemah, neither of whom had been appointed Deputy Prime
Minister, in charge of the Government during his absence abroad.
But as they were bitterly jealous he did not wish to chose which of
the two should be acting as his Deputy. He would like to leave the
decision to me. I am afraid I answered very firmly that it was not

[567] J.B. Danquah (1895–1965), leading Ghanaian politician and political opponent of
Nkrumah; later arrested twice on charges that he was subverting the government. Died
in prison in 1965.

198   GOVERNOR GENERAL OF GHANA: 1957–1960

one of my constitutional duties to appoint his Ministers, and that he would really have to do it himself. I heard no more about the matter. In this instance, I do not think he could have expected this 'try-on' to work.

I was glad to find Nkrumah wanted my views about the draft Constitution. It was to be a presidential type of democracy, similar in this respect to the United States of America, with no ministerial responsibility to Parliament. As I knew it would be useless to suggest any limitation to the powers of the President, I made a suggestion about safeguarding the independence of the Judges, which Nkrumah appeared at the time to approve. I pointed out to him that removal from office with the concurrence of two-thirds of the National Assembly would be a pretty flimsy safeguard in an Assembly dominated by one Party, unless the grounds for removal of a Judge were clearly specified. Nkrumah saw the point immediately, and agreed to the insertion of the words 'on the grounds of stated misbehaviour or infirmity of body or mind' in the relevant clause of the Constitution. But in spite of Nkrumah's acceptance of my proposal, it was amended by his Party in the National Assembly so as to exclude the Chief Justice. This was to have important consequences after I left Ghana. For it made possible the dismissal of the Chief Justice, Sir Arku Korsah, in December 1963, after the Special Court over which he had presided had acquitted three men accused of the attempted assassination of the President in Northern Ghana. The Constitutional safeguard which still protected other High Court Judges was removed in June 1964, when two amendments were made to the Constitution after a referendum, one of which gave the President power 'to dismiss a Judge of the High Court at any time for reasons which appeared to him sufficient'.

The Republic came into being at midnight on the day I left Ghana at the end of June 1960. Nkrumah wanted a British representative to attend the midnight inauguration ceremony, when he would take the oath as President of Ghana. The United Kingdom Government agreed to do so, and the Foreign Office proposed to send out a senior Minister, the Earl of Dundee,[568] who sat in the House of Lords. I discussed this proposal with Nkrumah, and he seemed very put out about it. The Minister in question was not a member of the Cabinet, and he had never even met him. I asked Nkrumah whom he would prefer if a Cabinet Minister was available. He replied that he would like Quentin [sic] Hogg, now Lord Hailsham. They

[568] Henry James Scrymgeour-Wedderburn, 11th earl of Dundee (1902–1983), Conservative peer and junior minister; minister without portfolio, 1958–1961.

had travelled together to Balmoral, and he had found him a most entertaining companion. He regarded this request as not at all unreasonable, because the other African countries would all be represented at Cabinet level. I therefore wrote to Mr MacMillan who agreed with considerable reluctance to this proposal, I will quote one passage from his reply:

> The inauguration of the Republic ... calls for no particular rejoicing on our part. All the more because the form of Government that is being abandoned is one to which our people are deeply attached.

This was in a letter to me from the Prime Minister in the beginning of April. However in the end he proved vulnerable to persuasion, and Quentin arrived in Ghana in the afternoon of my final day. I had the pleasure of completing his wardrobe with a pair of bathing drawers, which enabled him to refresh himself with a dip in my pool before attending the evening celebrations.

To me personally Kwame Nkrumah was always the most considerate of friends. He never refused me anything where my own convenience was concerned, for example he allowed me a long spell of home leave after an attack of jaundice, saying that I would recover sooner in London. When I left Ghana in 1960 he gave me a piece of African sculpture, a fine head in ebony, which he knew I admired. I should like to quote from the note that he sent with his gift:

> I have been wondering for some time what I could give you as a personal gift. The idea has come to me that you might like to have a carving which has been in your Lodge and which I believe you have grown fond of. If you would accept this, and if you think that you will be able to find room for it in your English home, I would be delighted to present it to you. It is something that I too greatly admire and this makes me all the more happy that you should have it. Also it will remind you of Ghana and the days you have spent with us.
>
> With kindest regards,
Yours ever,
Kwame Nkrumah

He was a good listener and listened carefully to what I said in our talks together, and did not take offence when I disagreed with him. He was always good company and he liked nothing better than a really hearty laugh, when his whole body shook with enjoyment of a joke. If he wanted to tell me something even slightly disagreeable, he did so through my Private Secretary. He must have suspected at first that I might interfere in politics, as he forbade his Ministers to see me without his written permission.

One of his greatest assets as a politician, especially when he led the Nationalist Movement before independence, was from the accounts I heard from eye witnesses, of his spell binding 'stump' oratory. He entirely eclipsed Danquah and the older generation of Nationalist leaders, who were far too intellectual to indulge in mob oratory. His speeches in Parliament and on formal occasions always read well but lacked spontaneity, as he never engaged in the cut and thrust of debate. They were carefully prepared in advance, and read aloud to his audience.

Just before I left I received a farewell letter from Sir Michael Adeane:

Buckingham Palace,
23.6.60
Private

My Dear Billy,

... I don't suppose that you are aware yourself in Accra how very successful your term of office seems from here, but I can assure you you need have no doubts. I doubt myself whether the really excellent understanding which exists between the Queen and her Ghanaian Prime Minister – shortly to be President – could have been achieved by any one else but you ...

Yours,
Michael Adeane

The heavy programme for my last day included a farewell broadcast to the Nation, a farewell party for the Corps Diplomatique, and a ceremonial departure from the Airport, carefully timed to remove me by midnight from the local airspace of Ghana. All these items were set out on a printed programme which ended with the unflattering words 'Governor-General departs. General rejoicing.' I was reassured by the hope that the rejoicing might be for the advent of the Republic and not for my departure. Just before take-off from Accra Airport, I boarded my plane after the last handshake with Nkrumah, and the guns began to boom out their parting salute. To my dismay, the plane did not begin to move. I had visions of engine trouble, causing me, like Cinderella, to be caught at the ball after midnight, when the Republic would have come in. So I summoned the stewardess, and asked her to find out from the Captain what was wrong. The explanation she returned with allayed my anxiety. He was only waiting for me to change from my uniform into a comfortable tropical suit. I told him to take off immediately, and I have no doubt the waiting crowd was as relieved as I was when the plane was safely airborne.

And so I left Ghana in 1960, after three of the most exciting years in my life, with a deep sense of gratitude for the friendship and kindness that seem a national trait. But I left with grave doubts about the future. I could only visualise a country plunged more deeply into debt by Nkrumah's extravagance and haunted by the fear and insecurity of his ruthless egotism. He was a classic example of the truth of Acton's aphorism that 'power corrupts, and absolute power corrupts absolutely'.[569] I was therefore not surprised, but greatly relieved, when I heard in 1966 that he had been toppled by a relatively bloodless army coup.

It was not unexpected that Nkrumah had made no provision for a successor. His little son had been taken by his Egyptian mother[570] to the security of her homeland, and for a number of years one military president succeeded another. It was not until the revival of a limited parliamentary system under the aegis of Flight Lieutenant Rawlings,[571] an air force officer backed by the armed services, that a period of political stability was restored, apart from the brief period of Busia's parliamentary rule. But the ultimate authority was still autocratic, and the democratic institutions little more than cosmetic.

1970: A Brief Return to Ghana

I returned to Ghana in November 1970, during the brief Parliamentary interlude of the Busia Government. I was invited by the Ghana Branch of the Commonwealth Parliamentary Association to lead a Parliamentary delegation from the United Kingdom Branch on a short visit at the invitation of our Parliamentary colleagues in Ghana. My own colleagues from the House of Commons were John Maginnis,[572] Trevor Skeet,[573] James Tinn,[574] and Bruce Millan.[575] We spent a fortnight in Ghana from 6th November to 20th November, visiting every Region except the Upper Region and Brong-Ahafo. We saw everything we wanted to

---

[569] Quotation from late 19th-century writer John Dalberg-Acton, 1st Baron Acton.

[570] *Mrs Nkrumah was Egyptian. It was impossible for Nkrumah to marry a Ghanaian as the 'market mammies' (main shop-owners in Accra) would have been madly jealous. So his marriage was arranged by a mutual friend in Egypt. He wanted a son.* Fathia Nkrumah, née Ritzk (1932–2007).

[571] Jerry Rawlings (b.1947); Ghanaian air force lieutenant and politician; led a coup d'état in 1979; head of state, 1979, 1981–2001.

[572] John Maginnis (1919–2001), Ulster Unionist MP.

[573] Trevor Skeet (1918–2004), later Sir Trevor Skeet; Conservative MP.

[574] James Tinn (1922–1999), Labour MP.

[575] Bruce Millan (1927–2013), Labour MP and minister; secretary of state for Scotland, 1976–1979.

see except the wild animals in the Damongo Game Reserve, which were hidden from view at that time of the year by the long grass. I was delighted to meet a number of my old friends, including Mr Madjety, former Commissioner of Police until dismissed by Nkrumah, and now Leader of the Opposition. I also met Mr Braimah,[576] former Opposition Member of Parliament, now Chief Executive of the Northern Region, and also my dear old friend Judge Ollenu [sic],[577] then Acting President of Ghana.

There was everywhere we went an atmosphere of freedom unknown to the Nkrumah years. People could say and think what they liked without fear of the consequences. It was refreshing to find that the Opposition not only criticised the Government, but had their criticism fully reported in the Press. I remember how the one Opposition newspaper, the Ashanti Pioneer, was snuffed out shortly after my first arrival in Ghana, and I was delighted to find that its successor, the Pioneer, was circulating freely throughout the country. All the basic freedoms of democracy: freedom of thought, publication, and association; had come back, and there were no longer any political prisoners. I was pleased to hear that there had been no intimidation or cheating at the last General Election. The most deeply depressing experience in my time had been the detention of political opponents in prison without trial. Now the refugees from persecution, like Joe Appiah,[578] could safely return from the United Kingdom.

I was glad to find that the Paramount Chiefs were allowed to make a useful contribution to the life of the country again, through such national institutions as the Council of State, and the National House of Chiefs, and were no longer subject to political pressure from the local representatives of the central Government. I was particularly pleased to meet several Chiefs who were not politically acceptable when I was in Ghana.

The rapid economic development of the country since I left in 1960 had also been remarkable. The Volta project was then still on the drawing board. Now it had become a vast power and industrial complex. I remembered Tema as a fishing harbour. It had now outstripped Takoradi as the largest port in the country, and the site for the main industrial development of power from the Volta. Of

---

[576] J.A. Braimah, Ghanaian politician; MP and later Northern Region administrator, 1969-1972.

[577] Nii Amaa Ollennu (1906-1986); Ghanaian judge and politician; justice of the Supreme Court of Ghana; and acting president in 1970.

[578] Joe Appiah (1918-1990), Ghanaian politician; MP who was once a close ally of Nkrumah before falling out with him in the 1950s.

course it had been a disastrous mistake to place the main emphasis on the development of industry, as a sort of miraculous short-cut for a third world country to the prosperity brought about by the industrial revolution in the developed countries. It had been recognised too late that an agricultural country must rely on the exploitation of its natural resources, namely cocoa in the case of Ghana, although it also had valuable minerals in the shape of gold, oil, and bauxite.

The fragile democracy I found in 1970 did not long survive runaway inflation and rocketing prices. Kofi Busia was toppled by another Army coup in 1972. His austerity Budget in 1971 had hit the Army Officers very hard, and the last straw was a 45% devaluation of the currency. These measures were due to the crushing debt burden he had inherited from the Nkrumah years.

XIII
THE MOLSON COMMISSION:
UGANDA AND THE LOST COUNTIES OF
BUNYORO: 1961

Soon after I left Ghana I found myself with another and much more difficult and challenging assignment in Africa. This was a mission to Uganda to sort out the differences between the Kingdoms of Buganda and Bunyoro before the country became independent in October 1962.

The first attempt to solve this problem was made by the Uganda Relationship Commission, chaired by Lord Munster, in 1961. Lord Munster was Parliamentary Under-Secretary at the Colonial Office when he was sent out by the Colonial Secretary, Mr MacLeod [sic],[579] to report on relationships between the peoples of Uganda. He was accompanied by two officials from the Colonial Office, Mr Marshall and Mr Wade.[580] He himself paid short visits to Uganda in 1960 and 1961 but went home sick in February, 1961, while remaining titular Chairman of the Commission. The Report was therefore made de facto by the two officials. Their recommendation about the so-called 'lost counties of Bunyoro' was to propose a referendum in the disputed areas as: – 'this problem is in a class by itself. The 1959 Census shows a clear majority of Banyoro in two of the counties claimed, and of Baganda in the remaining area. The figures are thought to be reasonably accurate.' These counties were lost to Bunyoro in the wars which preceded the pacification of the Protectorate and were incorporated in Buganda territory under the 1900 Uganda Agreement, to which the British Government was a signatory.

However no referendum was held and, since that time, there had been no less than five Petitions to the Secretary of State from the Omukama of Bunyoro between 1943 and 1954, claiming territory he had lost to Buganda. So the Prime Minister, Mr MacMillan,

---

[579] Iain Macleod (1913–1970), Conservative MP and minister; secretary of the state for the Colonies, 1959–1961 and chancellor of exchequer, 1970.

[580] H. William R. Wade (1918–2004), later Professor Sir H. William R. Wade, Cambridge law don, not a colonial office official.

decided to appoint a Commission of Privy Counsellors to visit the country and report on the differences between the two Kingdoms, and thereafter recommend what action should be taken to remove these differences before independence. His concern was that: – 'as independence comes nearer, the tension has been rising, and the Munster Commission ... gave a warning that, with other areas tending to sympathise with Bunyoro, [the differences] might even lead to a civil war'.[581] We were given a free hand to find a solution by agreement between the parties, or, failing this, by an imposed settlement. We were appointed by the Prime Minister on December 20, 1961.

'Having regard', as our terms of reference began,

> to the paramount need for the people of Uganda, including Buganda, to move together into independence in conditions which would ensure them peace and contentment, to investigate allegations of discrimination of the kind contained in the Omukama of Bunyoro's petition and grievances referred to in the Munster Report concerning areas in Buganda which are named below ... to advise whether, and if so, what measures should be taken to deal with the situation.

The Commission was immunised against Party politics by including one Labour member, myself, as well as two Conservatives, Lord Molson[582] and Lord Ward of Witley.[583] Lord Molson, as a Conservative and an ex-Minister, was Leader of the Party.

By a curious co-incidence I was already familiar with some of the troubles in Uganda. In 1953 the Buganda Parliament, called the Lukiko,[584] had demanded independence from the rest of Uganda. The Governor, Sir Andrew Cohen,[585] for many years the brains behind the Colonial Office, now in the field something of an old style paternal autocrat, promptly deposed the Kabaka, the King of Buganda;[586] and sent him into exile in the United Kingdom. He lived in London in far from regal style, and I asked him to lunch one day at the House of Lords. We had only reached the soup stage of our meal when the tears started falling into the soup bowl in front of him. I concluded that his undoubted sense of injury was

---

[581] *Letter from Mr MacMillan to me dated 6 December 1961.*

[582] Hugh Molson (1903–1991), later Lord Molson, Conservative MP, peer and junior minister.

[583] George Ward (1907–1988), later Viscount Ward of Wiley, Conservative MP, peer and minister; secretary of state for air, 1957–1960.

[584] Or Lukiiko, the parliament of the kingdom of Buganda.

[585] Sir Andrew Cohen (1909–1968), Colonial Office and Service, governor of Uganda, 1952–1957.

[586] Mutesa II of Buganda (1924–1969), Kabaka of Buganda, 1939–1969 and first president of Uganda, 1963–1966.

genuine, but that of a rather weak character. My embarrassment was much enhanced when I saw, striding past my table, but fortunately without noticing my guest, the Governor himself, in the company of one of my colleagues. The Kabaka was allowed to return to his Kingdom two years later, but only on condition that he would become a constitutional monarch, taking no part in politics, and that Buganda would remain part of Uganda.

Now let me return to the actual business of the Molson Commission. Our purpose was to persuade the Kingdoms to settle their differences by agreement and, failing this, to recommend to Her Majesty's Government the terms of an equitable settlement it would then be obliged to impose before independence, while Uganda was still a Protectorate. We were keenly aware that the United Kingdom was responsible for averting the risk of serious disturbances or even a civil war after the country had become independent.

We arrived in Uganda on January 8, 1962 and spent most of January in Uganda, hearing evidence from the Kabaka, and the Omukama, each represented by Counsel. One of them was John Foster Q.C.,[587] an old friend and Fellow of All Souls, who had been attached to the Washington Embassy during the war. There was a very large number of witnesses. As we drove through the disputed areas it was rather amusing to see posters along the roadside with the biblical flavour of the injunction 'Oh Lords Deliver Us!'

My short stay in Uganda was not confined to sessions of the Commissioners. We found time in the early morning to watch the processions of wild animals in the game park that came down to the drinking holes in one of the rivers at dawn. This was a special pleasure for me, as there had been little wildlife in Ghana, and apart from some bird watching in the vicinity of Accra, I saw almost no wild animals. In those days at any rate in Uganda, unlike Kenya, where the tourists from Nairobi had turned the game park into something more like a zoo, with lions lying by the roadside as the cars drove past, the game park was a place where you could still enjoy the wildlife of Africa unspoilt by European or American intruders.

I must not fail to put on record the unfailing kindness of the Governor, Sir Walter Coutts,[588] or the benefit we derived from his wide advice during the talks we had with him at Government House before and after our official duties. I shall never forget the beauty of the rugged countryside, the pleasure of working in a

[587] John Foster (1903–1982), later Sir John Foster, Conservative MP and barrister.
[588] Sir Walter Coutts (1912–1988), Colonial Service; governor, 1961–1962, and governor general of Uganda, 1962–1963.

tropical climate tempered by its altitude, or the friendliness and help-fulness of the many Ugandans and Europeans we met as we travelled about the country.

We decided that the only way to achieve a just and lasting settle-ment of the dispute would be by a limited transfer of territory. We therefore recommended that the lost counties of Buyaga and Bugangazzi should be transferred to Bunyoro, but there should be no change in the status of the territory to the East of these counties, where the Bagandas were in a majority. The town of Mabende, where there was a predominantly Baganda population, should be administered by the central Government. The main reason for the transfer of territory was an overwhelming majority of Banyoro inhab-itants. In Buyaga there were 33,000 Banyoro against 2,000 Bagandas. While in Bugangazzi there were 16,000 Banyoros against 2,000 Bagandas. We did not take a plebiscite because there had already been a recent count.

Our Report was signed and presented to the Prime Minister on March 2, 1962. I have never been able to understand why Mr MacMillan and the Cabinet, having asked us to recommend a solu-tion of the problem, immediately refused to give it a reasonable chance of success. In June 1962 the then Colonial Secretary, Mr Maudling,[589] announced in the House of Commons that he had decided that there would be no immediate transfer of territory. In other words, Uganda would be left to decide after independence, which was exactly what we wanted to avoid. I agree with the views expressed by Mr Kirkman in his excellent book on 'Unscrambling an Empire'[590] : –

> The Cabinet decision to allow Mr Maudling to ignore the solemn recommen-dations of a Commission appointed by the British Prime Minister specifically to make recommendations, was an act of cynical irresponsibility, a gamble that came off but ought never to have been made.

The gamble came off, in spite of the pusillanimous indecision of the British Government, because of the statesmanship of Dr. Obote[591] after Uganda had become an independent country. In 1964 his Government put forward a Bill providing for a referendum in the lost counties in the same year, in which the vote went overwhelmingly

---

[589] Reginald Maudling (1917–1979), Conservative MP and minister; secretary of state for the Colonies, 1961–1962; chancellor of the exchequer, 1962–1964; and home secretary, 1970–1972.

[590] Bill Kirkman (b.1932), journalist and writer, author of *Unscrambling an Empire* (1966).

[591] Milton Obote (1925–2005), Ugandan politician; prime minister, 1962–1966, and pres-ident of Uganda, 1966–1971 and 1980–1985.

to Bunyoro. He softened the blow for the Kabaka by making him Head of State of the new country of Uganda. Our Commission had at any rate pointed the way to what successive British regimes had failed to achieve, and left our African successor to bring about the agreed peaceful conclusion for which we had always hoped.

XIV
THE HOUSE OF LORDS: PAST, PRESENT AND FUTURE

The House of Lords when I took my seat shortly after my father's death of pneumonia in 1931 – which took place a few years before the discovery of penicillin and other antibiotics – was a very different place from what it has become over 60 years later.

I have now become the longest active member, having served continuously in Government or Opposition or as Chairman of Committees, apart from a short break during the war years, and my time in Ghana as Governor-General.

It was at that time an entirely hereditary chamber, apart of course from a handful of Bishops and Law Lords. The Labour Party, as the official Opposition, could only man two Benches, including the Front Bench, and in 1938 could still muster no more than 15 Peers. They were greatly outnumbered by the 80 Liberals, also of course on the Opposition side of the House. In fact, I remember a protracted argument between my Leader Lord Ponsonby, and the Leader of the Liberal Party, the Marquis of Crewe,[592] about which party was entitled to occupy the Opposition Benches immediately facing the Ministers sitting on the Government Front Bench. It was decided in favour of Lord Ponsonby, because the Labour Party was the official Opposition and occupied this position on the Opposition Front Bench in the House of Commons. The Conservative Party had even then a permanent majority of between 300 and 400 Peers in the House.

Perhaps even more striking than the differences in composition was the difference in our working hours. In those days the Law Lords used to sit and deliver their Judgments and heard all appeals in the Chamber before legislative business had begun in the afternoon, so we never started our work before 4.30 pm at the earliest. We rarely sat on a Monday, never on a Friday, and we almost always adjourned by 7.30 pm, so that every noble Lord could get a hot bath

---

[592] Robert Crewe-Milnes, 1st Marquess of Crewe (1858–1945), Liberal peer and minister; Liberal leader in the House of Lords, 1908–1923 and 1936–1944; secretary of state for India, 1910–1915; and secretary of state for the colonies, 1908–1910.

and change into a dinner jacket suit before dinner, and prepare for a long weekend at his country seat.

This, indeed, was a life of leisure, compared to our present strenuous daily routine, with legislative business or general debates starting as a rule in the early afternoon. We regard ourselves now as somewhat lucky if the House rises in the early evening. Another illustration of our leisurely life was the fact that in those days the Lord Chancellor had only two Deputy Speakers, the Chairman of Committees and Lord Airedale,[593] instead of the 20 odd he has now.

So far I have only mentioned the legislative and deliberative preoccupations of the House when it is sitting in the Chamber. But apart from the sessional Committees concerned with our domestic arrangements, procedure, and administration, we now have a number of subject 'Committees' which meet in the morning and very often sit all day. I shall deal later on with the more detailed work of these Committees.

Another field in which there has been a substantial increase in the work of the House is that of Private Bills. These are Bills promoted by individuals, or bodies such as Local Authorities, petitioning Parliament for powers which they cannot exercise under the General Law. A recent example is the London Underground, authorising the construction of the extension to the Jubilee Line. Like Public Bills, they have to pass through both Houses of Parliament, but as they do not emanate from the Government they are not handled by Ministers. They are therefore the responsibility in both Houses of a politically neutral officer of each House, the Chairman of Ways and Means in the Commons; and the Chairman of Committees in the Lords. These Officers are also the Senior Deputy Speakers in their respective Chambers.

There can be no doubt that the House worked much harder in the 80's and 90's than it did in the 30's. As late as 1956 the average daily attendance was 104, and the number of sitting days 130 in the year. The corresponding figures in 1985 were 315 and 142 respectively.[594] But the vital question is whether it has become a more efficient and useful legislative body. This can best be judged by the extent to which it has been able to complement the work done by the House of Commons, both on Public Bills and Select Committees, and in general debate on issues of national importance. There has been an enormous increase in the number of amendments made

---

[593] Oliver Kitson, 4th Baron Airedale (1915–1996), Liberal peer, deputy chairman of committees, House of Lords, 1961–1996; deputy speaker 1962–1996.

[594] In 2016–2017 the average daily attendance was 484 and the number of sitting days 141.

by the Lords during the Committee and Report stages of Public Bills, and a great majority of these minor alterations have been accepted as improvements by the Commons. The Lords rarely, insists on an amendment rejected by the Commons.

The influx of talented representatives of the professions is a striking and remarkable change since I took my seat early in 1932. It has been mainly due to the Life Peerages Act of 1958,[595] which has also made possible the establishment of the Select Committees which in recent years have added so much value to the detailed scrutiny of Government policy. Their presence is signified by the growth in the number of Independent Cross-Bench Peers, which by 1984 had already exceeded the combined total of Labour and Liberal Peers. Since the abolition of the University Seats[596] there have been few Independents in the House of Commons. So they also serve a useful purpose in representing a considerable cross-section of public opinion without any firm Party attachment.

A joint Select Committee of both Houses (on which I was lucky enough to be chosen to sit) recommended to Parliament that the succession to an hereditary title could be relinquished during the successor's lifetime. Parliament accepted our advice, and several Peers by succession have done so for different reasons – such as a career in the House of Commons,[597] the expense of being a Lord, or an objection to titles – without attracting much public attention. It would certainly have made it easier for me if Legislation of this kind had been passed some years earlier.

I do not find that the House has become more informal in its habits, or more inclined to take advantage of the absence of a Speaker to enforce the rules of procedure. I remember that Lord Onslow,[598] and before him Lord Donoughmore,[599] used to wear a frock coat as Chairman of Committees, but their successors have not followed what may have been an uncomfortable formality of the House in the 19th Century. Any transgression of the rules of procedure is still easily contained by a few words from the Leader of the House, or an occasional shout of 'Order, Order'. It is striking how soon well known hecklers from the House of Commons have accepted

[595] This Act enabled peers to be appointed for life.

[596] In 1950.

[597] *It was only possible for Lord Hume[sic] to become Prime Minister because he relinquished his title to sit in the Commons.* Lord Stansgate (Tony Benn) was the first hereditary peer to disclaim his peerage in 1963. Alec Douglas-Home, 14th earl of Home followed suit not long afterwards.

[598] Richard Onslow, 5th earl of Onslow (1876–1945), Conservative peer and minister: lord chairman of committees, 1931–1944.

[599] Richard Hely-Hutchinson, 6th earl of Donoughmore (1875–1948), Conservative peer and minister, lord chairman of committees, 1911–1931.

the self-discipline of the Lords. A few elderly Back Bench Conservative Peers still wore top hats in the Chamber, I remember among them Lord Banbury of Southam.[600]

I would like to record my impression, and after all these years it can only be an impression, of some of my colleagues in the House of Lords before the war. I have already mentioned my Leader, Lord Ponsonby of Shulbrede, much respected even by those who most abhorred his opinions, to whom I owe a large debt of gratitude for my initiation into the procedure and personalities of the House. There was no Deputy Leader of the Opposition, so his second-in-command was our Chief Whip, Lord Marley.[601] A former officer in the regular army, he retained some of its external habits. The brisk walk, the upright figure, the smart appearance, accompanied a genuine feeling for the underdog shared by his delightful wife whose warm heart and unfailing support gave him a happy home background. But his revolutionary socialist views led to serious criticism in the House when his American lecture tours were reported in the British press. He was certainly used by the Communist Party in the US to put their case to large audiences from coast to coast. It was represented to my Leader that the House of Lords was being brought into disrepute by a British Peer preaching the communist doctrine of the Soviet Union, advocating at that time world revolution, in the United States. Marley was obliged to resign.

Another figure whom I remember vividly from the time I first took my seat in the Lords was the Leader of the Liberal Party, the Marquis of Crewe. In appearance, with his elastic-sided boots, his tail coat, and his stick-up white collar, he was a survivor from the Edwardian era. But his whole life testified to his genuine Liberalism, a patrician born into a cultured literary family who was more of a radical than a whig. From his appointment by Gladstone, at that time a fervent Home Ruler, as Viceroy of Ireland until his retirement to become Leader of the Liberal Party in the House of Lords [for the second time, in 1936], he had sat in every Liberal Cabinet since the Liberal election victory in 1906. In the long struggle between the Lords and Commons over the passing of the Parliament Act,[602] he did not hesitate to support his party, and

---

[600] Frederick Banbury, 1st Baron Banbury of Southam (1850–1936), Conservative peer.

[601] Dudley Aman, 1st Baron Marley (1884–1952), Labour peer, Labour chief whip in the House of Lords, 1930–1937.

[602] The Parliament Act 1911. The law came about as a consequence of the political crises between the Liberal Government and the Conservative-dominated House of Lords. The Act effectively ended the veto power of the Lords and replaced it with a delaying power of two years on bills. This was reduced to one year with the Parliament Act 1949.

share with his small group of Liberals in the Lords the final threat of creating enough Peers to carry the Bill. His speeches in the Lords were always heard with respectful attention on all sides of the House. He was, however, handicapped by a slow and painfully hesitant delivery. One of his female relatives is supposed to have remarked that she hoped her delivery would not be as difficult as that of her noble kinsman.

In the years before the last World War the House was predominantly concerned with agriculture, which reflected the landed or farming interests of most of its members. There were always two parliamentary Under-Secretaries at the Ministry of Agriculture, and one of these had to be in the Lords to reply to the frequent questions and debates on this subject. I had a short spell in this capacity during the 1951 Labour Government,[603] and I much enjoyed my travels around the country to meet the County Agricultural Executives, when I was expected to exhort farmers to grow more food to make up for the food shortage that had persisted for so long after the war. I found a good friend in the Secretary of the Agricultural Workers Union, George Brown,[604] later himself in the Lords, and did what I could to support his claim for an improvement in the wretched wages of the agricultural labourer. I am sure the infinite patience farmers learned from exposure to the trials and tribulations of nature taught them to cope with an ignorant Londoner like myself, speaking from a Whitehall brief prepared by civil servants who knew as little as I did about practical farming. I also remember the last occasion on which a Peer was tried on a criminal charge by his Peers as required by law. The Court assembled in the Royal Gallery, and the Lord Chancellor, as Lord Steward, with his fellow Law Lords presided. The Defendant in this case was Lord de Clifford,[605] who was charged with an offence arising from a road accident. He was acquitted by the

---

[603] Listowel was a parliamentary secretary to the Ministry of Agriculture and Fisheries from November 1950 till October 1951.

[604] George Brown, later Lord George-Brown (1914–1985), trades unionist and later Labour MP and minister. Brown was not secretary of National Union of Agricultural and Allied Workers, but did do some work with agricultural workers through the Transport and General Workers' Union and sat on the War Agricultural Executive. He also served as a parliamentary secretary to the Ministry of Agriculture and Fisheries, 1947–1951; later first secretary of state, 1964–1966; foreign secretary, 1966–1968; and deputy leader of the Labour Party, 1960–1970.

[605] Edward Russell, 26th Baron de Clifford (1907–1982). In 1935 Lord de Clifford was involved in a car collision, which resulted in the death of the other driver. As a peer he could only be tried in the House of Lords. The Lord Chancellor, the 1st Viscount Hailsham, as Lord High Steward, presided over the trial which delivered an acquittal. This was the last such trial and the Criminal Justice Act 1948 among other measures abolished the right of peers to be tried in the Lords.

Jury of his Peers. I did not myself participate in the trial, as I did not wish to be party to what was obviously an anachronistic procedure. This procedure was extinguished in 1948 by legislation requested by the House of Lords.

When I returned to the House of Lords in 1960, after I had completed my three years service in Ghana, I took my place, after a provisional interval of political neutrality observed before and after my appointment, on the Front Opposition Bench. I first served under Lord Jowett [*sic*], when I assisted as an ex-Postmaster-General in dealing with the Broadcasting Bill. We both warned the House at the time about the risks of allowing advertisements to pay for the new Commercial channels, which would compete with the BBC, and might lower its standards by threatening to take away listeners to public service programmes.

It was not until 1965 that an opportunity occurred of doing something more constructive and useful for the whole House. This was an offer to succeed Merthyr[606] as Chairman of Committees. He had been anxious for some time to retire, in order to enjoy his few remaining years on what he called his 'boat' – which was in fact a very comfortable luxury yacht which he sailed on the Mediterranean. At that time his principal assistant had been Lord Airedale. The essential qualification for this post, apart from regular attendance, was to be sufficiently unabrasive, and not to antagonise any substantial section of the House. Airedale had unfortunately fallen out as a robust and active Liberal with some of my Labour colleagues, and they also took the view that it was time for a member of the official Opposition Party to claim this important office. The Labour Party was the only Party in the House not to have provided a Chairman of Committees from among its numbers, and my Leader, Lord Longford,[607] decided to put my name forward. He first ascertained that the Conservative Party would not object. Their Leader, Lord Carrington,[608] was entirely agreeable, but he was slightly doubtful about some of his Conservative followers, particularly an ex-Lord Chancellor, who had some influence in the Party. However, he and I had been nodding acquaintances at Eton, and I am afraid that this removed the doubt about my suitability. My nomination was therefore supported by all the Party Leaders,

---

[606] William Lewis, 3rd Baron Merthyr (1901–1977), lord chairman of committees, 1957–1965.

[607] Francis Pakenham, 7th earl of Longford (1905–2001), Labour peer and minister; leader of the House of Lords, 1964–1968, and secretary of state for the colonies, 1965–1966.

[608] Peter Carington, 6th Baron Carrington (1919–2018), Conservative peer and minister; Conservative leader in the House of Lords, 1963–1970 and 1974–1979, and foreign secretary, 1979–1982.

and I was elected by the House nemine dissentiente.[609] I was already familiar with some of the duties of the Woolsack[610] – as the Chairman of Committees was also a Deputy Speaker – because when I was Chief Opposition Whip it was the custom for one of the two Party Chief Whips, who were obliged to stay in the Chamber until the House rose at the end of its daily proceedings, to occupy the Woolsack if the Lord Chancellor was not present at the finish.

The office to which I had succeeded in 1965 had a long pedigree, and was second in importance among the Officers of the House to that of the Lord Chancellor as Speaker. An official Chairman of Committees was only formally appointed for the first time by the House, in a series of resolutions passed on July 23rd, 1800, which still govern the appointment and the functions of the present Chairman. He is still chosen by the House at the beginning of every new session, he still presides over Committees of the whole House and over Committees on Private Bills, and he is still a salaried officer of the House.

The origin of the official appointment of a Chairman of Committees is an interesting example of the slow evolution of parliamentary procedure. It was no more in fact than open recognition of what had for a very long time been the actual practice of the House. From at least the middle of the 18th Century there had been one Lord who was usually chosen to take the Chair in Committees of the whole House and in its Select Committees. It seems that there were usually a number of impoverished Lords who were in hope of Government largesse in giving so much of their time to the work of the House. From the session that began in January 1795, until his formal appointment as Chairman of Committees in 1800, Lord Walsingham[611] had continued to occupy the same position and to discharge the same duties in the House and its Select Committees. His experience of Private Bill Committees went back to 1782. After 1800 Walsingham was re-appointed annually in every session until 1814, when he retired on account of 'ill health and infirmity'. At least he had the support of qualified Counsel during his later years, for in 1808 the House resolved upon a Humble Address to the Crown representing 'That the office of Counsel to the Chairman of Committees of the House of Lords is an office to which very material duties are annexed' and praying for his 'better remuneration'. In recent years

---

[609] Without dissent.

[610] The seat of the lord chancellor, and since 2006 that of the lord speaker in the chamber of the House of Lords.

[611] Thomas de Grey, 2nd Baron Walsingham (1748–1818), MP, peer and minister; lord chairman of committees, 1794–1814.

the number of Private Bills have increased to such an extent that my lucky successor, Lord Aberdare,[612] was able to benefit from more professional legal advice than I had.

Walsingham's retirement in 1814 was marked by a suitable eulogy in a 'Humble Address' to the Prince Regent,[613] commending 'His Lordship's eminent and essential services to His Royal Highness's most gracious consideration'. The Prince Regent's response was equally laudatory, and asked the House to concur in the grant of an annuity of £2,000 per annum. None of Lord Walsingham's successors have, unluckily, been equally fortunate.

During the whole of my time as Chairman of Committees I heard no-one cast the slightest doubt on my political neutrality, in spite of my past record as a Labour Minister of the Crown. At the start of the new session following the defeat of the Labour Government in 1970, I was immediately assured that Conservative Ministers in the Lords wished me to carry on. My workload of Private Bills was increasing so rapidly that I had to ask for some assistance. I was delighted when the House appointed one of our few women Peers, Priscilla Tweedsmuir,[614] to assist me as the principal Deputy Speaker. This she did though her main task was to chair the recently appointed European Communities Committee. It was good that the officers of the House should not continue to be an entirely male preserve, and she herself was not only an ideal colleague but had a lightness of touch which I much envied in enlivening even the dullest Committees.

Although as a rule our hours of work were considerably shorter than they are now, we had the occasional all-night sittings, when the Government wanted to pass a Bill of special urgency through all its stages in the House. Priscilla and I divided the night's work between us, as we felt it would be unfair to involve any of the unpaid Deputies. We did short stints of two hours each between 9.00 pm and 7.00 am, so as to avoid the risk of falling asleep while off [on?] duty! Her early death was a tragic loss to us all.

When I retired from my post in 1976, I sat for a short time on the Cross-Benches, which emphasised the neutrality I had assumed for the past 11 years. Since then I have had more time to consider the

---

[612] Morys Bruce, 4th Baron Aberdare (1919–2005), Conservative peer; lord chairman of committees, 1976–1992.

[613] Later King George IV.

[614] Priscilla Buchan, Baroness Tweedsmuir of Belhelvie (1915–1978), Conservative MP and later peeress and minister; minister of state in the Scottish Office, 1970–1972; deputy chair of committees, 1974–1977; and chair of the select committee on European Communities, 1974–1977.

future of the House of Lords and its proper function in our parliamentary system, and I shall now set out a few of my own thoughts on this subject.

I am convinced that the House of Lords can still justify its existence by the need to revise legislation coming to it from the House of Commons. Parts of some Bills are often withheld altogether from parliamentary scrutiny by the use of the 'closure' or 'guillotine' in the House of Commons. Less controversial Bills are often introduced and pre-digested in the Lords before they are passed on to the Lower House. In this way it does succeed in complementing, without attempting to rival, the elected Chamber. No more delay can be justified than that required for the considered opinion of both Houses to be expressed on the Government's legislative proposals. Without careful scrutiny of the drafting and substance of every clause of a Public Bill in the Lords, the Commons would probably have to add at least another stage to every important measure.

Owing to the pressure of Government business in the Commons, the Lords has always had more time to discuss matters of public importance, such as unemployment, education, housing, or foreign affairs, which Opposition Leaders or Back Benchers wish to raise, and to allocate one day in the week when debates take precedence over public legislation. We are particularly fortunate to have many of the leaders of the professions, who do not have to attend regularly, but come to give their advice on subjects requiring their expertise, such as ex-diplomats on foreign policy, or retired Field Marshals or others eminent in military matters on defence. Before the last World War we had naturally fewer representatives of the Armed Services. The contribution of these experts from many different fields can only be expected to continue so long as the Lords maintains its relative immunity from the Party battle that must and should dominate debate in the elected Chamber.

Much of the useful but least conspicuous work of the Lords is done by its Select Committees. The reports of these Committees are published and debated by the House, where the Minister representing the Government replies to the debate. The most important of these Committees was set up after we joined the European Community, and is called the European Communities Committee. It has no less than six sub-committees, each of which deals with a different aspect in the field of legislation covered by Brussels, such as finance, transport, agriculture, environment etc. Most of the sub-committee members are co-opted for their special knowledge of the subject dealt with by the Committee. This gives their Reports special authority, and sometimes they are more widely read then those of the Commons.

We also have a Committee on Science and Technology, which includes members of the Royal Society and one Nobel Prize winner. It is a pity that we do not have more of these expert Committees, on other vital topics, such as health, education, unemployment, or foreign affairs. There is certainly room for a further expansion of the work of our Select Committees but the House is careful not to duplicate work done by Select Committees in the House of Commons.

It is of course desirable for any changes in the powers or composition of the Lords to be acceptable to both the major political Parties, Conservative and Labour, and to the Liberal Democratic Party so long as it is represented in Parliament. As long ago as 1968 an Inter-Party Conference on the reform of the House of Lords produced an agreed report, embodied in a White Paper and published in November of that year, which included the recommendation that in future membership should be by creation alone, and the succession to a hereditary Peerage should no longer carry with it a right to a seat in the House of Lords.[615]

If the proposals in this White Paper had been approved by Parliament, the main problem of reform of the House of Lords would have been almost completely solved 20 years ago. Its recommendations went first to the Lords, where they were accepted by a majority of 251 votes to 56 votes in favour of the proposals in the White Paper. In the Commons it was also carried by a smaller majority. The Government then introduced the Parliament number 2 Bill which received a Second Reading, but was bogged down in Committee, mainly due to filibustering speeches by Michael Foot[616] and Enoch Powell[617] from opposite ends of the political spectrum. Their obstructive tactics were successful in obtaining the withdrawal of the Bill, which the then Labour Government decided would take up too much parliamentary time. Thus the latest opportunity to reform the Lords fizzled out. By 1977 the Labour Party had reverted to its traditional policy of outright abolition, though since then it has had second thoughts about a non-hereditary indirectly elected Second Chamber.

But the present degree of dilution of the hereditary Peerage is by no means sufficient to give a Labour Government a reasonable chance of getting its legislation through a chamber with an inbuilt

[615] The House of Lords Act 1999 removed hereditary peers from being able to sit in the Lords with the exception of 92 hereditary peers elected among their number and those holding the offices of earl marshal and lord great chamberlain.

[616] Michael Foot (1913–2010), Labour MP and minister; leader of the opposition and leader of the Labour Party, 1980–1983.

[617] Enoch Powell (1912–1998), Conservative MP (and later an Ulster Unionist MP) and minister; financial secretary to the Treasury, 1957–1958.

Conservative majority. For this we shall need to go back to the White Paper of 1968, which advocated a two-tier structure of Peers, with voting powers and non-voting Peers, which would include most of the hereditary Peers, with the right to speak but not to vote. Succession to a Peerage would no longer confer membership of the House of Lords, but existing hereditary Peers would remain as non-voting members for their lifetimes. The voting Peers would constitute the working House. It could of course include the young and bright hereditary Peers, who have already done such excellent work in recent years, if they are granted voting rights.

This immediately raises the question of how and by whom the voting Peers should be chosen. From this it can be seen that I favour appointment rather than election for a reformed House of Lords. It seems to me that any form of election, whether direct or indirect, would be regarded as a threat by the House of Commons. It is most important that the legislative supremacy of the House of Commons, as the only elected Chamber, should be upheld in appearance as well as in fact. A further consideration is that the House of Commons would be most unlikely to pass a Bill that would considerably strengthen the authority of the Upper House.

The obvious difficulty about appointment is the extended power of patronage this would give the Prime Minister. Prime Ministers of all parties, from Lloyd George to the present day, have shown they cannot be trusted not to favour their friends or Party supporters. Of two recent Prime Ministers it can be said that one was unduly kind to his friends, and that another favoured those who were closely associated with companies that gave large contributions to Party funds. At present the only constraint on the Prime Minister's exercise of patronage is imposed by the Political Honours Scrutiny Committee, which can veto obviously unsuitable candidates. But the function of this Committee is to prevent undesirable appointments, rather than to propose the best candidates. For that purpose a stronger and more representative Committee should be appointed. What is needed is a body of elder statesmen and privy councillors, not themselves directly involved in day-to-day Party politics, which would be acceptable to both Houses, and have the approval of the Lord Chancellor and the Speaker of the House of Commons. This surely would be the most satisfactory way of securing life Peers from every walk of life, who would be chosen on their personal merits and their record of public service.

The non-voting Peers, would have except in this respect, exactly the same rights as other Peers, and there is no reason why they should not vote on matters arising in Select Committees of the House or on Private Bill Committees. As they would not continue to constitute the great majority, non-voting Peers might speak more often than voting Peers on Motions or Bills before the House, and their expert knowledge on subjects to which they are personally or professionally concerned would continue to be a unique contribution to Parliamentary debates. In the course of time the Chamber would ultimately become a Chamber of life Peers, as the successors to hereditary Peerages would no longer have the right to a seat in Parliament. They would be Peers of the Realm, but not Peers of Parliament.

An exception should of course be made for the Bishops of the Church of England. Whether or not the Church should be separately represented in the Lords, is a matter for public opinion to decide. There are some who favour disestablishment. But so long as the Protestant Christian Church remains established I have often thought, especially in view of our large ethnic minorities, that other forms of worship should be represented. The Bishop of Durham has recently said he would have no objection to seeing Roman Catholic Bishops or the non-conformist Moderator in the House of Lords. The main religious denominations: Catholic, Jewish, Non-conformist, Moslem, Hindu; should choose their own representatives as Life Peers.

So much for the composition of the Lords, as I would like to see it. A chamber of life Peers, male and female, comprising voting Peers with a right to speak and vote, and non-voting Peers with only a right to speak, while taking part in all the other activities of the House. I would expect the large contingent of Cross-Bench Peers to maintain their independence of Party affiliation. It is unlikely that any Party would have an absolute majority of voting Peers, but it would become a constitutional convention that the Government of the day should not be obstructed by the unreasonable use by the Lords of its delaying powers in obtaining consent for their legislation. It would probably be essential to fix a retiring age, in order to prevent the House from growing to an unreasonable size or an excessive age.

After a radical change in composition there would be less need for any substantial diminution in its present powers. The most contentious of these powers is the right to veto subordinate legislation. The administrative decisions of Ministers which are sufficiently important require parliamentary sanction of a negative or affirmative character. The negative order becomes law within a limited period of time unless it is annulled. The affirmative order comes into force after the express approval of both Houses. It is surely anomalous that the Lords should have the right to veto any form of legislation. It should be sufficient for them to express views which Ministers would take into account, and allow them to be over-ridden by the House of Commons if they disagree. This is in fact what happens usually in practice, as the power of rejection is too dangerous to use by the Lords, and no Ministerial Order can be amended. It might be said that the Lords should at least be able to delay subordinate legislation but there has been no demand for this additional degree of control over Ministers.

The limit of one year's delay for Public Bills approved by the House of Commons has not caused any serious conflict between the Houses. The most recent example of a Bill passed by the Commons over the heads of the Lords was the War Crimes Bill.[618] Its retrospective character condemned it in the Lords, where the legal profession is stronger, but the Commons took an opposite view and the Bill received the Royal Assent after the statutory lapse of time.

I think a certain amount of modernising could be done now with the consent of the House. The Lord Chancellor's duties are our only survival from the days before the division of powers. He is a Judge, a Cabinet Minister, Head of the Judiciary and also Speaker of the House of Lords, and he combines the duties of all these offices in his own person. Other countries have a Minister of Justice, responsible for a Department dealing with the Judiciary and the Courts. I can see no strong reason for not transferring the Lord Chancellor's present departmental duties to another Minister, answerable to either House.[619] This would give him more time for his judicial functions, and for presiding over the House of Lords from the Woolsack. It would avoid the present system of appointment of some 20 Deputy Speakers, none of whom could be so well versed in the procedures of the House as an almost whole-time Speaker. It always amazes me how successfully Lord Chancellors have survived their intolerable workload, which has steadily increased with the longer sittings of the House. I can only remember one occasion when a new Lord Chancellor seemed rather visibly dependent on prompting from the Clerk at the Table, who had to run to the Woolsack with the necessary procedural advice.

There is one way in which Governments seem deliberately to prevent the Lords from giving proper consideration to their Bills. They do this by applying the existing rule of law that all unfinished Public

---

[618] The War Crimes Act 1991.

[619] Reforms since 2005 have seen the roles and powers of the lord chancellor change. There is now a secretary of state for justice and a Ministry of Justice; a lord speaker to preside over the Lords. The positions of the lord chancellor and justice secretary have been held by the same person recently, who came from the House of Commons.

Bills expire at the end of a parliamentary session. They cannot be revived until the following session, when they are re-introduced. On the other hand, Private Bills are often 'carried over' from one session to another, as the prohibition applies only to Public Bills. But I am afraid it is hard to imagine any Government altering a rule that is so much to their advantage but some useful Bills would pass into law if they were allowed to run for two sessions instead of only one.

The House of Lords is a courteous and friendly place. Its courtesy is not a mere formality, because it is an expression of the friendly feeling and respect which cuts right across Party lines. It is because issues are usually debated on their merits, and without regard to scoring Party points, that there is so little hostility between the Parties. Another factor is the large number of Cross-Benchers. There are usually more Cross-Benchers amending in the course of a single Session than members of either the Liberal or Labour Parties. The fate of a Government can be decided in the Commons. In the Lords the Government can frequently be defeated without any loss of public support, as such defeats are due to a combination of members from all parts of the House.

Its proceedings can be deadly dull, but in almost any debate you can hear a speaker who really knows what he is talking about, and regular attendance is a liberal education. However outrageous an opinion, it is there to be heard, and if you disapprove you leave the Chamber, you don't shout the speaker down. Its usefulness in amending the drafting and the substance of public Bills gives it a unique place in our Constitution.

So long as the Lords continue to assist and complement the work of the House of Commons, its usefulness will not be questioned. But its survival will depend on its willingness to play a constitutional role that in all matters of Government policy gives the last word to the elected Chamber, and prefers persuasion, influence, and collaboration to the exercise of its diminished and strictly limited political powers. I hope the House survives as an example of courteous, rational, and civilised debate and discussion of public affairs, and I am deeply grateful for all the tolerance and kindness I have personally received from all quarters during a span of over 60 years.

Appendix

SELECTED PERSONAL CORRESPONDENCE BETWEEN THE LAST SECRETARY OF STATE FOR INDIA, LORD LISTOWEL, AND THE LAST VICEROY OF INDIA, LORD MOUNTBATTEN, CONCERNING THE END OF BRITISH RULE IN INDIA, APRIL–AUGUST 1947

1 Mountbatten to Listowel: 24th April 1947

Dear Listowel,[620]

In my letter of the 17th April I said that your predecessor's letter of the 12th April had just arrived; his letter of the 18th April has just reached me, and so in this letter I am replying to the points mentioned in both these communications.

2. I followed up the publication of the joint statement by Gandhi and Jinnah by writing to Patel[621] and asking him to take steps to ensure that the press took an objective line in reporting events in the country at the present time, and did not add to our difficulties by tendentious and one sided reports. I have just had a reply from Patel giving me a copy of the instructions which have been sent out to the press, but like all party leaders he found it impossible to complete his letter without a violent attack on the attitude of Jinnah and the Muslim

---

[620] All Mountbatten's letters but the last are written from the Viceroy's House, New Delhi, and all Listowel's letters from the India Office in London. They can be found in the British Library's India Office Records and Private Papers section under the reference MSS Eur C357. Volume XII of *The Transfer of Power 1942–47: Constitutional Relations between Britain and India*, Nicholas Mansergh, editor-in-chief (London: HMSO, 1983), is a particularly good resource for the high politics of the final days of British rule in India and Listowel's part in it. It complements this appendix very well.

[621] Vallabhbhai Patel, commonly known as Sardar Patel (1875–1950), Indian Congress politician, Home Member of the Interim Government, 1946–1947; after independence, deputy prime minister and minister of home affairs, 1947–1950.

League. I am, however, satisfied that we have made a step forward, and the statement by Gandhi and Jinnah and the favourable press it has received in India, should be a great help to us in the coming weeks.

3. Patel has also figured in another incident I feel I must report this week. He has always been one of the Congress leaders who have stated publicly that he is anxious to keep British officials after the transfer of power in June 1948. He has, however, never shown any practical signs to support these statements, and his attitude has been made particularly clear in the case of the appointment of a relief for Mr. Porter, Secretary of the Home Department, who is going home on seven months leave.

4. The obvious person to succeed Mr. Porter is Mr. Williams,[622] the Joint Secretary of the Home Department, who is a competent official with Home Department experience and 24 years service in the I.C.S. Patel, however, proposed that Mr. Banerji, who is now Secretary of the Commonwealth Relations Department, should be appointed in Mr. Porter's vacancy, and this can hardly be resisted as Mr. Banerji is senior to Mr. Williams.

5. Mr. Banerji is not, however, a particularly competent official, and Mr. Williams having heard of the recommendation has asked to be allowed to go home on leave. Mr. Williams, as Joint Secretary of the Home Department, is concerned with Service questions, compensation, proportionate pension, terms of repatriation and so on. He is thus a key man at the present time, and with the greatest regret I have had to turn down his application for leave; though in the circumstances it would be too much to expect that we can get the best out of him. I feel very sorry for him.

6. Meanwhile I think you should know that since Patel had not referred the question of Mr. Porter's relief to the Selection Board I asked that this should be done. As a result the Home Member[623] wrote on a minute the following remarks:

> I am not surprised that the Selection Board felt embarrassed at the indication of my preference, I myself feel equally embarrassed in having to deal with this matter once again in the light of the Selection Board's comments. In the very nature of things, the Selection Board cannot appreciate the requirements of the Department in the same way as I can. I regard a reference to the Selection Board as both pointless and inappropriate.

[622] C.F.V. Williams, Indian Civil Service (ICS).
[623] Patel.

The appointment of a Joint Secretary to act in a leave vacancy is by no means an invariable rule. There are instances in which a Joint Secretary has not stepped into the place of Secretary in a leave vacancy. Apart from this, I regard the next six months, or even more, as most crucial from the point of view of the work which is entrusted to the Secretary of the Home Department. A more experienced and senior man is clearly necessary, and I am glad that the Selection Board have agreed on Mr. Banerji's complete suitability for the post, and in view of this their further remarks regarding the officiating appointment of the Joint Secretary in the Department seem quite out of place and uncalled for.

I could not overlook this insubordination, and have replied on the same minute sheet: –

I agree to the appointment of Banerji. There are some points about the tone and substance of the Home Member's minute which I think should probably be taken in Cabinet. I should like to discuss the matter with the Home Member at our next interview.

7. I saw him today on this subject and have recorded a condensed version of the interview in paragraph 31 of my Personal Report No. 4.

8. I fully see the point which was made by Pethick Lawrence about the appointment of a European barrister to a permanent vacancy in the Oudh Chief Court. Of course in this case, where the barrister concerned had been acting as Senior Additional Judge for two years, it would have been unfair to disappoint him; but I will certainly bear in mind in the future the undesirability of adding to the number of permanent European judges, if it can be avoided without undue personal hardship.

9. In his letter of the 12th April, Pethick Lawrence referred to the case of the Nagas. I discussed the matter with Clow,[624] when he was here for the Governors' Conference, and he said that the Naga National Council is self-constituted, but is as representative a body as can be found of the more educated Nagas, particularly of the Angami and Aos tribes.

10. In the copy of the memorandum which my predecessor sent you on the 4th March, the Naga National Council in their reference to an interim government meant an interim form of British rule. The placing of the hill tribes under a Central Indian Government would mean that they would be subject to politicians at Delhi, who would be even more unaware of their needs than the politicians in Assam,

---

[624] Sir Andrew Clow (1890–1957), ICS; governor of Assam, 1942–1947.

and to whom they would have no access. If they can be brought with suitable safeguards within the framework of the Assam constitution, they can themselves expect some share in the Government there and will have access to and influence over Government.

11. The question is not one which merely affects the Nagas. It affects in the same or only a slightly less degree all the excluded and partially excluded areas of Assam. The real problem is not preservation of the economic equilibrium. The excluded areas are all deficit districts and will have, as at present, to be supported by some other part of India. But the main problem is the protection of these people from exploitation, and the preservation of their way of living.

12. Clow has set out his views on the subject briefly in a pamphlet entitled 'The Excluded and Partially Excluded Areas of Assam', of which I attach an uncorrected copy.[625] It is being reprinted, and copies will be sent to you, but I thought it might be useful for you to have this copy in advance.

13. Your predecessor in his letter of 12th April referred to Bevin's discussion with Stalin on the subject of India, and I was interested to read the account of what they said. I took the opportunity during the Governors' Conference of discussing with them the Communist Party in India, and the possibility of financial aid being supplied by Soviet Russia. The Governors were all very doubtful whether such financial aid was being given, although Burrows'[626] Secretary referred to a report that the Russian Representative on the World Youth Delegation, which visited India early in the year, had handed over a sum of half a lakh of rupees, and had promised further payments for the Party's work in future. This was the subject of your Private Secretary's letter of the 17th April, to my Private Secretary, and is under further investigation in the light of the Foreign Office remarks. We were unanimously opposed to any attempt at declaring the Communist party illegal; a step which even in the height of the war was never attempted by H.M.G.

14. I have referred paragraphs 6 and 7 of your predecessor's letter of the 18th April to my Political Adviser, and will let you have comments in due course. I quite agree with the remarks that a special treaty relationship with the U.K., rather than Dominion status, is the only possible future for the Indian States, unless British India elects for Dominion status and they join the Union of India.

[625] Not included here.
[626] Sir Frederick Burrows (1887–1973), trade unionist and colonial administrator; governor of Bengal, 1946–1947.

15. I am forwarding herewith for your personal information the record of my meetings with the Governors:[627] additional copies are also being sent separately for circulation as may be required. As I said in my last report, it was a very successful conference, and I am sure we all got very good value out of it.

16. The Governors also unanimously recommended that everything possible should be done to assist British officers of the Indian Police to obtain employment when they retire from India. There are fairly good prospects for I.C.S. officers and for most members of the technical services, but police officers are badly placed because they seldom have University degrees, and their experience does not at first sight qualify them for appointments elsewhere under the Crown, except possibly in the Colonial Police forces, where there seem to be few vacancies.

17. Many of the British police officers are men of considerable ability with adequate secretarial training and experience. The Governors and I feel that they should not be automatically excluded from consideration for the Home Civil Service. After the last war several were taken into the I.C.S., one became Chief Commissioner of Delhi, and another is now an invaluable member of the Central Board of Revenue. I should say that a policeman with a really first class record would be a better choice for some Departments in Whitehall than an I.C.S. officer with a less good record.

18. I think special efforts should also be made to secure vacancies for police officers in business through the organisation that has been set up for the purpose, and I should be grateful if you would draw the attention of those concerned to this request by the Governors and myself.

19. Finally, I should like if possible to help British members of the Provincial Services, some of whom are likely to retire. Could it be arranged that the Re-employment Bureau which you have started should accept enquiries from Provincial Service officers and assist them in finding appointments.

20. I am forwarding herewith two copies of each of my first three Personal Reports[628] in response to the telegram from your Private Secretary. I am sorry that we have no more spare copies but I will send 8 copies of the Report in future.

Yours sincerely,

Mountbatten of Burma

---

[627] Not included here.
[628] Not included here.

2 Listowel to Mountbatten, 25 April 1947

My dear Viceroy,

I would like to tell you with what tremendous interest I have read your first three Personal Reports; I had not seen the first two at the time of their receipt. I hope you will agree with the suggestion which has, I understand, already been made to you that you should in future send sufficient copies of these reports to be circulated to all the Members of the India and Burma Committee, since they will clearly form an essential part of the background to the decisions which the Committee will be called upon to take during the next few months.

2. To turn to your third report, Pethick-Lawrence has already sent you a message of congratulation upon the achievement of the joint appeal by Mr. Jinnah and Mr. Gandhi for the renunciation of the use of force for political ends. I would like to associate myself with those congratulations and with the hope he expressed that the appeal may have some effect in reducing communal strife. I cannot help noting, however, that in paragraph 22 of the same Report you draw attention to the likelihood that, if any attempt is made to impose the Cabinet Mission Plan on the Muslim League, they will report to arms to resist it.

3. It was perhaps hardly surprising that nothing came of Mr. Gandhi's outline for a scheme for an Interim Government pending the transfer of power.

4. Your full and vivid accounts of your prolonged talks with Mr. Jinnah seem to lead remorselessly to the conclusion that there is only the remotest possible chance that the Cabinet Mission's plan can still be implemented. It is clear that this result is not for want of your having impressed upon Mr. Jinnah with 'ruthless logic' the probable consequences for the Muslims of insisting on a full-blooded Pakistan, however truncated. It is, of course, only natural that, as a corollary to the Muslim refusal to accept what they represent would be a Hindu Raj on the all-India scale, the non-Muslim elements in those areas which the Muslims regard as naturally destined to become a part of Pakistan are beginning to agitate for partition of provinces. The growing force of this agitation in Bengal, for example, is illustrated by paragraph 3 of Burrows' letter to you of 11th April (No. F.J.B.22).

5. There certainly appears to be an impressive consensus of opinion in official quarters in India as to the need for a very early declaration of H.M.G.'s intentions and I shall, of course, await with keen expectations a more explicit exposition of what you have in mind. I need hardly say, however, that I appreciate all too well the crucial nature of the recommendations which you will be making and you may rest assured that I have complete confidence that you will choose the right moment for making them.

6. It was very encouraging to learn that the Governors are happy about the decision reached in regard to compensation for the Services. In particular, the attitude that appears to have been adopted by Trivedi[629] and Hydari[630] leads one to hope that the decision not to grant compensation to Indian members of the Services except in special cases will not cause resentment on the part of Indian members of the Services.

7. I am sure that the Governors' Conference will have been of the greatest value to the Governors themselves, all of whom are carrying an exceptionally heavy and difficult burden at the present time. The Congress attitude to Jenkins,[631] Caroe[632] and Mudie[633] will only serve to increase the difficulty of their tasks and is greatly to be deprecated. It is also a sad reflection on the statesmanship of some Indian political leaders that the best proof of a Governor's success should lie in the equality of the violence with which he is accused of partisanship by either side.

8. The problem raised by Mr. Liaquat Ali Khan[634] in his letters to you of 7th and 13th April about the communal aspect of the reorganization of the Indian Army is a difficult one and it is to be hoped that your suggestion that the matter should be discussed by the Defence Committee will be acceded to and that the discussion in Committee will be a helpful one. The vital need for avoiding any step which may adversely affect the reliability of the army is well

---

[629] Sir Chandulal Trivedi (1893–1980), ICS; administrator; governor of Orissa, 1946–1947; after independence, governor of Punjab (India), 1947–1953, and governor of Andhra Pradesh, 1953–1957.
[630] Sir Muhammad Akbar Hydari (1894–1948), ICS; administrator; governor of Assam, 1947.
[631] Sir Evan Jenkins (1896–1985), ICS; governor of the Punjab, 1946–1947.
[632] Sir Olaf Caroe (1892–1981), ICS; governor of the North-West Frontier Province, 1946–1947.
[633] Sir Francis Mudie (1890–1976), ICS; governor of the Sindh, 1946–1947; after independence, governor of West Punjab (Pakistan), 1947–1949.
[634] Liaquat Ali Khan (1895–1951), Muslim League politician; first prime minister of Pakistan, 1947–1951; assassinated 1951.

illustrated by one passage in the Governor of Bihar's fortnightly letter to you of 5th April D.O.No. 86/G.B. where he says that, in his Province, a position has already been reached in which the government is only kept in power by the presence and loyalty of the army. This is indeed a significant admission.

9. In paragraph 6 of his letter of 21st April, Pethick-Lawrence referred to our policy in respect of the Indian States, and suggested that our only possible course at this stage is to stick to the lines of the Cabinet Mission's Memorandum on State's Treaties and Paramountcy. You may be interested to know that the American Embassy made an informal approach to the India Office the other day on the basis of reports which have been reaching the State Department from their representative in Delhi. The Embassy asked to be assured that H.M.G. are not contemplating departure from the Mission's plan in so far as the States are concerned, and in particular are not contemplating maintaining direct relations with the States after the transfer of power. The suggestion was that, if this were the case, the U.S. Government might have to consider modifying its present attitude of open support for British Policy towards India.

10. The main ground for this démarche seems to have been an interview in Delhi between Merrill and Nawab Mir Nawaz Jung,[635] the newly appointed Trade Commissioner for Hyderabad in London, whose status I understand the Hyderabad Government have shown a desire to raise to that of a quasi-diplomatic 'Agent General'. He apparently told Merrill that Hyderabad intended to remain a separate political entity, independent of any Indian Union, and wished to remain in alliance with the United Kingdom; he added that Bhopal would do the same. He claimed that his own appointment was intended as a covert means of sounding H.M.G. in the matter. He admitted, however, that Sir Mirza Ismail[636] is clever enough to create the basis of cooperative relations with the Congress successor regime, even if this is not intended to lead to any fusion with an Indian Union.

11. It was suggested to the American Embassy that the reference to Sir Mirza Ismail's disposition to work with Congress indicated that there might not be much in Nawaz Jung's claims: Hyderabad was perhaps chiefly concerned to raise its stock for bargaining purposes with the future leaders of India. In any case, nothing was known

---

[635] Mir Nawaz Jung, official in the service of the nizam and government of Hyderabad.

[636] Sir Mirza Ismail (1883–1959), official in certain Indian princely states; Dewan of Hyderabad, 1946–1947.

in the India Office of any abandonment of the Cabinet Mission's plan in respect of the States, and we did not contemplate continuance with them of special relations outside the Indian Union; paragraph 12 of the Statement of February 20th in fact implied no change in the Mission's plan. It was of course not beyond the bounds of possibility that before June 1948 the Viceroy might report that there was no possibility of the Mission's hopes as regards the States being realised, and in that event he might propose to H.M.G. some other means of fulfilling our undertakings. But no such proposition was before H.M.G.

12. This conversation was on the Chancery level and it was not apparently desired that the Ambassador should approach me formally on the subject. I am, therefore, passing on the report to you in the same informal manner. I should add that Merrill apparently reported very adversely on the speech made to the States Peoples Conference at Gwalior by Nehru, whose lack of statesmanship in this matter he deplored. He also reported that the feeling in Delhi was that the Cabinet Mission's plan in general no longer held the field, that there was no sign of leadership towards an All-India solution among British Indian politicians as a result of your talks, and that while some states had decided to join the Constituent Assembly, the majority showed little intention of doing so. You will of course treat these disclosures of what Merrill has been saying to his Government with all due discretion.

13. In paragraph 33 of your Personal Report No. 2 you mentioned the Polish refugees in Kolhapur. I find that the position in respect to the removal of these people, who I understand number about 4,700, not 9,000 is far from easy. The financial responsibility for their maintenance used to be borne by H.M.G. the Government of India acting as their agent. Last August financial responsibility was taken over by UNRRA [United Nations Relief and Rehabilitation Administration]. There have been recent representations that the funds from which the cost was borne were exhausted at the end of March, but is hoped that UNRRA will find ways and means to discharge their responsibility up to the end of June. After then it is expected that their functions will be taken on by the International Refugee Organisation [I.R.O.]. Strictly speaking, therefore, the decision about the future of the Poles in Kolhapur does not lie with H.M.G.

14. On the other hand you may count on the co-operation of H.M.G. in the removal at the earliest possible date of the wives and children of members of the Polish Forces who have joined the Polish

Resettlement Corps; and it is probable that at a later date the defini-tion of a 'dependant" will be extended to include other relatives. Many of the Poles in the Resettlement Corps, however, are likely to go to other countries such as Canada or Brazil, and there would be no point in moving their relatives till their destinations are fixed. Indeed, to bring them to this country would be a physical impossibility in existing circumstances.

15. I understand that a token move from India of about 100 wives and children of ex-Polish soldiers, who have joined the Polish Resettlement Corps and who have settled in this country, has already been initiated by the War Office who have been in correspondence with the Commander-in-Chief on the matter. But the soldier rela-tives of a large number of dependents in Kolhapur are still in the Middle East, and will not be brought here for some time yet. I am told that there can be no question of their dependents being moved till their men have been brought to this country, and have joined the Resettlement Corps, as not only have they no place to go to, but it also is a cardinal element in H.M.G's policy towards members of the Polish Forces that dependents should not be admit-ted to this country in advance. Otherwise the men might be tempted to refrain from joining the Resettlement Corps and to join the recal-citrants who have been causing H.M.G. considerable worry.

16. You will thus gather that the process of settlement is likely to be rather slow and that even after relatives have been taken out of India, a residue will remain for whom new homes will have to be found by IRO. In the meantime, of course, those Poles who desire repatriation to Poland will be moved by UNRRA or IRO.

17. From the point of view of the provision of shipping, the implica-tions of what I have said in the previous paragraphs are, first, that, as in the past, UNRRA will find berths for the few Poles who may still opt for repatriation in any ships, British or others which may have accommodation to offer, and, secondly, that no arrangements can be undertaken for shipping the remaining Poles, apart from the small number to be moved by the War Office, till their new homes are known.

18. I hope that in these circumstances your Government will not press for the removal of the Poles from India by a given date. You may be assured that I will do everything I can to help, but this is a problem in which the best will in the world must wait on opportunity.

19. May I, in conclusion, say how particularly pleased I am to learn of your decision to appoint three Indian A.D.C.'s and of the

unprecedented extent to which Indians are taking part in official functions. I am sure that changes of this kind, which are long over-due, will have a beneficial effect out of all proportion to their apparent importance.

Listowel

3 Mountbatten to Listowel, 1 May 1947

My dear Listowel,

Thank you for your letter of the 25th April. I particularly appreciate the kind and encouraging things you say, which are a great help as one is apt to feel rather cut off from Whitehall out here.

2. This letter is being taken home by Ismay and Abell,[637] who will be able to give you a first-hand account of the situation, which I am sure will be very helpful. I should like to take this opportunity to tell you how magnificently Abell has played in with our new team and what a grand example he has set to the old staff. He has volunteered to stay on although he has had to give up his magnificent office to Ismay. I could not wish for a more public spirited, competent or delightful P.S.V.

3. While Abell is away my Personal Secretary, Captain R. Brockman, CIE, CBE, R.N.,[638] will act as P.S.V.

4. I am forwarding herewith my Personal Report No. 5 for the past week, for distribution as usual. I have aimed at giving you the background of Ismay's mission in this Report.

5. Ismay will give you the background of the difficult situation in the N.W.F.P. [North-Western Frontier Province], and will explain how Nehru will only accept a referendum on the issue of whether the N-W Frontier Province is to join Pakistan or Hindustan,[639] and that if we try to force through an election merely as a result of pressure from the Muslim League civil disobedience movement, Congress

[637] George Abell (1904–1989), later Sir George Abell, ICS, and Whitehall civil servant; private secretary to the viceroy (PSV), 1946–1947.
[638] Ronald Brockman (1909–1999), later Vice-Admiral Sir Ronald Brockman, naval officer and administrator; personal secretary to Lord Mountbatten and private secretary to the governor general of India, 1947–1948.
[639] A name sometimes used for India (as opposed to Pakistan).

will refuse to take part in the election as a strong gesture of their disapproval.

6. I have also charged Ismay with seeing you personally on the subject of Olaf Caroe. I like him immensely and in my opinion he is a very competent loyal and honest official. But I have had to warn him that Congress are so bitterly against him that it may not be in the best interests of all concerned to retain him; though whilst he is there I have guaranteed him my fullest support. I still think that he is showing signs of the great strain under which any man in his position must suffer.

7. Thank you for telling me about Merrell's report on his interview with Nawab Mir Nawaz Jung. The line I am taking up here to the question of individual membership of the Commonwealth for parts of India is clearly shown in my Personal Report. I am working a very delicate manoeuvre to give Congress an opportunity of offering to come back into the Commonwealth in some form, which might possibly bear fruit, but it is too delicate a matter to write about at present. Ismay can give you the latest form.

8. The business of the sterling balances has been very difficult. Nehru took the line that neither he nor any of the Congress Members could possibly be snared to go home on the Sterling Balances Mission. On my advice Liaquat Ali Khan brought this to a head at the Cabinet yesterday, when it was agreed that if it was impossible for the British to send a Mission out here, we would send a Mission home about mid-June, which would include Liaquat Ali Khan, Matthai[640] and provisionally Rajagopalachari, though this is not yet firm.

9. I am so glad that the question of compensation for the Secretary of State's Services has now been finally settled. The result of the meeting of the Special Cabinet Committee has already been reported by telegram and two copies of the Minutes were sent to the India Office earlier in the week. The statement has been well received by the Indian Press. The statement will, I know, give the greatest satisfaction to all members of the Services out here and will be a great help in improving morale during the difficult months ahead. I shall be glad if you will express my thanks to your colleagues on the I. and B. [Indian and Burma] Committee who have been so helpful in arriving at this satisfactory conclusion.

---

[640] John Matthai (1886–1959), Indian economist and official; Industries Member in the Interim Government, 1946–1947; finance minister in independent India, 1949–1950.

10. In paragraph 5 of my letter of the 24th April, I referred to the case of Mr. Williams and the way that he had been passed over by Patel for the Secretaryship of the Home Department. I asked him for Williams to come as Secretary of the Governor-General's Secretariat (Public) where a vacancy occurs shortly, and where he would be of the greatest help in dealing with the many Service problems which are going to arise during the next year. Somewhat to my surprise, however, Patel at his interview with me this week, suggested that Williams should be appointed as Secretary of the Information and Broadcasting Department where a vacancy occurs shortly. This Department comes, of course, directly under the Home Member and this change of heart on Patel's part is surprising, as I am sure he has no real desire to keep on any Englishmen. I am, however, hoping he will release Williams to me, as we really need him, and Williams has no desire to continue serving under Patel.

11. Nehru has recently been taking a keen interest in the future of the Indian States, especially from the point of view of the people of the States, and in a recent letter to me he complained that the Political Department worked in secret and no-one knew what it was doing. In particular, he expressed anxiety regarding the relations of Hyderabad with Bastar and Berar. I think much of the trouble has been due to the fact that although Lord Wavell offered to arrange a meeting between Corfield[641] and Nehru at which the fullest information was exchanged, Nehru never followed this up and has developed a slight sense of grievance, although I think the fault was undoubtedly his. In the last week, however, he has had a very full talk with Corfield, covering such matters as the representation of the States in the Constituent Assembly, the working of the Political Department, the future of the Indian States and the relations of Hyderabad with Bastar and Berar. Corfield reports that the meeting was held in a very pleasant atmosphere and that Nehru had no critical comments to make.

12. I am taking the opportunity of sending Corfield home with Ismay this week for a brief visit which I hope will be helpful both to you and to him. You will, I expect, by now have seen the Minutes of the recent Residents' Conference, which were sent home last week.

13. Your Private Secretary's letter of the 17th April, 1947, and its enclosures, discussed a report from the C.I.O. [Central Intelligence

[641] Sir Conrad Corfield (1893–1980), ICS, political adviser to the viceroy as Crown Representative to the Princely States, 1945–1947.

Office] Calcutta, about aid from Russia to the Communist Party of India.

14. The D.I.B. [Director of Intelligence Bureau] obtained this report, and passed it on to the Home Department. I understand that it has not been followed up, and that the report is not regarded as completely reliable. I doubt whether this report by itself will have much effect on the Government of India, but the Home Member is almost as jumpy about Communists as American politicians; so that I think you may take it that their activities are being pretty carefully watched.

15. I am afraid I cannot offer any advice on the question your predecessor asked as to what use can be made of the report in Great Britain.

16. In my letter of the 24th April, I referred to the Indian Police and the desirability of special efforts being made to assist British police officers to obtain employment when they retire from India. I have since had a letter from Wylie[642] who suggests that in addition to Government administrative posts similar to those now offered to members of the I.C.S., Indian police officers would be suited for appointments of the following type: –

(i) Police appointments in the U.K. or Colonies.
(ii) Administrative or Police appointments in the German Control Commission.
(iii) Military Intelligence (particularly for officers with C.I.D. [Criminal Investigation Department] or Intelligence experience).
(iv) Security posts in Commercial organisations.
(v) Labour Welfare Officers.
(vi) Government departments such as Home (Police, Fire Service, Salvage Corps), Port of London Authority, Post Office (Investigation & Claims Branch), Prisons, Transport, Customs & Excise, Ministry [of] Labour.
(vii) Local Self-Government appointments in Town, Borough or District Councils such as Public Control officers.

17. Some junior Indian Police officers have also suggested that H.M.G. might offer facilities and assistance for University or Technical training on the same lines as assistance now being offered

---

[642] Sir Francis Wylie (1891–1970), ICS; governor of the United Provinces, 1945–1947.

to ex-Servicemen. I am sure that many junior officers would gladly welcome an opportunity for such specialised training, and I think this is a line of action which is well worth following up.

18. I have no doubt that many Indian Police officers whose services are shortly to be terminated, would willingly forgo any compensation if they could secure permanent employment with reasonable pay and prospects, and I feel there must be some demand in England or the Colonies for men with administrative and executive experience in positions of trust where a high standard of integrity is required.

19. I am asking Ismay to raise with the India Office the question of a greatly increased allotment of honours for the last New Year's Honours List during our time in India. He, Corfield and Abell are well briefed with my views. I do hope you will be able to give them your support.

20. In my letter of the 9th April, I mentioned how both my wife and I thought it most important that the British Council should be adequately financed for its work in India. I am sorry to have heard now through the High Commissioner that the Treasury have found it necessary to reduce the Council's grant, which means that the amount allocated for India will be about £53,000/-, a third of which will be spent on overhead charges in London. I realise how difficult the position must be from the Treasury point of view, but I do think that a larger investment in India at this time will pay great dividends. I do hope you will do whatever you can to see that the Council gets a good start here.

21. I am sure Auchinleck,[643] Ismay and Abell will be able to give you a picture which will convince you of the supreme need of speed, and I sincerely trust that you will be able to help forward the pace of the discussion, so as to release Ismay within a week or ten days at the most. The price to pay for any appreciable delay may well be a general communal eruption out here.

22. I was very glad to have Burrows up here; although he still looks to me to be pretty ill, his doctors tell me he is on the mend, and he has promised me that he will go up to Darjeeling on Sunday. In the meanwhile, he is going to suggest to Suhrawardy[644] that he should immediately form a coalition government and offer joint electorates

---

[643] Field Marshal Sir Claude Auchinleck (1884–1981), officer and administrator; commander-in-chief in India, 1941 and 1943–1947; supreme commander of Indian and Pakistani Forces, 1947.

[644] H.S. Suhrawardy (1892–1963), Muslim League politician; chief minister of Bengal, 1946–1947; and later prime minister of Pakistan, 1956–1957.

in the future. If he can bring this off, he should be on a good wicket to retain the unity of Bengal as an independent Province.

23. I have been averaging 17 to 18 hours a day for six weeks now, and my doctor wants me to go to Simla to get really rested and fit for the much more important discussions which will start when Ismay gets back. I think I shall go up after the next Cabinet and come down before the following one. I shall be in just as good touch with you at Simla as in Delhi.

Yours very sincerely,

Mountbatten

4 Listowel to Mountbatten, 3 May 1947

My dear Viceroy,

Thank you for your letter of 24th April and for Personal Report No. 4 and the records of your meetings with Provincial Governors which accompanied it. I am very glad that the Personal Reports are to be circulated to all the members of the I. & B. Committee – I obtained the Prime Minister's agreement to this – as I myself find them most informative and enlightening. The Prime Minister has just invited Lord Chorley,[645] Mr. C.P. Mayhew, M.P. and Mr. A.G. Bottomley, M.P. to join the Committee. Mayhew and Bottomley were members of the U.K. Delegation for last December's Conversations with the Delegation from the Governor of Burma's Executive Council and Bottomley subsequently attended the Panglong Conference. Chorley will, I am sure, be of great assistance to me in the House of Lords on Indian and Burma affairs. He was a member of the Parliamentary Delegation to India.

2. I read the full records of the Conference with Provincial Governors with the greatest interest and look forward to reading the report of the Conference with Residents, which you say is on its way. Records of such excellence prove the value of the additional staff which you have at your disposal. I was very glad to hear that the new-comers and the old hands had settled down so well together and that

[645] Robert Chorley, 1st Baron Chorley (1895–1978), legal scholar and Labour peer; lord-in-waiting, 1946–1950.

all are exhilarated rather than oppressed by the magnitude and urgency of the tasks confronting them.

3. Perhaps it is just as well that the episode over Mr. Porter's relief should have revealed Patel in his true colours so far as the employment of European officers is concerned, although episodes of this kind cannot fail to have adverse effects on service morale and efficiency. The truth of the matter is, I suppose, that the temptation to appoint an Indian for the first time as Secretary of the Home Department, even though the appointment was not the best that could be made on the merits of the case, proved too great for the first Indian holder of the Home Department portfolio. I hope that Mr. Williams, whose work as Joint Secretary of the Home Department is well-known and appreciated here, will be able to establish good working relations with Mr. Banerjee.

4. I am grateful to you for sending me an advance copy of Clow's pamphlet 'The Excluded and Partially Excluded Areas of Assam', which will be studied with interest here.

5. I find myself in whole-hearted agreement with the conclusion reached at the Conference of Provincial Governors to take no action on the suggestion that the Communist Party should be declared illegal. Such action would appear to be quite unwarranted, at any rate until there is much more conclusive evidence than exists at present that the Party is engaged in subversive activities that constitute a threat to the Government.

6. I shall hope to let you have in my next letter some information as to the prospects of European police officers obtaining other suitable employment when they leave India. I am also investigating the question whether the Re-employment Bureau which has been established here can assist retiring British members of the Provincial Services to find suitable jobs. There has, as a matter of fact, been some interest shown recently in Parliament about the future of British members of subordinate services in India and Burma who are not entitled to proportionate pension on premature retirement, and I have already asked that the whole question of their future should be looked into.

7. In paragraphs 13 to 14 of Personal Report No. 4, you refer to the case put forward by the Sikh representatives when you interviewed them. I shall hope to include in my next letter some comments on the Sikh complaints.

8. A speech of the kind made by Nehru at Gwalior is certainly not encouraging from the point of view of a peaceful settlement of India's future. It is indeed extraordinary that a man of his stature

can seriously contend that it is open to him to say publicly, in the capacity of President of the States Peoples' Conference, things which it is obviously quite improper for him to say as Vice-Chairman of the Executive Council. Not that ill-judged speeches are a monopoly of one side; Liaquat's published riposte to Nehru was in its way just as mischievous.

9. Auchinleck has arrived and I have already had a short talk with him. He is to see the Prime Minister on Monday morning and I hope will have an opportunity of talking to other Ministers. I have also this week had an interesting talk with Weightman.[646]

10. It is a great relief to all of us here, as it must be to you, that the Compensation announcement has been made and I would like to congratulate you upon the extent to which you secured concessions from your Cabinet and their agreement upon the form of the announcement. The terms have, broadly speaking, been accorded a remarkably favourable reception here. The statements in Parliament prompted few Supplementary Questions and press editorial comment gives the impression that the terms are regarded as having struck just about the right balance. It is, of course, possible that, when there has been more time for detailed study of the White Paper and the Tables, the Opposition may press for a Debate. Prima facie, this would seem more likely to happen in the House of Lords than in the House of Commons, but it is a good sign that Hailey, who raised the Question by arrangement in the House of Lords and who received an advance copy of the White Paper did not raise any question upon it. I have heard from the Prime Minister that Simon is satisfied.

11. The case of Mahbub Ali, the Political officer of Malakhand who failed to prevent Nehru being stoned during his visit to the Frontier a few months ago,[647] to which Caroe referred in his letter to you of 7th April. d.o. No. GH/37, illustrates well the vindictiveness on the part of Ministers against which the Indian Services have to contend, and the genuineness of the need for compensation for Indians in the special categories.

12. We have been a bit mystified here by the line taken by the Indian Representatives at the Wheat Conference, which ended on 23rd April. While it is, of course, generally recognised that the prime cause of the failure of the Conference was the insistence of the United States on an exorbitant price for wheat under the proposed

---

[646] Sir Hugh Weightman (1898–1949), ICS, served in Assam and Baluchistan.
[647] In October 1946.

agreement, some surprise is felt in United Kingdom circles at the extent to which the India representatives based their policy on the hypothesis that four or five years hence India will require to import little or no wheat. This hypothesis would appear to depend on

(1) acceptance of standards of nutrition no better than prewar;
(2) the success of a 'Grow More Food' campaign which depends on machinery, fertilisers, and above all, the education of the cultivators;
(3) restoration of rice imports, and
(4) the absence of civil strife on any major scale

(1), though probably inevitable, means the abandoning of a cherished and most desirable aim, whilst not one of the last three factors can be regarded as certain. In these circumstances India might have been expected to put her name down for level quantities of wheat of not less than 1 million tons for each year of the post agreement and, if she had done so, her position in the Conference would have been likely to be much stronger and far more acceptable in principle both to exporters and to the regular customers.

13. I am greatly looking forward to seeing Ismay and hearing his impression of the present position in India. Your telegrams 954-S and 955-S have only just arrived and there has not yet even been time to read them carefully, but it will make all the difference having the outline of your plan in advance of Ismay's arrival, and we intend to embark upon intensive discussions next week.

Listowel

5 Mountbatten to Listowel, 8 May 1947

My dear Listowel,

I am afraid this will be a shorter letter than usual as I am at Simla and have no letter of yours to answer.

2. Last week I referred to the passing over of Mr. Williams, the Joint Secretary Home Department, by the Home Member, Patel, in favour of Mr. Banerji, his own nominee, and I added that after my protest Patel proposed to appoint Williams as Secretary of the Information and Broadcasting Department. I am glad to say that Patel has now acceded to my request and agreed to release

Williams to become Secretary to the Governor-General (Public) in succession to Mr. Godbole who was leaving in any case. Mr. Williams is particularly well suited for this appointment as there will be a number of questions arising in regard to the Secretary of State's Services during the next few months, with which he has been dealing in the past in the Home Department. I am arranging for him to join at once, as this appointment has been vacant for the past week.

3. Patel has also been creating difficulties in regard to the Chief Commissioner of Delhi, Mr. Christie,[648] who is an Englishman. It is an open secret that Patel has wished for some months past to replace him by an Indian, but his appointment is on the Viceroy's patronage list and my predecessor refused to give way. Recently Patel has trumped up two charges against the Chief Commissioner, which came to me with recommendations that he should be called upon to resign.

4. I saw Patel and asked him point blank whether he wished that the Chief Commissioner should be replaced by an Indian; I told him that if he wished to get rid of Mr. Christie he should do so by coming to ask me outright for his relief and not to attempt to accomplish it by underhand methods. Patel somewhat surprisingly said that he was content for the Chief Commissioner to stay on provided he changed his ways, but I am sure that there will only be friction if Mr. Christie stays. I have therefore written privately to the latter telling him that I think I shall have to agree to Patel's wishes and have an Indian as Chief Commissioner; but I have made it clear to him that I should have no wish that he should leave his appointment immediately and that nothing will be done until he has told me when he would like to leave. I am sure he should be treated with every consideration because, in my opinion, he has done his job efficiently and fearlessly.

5. In paragraph 7 of your letter of the 18th April, you mentioned a letter from the Resident at Hyderabad about the steps to be taken on the death of the present Nizam,[649] and said that you thought that I might encounter difficulties with the Central Government if I considered it necessary to despatch troops to Hyderabad to support the State Forces at such a time. Since you wrote, I understand that the Political Department has sent you a copy of a letter to the Resident at Hyderabad, dated 29th April, which shows that the possibility that difficulties may arise with the Interim Government over

---

[648] William Christie, ICS; chief commissioner of Delhi, 1945–1947.
[649] Sir Osman Ali Khan (1886–1967), nizam of Hyderabad from 1911.

attempts to discharge our treaty obligations with the States is being borne in mind.

6. I saw Major General Lyne[650] just before I left for Simla and he reported to me the very satisfactory talks that he and the Indian representatives had had with the Maharajah of Nepal at Khatmandu [sic].[651] It looks as if with care the negotiations will be satisfactory and Gurkha troops will he provided for both the British and Indian armies, but I have impressed on Lyne the desirability of handling this matter with the very greatest care, as the position is not yet completely cut and dried.

7. Clow completed his five year period as Governor of Assam on the 4th May and Sir [M.] Akbar Hydari took over the next day. I shall be sorry to lose Clow as, although I have not been out here long, I saw enough of his work during the South East Asia campaign to appreciate him at his true worth. He leaves for England shortly and I hope you will take the opportunity of having a talk with him about the position in Assam.

8. Ismay has reported to me that the initial reception of my plan by the India and Burma Committee was very favourable and I am so glad that this was so. I am awaiting further news from home with some eagerness.

Yours sincerely,

Mountbatten of Burma

6 Listowel to Mountbatten, 9 May 1947

My dear Mountbatten,

Thank you for your letter of 1st of May covering Personal Report No. 5 which provided a most useful background to the visit of Ismay and his party. They arrived safely last Sunday afternoon and I think I may say that we have been making steady progress ever since with our consideration of your plan. There is certainly no disposition whatever here to question the need for an early decision as to the plan we are going to adopt for transferring power in June 1948 and the announcement of it. Apart from our consideration of the plan, I

[650] Major-General Lewis Lyne (1899–1970), British officer.
[651] Tribhuvan Shah (1906–1955), king of Nepal, 1911–1955.

have had most valuable talks with Ismay and Abell[,] and Ismay has also seen the Prime Minister.

2. I took the opportunity provided by a meeting of the India and Burma Committee yesterday to thank the Committee on your behalf for their help in arriving at a satisfactory conclusion to the discussions on compensation for the Services.

3. Nawab Nir Nawaz Jung, to whom reference was made in paragraph 7 of your letter, has now arrived in London and has lost no time in trying to build up his position as 'Agent-General' for Hyderabad in the manner that was expected of him. He has arranged a banquet at the Dorchester in honour of the Nizam's birthday and has sent invitations to other Cabinet Ministers besides myself. I thought it right (and I understand that Corfield, who has been consulted, concurs) to have it indicated to the Nawab that the nature of his post of Trade Commissioner is not such as to justify the public entertainment of Cabinet Ministers. It is clearly most undesirable to give him any undue encouragement.

4. I am hoping to have a good talk with Corfield tomorrow about States matters, on the basis of the minutes of the Residents' Conference which I have just received and am reading with great interest.

5. In paragraph 6 of my letter of 3rd May I promised to let you have some information on re-employment questions: in the meanwhile paragraph 16 of your letter of 1st May contained some suggestions on the matter made by Wylie.

6. We have realised from the beginning that it would not be easy to find careers for Police Officers. It was partly for this reason that the first officer of the Indian Services to be appointed to the staff of the Re-employment Branch was a retired Police Officer from the Central Provinces, who has since devoted most of his time to preparing the ground and planning for the future. The Re-employment Branch has already covered, on an exploratory basis, all the points mentioned by Wylie and some appointments have already been made from among the younger officers on leave preparatory to retirement both to security posts and to the Ethiopian Police. The question of re-training is also receiving particular attention.

7. With regard to the specific suggestions made in your letter there are very few opportunities in police work in the Colonies and, in view of the official promotion policy, practically none in the U.K. We expect to get some men into the Control Commission and

some into various temporary Government appointments, such as that of Food Enforcement Officer. But, though I have given instructions that the point should be taken up again with the Treasury, I very much doubt if there is any possibility of police officers being taken in to the Home Service through the Special Principals' Competition and vacancies in permanent Government Service in the U.K. are, therefore, only likely to fall to those who are successful in the Reconstruction Competitions for the Administrative Grade or who are prepared to go in at a lower level: I hope there will be a few of the younger men who will apply as private individuals for the Colonial Administrative Service – the police are not eligible as a Service for the special competitions – and we hope that some of them may be successful. We also hope that Local Government will take on a few – we have been having discussions about this recently; but the main body will undoubtedly have to go into business and it is on this that efforts are at present being concentrated.

8. You can assure Governors that the problem is being tackled energetically and that all the ground will be properly covered by the time the main body of police officers begins to leave India. We are also considering the possibility that a limited number of men might, assuming they can be spared, be brought home for interview for business appointments in due course. It goes without saying that employers are unwilling to make appointments unless they have seen the men first.

9. You ask whether members of the Provincial Services can make use of the Re-employment Branch. The position is that the Re-employment Branch in the India Office (which will, when our final plans take shape, be charged with policy and questions involving permanent Government employment only) could not legitimately be expanded beyond the field in which I have direct responsibility and obligations. It is, however, the intention that, when the Indian Services Section in the Ministry of Labour Appointments Office is functioning (probably in the autumn), Provincial Service Officers should be able to make full use of the facilities provided by that Section and by the unofficial committee which Lord Hailey intends to establish very shortly. I hope you will agree that these arrangements will provide what is needed.

10. I might also mention that the Re-employment Branch hopes before long to begin sending to Provincial Governments and other authorities concerned a monthly letter explaining some of the background to what is now being done to find alternative careers for members of the Secretary of State's Services.

11. You referred in paragraph 6 of your letter of 9th April and paragraph 20 of your letter of 1st May, to the British Council's proposals for their work in India. I need hardly say, that I entirely share your views and those of Shone[652] regarding the importance of the development of cultural relations with India and for this reason I am most anxious that the Council should make an early start with their representation in India and that whatever they do should be done well. It is most unfortunate that financial stringency should have led to a reduction in the original estimate for India for the present year but I shall not fail to impress upon the Foreign Office and the Treasury our joint conception of the needs of the situation with a view to obtaining a substantial increase in the grant for next year.

12. The amount finally allocated for this year has necessitated some modification of the proposals made in Sir Angus Gillan's[653] report. There has been some delay, owing partly to illness in the staff of the council, in submitting its revised proposals. These, though envisaging a more restricted field of immediate operations, are designed to build a solid foundation for the future development of its work in India. They are now being put into final shape as speedily as possible and we hope to get Treasury approval in the very near future to enable a start to be made next cold weather. I will let you know how matters progress.

13. I said in my last letter that I hoped to let you have my comments on your interview with the Sikhs described in paragraphs 13 and 14 of your Personal Report No. 4.

14. I suppose the basic fact of the situation is that the Sikhs have an exaggerated idea of their proper status in the future set-up. No doubt this is due to their historical position as the rulers of the Punjab, partly to the rather flattering treatment they have received from us as one of the great martial races of India, and partly to the fact that they consider that they have contributed out of proportion to their numbers to the economic wealth of the Punjab. On the other hand, they are a community numbering only some 6 millions out of nearly 400 millions and in the Punjab itself they number only 4 millions among 28 millions. On any democratic basis, therefore, they must definitely be regarded as a minority (and not even as a 'major' minority). Owing to the fact that in no single district of the

---

[652] Sir Terence Shone (1894–1965), diplomat; high commissioner to India, 1946–1947; first high commissioner to independent India, 1947–1948.

[653] Sir Angus Gillan (1885–1981), colonial service and official; served in the Commonwealth and Empire Division of the British Council, 1941–1949.

Punjab do they constitute a majority of the population, it is out of the question to meet their claims by setting up a separate Sikh State.

15. I understand that during the Cabinet Mission these considerations were put to the Sikhs in answer to their case but evidently if has all been like water off a duck's back. It was pointed out to the Sikhs, I am told, that even minimum Pakistan would include 1 million Sikhs and that therefore the alternatives for them were to be all together in Pakistan or divided between Pakistan and Hindustan. They were asked to say which they preferred. Their reply was that if there were Pakistan there must be Sikhistan. In short, they refused to face the facts. The Mission's plan had the great advantage from the Sikh point of view that the Sikhs would all remain within the Punjab (except those in the States). One would have thought that the right thing for the Sikhs to have done would have been to throw their weight into getting the Cabinet Mission's plan adopted and to that end to make terms with the Muslim League as to their position in Section B. There was, in fact, some skirmishing between the Sikhs and the League but it never came to anything. It may be that Jinnah adopted an unduly frigid attitude, but no doubt the Sikhs also asked for far too much. The Sikhs then clamoured to be given the same right as the Muslim and General communities in the Union Constituent Assembly, i.e. a majority of Sikh votes should be required for any decision on a major communal issue. The Mission naturally felt unable to accede to this demand. It would have given four Sikh voters a veto on any question of this kind. The Sikhs also asked for the same right within Section B. This could not be conceded without conceding it also to the major communities in all three Sections and it would have raised a demand for a similar right from the Depressed Classes.

16. I had not heard before of the Sikh contention that they were ruled out of voting on a major communal issue in the Union Constituent Assembly by the wording of paragraph 19 (vii) of the Statement of May 16th. I do not think this is a correct reading of that paragraph. The position, of course, is that decisions of the Union Constituent Assembly are by majority vote except where paragraph 19 (vii) applies, in which case the majority must contain a majority of each of the major communities. But since on a population basis the Sikhs are entitled to four votes only, it has to be recognised that it is almost inconceivable that the Sikh votes could actually sway a decision of the Assembly.

17. There is no doubt that the Sikhs are a very dangerous element in the situation. Under your proposals they will be divided and I do not think that any subsequent adjustment of boundaries can

possibly begin to satisfy the claims they put forward. I understand from Ismay that they are asking that the Lahore Division be kept out of the partition you propose pending a Boundary Commission at which Sikh claims would be considered. But Sikh claims are based not on population but on such factors as the economic position of the Sikhs in certain parts of the Punjab and religious sentiment applying to certain areas where there are Sikh shrines. Unless the Boundary Commission were told to give weight to these factors it could not do more than make marginal adjustments in the boundaries where the division by districts has included in the Muslim or Hindu areas small parts of districts in which Hindus or Sikhs or Muslims were in the majority. But if you are satisfied that a Boundary Commission, with terms of reference such as will help to keep the Sikhs quiet until the transfer of power, can be set up without provoking the hostility of the two major communities, I shall be very ready to support your view to my colleagues.

18. What the situation really calls for is a settlement between the Muslims and the Sikhs. Their interests are not necessarily irreconcilable and indeed have a good deal in common, as appears from the fact that they have worked together for many years under the Unionist party system in the Punjab. In this way the Sikhs would avoid being split up (which is their major interest) and the Muslims would get a larger and more viable Pakistan. But I fear the recent bloodletting has done much to destroy any chance of this, anyway for the present.

19. I understand from Leo Amery that he has already sent you a copy of his proposals for a 'United Commonwealth of India'. These proposals, which of course, have much in common with Jinnah's ideas as to the relationship of Pakistan with Hindustan, are interesting and not without some value but their practicability clearly depends to a very great extent on whether the major parties are capable of that degree of mutual trust and respect that underlies the relations between the United Kingdom and the present Dominions. No doubt, if there were full and real acceptance of partition by Congress, such relations could be established and made to work well, but if Congress only accept Pakistan in order to convince the Muslims that it is impracticable, and to force them ultimately into Federation, they could hardly do so.

20. One further point is perhaps worth mentioning. Amery's preference to 'the definite solution which they (i.e. H.M.G.) 'as arbiters, are compelled to impose' seems to imply an over-estimation of the part

which H.M.G. can, or indeed should, play in framing the shape of the future India. It would be impossible to impose the partition of India against the wishes of both major communities.

21. I was very glad to hear that you had decided to go to Simla for a short break. The intensive negotiations you have been conducting ever since your arrival in India, in addition to the innumerable interviews you must have had to grant on assuming the office of Viceroy, must have put a tremendous strain upon you and some degree of relaxation before the next and perhaps even more intense phase of negotiations is obviously most desirable for you.

Listowel

7 Mountbatten to Listowel, 15 May 1947

Dear Listowel,

Thank you for your letter of the 3rd May. I am glad that my Personal Reports are of interest and that they are to be circulated to all members of the I. & B. Committee. I am sending extra copies to cover the three latest additions to the Committee.

2. With all that has been going on I have not been following closely the proceedings of the International Wheat Conference, but will certainty look into the question of the line taken by the Indian representatives, and try and find out their reasons for not asking for imports of wheat. At first sight I am surprised that they had such an optimistic outlook.

3. In connection with the International Wheat Conference, am sorry to say that Hutchings, who was one of the Indian representatives, and who has just returned to Delhi, has just been informed by his doctor that he has a tumour on one lung and will have to return to England for an operation. I am afraid that he will be away for at least four months, which is a big loss as he is an outstanding man.

4. I expect you are aware that the External Affairs and Commonwealth Relations Departments of the Government of India are about to be amalgamated and Sir G.S. Bajpai[654] has been selected to be Principal Secretary of the combined

---

[654] Sir Girja Shankar Bajpai (1891–1954), ICS, and Indian Administrative Service; later secretary general of the Ministry of External and Commonwealth Relations, 1947–1952.

Departments. I think he is a very good choice as he has had plenty of experience of the type of work he will be handling.

5. The High Commissioner for India in London has in the past come under the Commerce Department of the Government of India, but it was decided by my predecessor that control should be transferred to the External Affairs Department. This was obviously a desirable step, and the more so in the changed circumstances which will result from the transfer of power in June 1948, when the High Commissioner will become the first Indian Ambassador. The transfer of control is now about to take place, and I have also approved plans for reorganising and strengthening the High Commissioner's staff. The appointment of a new High Commissioner is naturally being delayed until the political decision about the transfer of power to Indian hands has been taken.

6. I need not say how distressed I was to have to telegraph on Sunday explaining the entirely unexpected situation which had arisen in regard to the Plan[655] which Ismay brought home. I have just received the Prime Minister's telegram inviting me home for consultations and I am very hopeful that by the time I leave I shall have achieved some sort of agreement to the revised plan among the leaders.

Yours sincerely,

Mountbatten of Burma

8 Mountbatten to Listowel, 5 June 1947

My dear Listowel,

I see from his letter of the 26th May that Sir John Colville[656] kept you in the picture during my time in England of what was happening out here. My letter this week will be brief as I naturally have none from you to answer, and the last few days have been fully occupied with the meetings with the Indian leaders, to which I have referred in the attached Personal Report.

---

[655] This plan offered elements of self-determination and autonomy to a United India of States and Provinces, but Nehru on learning of it did not view it favourably. Mountbatten left for London on 18 May for consultations with the Cabinet and others.

[656] Sir John Colville (1894–1954), later 1st Baron Clydesmuir, National Liberal MP and minister; colonial administrator; secretary of state for Scotland, 1938–1940; governor of Bombay, 1943–1948 and acting viceroy, 1945, 1946 and 1947.

2. I think you will like to know that the Honourable Mr. Jagjivan Ram,[657] the Labour Member, is leading the Indian Delegation to the next Session of the International Labour Conference at Geneva on the 19th June, 1947. This will be his first visit abroad and Sir John Colville, who saw him recently, told me that he was quite excited about it. He is particularly looking forward to his visit to London and I should be very grateful if he could be given the opportunity to meet people and to see something of London, where I gather he intends to be from 27th June to 2nd July. He is a charming little man and quite remarkable for an 'untouchable'.

3. The question of dealing with outstanding appeals from the Privy Council after demission of power has been exercising attention out here. This is a matter for which provision must be made in the future constitutions drawn up by successor authorities and also I suggest might appropriately be included in any Treaty drawn up by H.M.G. with such authorities.

4. If the whole or any part of India remains within the Commonwealth then I understand that it is possible by agreement for the Privy Council to be used by Commonwealth members as the final appellate authority. This matter cannot be the subject of a definite recommendation at present, but I thought it might be useful if I mentioned it to you, in order that you could have a preliminary examination made at your end.

5. Sir John Colville returned to Bombay on Sunday; this is the fourth time he has officiated in the absence of the Viceroy in England and I have heard from all sides since my return that he has officiated once again with his customary ability and charm. I think Ramamurty [*sic*][658] had a very good fortnight's experience at Bombay and I have just received a useful fortnightly report from him, of which I think you have a copy. I understand that he brought 16 members of his family to live in Government House during his fortnight and had all three Government houses in the Bombay Presidency opened, and entertained lavishly.

Yours sincerely,

Mountbatten of Burma

---

[657] Jagjivan Ram (1908–1986), Indian politician and minister; Labour Member in the Interim Government, 1946–1947; minister and deputy prime minister in independent India, 1977–1979.
[658] Sir S.V. Ramamurthy (1888–1964), ICS; chief secretary to Madras, 1939–1943, and acting governor of Bombay, 1947.

9 Listowel to Mountbatten, 5 June 1947

I would like first of all to add to the message from the Cabinet already telegraphed to you by the Prime Minister an expression of my personal congratulations on what you have achieved. Although no well-informed person would be so foolish as to minimize the risks attendant upon the policy that has been announced or the scope for mischief still left to fanatics and those elements in Indian politics which do not sincerely desire a settlement broadly acceptable to all the main parties, there can be no denying that at the present moment the prospects of such a settlement appear to be more real than they have ever been before and we are all deeply conscious of the degree to which this is due to you personally. I greatly hope that during the coming critical months you may be enabled to complete the work which you have so successfully begun.

2. It was of the utmost value that the Prime Minister and I were able to preface our reading of the announcement in Parliament by saying that the plan[659] had been received favourably by the leaders of all parties. It was, of course, only after the announcement had been made that we received your telegram reporting in detail the course of your meeting with the leaders of the three parties on the morning of 3rd June and learned of the awkward corners you had had to turn with each of them and of the help you received from V.P. Menon[660] in dealing with Nehru and Patel. It looks very much from here as if Gandhi, having failed in his efforts to sabotage agreement on this occasion, has now thought it wise to try and get in on the ground floor before it is too late; but, even if this is the correct interpretation of his actions, his support will be no less valuable for that. There would seem to be good ground for hoping that acceptance of the plan will now be ratified by the All-India Committees of Congress and the Muslim League since a failure to ratify on the part of either would involve the throwing over of its Working Committee and an immediate prospect of large scale civil strife. If the plan is ratified, the broadcast appeals of all three leaders should contribute substantially to the preservation of order during the transition period.

3. Thanks to the promptitude with which you informed me of the changes in the text of the announcement, all the arrangements went very smoothly at this end and we actually succeeded in getting

---

[659] The so called 3rd June Plan accepted the principle of partition of British India and that the successor states of India and Pakistan should be granted dominion status.

[660] V.P. Menon (1894–1966), ICS, and Indian Administrative Service; reforms commissioner, 1942–1947 and secretary at the States Ministry, 1947–1951.

the White Paper released immediately after the actual making of the announcement. You will doubtless have seen full press reports of the reception of the announcement in both Houses and will, I know, share my pleasure at the compliment paid by Winston Churchill to the Prime Minister, which created a very favourable impression in the House. I hope you noticed the pleasant tributes paid you in the Lords by Bobbety Salisbury and Perth.[661] Thanks very largely to Joyce's efforts, the publicity arrangements at this end proved most satisfactory and the maximum possible coverage was obtained both from the B.B.C. and the Press. Perhaps you were able to listen to the B.B.C.'s 9 p.m. broadcast which contained an excellent summary of the plan besides the Prime Minister's broadcast and relays of your broadcast and of extracts from the broadcasts by the Indian leaders. The press reactions have been uniformly favourable, save only for the 'Daily Worker'!

4. As you have pointed out in one of your telegrams, it will be of vital importance to ensure that there is no 'resting on oars' now that the announcement has been made but that all necessary consequential action is pressed ahead as fast as possible. You may rest assured that we shall do all we can at this end to help you retain the initiative and make full use of the advantage gained.

5. I was very grateful to you for keeping Rance in touch with developments in Delhi in the final stages. We have just received a telegram from him reporting the first reactions of his Council to the Indian announcement which are not unpromising. If, as we really believe, it would be as advantageous to India and Burma themselves as to this country that they should remain within the Commonwealth, everything will depend on our ability to bring home to the leaders of both countries during the next few months the validity of this belief.

6. To turn to other matters, you will be glad to hear that, on a joint memorandum from the Colonial Secretary and myself, the Cabinet his week agreed to raise the ban on the admission of persons of non-European descent to permanent engagements in the Royal Navy and the British Army and an announcement to this effect was made in Parliament yesterday. This change of policy is, of course, of much greater significance to the Colonies than to India but, so far as India is concerned, it will be a real gain both in principle and because it will enable Indians resident in this country to join all three Services.

---

[661] Eric Drummond, 7th earl of Perth (1876–1951), diplomat and international official.

7. While you were with us in London, Colville wrote to me on the 22nd May asking that all possible help should be given to Hamilton, your Chief Conservator of Forests, when he arrived in the United Kingdom on the 9th June to investigate the chances of finding other employment for I.F.S. [Indian Forestry Service] officers when their present careers are terminated.

8. As you will see from the attached memorandum[662] (which has already been circulated to all I.F.S. officers on leave in this country and is in course of circulation in India and Burma), specially liberal concessions have already been obtained by the India and Burma Services Re-employment Branch for I.F.S. applicants for appointment under the Forestry Commission. We have also, after discussion with the Colonial Office, now agreed a memorandum offering appointments in the Colonial Forest Service and this will be distributed within the next week. I am told that your people have also been given details of a small number of appointments in Southern Rhodesia.

9. I think it will be clear from the above that most of the ground mentioned in your letter has already been covered, but we shall, of course, be very glad to see Hamilton and to put him in touch with the people concerned. No doubt his long experience of Indian conditions will provide them with valuable background.

10. I recently held a meeting here for the purpose of enabling the Minister of Education and myself to hear from the President of the Royal Academy and the Chairman of the Executive Committee of the Indian Art Exhibition 1947/48 the present state of the preparations for the exhibition. You may care to have the enclosed copy of the note of the discussion[663] from which you will see that at the date of the holding of the meeting the prospects for the exhibition were encouraging. Subsequently I received a letter from Sir Walter Lamb[664] about the failure of Udaipur and Gwalior to co-operate on which I have sent you a telegram (No. 67); I hope that it will be possible to get round this difficulty. You may also like to have the enclosed copy of a letter which George Tomlinson[665] has written to Maulana Azad[666] about the Exhibition. Anything you are able to

[662] Not included here.

[663] Not included here.

[664] Sir Walter Lamb (1882–1961), secretary to the Royal Academy of Arts, 1913–1951.

[665] George Tomlinson (1890–1952), Labour MP and minister; minister of education, 1947–1951.

[666] Maulana Abdul Azad (1888–1958), Indian Congress politician and minister; after independence, minister of education, 1947–1958.

do by way of keeping an eye on the preparations for the Exhibition in India and assisting the Indian Committee to surmount any obstacles that arise would be most valuable. I know you share my desire to make the exhibition a resounding success.

11. I understand that it was at your suggestion that Chundrigar[667] originally decided to visit London on his way to Geneva. You will be glad to hear that we secured agreement to his being treated as a guest of H.M.G. during his stay and that, before leaving for India, he wrote me a letter which showed that he had enjoyed his visit. A number of social functions were arranged in his honour.

12. At your request Ismay brought to my attention while he was in London your desire to obtain a generous allotment of honours for the next two lists and I assured him that, although proposals of this kind have to be submitted for the approval of the Committee on the Grant of Honours, Decorations and Medals, I would consider your proposals when they are received with the utmost sympathy and give them all the support I could. You will no doubt have already realised that the likelihood that the successor authorities in India will have obtained Dominion status before the end of the present year has a bearing on this question and that it may be that your wishes in regard to honours will have to be met by a special 'Transfer of Power List' in advance of the next New Year List. Doubtless I shall be receiving your recommendations on this matter before long.

13. There is one other point in connection with honours which has been outstanding for some time. In his letter to Pethick-Lawrence of 12th March, Wavell asked whether any objection was seen to his asking Shone to comment on recommendations for honours in favour of members of the British Mercantile community in India received from recommending authorities and also, if he (Shone) wished, to send in names himself to the Viceroy. This suggestion has been examined here from the point of view of the procedure at present followed in the Dominions and no objection is seen to its adoption.

Listowel

---

[667] This probably refers to I.I. Chundrigar (1897–1960), Muslim League politician; Commerce Member in the Interim Government, 1946–1947; prime minister of Pakistan, 1957.

10 Mountbatten to Listowel, 12 June 1947

Dear Listowel,

Thank you so much for your letter of the 5th June and for the good wishes and congratulations which you were kind enough to send me. I must say that everything has gone very well so far and, although we are not out of the wood yet, I have every hope that the good start we have made will be continued.

2. The All India Muslim League Council held their meeting on Monday the 9th June and I have referred to this in more detail in my weekly report attached. The All India Congress Committee meeting takes place next Tuesday the 17th June and, although both Nehru and Patel have written to me about the Muslim League resolution, I feel I will be able to solve this difficulty by further personal negotiation.

3. We might have had a little trouble with Gandhi but, as I have described in my report, I think we can now count at least on some form of co-operation from him. Nehru and Patel of course also worked on him hard.

4. Gandhi also told me that there was a lot of loose talk going about that His Majesty's Government might have different agreements with Hindustan and Pakistan which would possibly tend to favour one over the other. He felt, therefore, it was important that an announcement should be made to the effect that it was His Majesty's Government's wish either to enter into tri-partite arrangements with both the Dominions, or to have similar bi-lateral agreements with each of them: and that, in any event, there would be no question of differentiation. One solution might be for this to be referred to by the Prime Minister in the House.

5. I have read Hansard for both Houses of Parliament; I am so glad that the plan had such a favourable reception, and am most appreciative of all the kind things that were said. I was particularly pleased at Winston's very nice reference to the Prime Minister. The publicity arrangements at this end were also most satisfactory and I have written specially to Vallabhbhai Patel to thank him for the assistance which was given by All India Radio and the Information and Broadcasting Department, particularly in regard to my press conference.

6. There has been no relaxation of the pace here and we have pressed on hard all the week in ensuring that the leaders and the Cabinet

face up squarely to the administrative consequences of partition. The pace is so hot that we are still three or four lengths ahead, but certainly June in Delhi is not a month in which anyone – British or Indian – can be expected to give of his best.

7. Thank you so much for the information you have given me about the employment for the Indian Forest Service officers after the transfer of power. I was very glad to see the arrangements which have been made for applications for employment in the Forestry Commission and to hear that further appointments are in prospect with the Colonial Forest Service. There is no doubt that the ground has been very thoroughly covered and I think that Hamilton should be well satisfied with what has been done. But no doubt, as you say, he will be able to provide some additional background and perhaps help with some of the details.

8. I am sorry I am not in a position yet to reply to your telegram No. 67 about the failure of Udaipur and Gwalior to co-operate in the Indian Art Exhibition 1947/1948. I have shown what you have written to my wife and we are going to keep in touch with Maulana Azad, and his opposite number when Pakistan is formed, in order to be able to give any help we can in this matter. At the present time I agree with you that it is most desirable to make this Exhibition a great success.

9. I notice in your letter of the 5th June you refer to the possibility of a special honours list in advance of the New Year list 1948. I am very keen to have a special allowance of honours particularly for those who helped to put the agreement through and should have liked to have had the names included in the New Year's Honours List 1948. But before I reach any decision on this point I should be glad if I could be informed whether it is the intention that the Star of India and the Indian Empire Orders should lapse on the 15th August this year. Naturally it would be preferable for all concerned to receive honours in these two Orders rather than in other British Orders which are available, but this may prove difficult if the Indian Orders have lapsed on the 15th August, unless arrangements can be made for a special allocation for the New Year List 1948. I should be very grateful if I could receive an early decision on this point. [Handwritten – Personally I feel strongly they should certainly not be allowed to lapse for the present].

10. In letters to your predecessor I have referred more than once to the position of Caroe in the Frontier Province. As you know, I have been pressed continuously and most strongly by the Congress party for his removal. These representations have recently been renewed

to the effect that there is no hope of peace, nor of a fair and orderly referendum in the Frontier Province so long as Caroe is Governor, and I therefore decided that the time had come when I must, for the moment at any rate, replace him.

11. I attach a copy of my letter[668] to Caroe and I have just heard from him to say that he accepts my suggestion and that he would like to go on leave to England to settle affairs consequent on the recent death of his mother. This seems the best solution for a difficult problem.

12. In one of my past letters to your predecessor I referred to the American Ambassador Elect to India and to the impression he had created at his first press conference. I do not know whether it has been reported in England, but Mr. Grady[669] has managed to say the wrong thing again, this time on his arrival at Singapore, where he told reporters that 'We hope to be of assistance to India in her fight for independence'. If this statement had been made before the 3rd June it would, to say the least of it, have been tactless, but at the present time it is, of course, merely pointless. One of the high ranking members of the Congress hierarchy, referring to this statement, said to me 'Some people take time to grow up'.

13. I wonder if you can tell me whether there is any more information about the prospects of further employment in the Colonial Service in the case of Irrigation Engineers. Mr. C.F.V. Williams, my Public Secretary, attended a meeting at the Colonial Office on the 2nd August, 1946, at which it was stated that the prospects of employment in the Colonial Service were good in the case of medical officers and technical officers, such as engineers, but there was some doubt in the case of irrigation engineers. I have been asked whether there is any further information on this subject, and the Chief Engineer, United Provinces, has recorded the following note, which he sent to the Governor, Wylie: –

> I shall be grateful if you will inform the authorities who are dealing with the selection of Civil Engineers for re-employment that Irrigation Engineers in India have to design and construct their own buildings, including water supplies and sanitation, roads and river training works. In addition, they have to design and construct dams, weirs, barrages and canals. On the latter they have to design and construct bridges, falls, aqueducts, draining syphons or level crossings. In recent years in the United Provinces, Civil Engineers, have, in addition had to design and construct power houses, both hydro

---

[668] Not included here.
[669] Henry F. Grady (1882–1957), American diplomat; US Ambassador to India, 1947–1948.

and steam, transmission lines, tubewells complete with water distribution systems consisting of lined and unlined channels or unreinforced concrete pipes. Irrigation Engineers from India should, therefore, be capable of dealing with almost any Civil Engineering problem.

14. There certainly seems to be something in what he says and perhaps this might be passed to the Colonial Office.

15. I may not be sending you a Personal Report next week as I am going to Simla from Friday evening the 13th to Monday morning the 16th inclusive, and to Kashmir from Wednesday the 18th to Monday the 23rd inclusive, returning to Delhi in time for the visit of the Chief of the Imperial General Staff. I have promised Nehru to try and smooth over some of his recent difficulties with the Maharajah, as the latter is a very old friend of mine.

Yours sincerely,

Mountbatten of Burma

P.S. [Handwritten] Ismay has had a better brain wave than para.11 re Caroe & I attach a copy of the letter[670] I've just written to him. M of B.

11 Listowel to Mountbatten, 13 June 1947

Dear Mountbatten,

Thank you for your letter of 5th June enclosing Personal Report No. 8, which I, and I am sure all my colleagues, have read with the keenest interest. I have also been most interested to read the full records of your crucial meetings with the Party leaders and with the members of the States Negotiating Committee. It is clear that you achieved a tactical success by at once bringing the leaders up against the administrative consequences of partition.

2. On receiving your telegram No. 1348-S of 7th June about the proposed Arbitral Tribunal, I at once approached the Lord Chancellor about a possible Chairman. It seems that, apart from any other consideration, the members of the Judicial Committee of the Privy Council are all ruled out on account of age since 69 ought,

---

[670] Not included here.

I think, to be regarded as an absolute maximum and 55 would probably be the optimum age. As you doubtless realise, the pressure upon High Court Judges at the moment is very heavy and the Lord Chancellor can hold out no hope of one being made available for your purpose. An approach is, however, being made to Sir Cyril Radcliffe[671] who would, I think, fill the bill admirably. Apart from his great legal abilities, he has just the right personality and acquired during the war administrative experience which would be likely to be of great assistance to him. Of course, he may well feel unable to leave the Bar, even temporarily, so soon after returning to it, however worth while your job can be made to appear, but there is just a possibility that he might be attracted by it.

3. I am also having the question of the manning of the Boundary Commissions, raised in your telegram No. 1364-S, looked into and the suggestion about U.N.O. taken up with the Foreign Office. Clearly, the handling of this Boundary Commission business is going to be of crucial importance. It seems as if the Sikhs may try to get back at the Boundary Commission stage some of the ground which they surrendered over the announcement of policy. It is to be hoped that the staking out of claims, as, for example, for the River Chenab line, in advance of the findings of the Boundary Commissions will not get out of hand since, once claims of this kind have been staked out, withdrawal is apt to prove difficult without loss of face.

4. I was interested in what you say in paragraph 30 of Personal Report No. 8 about Suhrawardy's plans for the economic development of Eastern Bengal. It looks as if Eastern Bengal will be a pretty poor show economically and will require a good deal of development economically if it is to live. I am not surprised that American businessmen should already be making offers to Suhrawardy, because it is their tendency in fluid conditions, such as obtain at present in India, to make such offers, in order to get their foot in on the ground floor, but without necessarily having any intention of carrying the matter through. Doubtless interest which American businessmen are now taking in India generally will be reflected in a certain number of orders, availability of dollars permitting. But British exporters have great advantages, flowing from their long connection with India, the organisations which they maintain there, and the fact that the Indians are accustomed to their products. They are tending to mark time at present but I think that we shall find that when they

---

[671] Sir Cyril Radcliffe (1899–1977), later Viscount Radcliffe, jurist and official; headed the Punjab and Bengal Boundary Commissions, 1947; lord of appeal in ordinary, 1949–1964.

talk business they will do so seriously. We shall have to consider in due course what encouragement we should give them to help build up Pakistan economically to enable it to stand on its feet. I agree that the matter is one for Shone to handle.

5. I was a little surprised to see Ismay's telegram to Monteath[672] No. 1354-S about Caroe. When I mentioned the matter to you at Northolt, I understood that the Prime Minister did not wish any action taken in the matter for the time being. I can quite understand, however, that, if the public agitation for Caroe's removal had subsided, you consider it politic in all the circumstances to meet Congress criticisms on this score and, in particular, to forestall any allegation that a referendum conducted under the local direction of Caroe would not be carried out with complete impartiality. I have already obtained the Prime Minister's consent to my approaching the Palace with a view to obtaining the King's informal approval and I shall hope to be in a position to telegraph to you within a day or so. At the same time I feel very strongly, and the Prime Minister agrees with me in this, that it would be most unwise that Caroe should be allowed to resume the Governorship of the North West Frontier Providence if he once relinquishes it. Surely such action would be taken as implying that we ourselves believe that Caroe is prejudiced in favour of the Moslem League and therefore ought not to be in office during the holding of the referendum.

6. The Prime Minister recently held a meeting of the Ministers concerned to discuss the future of the India and Burma Offices. As a result of the meeting Sir Edward Bridges[673] was instructed to arrange for the preparation of a detailed scheme for the establishment of a Commonwealth Relations Office to which would be assigned, not only the duties at present entrusted to the Dominions Office, but also the affairs of India, Burma and Ceylon, if those countries, on attaining their independence, desire to retain a link with the Commonwealth. It was recognised that it would be possible, and probably necessary, to provide, within the new Department, for what would in effect be separate sub-departments to carry out our special responsibilities to India and possibly Burma, which for some considerable time would be likely to differ in tiny ways from

---

[672] Sir David Monteath (1887–1961), civil servant; under-secretary of state for India and for Burma, 1941–1947.

[673] Sir Edward Bridges (1892–1969), later 1st Baron Bridges, civil servant; secretary to the Cabinet, 1938–1946; permanent secretary to the Treasury and head of the home Civil Service, 1945–1956.

any which we have to exercise in respect of other countries, whether within or without the Commonwealth.

7. All concerned here have been pressing ahead as fast as possible with the preparation of the draft Indian Dominions Bill. According to present plans, the draft Bill will be considered by the India and Burma Committee on Tuesday morning next, a copy being sent to you before the week-end so that you may have it available by the time that the views of the Committee reach you by telegram. The time-table in regard to the Bill is of course going to be very tight indeed and great care will be required at every stage to ensure that nothing is allowed to upset it.

8. You will remember that at the meeting of the I. & B. Committee on 22nd May, at which you were present, it was agreed that, on the grant of Dominion status to one or more successor States in India, the offer of facilities for Indian Officers to attend the Imperial Defence College [IDC] and the Joint Services Staff College should be renewed. This matter has been taken up with the Ministry of Defence who have been consulted at the same time about the possible renewal of the invitation to India to attend the Commonwealth Advisory Committee on Defence Science and on the subject of the disclosure of classified information to India. I have asked that these matters should be approached with the desire to do everything possible to convince Indians of the advantages to be derived from membership of the Commonwealth.

9. You may care to know that of late we have rather gone out of our way to keep in close touch with the 'Joint Committee on India" which is a co-ordinating body for British commercial and industrial organisations with interests in India. It seemed very desirable to let the Committee feel that they were being given the opportunity to express their views while the draft Bill was still in a fairly fluid state and I am glad to say that Stafford Cripps has agreed to be with me tomorrow when a deputation from the Committee is calling on me.

10. I am very glad that it has been possible to obtain the agreement of the Foreign Office and the Prime Minister to the Government of India's scheme for a temporary Indian diplomatic establishment in London to handle India's relations with a number of smaller countries in Europe. Krishna Menon[674] was able to see both

---

[674] V.K. Krishna Menon (1896–1974), Indian diplomat and minister; secretary of the India League (London), 1927–1947; Indian high commissioner to London, 1947–1952 and minister of defence, 1957–1962.

McNeil[675] and Bevin on this question when he was over here and I have just sent a telegram to Nehru conveying H.M.G.'s agreement.

11. In paragraphs 9 to 12 of your letter of April 24th you referred to the Nagas and to Clow's pamphlet on 'The excluded and partially excluded areas of Assam'. The problem of these areas is very similar to that of the frontier areas of Burma; and there is some resemblance between the suggestions in Clow's pamphlet and the observations in Part 3 of Chapter 3 of the report of the Burma Frontier Areas Committee of Enquiry. I enclose three copies of this report,[676] and suggest that you may like to send one to Hydari. The report would probably also be very useful to the Sub-Committee of the Advisory Committee of the Constituent Assembly which is dealing with the future administration of the tribal and excluded areas.

12. Talking of Burma, it now looks very much as if the Burmese are going to shun the Indian example and decide for complete independence outside the Commonwealth. Whilst this decision is of course greatly to be regretted, it has to be recognised that it is probably due to the fact that the Burmese rank and file are completely ignorant of the meaning of Dominion Status which they regard as an inferior brand of independence and that the leaders of A.F.P.F.L who probably themselves would prefer that Burma should remain inside the Commonwealth, do not feel certain enough of their position to give a firm lead in that direction. Certainly, if the result of their endeavouring to do so was their own overthrow and the coming into power of the Communists, we should have still greater cause for regret.

13. I was very glad to hear that Mr. Jagjivan Ram would be visiting this country on his way to Geneva and you can rest assured that we will do all we can to make his visit a success. I shall greatly look forward to meeting him myself. This week I have seen General Savory,[677] the Nawab of Bahawalpur[678] and Mr. B.C. Roy.[679]

Listowel

---

[675] Hector McNeil (1907–1955), Labour MP and minister; parliamentary under-secretary of state, Foreign Office, 1945–1946; minister of state, 1946–1950, and secretary of state for Scotland, 1950–1951.

[676] Not included here.

[677] Lieutenant General Sir Reginald Savory (1894–1980), British Indian Army officer.

[678] Sir Sadiq Muhammad Khan Abbassi (1904–1966), nawab of Bahawalpur from 1907.

[679] Bidhan Chandra Roy (1882–1962), Indian physician and politician; chief minister of Bengal (India), 1948–1962.

12 Listowel to Mountbatten, 20 June 1947

Dear Mountbatten,

Thank you for your letter of 12th June and your Personal Report No. 9.

2. Since I last wrote the All-India Congress Committee [AICC] has ratified the Congress leaders' acceptance of the announcement of 3rd June so that another potential obstacle to progress has been surmounted. It is clear from your Personal Report that it was by no means plain sailing and that once again the successful outcome was in large measure due to your own initiative. It was perhaps hardly surprising that, with the example before them of what had happened in regard to the Cabinet Mission's plan, the Muslim League were chary about committing themselves to a definite acceptance of the announcement until they knew where the A.I.C.C. stood.

3. It is also clear from your letter and report that Gandhi will continue to require very careful watching and handling, though it is to be hoped that the stage has now passed when it was within his power to sabotage the whole plan. It has to be recognised, however, that injured vanity might still impel him to try to do so.

4. I have given some preliminary consideration to his point about agreements between H.M.G. and the two Indian dominions which you mentioned in paragraph 4 of your letter but am not yet entirely clear as to how we should proceed in regard to it. It may very well prove the right course that the Prime Minister should say something on the point in the House but the terms of any statement will require to be very carefully thought out and I am not at all sure that it won't have to be on lines rather different from what Gandhi would like.

5. I am also having the proposals you made about honours in paragraphs 9 of your letter and in your telegram No. 1429-6 examined as a matter of urgency and shall hope to be able to let you have an answer at an early date.

6. I am sorry that it took a little time to fix up at this end the change in Governorship in the N.W.F.P. but in the result a premature leakage seems to have been avoided. I had myself thought, as you know, that it would have been better that Caroe should resign outright from the start but I can see the advantages of handling the matter on the lines finally adopted and I am glad to know that you yourself do not

contemplate Caroe resuming office as Governor unless a recommendation in his favour were made by the Pakistan government.

7. In paragraph 13 of your letter you asked for further information about vacancies for Irrigation Engineers in the Colonial Service. I attach a copy of a memorandum[680] which has recently been issued on this question, from which you will see that Irrigation Engineers are eligible for consideration equally with other officers of the I.S.E [Indian Service of Engineers]. With regard to the desirability of impressing their general qualifications on the Colonial Office, Dawson, who was Chief Engineer in the United Provinces and presumably recorded the note sent on to you by Wylie, called on the Re-employment Branch on the 16th June and repeated his points. He was given a copy of the memorandum and the point was subsequently discussed with the Colonial Office on the telephone.

8. I feel sure that the interests or irrigation specialists will not be overlooked in making appointments, but I have asked that Dawson's note should be passed on to the Colonial Office to make sure that his case is given due weight.

9. In addition to your letter and Personal Report I have received during the past week the reports of your various meetings with the Indian leaders about the administrative implications of partition, for which I am most grateful. It seems that you have been able to achieve considerable progress in spite of unseemly wrangles. I note that it was agreed at your meeting on 13th June that Patel and Liaquat Ali Khan should consider together the composition of the Arbitral Tribunal; possibly, however, the services of a distinguished outsider as Chairman may still be required. You will have received my telegram No. 71 about Radcliffe who, as I said in my previous letter, ought to fill the bill admirably if he is acceptable. I am glad that the idea of consulting U.N.O. about the composition of the Boundary Commissions has been abandoned and it will probably be best if a reference even to the President of the International Court of Justice is also avoided as it would inevitably involve delay.

10. We feel every sympathy with you and your staff having to work at such intensity at the height of the hot weather. All concerned here, particularly those engaged on the Bill, have also been set a very fast pace, and it may interest you to know that the Cabinet Secretariat staff worked until 5 a.m. on Wednesday morning producing the minutes of a meeting of the Cabinet Committee as a basis for communicating to you the Committee's comments on the draft Bill.

---

[680] Not included here.

11. It is clear from the A.I.C.C. Resolution on the subject and from various other pointers that the Congress are working up opposition to policy towards the States and, in particular, to our declared intention not to hand over any degree of paramountcy to the successor authorities in India. Some comment on this issue is beginning to appear in the Press here and diverse opinions are expressed. You ought to know that Stafford Cripps recently received a letter on the subject from Rajagopalachariar [sic] in which he challenged alike the legal, historical, political and moral bases for the doctrine of the lapse of paramountcy. The only possible line to take in reply to such representations is, of course, that, from an historical and constitutional point of view, the Cabinet Mission's statement of 12th May, 1946, was and remains right. Thus, there can be no doubt that the relations of the States have always been with the Crown; the point is argued at some length in the Joint Opinion of 24th July, 1928, by Leslie Scott[681] and other eminent Counsel given to the States (cf. in particular paragraph 7(1) of Appendix 3 to the Report of the Butler Committee[682]). Before 1935 the Government of India was, of course, used as the agent of the Crown for conducting these relations; but this function was not to be confused with that government's executive functions as the Government of British India. At the same time it is imperative that our policy should take full account, as it has, in fact, done, of the practical consequences of the principle by which it has had to be determined. Thus, we have scrupulously avoided, and must continue to avoid, doing anything which might be taken by individual States as an encouragement to them to stand out of the new Indian set-up – this, I am sure you will agree, applies particularly to Hyderabad, Travancore and any other States which are reported to have declared their intention to assert independence – and we must clearly give any assistance in our power towards the working out of satisfactory new agreements between the States and the successor authorities. The letters to Residents which it was agreed should be despatched at your meeting with the Indian leaders on 13th June may be expected to help in bringing about the desired result.

12. I thought it would be helpful to you to receive in advance the text of the announcement on Wednesday in Parliament about the future of Ceylon. It may interest you to know that the agreements which it is contemplated should be negotiated when the new Government is in

[681] Sir Leslie Scott KC (1869–1950), jurist and Conservative politician; legal adviser to the Chamber of Princes, 1927–1931.

[682] Committee headed by Sir Harcourt Butler, which examined the relationship between British India and the Princely States. Its report was presented in 1929.

office will relate to defence, external affairs and safeguarding of minorities.

13. I was not at all surprised to receive your telegram No. 141-S about the food situation. Both Pethick-Lawrence and I have lost no opportunity in recent months of impressing upon the Minister of Food the desirability of doing all we possibly can to help India over food and about a month ago I circulated a memorandum to the Cabinet Committee warning them of the facts. I was, therefore, able, on receipt of your telegram, to follow up on my previous representations with a further memorandum inviting my colleagues to ask the Minister of Food, as a matter of political urgency, to arrange for the diversion to India of some quantity of wheat or flour, even at the risk of slowing down the rebuilding of our own stocks, and to ask the Secretary of State for the Dominions to instruct the U.K. High Commissioners in Australia and Canada to urge those Governments as a matter of Commonwealth interest to do everything they can to assist India at this moment. I shall hope to let you know the outcome of my efforts very shortly.

14. On the subject of food I was interested to see what Ramamurty said in his fortnightly letter to you of 30th May (No. 83). Although you have hinted to me that Ramamurty acted rather lavishly during his short spell as Governor of Bombay, it appears from the letter referred to that he approached his responsibilities in an energetic and constructive manner.

15. At the beginning of the week I attended the opening of the Fifth Commonwealth Forestry Conference. This Conference is being attended by a large Indian Delegation under the Inspector-General of Forests and I am arranging that the Delegation should be suitably entertained by the India Office.

16. You spoke to me when you were in London and have since telegraphed to me (No. 1366-S dated 9th June) about the case of the civilian ex-service clerks serving in G.H.Q. (India). Their case was also raised with Monteath by Auchinleck during his recent visit. The case of these civilian clerks is admittedly, on the face of it, a hard one and I entirely appreciate the considerations which impel you and the Commander-in-Chief to do all you can to secure for them the best terms obtainable. I can assure you that all of us here have approached their case with the utmost sympathy and desire to assist them but I am afraid that we have found it impossible to avoid a final conclusion that, so far as compensation at any rate is concerned, their case cannot be distinguished from that of other Europeans – some also after discharge from the Forces – who are serving as civilians

under engagements with one or other government in India, for example in the Provincial Police Force. You will doubtless have noticed that it is recognised in the extract from a letter from Mr. W.J. Wood to Mr. A.E. Phillips which Ismay sent to Scoones[683] that one reason for the refusal in 1933 to allow these men to revert to military service was the desire to preserve their better prospects as civilians. It may be that the good intentions of the government in this matter have been frustrated by events but it would not seem right to undo the past for one small category of a large class, whatever special merits they may possess. The only wise course seems to be to make no exception to the general principle that compensation is admissible only to the Secretary of State's Services or to officers appointed to posts by the Secretary of State.

17. There remains the question of the future employment of these men and their pensions. So far as their employment is concerned it seems probable that the services of most of them will be badly needed in the G.H.C. of one or other of the Indian Dominions and that there is therefore a good prospect of their being able to serve out their time. Those, however, who do not continue so to serve will be able to look to the Military Department of this Office and the Appointments Department of the Ministry of Labour (the staff of which includes an officer of the Indian Army) – who work in close co-operation – for assistance in finding alternative employment.

18. As regards pensions, it is, of course, the intention to make provision in the Treaty for the payment of pensions of this kind. I do feel, however, that there is a good case for endeavouring to persuade the Government of India to concede to these men the right to retire on proportionate pension once the transfer of power has been made, since it cannot be denied that conditions will be very different for them and they may be exposed to the risk of a reduction in their emoluments. I should therefore have no objection to your taking this point up with Patel if you wish to do so.

19. I am glad to know that you have been able to get up to Kashmir for a few days which will, I hope prove most refreshing to you and Lady Mountbatten.

Listowel

---

[683] General Sir Geoffrey Scoones (1893–1975), British Indian Army officer and official.

13 Mountbatten to Listowel, 27 June 1947

Dear Listowel,

Thank you for your letters of the 13th and 20th June, 1947; I did not write to you last week as I was away for brief visits to Simla and Kashmir.

2. I was very glad to hear of the possible appointment of Sir Cyril Radcliffe. I saw a certain amount of him when he was Director-General at the Ministry of Information during the war and formed a high opinion of him. I have put the matter in confidence to the leaders and I hope to let you have a reply shortly to your telegram.

3. There is, as might be expected, some difficulty in finding a Chairman for the Boundary Commissions, for the setting up of which the Leaders have just agreed, and, as the Arbitral Tribunal will probably not have much to do in the early stages, Jinnah has suggested that Radcliffe, if he proves acceptable, might perhaps serve in the first instance as Chairman of both Boundary Commissions to sit only to settle disputes within the Commissions. This is so far a purely tentative proposal. If anything comes of it I will let you know by telegram.

4. I was interested to read of the proposal for the establishment of a Commonwealth Relations Office to take over the duties at present entrusted to the Dominions Office and the India & Burma Office. I feel that this change of name will be a popular move as the title 'Dominion' seems to be going out of fashion these days and becoming almost unpopular.

5. I am glad to note, from Press accounts, that there is now a possibility that Burma may follow India's lead and ask for Dominion status in the first instance.

6. In this connection, I was interested to read the suggestion put forward by Rance in his telegram No. 161 of the 11th June, suggesting that the time was now ripe for investigation of a form of association within the British Commonwealth. I feel that the British Empire must move with the times and that it might well prove possible to find a somewhat looser form of association on the lines that Rance suggests. There are other parts of the Empire which might be placed in a similar position to India, Burma and Ceylon in the next few years, particularly the West Indies, where some form of federation seems to be quite possible in the future.

7. At this point may I say how much I appreciate your giving me advance information of the Colonial Secretary's announcement about Ceylon. One of the first things I had to do after reaching Kandy in April 1944, was to advise H.M.G. that an inquiry into the political future of the island was an urgent necessity if trouble was to be avoided in one of our principal bases in the Far East. The result was the Soulbury Commission[684] and I have retained an interest in Ceylon's affairs from that time.

8. I am so glad to hear that the Ministry of Defence are being consulted about the possible renewal of the invitation to India to attend the Commonwealth Advisory Committee on Defence Science and on the subject of the disclosure of classified information to India. These points, together with the offer of facilities for Indian Officers to attend the I.D.C. and the Joint Staff College, Chesham, will make a very good impression out here and will be a great help in convincing India of the advantages to be derived from membership of the Commonwealth.

9. Thank you also for your reply about Honours and Awards. I feel that the best solution is to include the final Indian List with the New Year's Honours List 1948 and to back date it to the 14th August, 1947. It will thus, I think, attract less notice and will not appear as if we are celebrating our departure by a triumphant Honours List.

10. I am glad to hear that the interests of Irrigation Engineers have not been overlooked. I felt sure that the Colonial Office had the matter in hand; I am grateful to you for the memorandum which you have forwarded to me and which I will see is made available to all concerned.

11. Wylie has written me a long letter about certain U.P. [United Provinces] Officers who had retired on proportionate pension between the 1st January 1947 (when proportionate pension was re-introduced) and the 30th April 1947 – the date of the announcement on compensation. I have replied to him regretting that it will not be possible for me to give a certificate to nine officers who had retired between these dates, as, by the terms of paragraph 10 of the announcement, these officers are expressly debarred from receiving compensation. Four of these officers are, however, candidates for alternative employment under the Crown and I promised Wylie that I would write to you and ask that everything possible should be done

---

[684] Commission headed by Lord Soulbury in 1944–1945 to propose constitutional reforms for Ceylon.

to help these officers as they all have first-class records. Their names are : –

> Mr. A.P. Hume (1927). He was Collector at Benares –a most disheartening place for any official under present conditions – before he retired on proportionate pension in February of this year. He is a candidate for alternative employment under the Crown.

> Mr. H.T. Lane (1937). He was Collector at Ballia, one of the worst districts in the U.P., when he retired on proportionate pension on 15th April, only a fortnight before the Secretary of State's 'terms' were announced. He is a candidate for alternative employment under the Crown.

> Mr. A.C. Cowan (1932). He was Collector of Azamgarh, if possible a worse district than Ballia, when he applied for proportionate pension. There tragically enough from his point of view he actually still is. He is a candidate for alternative employment under the Crown.

> Mr. A.I. Bowman (1937). He retired on proportionate pension in January of this year and is a candidate for alternative employment under the Crown.

12. Paragraph 10 of your letter about the late hours worked by the Cabinet Secretariat staff reminded me of the war years in Whitehall, and, although we have not yet managed to achieve as late an hour as 0500, it is only with the greatest difficulty that I manage to avoid after-dinner work and 'midnight follies' are all too frequent. But in spite of it all the whole party out here are as keen and cheerful as ever.

Yours sincerely,

Mountbatten of Burma

14 Listowel to Mountbatten, 27 June 1947

I have no letter from you to answer this week – not that I was expecting one after what you said in the last paragraph of your last letter.

2. In paragraph 4 of your Private and Top Secret letter of the 12th June you said that Gandhi was pressing for an announcement to be made to the effect that H.M.G's wish was either to enter into

tripartite arrangements with both the new Dominions or to have similar bilateral agreements which each of them and that in any event there would be no question of differentiation. You suggested that this might be referred to by the Prime Minister in the House of Commons in his speech on the Second Reading of the Bill.

3. This proposal of Gandhi's seems to me to be of such importance that I have put the matter before the India Committee. We all felt strongly that we should be extremely guarded in dealing with it.

Clearly one of the main objections to partition from the Congress point of view has been the danger that Pakistan would fortify itself with outside assistance from ourselves, the Americans or others. It seems to have been the fear of this happening through Pakistan remaining in the Commonwealth which in the end brought Congress to agree to temporary Dominion status and several utterances have been made to the effect that anyone who indulges in giving support to Pakistan will incur the hostility of Congress. The Congress would hardly pay so much attention to this point if they did not regard it as a serious danger.

4. Our position is that we want good defence arrangements with India as a whole and from our point of view it would be much best if they were on the same basis with both the Dominions and if the Commonwealth relationship provided the nexus between the two. But we feel that we should be very careful not to say that we shall not in any circumstances have closer relations with Pakistan than with India. Once we have said that, it will be open to the Congress to refuse any definite arrangements with us in regard to defence and other matters and then to say that we are precluded from having any better relationship with Pakistan. The best hope of getting an effective relationship with the Congress derives from their fear that if they do not play up we shall have differential and better relationships with Pakistan and possibly with non-acceding Indian States. The probability is that this is the strongest bargaining point we have with the Congress and it is one that may continue to operate for a substantial period. We feel that we should be very ill-advised to throw it away.

5. Further we do not think that we should say at this stage that it is our wish to enter into tripartite arrangements. Of course, if all parties were co-operating fully a tripartite arrangement would be the best but there can be a great deal of difference in the way in which an identical agreement is operated by two different parties. If we had a tripartite agreement all the arrangements under it would require the assent of the three parties. If, on the other hand, we had separate

agreements with Pakistan and India we should be free, even though the agreement were in identical terms, to develop our relations with Pakistan under the agreement without India having the right to object. In practice, formal agreements about defence matters cannot contain more than general principles and what really matters is the kind of arrangements which are reached between the Chiefs of Staff or between the Governments in implementing the general agreement. Clearly Ghandi's idea is that we should commit ourselves before we even begin to negotiate not to have any arrangements with Pakistan different from those which we have dealt with Hindustan. Once we have said that, Hindustan can decide what arrangements, if any, we shall be committed to have with either of the new Indian Dominions.

6. At the same time we recognise that it is of immense importance to have, if possible, good and close relations with the new India and we agree that the Prime Minister in the Debate on the India Bill should refer to our desire to have close and effective arrangements with both the new Dominions in all fields and particularly in the defence and economic field on a basis of free negotiation. It might be added that what we hope for is to have equally good and close arrangements with both the new States in India.

7. I regret that I have not yet been able to let you know the outcome of my efforts reported in para.13 of my last letter to obtain from H.M.G. a gesture in the matter of food, but I am not letting the matter rest and shall hope to reply to your telegram soon.

8. We are indeed grateful to you for your prompt reply to our latest telegrams to you about the draft Indian Independence Bill. The receipt of your telegrams No. 1598-S this morning has made it possible for the Prime Minister to send copies of the draft Bill to Opposition Leaders before the weekend with a view to discussing it with them on Monday afternoon. It is to be hoped that after that discussion the way will be clear to authorise you to discuss the Bill with Indian leaders.

9. Thank you for your letter of 20th June (1446/18) enclosing one you had received[685] from Bhopal[686] forwarding a statement of views upon H.M.G's policy towards the States. It is certainly to be regretted that any of the Princes should feel as he does about our policy but much of what they criticise is an inevitable

---

[685] Not included here.
[686] Sir Hamidullah Khan (1894–1960), nawab of Bhopal from 1926; chancellor of the Chamber of Princes, 1944–1947.

consequence of the termination of British rule in India rather than a result of the particular way in which we have thought it best to handle matters.

10. You will like to know that the discussions with the Burmese Goodwill Mission which is here at present have been on a very friendly basis although it has now become quite clear that, in spite of what appear to be their own personal inclinations, the AFPFL leaders feel bound by the ignorances and prejudices of their rank and file to persist in their determination to take Burma out of the Commonwealth. It has been made clear to them that there can be no question of legislation to transfer power during the present Session except on the basis of dominion status for a reasonable period of time and that, if it is a question of transferring power to a sovereign republic, H.M.G. cannot do more than promise to introduce legislation next Session and secure its enactment as soon as possible.

Listowel

15 Mountbatten to Listowel, 4 July 1947

Dear Listowel,

Thank you for your letter of the 27th June. I quite see the point of view expressed in the first few paragraphs of your letter. I, of course, entered into no commitment with Gandhi beyond promising to refer the matter to you. The line the Prime Minister intends to take, as described in paragraph 6 of your letter, may not satisfy Gandhi, but I feel it will have a reasonably good effect out here.

2. I am sorry to hear that it appears likely that Burma will leave the Commonwealth. I am sure, from their point of view, it will be a retrograde step; there is much we could have done to help them and their departure can only result in the end in their being a more backward country than they would have been with our assistance.

3. Can you not go ahead on the basis of an interim Dominion period as in India and Pakistan until Burma have completed their new constitution and completed the legal drafting? If you were to rush legislation through now this session and made it last until such time as the new constitution were accepted, I feel sure Rance could convince them of the advantages in the meanwhile.

4. You will remember in my letter of the 5th June I referred to the question of outstanding appeals with the Privy Council. I am glad to see that Clause 9(c) of the draft Bill allows for the continued use of the Privy Council. The question of outstanding appeals to the Privy Council and also whether the Privy Council is to be used in future for appeals is at present being considered by the expert Sub-Committee of the Partition Council dealing with legislative matters.

5. Nehru has shown to me a copy of his letter to you dated 20th June, in which he asked that arrangements might be made for the acting High Commissioner for India to meet the Colonial secretary in regard to proposals concerning Indians resident in East Africa, West Indies, Fiji and Mauritius. I do not, of course, know the background of the case, but anything that you can do at the present time to meet Nehru's request will be a great help to me in view of his peculiar frame of mind and the difficult negotiations I have on hand.

6. This letter and attached Report are rather shorter than usual, but I have had a very full week and a particularly difficult one dealing with the Indian Leaders in regard to the draft Bill and the Reconstitution of the Interim Government. The latter, as you will have realised from the exchange of telegrams, has been, I think, the most difficult matter I have had to handle since I came out here.

Yours sincerely,

Mountbatten of Burma

16 Listowel to Mountbatten, 4 July 1947

I am writing this letter whilst we are still in the throes of launching the Bill. Copies of the Congress and Muslim League comments on the Bill and of your views on those comments only became available shortly before a meeting of the Cabinet Committee was due to be held at 9.30 p.m. last night. The Committee sat until midnight by which time the final terms of the Bill had been decided upon and it was just possible to get a copy to the Clerk at the Table by 1 a.m. this morning, which was the latest possible time if the programme was to be adhered to. The Bill was printed off during the course of the night and was formally presented by the Prime Minister at 11 a.m. this morning. Copies were made available in the Vote Office at 2 p.m. and the Prime Minister and I immediately held a Conference with the Lobby Correspondents. I have also this afternoon had Press Conferences with the Indian correspondents and the Empire and Foreign Correspondents.

2. The Congress insistence on a change in the Interim Government, which has made it necessary for us to telescope still further an already foreshortened programme, appears at this end as most unreasonable but the risks of not making any attempt to meet them were undoubtedly too great to be run. We must now do our utmost to achieve our target date of 20th July although it is not going to be easy.

3. You will remember that at your request the clause that appeared in the original draft of the Bill stating that any sums falling [failing] to be paid as a result of the passing of the Act out of the Revenues of India should be paid out of those Revenues, was omitted. You may be interested to see a memorandum, of which I enclose a copy,[687] setting out the problem which the clause in question was designed to solve. The difficulty has been got over, as proposed in the memorandum, by means of a Motion to the effect that Standing Order 67 and the practice thereunder should not apply to proceedings on the Indian Independence Bill. This Motion was moved by the Lord President[688] this morning at the time of the presentation of the Bill. It may be helpful to you to have this background information in case questions are raised on the point in India.

4. I was glad to get your letter of 27th June covering Personal Report No. 10. It is certainly excellent that you have succeeded in getting Radcliffe as Chairman of the Boundary Commissions. He is approaching the whole matter in a most public-spirited manner and will, I have little doubt, fill the role admirably. As you have already been informed by telegram, he is hoping to leave for Delhi on Sunday and Lady Radcliffe hopes to join him about 10 days later.

5. I thought you would like to have advance telegraphic warning of the change in the title of the Dominions Office. The change has, of course, been prompted by developments in India but it was considered desirable from the point of view of the existing Dominions to make the change as far in advance of August 15th as possible in order to make it less obvious that the change had been dictated by events in India.

6. I am glad to be able to tell you that definite progress has already been made with the cases of two of the four officers referred to in

---

[687] Not included here.

[688] Herbert Morrison (1888–1965), later Lord Morrison of Lambeth, Labour MP and minister; home secretary, 1940–1945 and lord president of the council, 1945–1951.

paragraph 11 of your letter dated 27th June. Hume as accepted an offer of permanent employment in the Home Civil Service and is shortly going to the Department of Health of Scotland. Lane has also just been declared successful for the Home Civil Service and we hope that he will accept.

7. As regards the other two, Cowan, who is a candidate for the Reconstruction Competition, is likely to be interviewed for the Home Civil Service shortly and Bowman who is apparently doing a temporary job with a Youth Organisation in Scotland has not applied for any Government employment except the vacancies under the British Military Administrations in North Africa. The War Office have not yet decided whether to make him an offer. You can rest assured that they will both be given any assistance possible in obtaining further employment.

8. Congress seem out to cause trouble over the States though it is good news that the new States Department has been entrusted to Patel with V.P. Menon as Secretary. As you say, it would have made things very difficult indeed if Nehru had insisted upon taking this on himself. As you are doubtless aware, Zafrullah Khan[689] is now in London and is busy putting Bhopal's case before individual Ministers. Incidentally, I believe that Amery sent you a copy of his address to the Royal Empire Society on 18th June. In a letter to me covering a copy of it he laid emphasis on the distinction between paramountcy – based on treaties and other arrangements between the East India Company and the Princes, developed since by usage and sufferance of the Government of India – and the bond of allegiance between the Princes and the Crown, which was a new relationship introduced when Queen Victoria assumed direct government over India. Still further strengthened by her proclamation as Empress and by subsequent Royal Durbars. On Amery's suggestion I asked Patrick[690] to let me have a note on this question and I enclose a copy[691] as I think it will be of interest to you. I am sure that it will be politic to avoid at this juncture any recognition of a continuing formal relationship between the Princess and the Sovereign, although in practice the exchange of courtesies between them will doubtless continue.

9. It is clear from your latest report that nerves are getting on edge in Delhi – an inevitable consequence, I suppose, of a combination of

[689] Sir Zafrullah Khan (1893–1985), Indian (and later Pakistani) jurist and politician; foreign minister of Pakistan, 1947–1954.

[690] Sir Paul Patrick (1888–1975), civil servant; assistant under-secretary of state for India, 1941–1947.

[691] Not included here.

over-work and excessive heat. I have no doubt that, if any opportunity presents itself of inviting the key people to the cooler atmosphere of Simla for a few days, you will take advantage of it.

10. It was good news to hear of the invitations to Colville and Nye[692] to stay on and I hope that they will be willing to do so.

11. I have just heard that Ismay is arriving next week. We shall, of course, be delighted to see him again.

Listowel

Since writing this letter I heard, with much relief, that you have succeeded in getting the change in the Government postponed until July 20th.

L.

17 Mountbatten to Listowel, 11 July 1947

My dear Listowel,

Thank you for your letter of the 4th July. I was interested to read the details of how the Congress and League comments on the Bill were dealt with in London. As I said in paragraph 5 of my Personal Report No. 11, all of us here were most grateful and appreciative of the way these comments were dealt with so expeditiously. I can only repeat once more my admiration and gratitude.

2. Thank you so much for details of the future of the four officers I referred to in my letter of the 27th June. I am glad to hear that they all have employment in sight or good prospects and I am informing Wylie accordingly.

3. As you surmise, Amery did send me a copy of his address to the Royal Empire Society on the 18th June. He has subsequently sent me his latest book on the Commonwealth, but as I am too busy at present to look into it in any detail, I have asked Morris Jones[693]

---

[692] Lieutenant General Sir Archibald Nye (1895–1967), army officer, colonial administrator and official; governor of Madras, 1946–1948, and high commissioner to India, 1948–1952.
[693] W.H. Morris-Jones (1918–1999), academic; constitutional adviser to the viceroy, 1947; director of the Institute of Commonwealth Studies, University of London, 1966–1983.

(Constitutional Adviser) to let me have his comments. I hope soon to read Amery's address, the relevant chapter in his book and Patrick's note which you have been kind enough to send me.

4. I shall be interested to hear who exactly will look after the interests of India in the Commonwealth Relations Office, and through whom it will be possible to have my private letters sent in the future.

Yours sincerely,

Mountbatten of Burma

18 Listowel to Mountbatten, 18 July 1947

Dear Mountbatten,

It is, I fear, a fortnight since I wrote to you and in the meanwhile I have received two of your letters and personal reports. At the end of last week, when a letter was due from me, we were all preoccupied with piloting the Bill through Parliament and I felt it would be better to defer writing until that process was completed.

2. In your letter of 4th July you asked whether it would not be possible to follow in the case of Burma a procedure similar to that adopted in regard to India, namely, to rush through Parliament during the present Session legislation on the basis of dominion status for Burma in the hope that it might still be possible to convince the Burmese of the advantages of remaining in the Commonwealth. I can assure you that the possibility of following this course was fully weighed and that it was with the utmost reluctance that we finally decided that it could not be for the reason that, whether out of honesty or on other grounds, the Burmese leaders made it perfectly clear that there was no possibility of their changing their minds about leaving the Commonwealth and that if power were transferred forthwith on the basis of dominion status, Burma would ask for complete independence at the earliest possible moment thereafter and without making any show at giving dominion status a fair trial. Apart from any question of the prostitution of dominion status, it was at least doubtful whether the Opposition would co-operate to the extent of treating any such legislation as non-controversial and legislation this Session was out of the question on any other basis.

3. In the same letter you referred to Nehru's interest in the appointment of Indian agents in East Africa, the West Indies, Fiji and

Mauritius. As a matter of fact, I received a personal letter from Nehru on this matter and am glad to say that the Colonial Office have now agreed in principle to the appointment of such agents, the question of their exact function being left open for negotiation between our High Commissioner in India and the Government of India. I have replied to Nehru's letter on these lines.

4. In paragraph 2 of your Personal Report No. 11 you gave us the background to the announcement of 1st July about the partition of the Armed Forces. This announcement naturally took us rather by surprise as we had had no preliminary warning of it but examination of its details revealed no apparent defects. The part played by Trivedi in achieving this important success illustrated well the vital importance of the personal factor in the handling of Indian affairs at the present time.

5. I would like to say here how full of admiration I am for the public-spirited and generous way in which you have faced the question of the Governor-Generalships of the new Dominions.[694] The whole affair must have been most baffling and exacting to your personally, but, as you know, everyone here without exception believes that the right course is the one you have so unselfishly decided to follow.

6. I am very sorry that it was not possible, as you suggested, to announce appointments to Governorships during the passage of the Bill through Parliament but I hope that an announcement of at any rate some names will be possible very soon. While it is excellent that Cunningham[695] is willing to return to Peshawar, it is perhaps rather surprising that Killearn[696] feels at all attracted by East Bengal but it would certainly help to raise the status of Eastern Pakistan in the eyes both of Indians and of outside world if he were finally to accept.

7. I hope you will not have been too disappointed about Slim's refusal to accept the invitation to be Commander-in-Chief of the Army of the new Dominion of India. Personally, I formed the new impression that Slim's conviction that he was not in fact the right person for the job was sound and from all that I can hear I think that

---

[694] This was the question of whether there should be a joint governor general of India and Pakistan (Mountbatten's preference and a role he wanted) or two separate ones.

[695] Sir George Cunningham (1888–1963), colonial administrator; governor of the North-West Frontier Province, 1937–1939 and 1939–1946. He returned to be governor of the North-West Frontier Province, Pakistan, 1947–1948.

[696] Miles Lampson, 1st Baron Killearn (1880–1964), colonial administrator; high commissioner in Egypt and the Sudan, 1934–1936; ambassador to Egypt and high commissioner to the Sudan, 1936–1946; and special commissioner to South East Asia, 1946–1948.

Lockhart,[697] of the appointment is offered to him, would be a more suitable choice.

8. The future of the Interim Government must have been a perpetual anxiety to you in recent weeks but it is to be hoped that your latest device for bridging the time that remains before 15th August will meet the case.

9. Krishna Menon came to see me on Tuesday. It has to be admitted that in the past the impression he has created in home circles has been by no means favourable but, in view of his selection as High Commissioner in the United Kingdom for the new Dominion of India, it is encouraging to know that his services have been of such assistance to you in the difficult negotiations in Delhi in recent weeks. I am arranging for him to meet some of the Opposition leaders to whom at the moment he is by no means persona grata. The great need at India House at the moment is, of course, for someone at the top with real organising and administrative capacity. I rather doubt whether Krishna Menon will supply this need but perhaps he will be wise enough to realise that, if he wishes to concentrate on higher policy, he must find someone as his deputy who will carry out the re-organising of the office that will be required.

10. In view of what you reported in paragraph 13 of your Personal Report No. 11, it is indeed fortunate that the period to 15th August is so comparatively short. The strain upon you and your staff during this critical period must, I am afraid, be almost unbearable but I trust that after 15th August there will be a relaxation of the tension.

11. I entirely agree with you as to the great political importance of our providing the cruiser which the Congress members of your Cabinet have agreed that they should have. At the moment we are rather held up by the fact that the official telegram from the Defence department, promised in paragraph 18 of your Personal Report No. 11, has not yet been received and the Admiralty (whose ways will be familiar to you!) stoutly refuse to make any move except on the basis of an official request. The matter was raised in the House of Commons during the Debates on the Bill and the Prime Minister undertook to inform Commander Noble (M.P. for Chelsea)[698] of the decision finally reached in the matter.

[697] General Sir Robert Lockhart (1893–1981), British officer; commander-in-chief of the armed forces of the Dominion of India, 1947–1948.
[698] Allan Noble (1908–1982), later Sir Allan Noble, Conservative MP and junior minister; parliamentary under-secretary of state for Commonwealth Relations, 1955–1956.

12. In paragraph 4 of your letter of 11th July you ask about the new set-up in the Commonwealth Relations Office and to whom you should address your private letters after 15th August. Ismay is fully informed on these matters and will explain the position to you on his return.

13. An intense effort will certainly be required of Radcliffe if the work of the Boundary Commissions is to be completed by 15th August. I have always had a feeling that the reactions of the Sikhs to the decisions of the Punjab Boundary Commission would be one of the most critical danger spots in the process of transferring power and I hope that the services of Major Short, over whose appointment the Treasury have been most helpful, will be of some assistance in this connection.

14. In my telegram No. 9035 of 14th July I sent you a message for transmission to Sir C.P. Ramaswami Aiyer[699] in reply to identical telegrams which the Prime Minister and I had received from him. It is clear that Travancore is going to require very careful handling indeed and that we must avoid any statement which would give the State leverage in asserting its independence or economic autonomy. The Report No. 12 in paragraphs 27–32 of your Personal Report No. 12 on the discussions with the representatives of Hyderabad is very encouraging. I do indeed hope that you are right in believing that, if you can get Hyderabad to abandon the idea of complete independence, this would set an example which no other State, not even Travancore, could resist.

15. To-day the Indian Independence Bill has received the Royal Assent and we have fulfilled our intention with two days to spare. I was able to be present for part of the Second Reading Debate in the House of Commons and was, of course, present throughout the talking of all stages of the Bill in the House of Lords on Wednesday but could not find the time to attend the Committee Stage or Third Reading in the Commons. On the whole the Opposition in both Houses have been most co-operative and constructive in their criticism. It looked at the last moment as if the programme might be delayed in the House of Lords by the tabling of some amendment by Lord Rankeillour[700] but in view of the course of the debate he did not even move them.

---

[699] Sir C.P. Ramaswami Aiyer (1879–1966), Indian official; Dewan of Travancore, 1936–1947.
[700] James Hope, 1st Baron Rankeillour (1870–1949), Conservative MP and peer.

16. Ismay left this morning. His presence has as usual, been most valuable and he will be able to bring back to you first-hand impressions of the atmosphere in both Houses of Parliament.

17. To turn to other matters, it is unfortunate that Nehru has not responded to Smuts's[701] efforts to secure a détente between the Government of India and the Union [of South Africa] about the Indians in South Africa. He appears to be unwilling to co-operate unless Smuts accepts the implications of the U.N.O. Resolution, i.e. admits that U.N.O. has the right to intervene in matters of this kind, that the arrangements entered into between the Union and India in the past have the status of international obligations, and that consequently the Asiatic Land Tenure Act[702] will have to be suspended or withdrawn. This, however, might mean political suicide for Smuts. He has already lost an important by-election mainly because of his alleged liberal attitude towards Indians, and if he goes further his fall at the 1948 election in the Union seems certain.[703] The result would be the return to power of Malan[704] and the Nationalists, whose extreme views towards Indians are well known. This is surely not in Nehru's interests.

18. It would be very desirable to avoid at the next meeting of the U.N.O. Assembly a repetition of last year's controversy. The State Department, who like ourselves are uneasy about the position, have suggested to the Canadians that they might try to find out what the position is and we have privately advised the Canadians to make discreet enquiries both from the Union and from the Government of India as to the line each proposes to take. Bottomley, the Parliamentary Under Secretary of State in the new Commonwealth Relations Office, will take any opportunity he has in the course of the visit he is now paying to South Africa to talk the matter over with Smuts, I gather that Smuts has had considerable success with the moderate Indian leaders in South Africa, who are alarmed at the reaction in South Africa to the U.N.O. Resolution and have formed a new organization with the object of co-operating with the Union Government.

---

[701] Field Marshal Jan Smuts (1870–1950), South African army officer and United Party politician; prime minister of South Africa, 1919–1924 and 1939–1948.

[702] Asiatic Land Tenure Act 1946. The South African law restricted land ownership and voting rights of South African Indians.

[703] Which is indeed what happened.

[704] Daniel F. Malan (1874–1959), South African politician and National Party leader; prime minister of South Africa, 1948–1954.

19. All this is, of course, very confidential to yourself. You will doubt-less use any opportunity you get to guide Nehru on the path of moderation.

20. You mentioned in your letter of 5th June that the Hon. Mr. Jagjivan Ram, the Labour Member, would be visiting London after the end of the meeting of the International Labour Conference in Geneva. He actually arrived in London the 8th July and we were able to arrange that his time in London was used to the maximum advantage. In addition to interviews with the Prime Minister, Bevin, Cripps and Alexander as well as with Henderson and myself, Ram was taken to see various Ministry of Labour train-ing centres etc., and also attended a Garden Party at the Palace as well as being present in the Commons for the Second Reading debate on the Indian Independence Bill. We also gave him a small official lunch which was attended by Nanda, the other Indian Delegate in Geneva, as well as Lall, the Secretary of the Labour Department and the principal members of the Indian Sterling Balances Delegation. Ram seemed to have enjoyed himself and I think that he will consider that his trip to London has been well worthwhile. We were, of course, grieved to hear of the air crash at Basra but are thankful for his miraculous escape.

21. Yesterday we gave a Luncheon Party to the Indian and Burma delegates to the Empire Forestry Conference. It was a very successful occasion and from all accounts the delegates have played a most valu-able part in the Conference's deliberations and have been very impressed by the arrangements made. They have also, I am glad to say, greatly enjoyed their stay in this country.

22. I was consulted by Lord Robinson,[705] Chairman of the Conference, as to whether, from a political point of view, it would be a wise gesture to give India the opportunity of inviting the next Conference (in 1952) to be held in India. The Indian Delegation had indicated that they would like the matter left over for two years so that India, if so disposed, might then issue a firm invitation. I informed Robinson that, from a political point of view, it would cer-tainly be most advantageous if it proved possible for the next Conference to be held in India and that I, therefore, hoped that it would be possible to arrange for the question to be left open for a year or two by which time it was to be hoped that the situation in India would be clearer.

---

[705] Roy Robinson, Baron Robinson (1883–1952), chairman of the Forestry Commission, 1932–1952.

23. I am most grateful to you for what you have been able to achieve in the matter of Gwalior and Udaipur and the Indian Art Exhibition. You will, I think, like to see the enclosed copy of a letter[706] from the President of the Royal Academy which appeared in 'The Times' on Tuesday last and the Question and Answer in the House of Commons on 15th July of which I also enclose a copy.[707] The arrangements for the Exhibition are, I think, for the moment at least proceeding smoothly.

24. When I saw Amery the other day he threw out the suggestion that you might find it helpful to have on your staff during the next few months someone who was versed in Dominions procedure. The idea struck me as a good one and Ismay, to whom I mentioned it this morning, thought that it might meet your need if you were to have the advice of such a person even for a month or six weeks; it would probably be very difficult, if not impossible, to spare anyone for longer. I am making some quite tentative enquiries but if you feel that the idea is worth pursuing, it would be helpful if you would let me know.

Listowel

P.S.

Since writing paragraph 9 above I have met Krishna Menon at lunch and he would be very grateful if you would take an opportunity of mentioning to Nehru that I am, at my own suggestion, arranging for him (Krishna Menon) to meet Opposition leaders in view of the fact that, as High Commissioner, he will be brought into official contact with them.

19 Listowel to Mountbatten, 25 July 1947

Thank you for your personal report No. 13 which, as usual, I have read with the greatest possible interest.

2. We were delighted last night to get your telegrams 2195-S and 2196-S and you are indeed to be congratulated on securing the agreement of the Partition Council to this important statement. It is to be hoped that it will have a calming effect throughout all the areas

---

[706] Not included here.
[707] Not included here.

affected by partition and will help to discourage any large-scale migration of Muslims to Pakistan and Hindus to the territories of the future dominion of India; it has been disturbing to learn from Indians I have met in this country recently that such migration will be the natural tendency. It is also encouraging to learn from your latest personal report that Radcliffe has formed a favourable impression of the members of the Bengal and Punjab Boundary Commissions.

3. I sincerely hope that the absence of any information to the contrary can be taken as meaning that your solution of the problem of the Interim Government during the period that remains to August 15th is working out satisfactorily in practice.

4. I was delighted to learn of the arrangement you have been able to make with Admiral Palliser[708] about the shipping of the exhibits for the Indian Art Exhibition. It is particularly satisfactory that the Admiralty have arranged specially to divert an oiler for the purpose. There now appears to be good reason to hope that the Exhibition will be a real success.

5. I was also very glad to hear that all the leaders have so warmly welcomed the suggestion that Ismay and some of your staff officers should remain on with you during the transition period. As you say, Ismay may prove of the greatest help as a link between you and Jinnah.

6. I think we can regard the arrangements you have come to with the leaders about flags as satisfactory. It is clearly desirable to avoid pushing them so far in the direction of accepting the 'externals' of dominion status that they will forfeit the confidence and support of their followers.

7. Since I last wrote there have been the tragic events in Rangoon. Aung San is, of course, a tremendous loss both to Burma and to us, since we had put our confidence entirely in the will and ability of A.F.P.F.L. to take over power from us and exercise it worthily. At the same time it is indeed fortunate that Thakin Nu who, though not perhaps of quite the same calibre as Aung San, is undoubtedly a man of fine character and a potential leader, should have been spared and should so recently have visited this country and made the acquaintance of Ministers. It is, of course, disquieting that any degree of suspicion should attach to British officers over the theft of arms and ammunition from the Base Ordnance Depots and

---

[708] Admiral Sir Arthur Palliser (1890–1956), naval officer; commander-in-chief of the East Indies Station, 1946–1948.

regrettable, though not altogether surprising, that this suspicion should have helped to engender some degree of anti-British feeling. I have considerable confidence, however, that Rance and Thakin Nu between them will succeed in keeping the ship level and on its course.

8. A member of my staff has been shown confidentially by a member of the American Embassy the instructions issued by the State Department to the U.S. Ambassador at Delhi about the attitude that he and American officials should observe towards the Indian States. The State Department have indicated that they do not wish any formal dealings to occur between American representatives and the governments of Indian States while the negotiations for the inclusions of the States in one or other of the two Dominions are continuing. They recognise that at some later time it may be necessary for the U.S. Government to determine its attitude towards any States which remain outside the two Dominions but they attach importance to their remaining uncommitted so long as there is any prospect of the States who have asserted claims to independence entering into political arrangements with one or other Dominion. This is very satisfactory. There are indications, however, that the attitude of the French Government, particularly in regard to Hyderabad, may not be quite so sound but the Foreign Office are taking such steps as they can to prevent the French going off the rails.

9. After getting your private telegram 1960-S of 15th July, I saw Sir William Haley of the B.B.C. about the Corporation's plans for their programme dealing with the transfer of power in India. Haley appreciated the possible difficulties but I rather got the impression that he did not feel that they were sufficiently great to deflect the Corporation from their path. It is, I think, a good thing that the programme (as distinct, from mere reporting of events) is not to be begun until some time next spring and that no public announcement will be made about it before the New Year and I think that Haley would be quite prepared to review it, if events in the meanwhile pointed to the desirability of doing so. I also took the opportunity putting to Haley that it would be desirable that he should obtain the consent of the governments of India and Pakistan to the activities of the Corporation's representatives in India in connection with their projected programme.

10. I telegraphed to the Finance Department of the Government of India on the 19th July, No. 9306, asking that the Central and Provincial Governments should be invited to reconsider their attitude on the question of applying the Pensions (Increase) Act, 1947 to Indian pensioners in the U.K. I hope you will take any opportunity that offers itself for influencing the Indian leaders to change their

minds on this matter. The question has already aroused considerable interest in this country, both inside and outside the Parliament, and I fear that the refusal of the Indian leaders to extend the benefits of the 1947 Act to their pensioners in this country may afford an opportunity to throw doubts on the sincerity of the undertaking of the new Governments to maintain existing conditions of service.

11. In my last letter (paragraph 22) I mentioned the possibility that matters might be so arranged that it would be left open to India to issue an invitation for the next Empire Forestry Conference to be held in India. I am glad to say that the Resolution eventually passed by the Conference on this point was so framed as to give the future government of India the opportunity of doing so.

12. In my last letter I also mentioned (paragraph 13) that the promised official telegram from the Defence Department about the cruiser for India (Hindustan) had not yet been received. I am afraid I owe you an apology for this as the telegram had, in fact, been received on the 15th July but I had not seen a copy. This matter will, of course, now be pressed forward.

13. In conclusion, I might mention that on Friday last, after acting as a Royal Commissioner for the purpose of the King's Assent to the Indian Independence Bill, I attended a very successful inaugural luncheon of the newly formed association of Indian Journalists in London. It was altogether a very successful affair and the Association, which should be of the greatest assistance to us in the future, could not have had a more auspicious inauguration. This was largely due to your message, which I read to the gathering.

14. I have now arranged a luncheon for Krishna Menon on 5th August, to which prominent figures in all three Parties in the Lords and Commons have been invited. Menon would be reassured to know that you have mentioned this to Nehru, and that it has his approval.

Listowel

20 Mountbatten to Listowel, 25 July 1947

My dear Listowel,
Thank you so much for your long letter of the 18th July, which I read with much interest.

2. I am sorry to hear that the Burmese leaders during their recent visit to the U.K. made it perfectly clear that there was no possibility

of their changing their minds about leaving the Commonwealth. In the circumstances I fully appreciate that there is no possibility of rushing legislation through in the same way as has been done in the Indian Independence Bill, as it is obvious that there would be no chance of the Opposition co-operating on such terms.

3. But I am still worried whether at some future date we shall not find the Union of India wishing also to leave the Commonwealth – after all their vowed intent is still a sovereign independent republic – and I hope this matter is receiving consideration at home. In an earlier letter I suggested the possibility, to which Rance had also referred, of some looser form of association within the British Commonwealth, and I am putting the staff out here on to thinking about this and trying to find out the way in which more prominent Indians are thinking. I have been wondering whether some form of common citizenship, as was proposed for France and England in the summer of 1940, might be a possible solution and I shall be grateful for any thought on this matter from you at home.

4. In speaking of Burma I need hardly say how distressed and shocked I was to hear of Aung-San's death.[709] In my opinion, he was far and away the outstanding man of that group and I had hoped that he would occupy an outstanding position in Burma for many years to come. I do not think any of the others are up to his standard, and, although no one is irreplaceable, I fear that affairs in Burma will be much more unsettled now that he is dead. I suppose there is no chance of persuading the new Government to give Dominion status a trial.

5. I am sorry the announcement about the partition of the Armed Forces took you by surprise. Had there been time I would certainly have kept you informed, but it was a delicate matter securing agreement on so complicated a subject. Not only the political parties but also the Commander-in-Chief had to be carefully handled. With the valuable help of Ismay and Trivedi I managed to secure an agreement, and it was essential that once the negotiations were completed the formal decision of the Partition Council should be recorded and the announcement made. This was one of the biggest hurdles we have jumped since I came out here, and had I known I should have to jump it so soon I would have let you know, though clearly it was for the Partition Council to make the decision.

6. Jinnah has offered East Bengal to Killearn, who with Lady Killearn has been staying with us. They are now on a visit to

[709] Assassinated on 19 July 1947.

Dacca to see if they can find adequate accommodation, and I think the final answer will probably depend on that, for they have a family of small children and there are practically no modern sized houses in that one-horse town.

7. I was very sorry that Slim decided not to accept the appointment of Commander-in-Chief, India; I have had a very nice letter from him and I fully see his point of view. I understand that he felt he had been away from India too long, that he did not know the new Government or the new set-up and that he felt he would not fit in. I know him so well that I am sure there is nothing anti-Indian about him but that this is a perfectly straightforward honest opinion. Fortunately in Lockhart we have a most capable substitute.

8. I fully appreciate all that you say about Krishna Menon. I was aware that he is 'persona non grata' in many circles at home, and I would not say that he was popular or entirely trusted here. But he has been the very greatest help to me in the past difficult four months. Fortunately I made his acquaintance some years ago in England when he was very much an outcast because of his left-wing views and activities. He has never forgotten this and I have found him a valuable contact between Nehru (whose complete confidence he has) and myself, and through him I have been able to be particularly well informed about the trend of Congress thought and opinion. I need not stress how useful this has been to me since I came out. In fact with V.P. Menon and his close contact with Vallabhbhai Patel I have been able to know all that has been going on in both 'camps' in the Congress Party.

9. With reference to the postscript in your letter I am passing on to Nehru Krishna Menon's message about his meeting with the Opposition.

10. The official telegram about the cruiser must have crossed your letter, as it was despatched by Defence Department on the 14th July, telegram No. 2457. I am afraid as regards personnel it will not give the Admiralty all details they require. But at least it will let them know officially that India once again wishes to acquire the Achilles.

11. Thank you so much for the confidential information you gave me about Smuts and the Indian position in South Africa. This is not a matter which I have so far discussed personally with Nehru, though it has often come up in Cabinet. I will try and draw him out at some convenient opportunity, as I do not think this unsatisfactory state of affairs should be allowed to continue within the Commonwealth.

12. I am so glad to hear of Jagjivan Ram's programme at home and I am most grateful for all that was done to him on his initial visit to England. I am so glad that he survived the crash in the desert as he is a cheerful little man and I should have been sorry if he had been killed. I have not yet had full details of the crash, but I gather that through dust storms they were unable to land either at Basra or Shaiba and had to do a belly landing in the desert. I think they were exceedingly lucky that were not all killed.

13. I am certainly attracted to the idea of having someone on my staff, even for a short period, who is conversed in Dominion procedure and I shall be most grateful if you will go ahead with this. I think the earlier he can come out here the better and I think he will be a help not only to me but to the members of the Government.

14. You will recall the telegraphic correspondence we have had about a request for help in the matter of food, culminating in your telegram No. 8923 of the 11th July. I gave a copy of that telegram to Rajendra Prasad[710] and I enclose with this letter a copy of his reply[711] which covers the points raised. I do not know how far the insinuation that H.M.G. themselves gave barter inducements to Argentina is true.

15. The latest reports of the monsoon are slightly more favourable, and although the ration in Madras has had to be reduced further to 8 ounces a day, the situation in Bombay is slightly improved. As usual, much depends on the rainfall in the next two months, and I sincerely trust that we shall get through with the imports which are now in sight.

16. Representations have recently been made to me that the terms offered to I.M.S. [Indian Medical Service] officers for appointment to [the] Colonial Medical Service are unduly low and do not take sufficient account of their experience of tropical diseases. I am told that the D.G.I.M.S. [Director-General of the Indian Medical Service] has already addressed your Medical Adviser on the subject and I shall be grateful for anything you can do to secure more attractive terms for these officers, whose experience should be very valuable in the Colonies.

17. I have been reading Hansard both for the Commons and the Lords during the past week and I am filled with admiration at the way the Bill went through both Houses. If it is not out of place I

---

[710] Rajendra Prasad (1884–1963), Indian Congress politician; Food and Agriculture Member of the Interim Government, 1946–1947; first president of India, 1950–1962.

[711] Not included here.

should like to congratulate you and the members of the Government concerned heartily on this achievement. It is obvious that a very great deal of work must have been put in behind the scenes to smooth the passage of the Bill and to prevent the Opposition from raising controversial points, and I can assure you that I am most grateful to you for all that has been done. I need not say how high the British Government's stock stands out here at present for their honesty and good faith and the smooth and swift passage of the Bill has been the greatest help to me personally in my relations with the Indian leaders. If you see fit I should be very glad if you would pass my warmest thanks to all concerned.

Yours sincerely,

Mountbatten of Burma

21 Mountbatten to Listowel, 1 August 1947

My dear Listowel,

Thank you so much for your letter of the 25th July, and for all the information you sent me, which I read with great interest.

2. My Press Attache, Campbell-Johnson,[712] visited London recently with Ismay and was able to have an interview with Sir William Haley. He was able to put my point of view across, although he tells me that he did not think that anything he said would make any great change in the Corporation's plans. But Campbell-Johnson is in very close touch with the B.B.C.'s head man out here, Stimson,[713] and I am sure that in the end we shall be able to get the right slant on things.

3. I will certainly tell Nehru about the luncheon party you are arranging for Krishna Menon on the 5th August. I see, however, that Krishna Menon has been instructed to handle India's case on behalf of Indonesia before the Security Council of U.N.O. and I am wondering whether this will now make some alteration to your arrangements, and may indeed result in Krishna Menon being away from London on the 15th August, when he should be taking over as High Commissioner.

[712] Alan Campbell-Johnson (1913–1998), press attaché to the viceroy and governor general of India, 1947–1948.
[713] Robert Stimson, journalist.

4. In paragraphs 16 to 18 of your letter of the 20th June you dealt with the case of civilian ex-service clerks serving in G.H.Q.(I). Ismay tells me that he conveyed to you while he was in London my strong conviction that these clerks are entitled to special consideration in the matter of entitlement to compensation. I have since had a further talk with Auchinleck, who feels as strongly as I do that it would be most unjust to these men to deny them compensation. For reasons which Ismay gave you their case can be distinguished from that of others employed by the Government of India or Provincial Governments. I trust, even at this late stage, that you have found it possible to reopen the case.

5. Your predecessor in paragraphs 5 to 10 of his letter of the 9th May, 1947 referred to possible future employment for police officers. With reference to paragraph 8 of that letter, I wonder if you can give me any further information regarding their future prospects, particularly in the business world.

6. I have told both Nehru and Jinnah of Lord and Lady Addison's plans for passing through India on the way to the Conference in Canberra.[714] Jinnah has asked me to say that he would welcome seeing Lord and Lady Addison at Karachi both on the 18th August and on the 27th October. Nehru also expressed great pleasure at the prospect of this visit and in response to his suggestion I am getting in touch with Rajagopalachari, to see whether on the outward journey the latter will be able to put up Lord and Lady Addison in Calcutta.

7. I asked Nehru whether he himself could attend the Conference in Canberra, or send a high level representative. He told me he intended sending Mr. Rama Rau,[715] who had gone as Indian Ambassador to Tokyo, and that he would probably give him a subordinate official from Delhi to put him in the picture. I urged that he should send one of his Cabinet Ministers from Delhi to such an important Conference, and he agreed he would have liked to do so, but for the fact that it would mean leaving within a day or two of the formation of the new Government, when nobody would have got a grip of their new portfolios, or of the situation.

Yours sincerely,

Mountbatten of Burma

---

[714] Commonwealth Conference on the Japanese Peace Treaty in Canberra, August–September 1947.

[715] Sir Benegal Rama Rau (1889–1969), Indian diplomat and official; Indian ambassador to Tokyo, 1947–1948.

22 Listowel to Mountbatten, 2 August 1947

Thank you for your letter of 25th July enclosing Personal Report No. 14.

2. I very much hope that within the next two or three days it will be possible to issue the announcement about the formal appointments of yourself and Jinnah as Governors-General and about the appointments of Governors. To-day's reference in 'The Times' to the intention of the Constituent Assembly to meet at midnight on 14th/15th August and, as their first act, invite you to be Governor-General of the Dominion of India, about which I have telegraphed to you, is rather disconcerting but I hope it can be got round. On the whole, I think that the two new dominions will get a good start so far as Governors are concerned. I must confess that the new Indian names for Governorships in India do not, with one notable exception, mean very much to me but the experience of Nye, Colville, Trivedi and Hydari should prove of inestimable value. The exception among the new Indian Governors to which I refer above is, of course, Rajagopalachari whose qualities should have ample scope in Calcutta. As for Pakistan, Cunningham will, of course, be a tower of strength. It was hardly surprising that Killearn eventually was obliged to decline Eastern Bengal and I fear that Jinnah may find it very hard to get anyone of the necessary calibre to take the job on. As regards Baluchistan, about which I telegraphed, Weightman was quite ready to travel from the North to discuss the matter with me although he was fully convinced that he ought not to take the job on.

3. I am hav[ing] some enquiries made about providing you with a 'Dominions' expert, but I would be misleading you if I were to hold out any concrete hopes at this stage of being able to meet your need.

4. In paragraph 16 of your letter you refer to the terms being offered to I.M.S. Officers on appointment to the Colonial Medical Service. I understand the position to be that the Colonial Office are prepared to recognise in full, for purposes of seniority, 'war' service performed by I.M.S. Officers but to give only three months seniority for every year of peacetime service. The I.M.S. officer going into the medical services of the Armed Forces, on the other hand, is able to count his full I.M.S. Service for purposes of seniority. I am considering taking this matter up with the Colonial Secretary personally.

5. I much appreciated what you said in paragraph 17 of your letter about the passing of the Indian Independence Act and I feel sure that all the officials and ministers concerned, to whom I have passed on your message, will appreciate it equally.

6. I must confess to having some doubts about the line which you took at your meeting with the delegation from Kalat on 19th July. The treaties of 1854 and 1876 do not lead to the inference that Kalat is an independent and sovereign state and it has, in fact, always been regarded as an Indian state. It figures as such in Part 2 of the First Schedule of the Government in India Act, 1935, and I have no doubt that, as a matter of law, Section 7 (1) (b) of the Indian Independence Act applies to our treaties with it. Consequently the leased areas lapse to Kalat and the future is a matter for negotiation between the State and Pakistan. We have been at pains in Parliament to discourage claims by States to be regarded as separate international entities and to accept such a claim by Kalat will surely encourage other States to press similar claims. There is, moreover, particular danger in admitting such claims by frontier States since it is easier for them to make their independence effective. Apart from the risk to the integrity of India and Pakistan, the emergency of new weak international entities is undesirable. It seems to me, therefore, that any possible simplification of the problem of the areas leased by Kalat is outweighed by the general considerations set out above.

7. I was greatly interested in your account of your talk with the Dewan of Travancore and of your further talk with the Hyderabad Delegation on its return from seeing the Nizam. C.P. Ramaswami Aiyyar is, by all accounts, a past master in verbal diplomacy, and I congratulate you on having brought him to admit openly the danger to Travancore of pursuing a policy of independence. The Nizam is, no doubt, a very different proposition, since he is an incalculable creature and may not be wholly susceptible to reasoned arguments in this matter. If however, what appears in a press message from Hyderabad in today's Times is well-founded, your efforts with both these States have been crowned with success and they have agreed to treat for accession to the Union of India.

8. I have telegraphed to you some comments on the speech you made on 25th July to the representatives of the States. It is still not altogether clear to me how the States can, in fact, be expected to complete by the 15th August the process of adherence to the constitution of India, even if this is limited to three subjects. The draft Instrument

of Accession of which you sent a copy, would seem to open up various questions, such as the method of administration of the federal subjects in the States, which would require their careful examination. No doubt also there may be hesitation among the British-Indian negotiators about accepting a reservation, such as you discussed with the Dewan of Travancore, of the right to secede in the event of the Union of India leaving the Commonwealth. I had myself rather expected that the most that could be achieved before the 15th August would be an agreement on the part of the Union of India authorities to extend external protection to the States which were in process of negotiating terms of accession. The conclusion of the Instrument of Accession must surely be dependent on the constitution having been so amended as formally to provide for the admission of Indian States, and a completed constitution might contain other elements which would affect the States, notwithstanding their accession being limited in terms of external affairs, defence and communications. If, therefore, in the long run it is found impossible to secure the final accession of the key States you mention before 15th August. I think we shall feel well satisfied if these and the rest agree to be represented internationally for the time being by the appropriate Dominions while the negotiations are in process of completion, and I should hope that Patel would prove reasonable on such an accommodation, which would not be at variance with paragraph 5 of the Cabinet Mission's Statement of 12th May 1946. Such an arrangement, together with the standstill arrangement in economic and financial matters provided for in Section 7 of the Indian Independence Act, would relieve us of responsibility for the States while acquitting us of any charge of having exercised undue pressure on them to enter the new Dominions on terms against their better interests.

9. Pakistan clearly has a much simpler problem in dealing with the small number of States adjacent to its territory, and individual negotiations with each of these is clearly possible. No doubt Kashmir will claim as a price of accession acceptance by Pakistan of the existing customs arrangement whereby it imports goods from abroad free of duty. I shall be most interested to hear how the negotiations with the States progress, and we shall be asking Shone and Grafftey-Smith[716] to keep us informed after the 15th August, more especially since Parliamentary interest in this matter is still keen.

---

[716] Sir Laurence Grafftey-Smith (1892–1989), diplomat; high commissioner to Pakistan, 1947–1951.

10. I am sorry I troubled you unnecessarily with a reminder (telegram No. 9711) about the Resolution on the Services. The wording of the Resolution finally agreed upon is as follows:

> ... That this House, on the occasion of the transfer to Indian hands of the responsibility for the affairs of India, wishes to place upon record its profound appreciation of the ability and devotion with which, during the long period of British rule, the Civil and Military Services of the Crown in India have served India and its peoples.

I understand that the Prime Minister is now exploring the possibility of associating the Opposition parties with the Resolution, which will be moved and voted in both Houses before Parliament rises at the end of next week.

11. I was, of course, interested in the report of the Union Constitution Committee of the Constituent Assembly presented by Nehru on 21st July. At this end the emphasis in the report on the objective of a sovereign independent republic strikes a somewhat incongruous note at this moment and it seemed possible that it might give rise to some awkward questions in Parliament seeing that the Indian Independence Act had been passed at unprecedented speed on the basis of dominion status. However, the report has had no awkward repercussions here so far.

12. I was interested in the reference in Dow's[717] fortnightly letter (D-O.No. 156-GB) to the possibility of a reunion of Bihar with Western Bengal. No doubt this is the right long-term solution. The coalfields and other material assets in Bihar, for example, the very important Ansansol Railway junction, would greatly help stimulate the prosperity of Calcutta and Patna would be able to revert to its former and natural obscurity but the amalgamation would put a lot of local politicians in Bihar out of business and is hardly likely to appeal to the Congress High Command as an immediate measure.

13. It is clear that between now and August 15th Ministers here will be deluged with requests of one kind or another for 'messages' for publication on 15th August. I think the best solution will be for a single message to be sent from His Majesty's Government to the Governments of the two new Dominions and that all other requests for messages should be declined. In this connection I have seen a telegram from Canada saying that the Canadian High Commissioner at Delhi has arranged with the Government of India that, since the posts of Prime Minister 'are still in the air', messages for the two new dominions

---

[717] Sir Hugh Dow (1886–1978), ICS; governor of Bihar, 1946–1947.

should be sent, not from Prime Minister to Prime Minister, but from Minister of External Affairs to the two Ministers of External Affairs and Commonwealth Relations at Delhi and Karachi. I should be very grateful if you would confirm by telegram that this is, in fact, the position and that H.M.G.'s message should, therefore, go from the Secretary of State for Commonwealth Relations to his opposite numbers in the two new dominions.

14. Linlithgow called to see Carter[718] this morning and mentioned, among other things, that there are some pictures, including Zoffany portraits, which Queen Mary lent to Viceroy's House. Linlithgow (who is, I believe, one of Queen Mary's trustees) suggested that something ought perhaps to be done about these pictures before 15th August but that, so far as he was aware, the matter had not yet been mentioned to Queen Mary. You will no doubt wish to consider whether anything should be done about this.

15. I am very glad you have been able to pay a visit to Bengal as I feel sure that your presence in Calcutta at this time will have had a heartening effect in political and administrative circles and a reassuring effect on the population.

Listowel

23 Mountbatten to Listowel, 8 August 1947

Dear Listowel,

Thank you for your letter of the 2nd August. Amongst the points that you mention is the question whether or not Kalat is legally an Indian State. On this point I have always been very careful not to commit myself personally. It has been made quite clear that it is only Kalat itself and the Pakistan Government which consider, for the purposes of negotiation, that Kalat is not an Indian State. In this week's Personal Report I give an account of my latest meeting with the Khan of Kalat.[719]

2. I enclose the draft communiqué[720] which was agreed in principle between Jinnah, the Khan and myself, but with the words underlined

---

[718] Sir Archibald Carter (1887–1958), civil servant; permanent under-secretary of state for India, 1947.

[719] Sir Ahmad Yar Khan Ahmedzai (1902–1979), khan of Kalat, 1933–1955.

[720] Not included here.

(which Jinnah wishes included and the Khan does not wish included) still a matter of negotiation between the three of us – unfortunately by letter as Jinnah and His Highness have now left Delhi.

3. I was invited by the Khan of Kalat to add to the communiqué that I also recognised he was an independent sovereign ruler. I replied that so far as H.M.G. were concerned they considered Kalat to be an Indian State, but since the two interested parties both agree I did not propose to interfere with this agreement.

4. I have been sent by the Maharaja of Sikkim[721] a memorandum regarding the cession of Darjeeling. I have not yet received the advice of the External Affairs Department on this memorandum, but I enclose a copy of it for your information.[722]

5. On the issues raised in my speech to the Chamber of Princes, we have already exchanged telegrams. But I feel that, especially with regard to your mention of this in your letter of 2nd August, I should somewhat elaborate my view-point, and am addressing a separate letter on this subject to you.

6. In my last week's Report, I referred to the continued rumours that the Sikhs were likely to make trouble after the Boundary Commission's award has been announced. On 5th August, Jenkins sent down a Police Officer with a verbal report. I took advantage of the fact that there was a Partition Council Meeting the morning he arrived to keep back Mr. Jinnah, Mr. Liaquat Ali Khan and Sardar Patel so that they could hear what he had to say. This Police Officer is a member of the Punjab C.I.D. Control Staff, which coordinates investigation of disturbances cases, special interrogation and intelligence from all sources. He gave an account of the statements which had been made by various instigators of disturbances who had been arrested after incidents. The man who had given away most information was an ex-member of the I.N.A. [Indian National Army],[723] and had during the war been at the Japanese spy school at Penang and sent to India by submarine. This man's statement involved Master Tara Singh[724] in the production of bombs and a Sikh plan to attack a certain headworks. Statements of other men who had been arrested involved Tara Singh in plans to wreck the trains carrying the Pakistan

[721] Tashi Namgyal (1893–1963), chogyal of Sikkim, 1914–1963.

[722] Not included here.

[723] Army formed of Indian nationalists that sought to expel Britain from India by military means with support from Japan during World War II.

[724] Master Tara Singh (1885–1967), Sikh politician.

Governmental staff from Delhi to Karachi and in plans to assassinate Mr. Jinnah during the celebrations in Karachi on 15th August. The evidence produced was so incriminating that Jenkins may have to arrest Tara Singh and the more hot-headed of his confederates shortly before 15th August.

7. I have recently been in communication with Wylie concerning the future of the [1857 Indian] Mutiny Memorials in the U.P. It is a matter on which the Metropolitan of India,[725] who was staying with me last week, is much concerned. Wylie has suggested –

   (a) The Residency at Lucknow. This should continue under the present arrangements whereby the proprietory rights vest in the Defence Department (who bear the cost of maintenance) and the management is entrusted to a small Committee of which the Area Commander is Chairman;

   (b) The Memorial Well and Gardens at Cawnpore. These are the property of a regular Trust composed of European business men. They have agreed to offer 30 acres of the site to the Municipality free of cost on condition that it should be kept for ever as a space and not be built upon. They are considering Wylie's suggestion that the remaining 10 acres, including the Well and the Graveyard, should be enclosed and handed over to the Allahabad Diocese Trust; but may prefer to go on managing the Well and Graveyard area themselves.

   (c) The Massacre Ghat at Cawnpore. The Cross on this is not a conspicuous object and Wylie is inclined to leave it alone.

These suggestions seem to me to be sound and I propose to tell Wylie when he comes to pay me his farewell visit tomorrow that I agree with him.

8. The Maharaja of Bundi[726] (a gallant young soldier who won the M.C. under me in the 14th Army) is an Honorary A.D.C. to the King, and most anxious to be invited to attend Princess Elizabeth's wedding.[727] The other three Honorary A.D.Cs. I believe are the Maharajas of Patiala[728] and Kolhapur[729] and the Nawab of Bhopal. Not more than one or two of these would be likely to attend if

---

[725] Most Reverend George Hubback (1882–1955), Anglican clergyman, bishop of Calcutta and metropolitan of India, 1945–1950.

[726] Bahadur Singh (1920–1977), maharaja of Bundi from 1945.

[727] Princess Elizabeth's wedding to Prince Philip in November 1947.

[728] Sir Yadvinder Singh Mahendra Bahadur (1913–1974), maharaja of Patiala from 1938.

[729] Shahji II Puar (1910–1983), maharaja of Kolhapur from 1947.

they received invitations, so the total number would be unlikely to exceed three. It would, I feel, be an excellent thing if His Majesty could see his way to issuing invitations to them.

9. I also hope that Dominion Prime Ministers will be invited, for it would be a great thing if we could get Nehru to come to London at such a time of national rejoicing. As I have been invited I could bring him with me in our York [aeroplane]. He is an inveterate sentimentalist, and I feel it would greatly help to strengthen Anglo-Indian bonds if he went. It would also give him an opportunity of meeting the other Dominion Prime Ministers.

Yours sincerely,

Mountbatten of Burma

24 Listowel to Mountbatten, 9 August 1947

Thank you for your letter of 1st August enclosing Personal Report No. 15. As this is the last weekly letter I shall be sending you I should like to say (and I know that all my colleagues (both Ministers and officials) would agree with me) how immensely valuable and enthrallingly interesting your weekly Personal Reports have been. They have gone a long way towards eliminating the effects of distance and have enabled us here to appreciate the atmosphere in Delhi to a degree which has enormously assisted us in carrying out our part in the events of the past months. I would like also, if I may be allowed to, to commend the drafting of the reports which has combined lucidity with graphic description in a high degree. Such touches as paragraph 56 of Report No. 15 have, moreover, served to reassure us that pressure of work has not impaired the detachment and sense of humour of yourself and your staff.

2. As this will be my last letter to you, I must also endeavour to tidy up any loose ends from our previous correspondence. Thus in paragraphs 3 and 4 of your letter of 10th July you referred to the question of appeals to the Privy Council after the transfer of power. No steps seem necessary here at this juncture for, until some contrary provision is enacted by one or both Dominions, appeals all continue to come to the Judicial Committee. We had already sounded the Lord Chancellor[730] about this question some time ago and he then

[730] Lord Jowitt.

held strongly that any move for cessation of appeals should come from India. It seems unnecessary to pursue the matter with him further until it is clear that one of the Dominions wishes to stop appeals to the Judicial Committee. In that event, of course, we may have to meet a desire that proceedings pending before the Judicial Committee should be continued to judgement and, to secure this, it might well be expedient to have a clause in a Treaty providing for the continuance of the Judicial Committee's jurisdiction in respect of those proceedings which could be implemented by legislation if necessary at both ends.

3. I was interested in what you said in paragraph 3 of your letter of 25th July about some looser form of association within the British Commonwealth to meet the case of Burma and perhaps later on of India. I can assure you that the wider implications and possibilities are not being overlooked and that some hard thinking is being done at this end on the question. But the problem of devising a form of association which is even looser than that at present binding the Dominions and which is yet not entirely meaningless or indeed, in the absence of a real measure of common purpose and interest, even dishonest, is no easy one. And the reactions of, and on, existing Dominions, and more particularly Dominions such as S.[outh] Africa or Canada, of any weakening of existing links are material factors. However, I agree as to the importance and urgency of the issue.

4. So far as concerns the particular and, indeed, somewhat technical aspect of citizenship to which you refer, as you probably know, following the Commonwealth Conference of experts earlier this year, a scheme is now being worked out by the various Commonwealth Governments which would give the U.K. and each Dominion its own citizenship.[731] The possession of one of these citizenships would be the only gateway to the status of British subject, which would remain a common status with, it is to be hoped, common privileges in each of the Commonwealth countries. From some points of view the creation of separate citizenships ought to help towards that form of association within the Commonwealth which you have in mind. In another sense, however, to hanker after any form of common citizenship is swimming against the stream. In any case the status of [a] British subject will remain a common status, though in the last analysis it will now, more than ever, mean simply a common allegiance to the Crown. And there, I take it, we are back at our starting-point.

---

[731] The British Nationality Act 1948 was one consequence of these discussions.

5. In paragraph 4 of your letter of 25th July you said that you supposed that there was no chance of persuading the new Government of Burma to give dominion status a trial. I am afraid that the effect of the assassinations will have been rather to accentuate the feeling of the leaders who have survived that, whatever their own predilections, their position vis-à-vis the rank and file of their supporters is not strong enough to make it possible for them to give a lead in the direction of remaining within the Commonwealth. It has to be recognised, too, that the suspicion (which, I regret to have to say, is not entirely unfounded) that the assassinations were due in some measure to acts of commission or omission on the part of members of the British Services, is another factor inevitably tending to reinforce the urge to 'cut the painter'.

6. It has taken much longer than we hoped to settle up the question of compensation for the Burma Services. We now expect, however, to be able to make an announcement in Parliament before the Adjournment (which, for domestic reasons, has had to be postponed until the middle of next week) and to lay a White Paper.

7. I am sorry that I have not yet got any news for you on the subject of a 'Dominions' expert but if, rather contrary to my expectation, it proves possible to help you, Carter will communicate with Ismay on the matter.

8. I am afraid I am still not in a position to comment on Rajendra Prasad's letter which was referred to in paragraph 14 of your letter of 25th July but which was inadvertently omitted from that letter and has only recently reached me. The questions raised in it affect at least three Government Departments here and the matter will take a little time to investigate. It is hoped to communicate on the subject with the U.K. High Commissioner in the Dominion of India in due course.

9. I am not surprised at what you say in paragraph 2[?] of your Personal Report No. 14 about the desire of the Princes not to be cut off from future intimate and honorific relations with His Majesty. The Princes' own feeling is natural enough but the reactions of Patel and his forecast of the attitude of the future Government of India are unexpected and, as you say, welcome.

10. As regards the future treatment of the Princes, we feel here that they cannot expect their existing personal relations with the Crown to continue on the same basis otherwise than within the Commonwealth and through the new Dominion Governments. Time alone will show how these will work out. It is, of course, agreed

that the fact that Indian Orders are to remain in suspended animation does not preclude the grant of honours by The King to Indian Princes in the future should the Dominion Governments recommend such a course. Therefore the way remains open for the bestowal of decorations.

11. As regards other honours such as appointments as Honorary Aides-de-Camp to The King and Honorary Ranks in the British Army, the present position as we see it can remain undisturbed. There is no idea cancelling existing appointments

12. The appointments of Honorary Aides-de-Camp to The King, since they are so limited in number are very highly prized. Unless any individual Prince took it upon himself to relinquish his appointment, it is not proposed to suggest to His Majesty that He should take any initiative in the matter. On the other hand it seems doubtful whether any new appointments need be made, should a vacancy occur by the death of an Honorary A.D.C. to The King.

13. The same applies to Honorary Ranks in the British Army which will be retained, though no new appointments or promotions would of course be made save on the recommendation of the Dominion Governments. I am not sure, however, that these may not wish future grants of honorary rank to be in their own Forces.

14. Possibly you will think it desirable to say something about this to Jinnah, though the Muslim League attitude towards Honours for Princes may not correspond with that of Patel.

15. Fortunately, Krishna Menon did not have to go to New York and was able to be present at the Luncheon which I arranged for 5th August and which proved a very successful occasion. Apart from Henderson and Pethick-Lawrence I invited R.A. Butler, Godfrey Nicholson,[732] Samuel and Hopkin-Morris.[733] I am sorry to say that a certain amount of opposition to Menon's appointment is showing itself here, more particularly in Indian circles in London. Menon certainly has a past to live down, but we will do all we possibly can to help him establish his position.

16. You revert again, in paragraph 4 of your letter of 1st August to the case of the civilian ex-service clerks serving in [unclear] I hope you appreciate that I entirely recognise that theirs is a very hard case, but the old adage about hard cases and bad law remains true.

---

[732] Godfrey Nicholson (1901–1991), later Sir Godfrey Nicholson, 1st baronet, Conservative MP.

[733] Rhys Hopkin Morris (1888–1956), later Sir Rhys Hopkin Morris, Liberal MP.

And I concur in the unanimous opinion of my Department, that a concession in this case, however much one may be tempted to make it on compassionate grounds, would make a dangerous breach in the general principles upon which these matters have been settled.

17. In paragraph 5 of your letter of 1st August you asked for further information about the prospects of obtaining employment for officers of the Indian Police, particularly in business. I am afraid that, as we all expected, this problem continues to be the most difficult of those falling to the Re-employment Branch here and it would be wrong to minimise the very great obstacles which lie in the way of an entirely satisfactory solution.

18. You may have heard that, when Linlithgow was the guest of honour at a recent Police dinner in London, he suggested that it was probably in the best interest of many of those present to continue in service in India or Pakistan, so doubtful were the prospects of finding a satisfactory alternative career in business in the U.K. I understand that his remarks created a deep impression and the decision of certain Provinces not to retain the services of any Police officers must, therefore, be all the more disappointing to those who are prepared to stay on.

19. As I have said before, we cannot know how things will work out for the Police until the men concerned are actually in the U.K. All we can do is to make sure that the ground is properly prepared and I am satisfied that this has now been done. The India and Burma Services Section mentioned in paragraph 9 of my letter of 9th May is now on the point of being set up in the London Appointments Office of the Ministry of Labour and will, from approximately August 15th, be in charge of the officer mentioned in paragraph 6 of the same letter. He will be joined later by an I.C.S. officer. The Section will receive first-hand information about the vacancies notified by employers to the Ministry and will be able to submit direct for consideration the names of suitable Indian Service candidates.

20. I am also glad to be able to tell you that Hailey has now formed his unofficial Committee[734] and the Committee has had its first meeting. As you may know, Hailey himself is about to undertake a tour on behalf of the Colonial Office and Anderson has agreed to act as Chairman in his place; the other members of the Committee are Linlithgow, Catto,[735] Scarbrough, Hailey himself, R.A. Butler,

---

[734] See Letter 6, paragraph 9.
[735] Thomas Catto, 1st Baron Catto (1879–1959), businessman and official; governor of the Bank of England, 1944–1949.

Woodrow Wyatt[736] and Alexander Murray. It has been decided to address a circular letter (which will be signed by Anderson personally) to a large number of firms and business concerns, public corporations and academic bodies, explaining our case in detail and asking for their help.

21. I know that the Services are assured of very great good-will and sympathy on the part of the members of this Committee and that they are determined to do everything possible to make sure that the claims of officers appointed by the Secretary of State receive the maximum consideration from business firms. Nevertheless, I do not think that, the present economic position being what it is, they would care to commit themselves as to the extent to which it will be possible to secure appointments. I understand that, at the first meeting, general agreement was expressed with Linlithgow's view, that officers who had the ability, the opportunity and the desire to continue in service in India should be encouraged to do so.

22. It was also suggested, that some kind of central agency might be established in India to investigate further the opportunities of employment there. We shall be glad to know whether anything has been considered on these lines and, if not, whether it is considered that such an organisation should now be established.

23. I hope that I have not painted too bleak a picture in the preceding paragraphs. So far as the I.C.S. and (to a lesser extent) the Technical Services are concerned, we are encouraged by the ease with which men of average or greater ability in the critical age groups have already been able to find themselves satisfactory alternative careers. It is in relation to the less able officers of the I.C.S. and to the main body of the Police in the critical age groups that we are still not content. I have already suggested to you that it may be wise to encourage many of these younger Police officers officers to train themselves entirely for a fresh career (using, if necessary, some of their compensation for this purpose); no doubt we shall be able to arrange for those of them who wish to do so to enter a university,

24. To complete the picture I should add that the Re-employment Branch in this Office will remain in being until the cases of all officers who are applicants for any form of permanent Government employment have been completed. It will also continue to act as a co-ordinating agency.

[736] Woodrow Wyatt (1918–1997), later Lord Wyatt, Labour MP.

25. It is very good of you to have done so much to try and arrange a pleasant and interesting passage through India for Addison and Cripps. I am sorry that Addison's schedule will not make it possible for him to meet anyone in India but he hopes to stay with Rance in Rangoon. I am very glad that Cripps will be spending a day with you in Delhi after you have had about ten days experience of your new office; he will no doubt be able to tell us much of interest on his return.

26. It is a pity that none of Jinnah's high level choices for the governorship of East Bengal have materialised but the temporary appointment of Bourne[737] should give more time for the right selection to be made. It is encouraging to read in paragraph 11 of Personal Report No. 15 of the progress being made with the establishment of the new capital at Dacca. The provision of suitable accommodation for the Governor seems a necessary condition of obtaining a man of the necessary calibre for the post.

27. Your account in Personal Report N.15 of your dealings with Nehru, Patel and Gandhi over Nehru's emotional urge to visit Kashmir is illuminating, if somewhat disturbing. Clearly, Gandhi will have a safe passage in Kashmir, even though the Maharaja[738] finds himself bound to join Pakistan. The realistic attitude of Patel is a great asset to the Congress Party but one cannot suppose that it will be possible for all time to prevent an open clash between such differing temperaments.

28. What you say in paragraph 34 of the same report about the readiness of both Nehru and Jinnah to receive the Chiefs of Staff or high powered representatives of them for discussions with the Joint Defence Council is most encouraging. I will see that the Chiefs of Staff are informed.

29. Your first and last contact with the Chamber of Princes seems to have been a fairly exhausting experience. No doubt the Rulers and Dewans of the bigger states are most of them capable of appreciating the great risks they run in attempting to hold aloof from the Dominion of India. They will have had time to appreciate that they cannot count on active support from the outside world in staking out a claim to independence. We are full of admiration at your success in having overcome the hesitations of so many States about acceptance of the terms of accession offered by Patel. To do them

---

[737] Sir Frederick Bourne (1891–1977), ICS; governor of East Bengal (Pakistan), 1947–1950.
[738] Sir Hari Singh Dogra (1895–1961), maharaja of Kashmir from 1925.

justice, the States have had little reason up to now to assume that the Congress and their friends have any intention of offering them a square deal. Their experiences while Congress was in power in the Provinces before the war and Nehru's repeated abuse of their Governments since he came into power have at least given cause for their adopting an attitude of caution about throwing in their lot for good and all with the Dominion of India. However, having come to realise their weakness if they attempt to stand alone and the growing sympathies of their subjects with the more progressive elements in British India, the more enlightened Rulers and their Ministers seem to have at last accepted the inevitable. I am sorry to hear that C.P. Ramaswami Aiyyer should have been so severely mauled on his return to Travancore, but no doubt his going out of business at any rate temporarily has had the valuable effect of deciding the Maharaja to call off his bid for independence.

30. The personal equation seems for the time being to have dictated the choice of Bhopal, Indore[739] and Dholpur.[740] If your own diplomacy succeeds in persuading them to throw in their lot with their brother Rulers, you will have achieved something which we at this end would not have thought possible a few weeks ago. Even so, there still remains the problem of Hyderabad and its most unaccountable Ruler. It still seems to me that in the case of this State Patel could afford to accept an interim political arrangement of the kind I referred to in paragraph 8 of my letter of 2nd August. So many considerations are necessarily involved in acceding to a constitution which has yet to be finalised, even for the limited range of subjects in question, that I cannot withhold some sympathy from the Nizam in being told that he has to make up his mind to sign on the dotted line by 15th August. However, by the time this letter reaches you it may well be that your efforts and those of Monckton[741] will have prevailed against the pressure brought to bear on the Nizam by his Muslim subjects, without it being necessary for the Dominion Government to grant him a locus poenitentiae.[742]

31. With reference to paragraph 54 of Personal Report No. 15, one cannot but regret on grounds of principle that the remaining I.N.A. prisoners will appear to have had their brutality condoned

---

[739] Sir Yeshwant Rao Holkar (1908–1961), maharaja of Indore from 1926.

[740] Sir Udaibhan Singh Deo (1893–1954), maharaj-rana of Dholpur from 1943.

[741] Sir Walter Monckton (1891–1965), later 1st Viscount Monckton of Brenchley, legal adviser to the nizam of Hyderabad, 1933–1936 and 1946–1948; later Conservative MP and minister.

[742] Opportunity to withdraw from an obligation or contract.

but, taking all in all, the arrangement now proposed for dealing with them is probably the most satisfactory one possible. At the same time it does seem important that the scheme should be put into effect as inconspicuously as possible, and that great care should be exercised to prevent publicity, which might have a serious effect on the morale of the army.

32. You will no doubt like to know how things are shaping administratively here. On 15th August the appointment of Arthur Henderson as Minister of State for Commonwealth Relations will be announced. It will be announced at the same time that the staff of the India Office will be amalgamated with that of the Commonwealth Relations Office and that Carter will serve as a Joint Permanent Under-Secretary of State for Commonwealth Relations. It has been arranged that as soon as possible after the 15th August Henderson, the Under Secretaries and nuclei of certain of the key departments of the India Office should move from their present accommodation into rooms in the Colonial Office building (immediately adjoining the Commonwealth Relations Office) which are being evacuated by the Colonial Office and were to have been taken over by the Foreign Office. It is very difficult to see how things will work out in practice but this move should help accelerate the process of integrating the two departments. You may also like to know that, with the same object in view, we plan to hold a social party for the staff of both Offices towards the end of September when the leave season is over.

33. I have agreed to receive next week a deputation from the Indian Police Association and the newly formed Indian Government Officers (Retired) Association. In order not to raise false expectations it has been made clear to both bodies at meetings with officials that there is really nothing more that can be done for the Services than has already been done, but I felt that it would be unfortunate to resist pressure that I should receive a deputation. The point on which the Indian Police Association are particularly keen to speak is the question of the increase of police pensions which, leaving aside any question of merits, is politically, of course, quite out of the question at the present juncture.

34. The Resolution on the Services quoted in paragraph 10 of my letter of 2nd August was moved in both Houses yesterday. In the Lords there were eloquent speeches by Bobbety Salisbury on behalf of the Conservatives, and by Reading[743] on behalf of the Liberals. The

---

[743] Gerald Isaacs, 2nd Marquess of Reading (1889–1960), Liberal peer and later junior minister.

Bishop of Salisbury,[744] Chetwode,[745] and Hailey also spoke. In the Commons, where the Prime Minister, Eden and Clement Davies spoke, the names of Churchill and Eden were associated with those of Ministers in sponsoring the resolution. I hope these resolutions will give satisfaction to the members of the Services, who will no longer entertain the slightest doubt about the whole-hearted appreciation of Parliament.

35. I have seen the copy of Spens's[746] letter to you of July 21st which Abell sent to Harris. It was only natural that the Judges should feel impatient over the delay which occurred in informing them how they stand in the new constitutional situation: and I am glad to note from your telegram No. 2957 of July 26th that a communication has now been made to them. This telegram also formed the basis of Henderson's reply to a Question in the Commons by Niall Macpherson[747] on August 4th.

36. I was grateful for your telegram No. 3200-S about the proposed messages to India and Pakistan on the 15th August. The messages will be sent to the U.K. High Commissioners with the request that they may be passed to the Prime Ministers of India and Pakistan respectively. The draft of the messages at present runs as follows:

> My colleagues in the United Kingdom Government join with me in sending on this historic day greetings and good wishes to the Government and people of India/Pakistan from the people of the United Kingdom. It is our earnest wish that India/Pakistan may work out its destiny as a free country in tranquillity and prosperity and, in so doing, make its full contribution to world peace and progress.

37. It seems at the moment as if the Government of India will have reason to be pleased with the terms of the agreement on sterling balances, which were far more satisfactory than I had dared to hope. Not unnaturally, it seemed at one moment as if the terms of the projected agreement might have to be modified to India's disadvantage in view of the coincidence of the negotiations with the economic 'crisis' in this country, but it now seems certain that this will not happen.

---

[744] Geoffrey Lunt (1885–1948), bishop of Salisbury, 1946–1948.

[745] Field Marshal Sir Philip Chetwode, 1st Baron Chetwode (1869–1960), army officer and official.

[746] Sir Patrick Spens (1885–1973), later 1st Baron Spens, jurist and Conservative MP; chief justice of India, 1943–1947.

[747] Niall Macpherson (1908–1987), later 1st Baron Drumalbyn, National Liberal MP and later junior minister.

38. I telegraphed to you recently about difficulties which had arisen over the embarkation of the exhibits for the Exhibition of Indian Art and I am very glad to hear through the Royal Academy that you have managed to smooth over these difficulties and that shipment is now taking place as arranged.

39. I am enclosing copy of a letter[748] from the Royal Academy in which they convey what I am sure will be good news to you, namely that the Prime Minister has agreed to be President of the Exhibition. The Royal Academy and the Committee of the Exhibition also ask me to convey to you as Governor-General of India, and to the Governor-General of Pakistan, the High Commissioner for India and the High Commissioner for Pakistan, their invitation to be Honorary Presidents of the Exhibition. I would be most grateful if you would accept the invitation to you as Governor-General of India, and would have transmitted to Jinnah, Krishna Menon and Rahimtoola[749] the invitations to them. It seems better that these should be communicated through you than from this Office.

40. The Academy have, I think, rightly raised the question whether the title of the Exhibition requires alteration with the coming into existence of Pakistan as a separate Dominion. I do not know whether you would feel justified in asking Jinnah whether, for reasons of convenience, he would be prepared to support retention of the existing title. If not, I would propose advising the Academy that the title might be amended to "Exhibition of Art of India and Pakistan". It would be a great help if you could let me know by telegram before the date of the transfer of power what you think about this.

41. I cannot end this, my last weekly letter, without paying a tribute to all that you and your staff have achieved in the few months since you left for Delhi. When one considers the intractability of the problems, great and small, requiring to be solved, the intensity and bitterness of feeling between the major communities affected and the sheer weight of the work to be got through, one realises the magnitude of what has been achieved by you and your staff. The Indian leaders and officials, civil and military, whose share in the process of transferring power has been indispensable, have made a remarkable contribution to the settlement. It must be with a sense of great relief that you see 15th August approaching and yet relief not untinged with

---

[748] Not included here.

[749] H.I. Rahimtoola (1912–1991), Pakistani diplomat and minister; first Pakistani high commissioner to London, 1947–1952.

regret at the ending of a great chapter and of concern at the thought of the unchartered seas that lie ahead.

Listowel

25 Mountbatten to Listowel, 16 August 1947

My dear Listowel,[750]

Thank you for your last weekly letter, dated 9th August. Although I understand you will have relinquished office as Secretary of State officially on the 15th August, I am addressing this letter to you in order that you may decide how the various outstanding points may be dealt with.

2. You asked in paragraph 10 of your letter of 25th July that I should use my influence to persuade the Central and Provincial Governments to reconsider their attitude on the question of applying the Pensions (Increase) Act 1947 to pensioners of Indian Services in the U.K.

3. I spoke to Rajagopalachari, while he was still Finance Member, and to Liaquat Ali Khan, but I am afraid it is doubtful whether they will agree as there is a good deal of feeling against increasing liabilities by way of pensions, etc. in any form. The matter will, however, be carefully examined.

4. I am sorry that Nehru made his rather embarrassing request to allow Sir N.R. Pillai,[751] Mr. K.P.S. Menon[752] and Mr. K.K. Chettur[753] to receive certain Peruvian Orders without letting me know. After I received your telegram of 26th July, however, I made enquiries and found that Nehru himself was by no means happy about the telegram which had gone to you. A letter from my Secretary to the Department, pointing out that the grant of

---

[750] In recognition that Mountbatten was no longer viceroy, but now governor general of the independent realm of India, the official residence was appropriately renamed, and at the top of this letter 'The Viceroy's House' has been struck through and replaced with 'Government House'.

[751] Sir N.R. Pillai (1898–1992), ICS, and later Indian Administrative Service and Indian diplomat.

[752] K.P.S. Menon (1898–1982), ICS, and later Indian Administrative Service.

[753] K.K. Chettur (1901–1956), ICS, and later Indian Administrative Service and Indian diplomat.

restricted permission to receive these Orders would be at variance with the practice followed by His Majesty's Government, and that it might be difficult to explain to His Majesty why Indian officials should be permitted to accept Orders from a foreign Head of State while declining to accept them from him, gave Nehru the opportunity he needed to withdraw the request. I understand that considerable pressure had been put upon Nehru to make the original request and he was glad of an excuse to withdraw it.

5. In my last weekly report (paragraph 43) I stated that I was sending to Mr. Jinnah a bowdlerized version of a paper, prepared by General Messervey [sic],[754] on the problems facing the Pakistan Army. In fact, I later discovered that General Messervey himself had sent Mr. Jinnah a copy of his own paper; and so my version was never despatched.

6. Thank you for the memorandum on the North-West Tribal Area and Afghanistan which you sent with your letter of August 1st. I discussed it with Cunningham on his way to Peshawar. We agreed that the present is not an appropriate time for me to open this matter with the Political Leaders.

7. There is nothing in the Frontier situation which made it necessary for me to speak of it before the 15th August, particularly since Mr. Jinnah made it clear in a statement to the Press on the 31st July that tribal allowances, etc., will be continued after the 15th August until the Pakistan Government can negotiate new agreements with the Tribes, and that control in the Political Agencies would be continued as at present.

8. I am sure it is necessary that the new Governments in Pakistan and India should start to function, and begin to feel the impact of events before they can shape their foreign policy.

9. Opportunity will undoubtedly occur in the next few months for consultation between the Pakistan Government and Afghanistan, and also H.M.G's representatives, about the Frontier policy. At the moment the Government of India are disinclined to own to any interest in the Frontier, and disclaim any responsibility for its affairs or defence. This attitude will, I hope, mellow as time goes on, and I trust that India, and more particularly, Pakistan, will come to appreciate the need for a common policy in this region, and will welcome the interest and support of H.M.G. in carrying it out. I would suggest

[754] General Sir Frank Messervy (1893–1974), army officer; commander-in-chief of the Pakistani armed forces, 1947–1948.

that background should be given to both the U.K. High Commissioners and they be instructed to pursue the matter as opportunity offers in the next few months.

10. The communiqué on the negotiations between Kalat and Pakistan, a draft of which I attached to my last letter, was published on 11th August, with the following amendments. Paragraph 1 should read : –

> The Government of Pakistan recognises Kalat as an independent sovereign State in treaty relations with the British Government, with a status different from that of Indian States.

In paragraph 2, the words 'treaties and' should be omitted.

11. I have referred, in paragraphs 1 and 2 of the attached Report, to the awards of the Boundary Commissions. I do not, however, think that these would be of sufficient interest to all the recipients of the 'V.P.R.' I am, therefore, sending you copies of these awards as Appendices I, II and III to this letter.

12. In paragraph 41 of my last Personal Report I mentioned that Ismay had made a statement to the Joint Defence Council about his conversations with the Chiefs of Staff in England, and it occurs to me that the Chiefs of Staff might wish to know what he said. I therefore enclose (as Appendix IV) a copy of the notes from which he spoke. You will see that, in agreement with me, he dealt with the subject on very general lines and made no mention of Naval or Air bases, etc. It would have been a mistake to do so at this stage, since it would have merely frightened them off. Even as it was, the Indian Leaders did not look too happy about the future prospects, and would not commit themselves further than to say that they would examine Ismay's statement carefully and then let us have their reactions.

13. I am all in favour of the Chiefs of Staff's Mission coming as soon as possible, but I do not want them to come before the two new Governments have got over their teething troubles, have got their Defence Departments more or less organised, and have begun to know and trust their British Commanders-in-Chief. As a rough guess, I should say that a suitable target for the delegation to arrive would be about the middle of October: but I will, of course, send a firm recommendation in due course.

14. I have asked Pandit Nehru's concurrence to proceed home for about a fortnight (from about 10th–24th November) to attend the wedding of Princess Elizabeth to my nephew.[755]

---

[755] Prince Philip, duke of Edinburgh.

15. I was very touched by your kind farewell telegram and deeply appreciated the very generous remarks that you made. Abell, my late P.S.V., left to-day by air and I asked him to go and see you and give you an account of the perfectly amazing scenes which occurred on the 15th August, and which I feel demonstrate the real good feelings that now exist between the British and the Indians.

16. I realise that during these last few weeks we have had to take the bit between our teeth. It is almost impossible to describe the atmosphere in which we have been living or the strain to which everyone has been subjected. Of the six British members of the 'operational staff' I brought out with me, four have been in bed recently for longer or shorter periods under the doctor's care. Mieville[756] has been quite seriously ill with thrombosis; Ismay is still in bed with a very bad go of dysentery; my two 'personal' (naval) secretaries, who now become my 'private' secretaries have both been in bed, the senior one, Brockman, having had a relapse through trying to get back to work too quickly.

17. It is impossible to over-estimate the value which George Abell and his gallant 'P.S.V.' team (John Christie,[757] Ian Scott[758] and Peter Scott[759]) have been to the 'U.K.' team. They had every reason for their noses to be put out of joint by the new set up, but they played up 100 per cent, and without them we could never have achieved the success which has come our way.

18. Before coming out I asked for a generous allowance of honours and I had at the back of my mind that if we made a success of this job I would like every member of my small team to receive recognition. Now that I myself (to my very great surprise) have received an Earldom, I feel it is all the more important that this recognition should be given to my staff. I will be sending in their names in the ordinary way for the Honours List, but I hope that you will be able to leave a note to the appropriate authorities that no one on my special list shall be turned down.

19. Old members of the I.C.S. out here say that never at any time has the India Office been quite so helpful, quite so quick and quite so

---

[756] Sir Eric Miéville (1896–1971), civil servant and Colonial Service; senior member of the viceroy's staff, 1947.

[757] John Christie (1905–1983), ICS, joint private secretary to the viceroy, 1947.

[758] Ian Scott (1909–2002), later Sir Ian Scott, ICS and later diplomat; deputy private secretary to the viceroy, 1945–1947.

[759] Peter Scott, ICS, assistant private secretary to the viceroy, 1947.

valuable as during the last few weeks. I certainly could not have wished for any better support.

Again all my most sincere and heartfelt thanks.

Yours very sincerely,

Mountbatten of Burma

INDEX

Numbers in bold indicate references to pages with notes containing biographical information.

320	INDEX

Bottomley, Arthur **143**, 145, 240, 285
Bourne, Frederick **309**
Boyd-Orr, John, Baron **49**
Braimah, J.A. **202**
Bravo, Lisardo Doval **59**
Bridges, Edward **263**
Bright, John **15**
British Guiana, *see* Guyana
British Honduras 168, 170–171
British Virgin Islands 168 171
Broad, C.D. 51n
Brockman, Ronald **235**, 317
Brook, Norman **135**
Brooke, Charles Vyner **166**
Brooke, Rupert **43**
Brown, George **215**
Brown, Isabel **76**
Brunei 167
Buganda 206–207
Bundi, Bahadur Singh, maharaja of **302**
Burdett, Francis **11**, 14
Burke, Wilfrid **112**
Burma xvi–xvii, xxiii, xxv, 135, 139–156, 173–174, 240, 241, 255, 256, 263, 265, 271, 276, 281, 286, 288, 291, 304–305, 307
Burnham, Forbes **169**
Burrows, Frederick **228**, 239
Burton, Harold Hitz **89**
Busia, Kofi **195**, 201, 203
Bustamante, Alexander xxv, **170**
Butcher, Herbert **88**
Butler Committee 268, 268n
Butler, Harcourt **154**, 268n
Butler, R.A. **107**, 120, 154, 176, 306, 307

Campbell, Gerald **88**
Campbell-Johnson, Alan xvii, **294**
Canada 14, 39, 87, 92, 96, 135, 136, 173, 182, 234, 269, 285, 299, 304
Caroe, Olaf **231**, 236, 242, 259–261, 263, 266–267
Carrington, Peter Carington, 6th Baron **216**
Carter, Archibald 300, 305, 311
Catto, Thomas, 1st Baron **307**
Caulfeild, James, 1st earl of Charlemont **4**
Cecil, Lord Robert **62**
Cecil, Lord William **52**
Ceylon, *see* Sri Lanka
Chamberlain, Austen **60**
Chamberlain, Neville 1, **78**, 79
Charlemont, James Caulfeild, 1st earl of **4**
Charteris, Martin **193**

Chaudhuri, J.N. **124**
Chiang Kai-Shek 62n **63**
Chiang Kai-Shek, Madame **62**
Chifley, Ben **93**
China x xv 61–64
Chetwode, Philip, 1st Baron **312**
Chettur, K.K. 314
Chorley, Robert, 1st Baron **240**
Christie, John **317**
Chundrigar, I.I. **257**
Churchill, Lord Randolph **150**
Churchill, Randolph **150**
Churchill, Winston x–xii, 1, **77**, 88, 91, 103, 105–106, 108, 111, 115, 119, 119n, 120–121, 123, 125, 130, 150n, 154, 174n, 188, 188n, 255, 312
Clegg, Arthur **63**
Clemenceau, Georges **91**, 91n
Clow, Andrew **227**–228, 241, 245, 265
Cohen, Andrew **206**
Cole, G.D.H. **36**
Cole, Margaret **36**
Coleridge, Samuel Taylor **93**
Colville, John **252**–253, 256, 280, 296
Commonwealth, The xvi–xix, xx, xxii, xxiv, 1, 89n, 106, 115, 121, 124, 128, 130, 135–137, 140–141, 143, 145–146, 150, 153, 154, 159, 161, 171, 173, 177–178, 182–183, 188, 192, 195–197, 201, 236, 253, 255, 263–265, 269, 271, 272, 274, 276, 280, 281–282, 284, 290–291, 295, 298, 300, 304–305, 311
Connally, Thomas **88**
Conservative Party (UK) x, xii, xx, xxi, xxii, xxvi, 1, 6, 21, 34n, 49, 50, 53, 62, 64, 87, 105n, 108–109, 123, 129–130, 154, 159, 163, 174, 174n, 176, 206, 211, 215n, 216, 218, 220–221, 311
Constable, W.G. **56**
Cooke, A.J. 44, 44n
Cooper, Frank **96**
Cornford, F.M. **43**
Coutts, Walter **207**
Corfield, Conrad **237**, 239, 246
Cranborne, Viscount (Bobbety), *see* Salisbury
Crewe, Robert Crewe-Milnes, marquess of **211**, 214
Cripps, Isobel xiii
Cripps, Stafford xii–xiii, xv, **91**, 91n, 106, 106n, 107, 120, 120n, 121–125, 128, 129, 131, 136, 143, 146, 150, 152, 155, 264, 268, 286, 309